Pageantry and power

Manchester University Press

Pageantry and power

A cultural history of the early modern Lord Mayor's Show, 1585-1639

TRACEY HILL

Manchester
University Press

Manchester and New York

distributed in the United States exclusively by Palgrave Macmillan

Published by Manchester University Press
Oxford Road, Manchester M13 9NR, UK
and Room 400, 175 Fifth Avenue, New York, NY 10010, USA
www.manchesteruniversitypress.co.uk

Distributed in the United States exclusively by
Palgrave Macmillan, 175 Fifth Avenue,
New York, NY 10010, USA

Distributed in Canada exclusively by
UBC Press, University of British Columbia, 2029 West Mall,
Vancouver, BC, Canada V6T 1Z2

British Library Cataloguing-in-Publication Data is available

Library of Congress Cataloging-in-Publication Data is available

ISBN 978 0 7190 9012 7 paperback

First published by Manchester University Press in hardback 2010

This paperback edition first published 2013

The publisher has no responsibility for the persistence or accuracy of URLs for any external or
third-party internet websites referred to in this book, and does not guarantee that any content
on such websites is, or will remain, accurate or appropriate.

Printed by Lightning Source

For Edwin, Georgia, Clare, Tom and Sarah

Contents

List of figures

Acknowledgements

In researching and writing this book I have been fortunate to receive what Munday calls 'friendly helpes and furtherances' from numerous people. I would especially like to thank Richard Rowland for sharing the 'formidable erudition' of his Heywood book with me prior to its publication, and for reading and commenting on this book in draft. Ian Gadd and Chris Ivic have also given very generously of their time and expertise (often at very short notice), and I cannot thank them enough. Other friends and colleagues at Bath Spa University, notably Bobby Anderson, Stephen H. Gregg, Mark McGuinness, Alan Marshall and Steve May, have given assistance, as have Maggie Collins, Alison Cox, Paul Davies and Penny Williams. Students on my 'Literary London' module over the last couple of years have offered a valuable reality check. I am also indebted to various scholars for their advice: Ian Archer, David Bergeron, Peter Blayney, Matthew Davies, Andy Gordon, Vanessa Harding, Gordon Kipling, Steve Longstaffe, Robert Lublin, Kim Martin, Julia Merritt, Lucy Munro and Elaine Tierney. The anonymous reader of my book must also be thanked for offering such rigorous and constructive comments. Affectionate thanks are due to my family and to Gill and Rob Silversides for their tremendous moral support, and to Caz Netherton and David Heath for civic hospitality and much besides. My cats also contributed in traditional style, even though sadly one of them did not live to see the final result of my labours.

I have travelled far and wide in the making of this book, and am indebted to the help of a large number of librarians and archivists. Particular thanks are due to all the staff at the Guildhall Library (my second home), especially John Fisher, Stephen Freeth, Andrew Harper, Wendy Hawke and Philippa Smith. Penny Fussell at the Drapers, David Beasley at the Goldsmiths and Alexandra Buchanan at the Clothworkers have also given generously of their time and expertise. I have been able to draw widely on the livery companies' records and appreciate their generosity in allowing me to quote from and use illustrations from their archives so freely. I am grateful to Bart Jaski and Wiebe Boumans of the University of Utrecht Library, to Tricia Boyd and Rona Morrison at the University of Edinburgh Library and to staff at the British Library, the Bodleian, the National Library of Scotland, the John Rylands University Library of Manchester, the Pepys Library, Magdalene College, Cambridge, the National Art Library at the V&A, the Huntington Library, the Folger Shakespeare Library, the Houghton Library, Harvard, and the Society of Antiquaries Library. Thanks are also due to Naomi van Loo at New College, Oxford, Joanna Snelling, Corpus Christi College, Oxford, Joanna Parker, Worcester College, Oxford, Catherine Hilliard, St John's College, Oxford, and to Sandy Paul and David McKitterick, Trinity College Library, Cambridge.

I would not have been able to complete the book (at least not in one lifetime) without the benefit of a British Academy Small Research Grant to travel to the US in 2008, and without financial support from the School of English and Creative Studies at Bath Spa University.

1

'From low-obscure Beginnings raysde to Fame': critical and historical contexts of the Lord Mayor's Show

The London Lord Mayors' Shows were high-profile and very lavish entertainments that were at the centre of the cultural life of the City of London in the early modern period. Staged annually in the course of one day in late October to celebrate the inauguration of the new Lord Mayor, the Show – or Triumph, as it was often called – was usually composed of an eclectic mixture of extravagantly staged emblematic tableaux, music, dance and speeches, together with disparate crowd-pleasing effects such as fireworks and giants on stilts.[1] The Lord Mayor proceeded by water to Westminster to take his oath of office before representatives of the sovereign, and then processed back through the City in all his finery accompanied by hundreds of others, including civic dignitaries, members of the livery companies and 'poor men' dressed in blue coats. The impact of the Shows has been testified to in various contemporary sources, perhaps most valuably in the eyewitness accounts that survive in surprisingly large numbers. The Shows themselves, as events, also survive – in a more complex way than one might assume – in the printed texts often produced as part of the event. These texts were produced by a body of professional writers, including Thomas Middleton, Thomas Dekker, Anthony Munday, Thomas Heywood, John Taylor and John Webster, who worked in collaboration with artificers and others to design and stage the entertainment. The Shows have a presence elsewhere in early modern culture too, featuring, often satirically, in a wide range of other dramatic and prose works. Their heyday (and the period covered by this book) was also the heyday of the early modern stage, when theatrical modes of celebration and entertainment were ubiquitous in the rapidly expanding city.

I will address the lived experience of the Shows in more depth

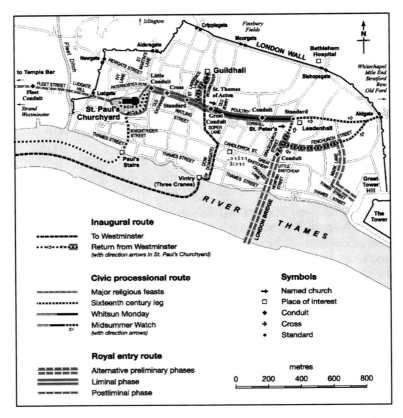

1 The route of the Lord Mayor's Show in the early modern period

in Chapter 3, and will discuss the ways in which the ceremonial elements of the day developed over time further below, but it is worth providing at the outset a brief overview of the structure and content of a 'typical' Lord Mayor's Day (one should note that the Shows did not follow exactly the same format every time, but they were broadly similar from year to year from the late sixteenth century onwards). First thing in the morning, both the new and previous incumbent Lord Mayors were escorted (normally from the Guildhall) in a formal procession across Cheapside and along Soper Lane down to the river Thames (see Figure 1 for the route of the Show). Here the party embarked on barges, usually at Three Cranes Wharf, to be taken up river to Westminster for the oath-taking in front of the representatives of the Crown at the Exchequer.

Occasionally, speeches were given to the procession as it passed by one or more of the pageant stations on the route through the City to the river for the first leg of the trip. The journey along the river to Westminster was marked by fireworks and cannon set off from the river banks, and the barges themselves were ornately painted and decorated with flags, banners, and the like; musicians usually travelled in the barges too. A series of emblematic figures and/or mythical beasts usually called the 'water show' entertained the Lord Mayor and his entourage on the river. On arrival at Westminster, the new Lord Mayor was presented by the Recorder of London to the Barons of the Exchequer for the royal imprimatur; this ceremony comprised reciprocal speeches (these are further discussed in Chapter 3). Following the actual oath-taking, the barges returned to the City, usually disembarking at Barnard's Castle or Paul's Stairs, a moment emphasised by cannon-fire.

At this point the pageantry which was so central a feature of the day's entertainment really got under way. Practice varied, but the usual arrangement was to stage emblematic pageants, featuring speeches and songs, at certain symbolic locations in the City, often existing edifices such as conduits. The mayoral procession moved from the river up to Paul's Churchyard, the location of one of the pageant stations. From there, the procession continued along Cheapside, where the pageant stations tended to be placed at the Little Conduit and at the end of Lawrence Lane, near the Standard. These pageants were either fixed or peripatetic. The next stage of the day, in the afternoon, was the formal banquet at the Guildhall, hosted by the new Lord Mayor and his sheriffs. After this feast, the pageantry continued as the Lord Mayor and entourage made their way back to St Paul's for a sermon marking the inauguration. By then, given that it was late October, darkness would have fallen, and one gains from the printed texts an evocative impression of the torchlit procession escorting the Lord Mayor back to his house at the end of the day, with one final speech of farewell and moral exhortation traditionally presented at 'his Lordship's gate'. The extraordinary effect of speech, music, song, pyrotechnics, cannonfire and the lavish costumes worn by the performers as well as the assembled dignitaries comes across very powerfully from the printed texts of the Shows, as well as from the eyewitness accounts further explored in Chapter 3.

These were, then, magnificent occasions. However, despite their undoubted importance in their own day, as well as for our understanding of early modern civic culture and for an appreciation of the full diversity of the careers of a number of high-profile writers, the Shows have too often been sidelined by modern scholars in favour of the professional theatre and courtly entertainments like the masque. Under the general heading of 'civic pageantry', even the more apparently glamorous royal entries, staged to celebrate accessions and visiting VIPs, have received scant attention, beyond the work of a few devotees like Gordon Kipling.[2] In the context of an urban population which was, in Glynne Wickham's phrase, 'addicted to spectacle', such an omission is hard to explain, and certainly almost impossible to justify.[3] Civic pageantry, in both its written and visual forms, offers a treasure trove of symbolic meanings and contemporary resonances. The printed works alone – of which thirty-one survive from a period of over fifty years – are rich documents, offering multiple insights into early modern culture and politics. As we'll see further below, the Shows could transcend the boundaries of the civic and parochial to comment on events of national significance. In addition, the Shows themselves were such *public* events, witnessed by thousands: Gary Taylor remarks that 'anyone could attend the annual Lord Mayor's pageant for free', and, as with playgoing, 'neither spectacle demanded literacy'.[4] As we'll see, both the printed texts and eyewitness accounts of the Shows testified repeatedly to the wide appeal of these entertainments. Therefore, as Richard Dutton argues,

> to ignore the civic pageants of the Tudor and Stuart period is to ignore the one form of drama which we know must have been familiar to *all* the citizens of London, and thus an important key to our understanding of those times and of the place of dramatic spectacle in early modern negotiations of national, civic and personal identity.[5]

John Astington puts forward an even wider claim: 'renowned in London culture', he writes, 'the shows formed one of the central icons by which London was memorialised in European civilisation at large'.[6]

So why has the Lord Mayor's Show been repeatedly sidelined? It appears that for generations of critics and scholars, pageantry – or at least that pageantry produced by and *for* the City – is both one-dimensional and relentlessly lowbrow. In this respect E. K. Chambers's view is typical and probably did much to entrench the view of the Shows' alleged mediocrity: 'a full analysis of all this municipal imagery would be extremely tedious', he writes, with his nose held high.[7] As a explanation of what might underlie Chambers's attitude, Ceri Sullivan has astutely noted a kind of scholarly snobbery about citizens and civic oligarchs, who are implicitly regarded as 'coarse businessmen'; such 'coarseness' has evidently, in the eyes of many scholars, rubbed off on the writers they employed and the works they commissioned.[8] Curiously enough, the involvement of playwrights in *monarchical* pageantry is not generally regarded as a stigma. Rather the reverse, in fact: Graham Parry says that it was 'appropriate' that Dekker and Jonson, 'two of London's leading dramatists', should have written parts of James I's 1604 royal entry.[9]

There is clearly an element of discrimation at work here about the status of these writers and their civic productions, although it is rarely so overt as in Chambers. Heywood, Dekker, Taylor and Munday, in particular, have too often been treated as a plebeian bunch of hacks (although one can only imagine how the Cambridge-educated Heywood might have reacted to his subsequent treatment as the 'citizen' playwright of the despised Red Bull playhouse). Sergei Lobanov-Rostovsky typifies this approach. Middleton, in particular, he argues, when compared to his contemporaries, advanced the formal literary and dramatic qualities of civic pageantry in ways which were beyond Munday, for instance. The livery companies' allegedly culturally illiterate preference for Munday in the years immediately following Middleton's 1613 Show, *The triumphs of truth* (a work which actually was, as we will see, a collaboration with the benighted Munday), is therefore seen by Lobanov-Rostovsky to illustrate their inability to tell good art from bad. In his view it demonstrates the livery companies' 'unease with the introduction of theatrical mimesis' into civic entertainments.[10] There is scant evidence for this argument, however. As I will show in Chapter 2, the reasons for choosing one team of producers over another were rarely aesthetic, as Middleton would have known just as his peers did. Lobanov-Rostovsky is aware that the Grocers' accounts reveal Munday and Middleton to have been collaborators in 1613, but he finesses this unfortunate fact (which he calls 'ironic') by underplaying Munday's contribution and by imagining that Middleton was 'forced' to work with him.[11] Indeed, the widespread critical preference for Middleton's first mayoral text quite possibly derives from the fact that more than some of its peers it resembles a stage play, the cultural form with which a number of commentators are most comfortable. As I will argue further below, however, the qualities of the Shows do not always cohere with the artistic values rated for drama; one should approach them with more nuanced critical criteria.

In fact, as the history of the making of the Shows eminently demonstrates, the production of culture in early modern London invariably went on in ways which have been frequently stigmatised as those relating to 'hack' writing, although, as Mary Osteen and Martha Woodmansee remark, 'we should never know this from our literary histories'.[12] Until quite recently the literary-historical canon tended either to exclude these writers entirely or to filter their civic works out. The works of John Taylor, for instance, are still very rarely discussed, and Julia Gasper has ably critiqued the ways in which Dekker's work (and his personality) have too often been patronised and dismissed as both 'popular' and 'naïve'.[13] Related to the question of the literary canon and its impact on our interpretations of these works is the issue of collaboration, which, as many have argued, presents problems for those who value sole authorship and artistic unity. My discussion of these works has thus been usefully informed by a lively series of recent publications on dramatic collaboration, including Heather Hirschfeld's *Joint Enterprises* and Mark Hutchings and A. A. Bromham's *Middleton and His Collaborators* (although the latter, strangely, do not discuss collaboration within Middleton's Shows); the massive *Middleton: The Collected Works* has also gone to some lengths to excavate the collaboration that lies behind so many of Middleton's works.

Another feature of mayoral Shows that may have led to their exclusion from critical attention is the way in which they were undertaken, from the initial commission to the staging on the river and streets of London. As Sullivan comments, the livery companies' bureaucratic and financial approach to the putting together of the Shows can be seen to make indecorously evident the 'taint' of treating 'art' as a commercial transaction.[14] Osteen and Woodmansee reflect on the ways in which 'Romantic ideology' has 'defined literature (and indeed the arts generally) in opposition to commerce'; this, they argue, has resulted in 'the belief in the separation of aesthetic value from monetary value that endures to this day' which has in turn had an impact on the critical assessment of the Lord Mayor's Show.[15] I would prefer to see the fact that the Shows breach this separation as a more positive opportunity to take advantage of the insights recently produced by what some have called 'a new economic criticism'.[16] Indeed, the case of the Lord Mayor's Show exemplifies what John Guillory has called 'the expressly economic institutions and practices' which underpin cultural production.[17] Perhaps this is the problem with the Shows, for some. This book, in contrast, will focus on the social, cultural and economic contexts in which the Shows were designed, presented and experienced. Utilising a diverse methodology that includes textual, historical, bibliographical and archival material, I will explore the Shows in all their manifold contexts.

We will see in due course the intricate ways in which 'culture' and 'economics' are entwined in the Shows. Indeed, the very fashion in which the Shows were commissioned and then brought to life on the streets demonstrates in revealing ways the operation of the literary and cultural markets in this period.[18] I would argue, in addition, that there is considerable interest in exploring texts and events so close to that which they represent. Indeed, their 'social purpose', in David Middleton and Derek Edwards's phrase, is entirely explicit and would have been understood in those terms by the domestic audience, unlike many other cultural forms in early modern London.[19] Sullivan rightly states that mayoral pageantry was one means of 'manag[ing] . . . the public image' of merchants.[20] William Hardin goes further still, arguing that the Show was 'one of the most powerful means of shaping the public's conception of London'.[21] The Shows were also an annual demonstration of the way in which, as Philip Withington puts it, 'the principle of election was ubiquitous' in the government of London (as we will see, this was an aspect of its government that was highlighted on Lord Mayor's Day). Withington goes on to argue that

> the precepts and practices of civic community – in terms of practical responsibilities and dependencies, ceremony and ritual, and its structuring of everyday living – formed an important context for a citizen's social relations and sense of self.[22]

Such a civic community, as he comments, 'carried obvious symbolic significance', a significance that was eminently exploited by mayoral pageantry.[23] In Charles Phythian-Adams's words, investiture into civic office had 'solemn and social attributes over and above the practical demands of annual executive position'.[24] Along with the street pageantry, the oath-taking and attendance at prayers and feasts associated with mayoral inaugurations constituted important aspects of this moment of transition.[25] The interconnection between power and culture in early modern London thus had many dimensions. The London mayoralty was therefore not simply an entity of civic power but always had its ritual and ceremonial dimensions. It is therefore of considerable interest to examine texts and events so attuned to the power structures of the City.

Patricia Fumerton has recently argued that in this period

'everyday life . . . expands to include not only familiar things but also collective meanings, values, representations, and practices'.[26] Although the Shows themselves were not 'everyday' events, as such, they certainly are excellent examples of 'collective practices' in this period. Furthermore, they were still closer to the quotidian lives of early modern Londoners than court or aristocratic cultures, for they celebrated people and entities – the Lord Mayor and the livery companies – that would have impinged on these people's lives rather more than the remote vicissitudes of court politics. Ephemeral events like the Shows have a particular ability to preserve the everyday; they operate as one contemporary, John Selden, remarked of other ephemeral works: 'More solid Things', he wrote, 'do not shew the Complexion of the times so well, as Ballads and Libels'.[27] The Lord Mayor's Show was also, importantly, a high-profile moment – the apex, in a way – within the *ongoing* processes of civic government, processes which were a central aspect of everyday life in early modern London. Unlike much more sporadic events such as the coronation entry, which by definition marked a momentous transition in the life of the country at large, the mayoral Show was what Manley calls 'a calendrical rite, a periodic collective ceremony, linked to an annual cycle of events'.[28]

Indeed, as a manifestation of collective practices, the Lord Mayor's Show was aided by its regularity. The very existence of an annual ritual which the citizenry could (almost always) depend upon happening helped, as Alan Fletcher writes, 'to structure the year and thus also to lend definition to individual citizens' sense of civic identity'.[29] The Shows can therefore be said to have functioned as an exercise in what has been called 'collective remembering'.[30] Although, as Robert Tittler comments, 'such memories may easily be induced or manipulated . . . in order to fit the requirements of the dominant or ruling element of a particular era', the invocation of a collective sense of the metropolitan past – for whatever reason – is undeniably a consistent feature of civic ceremony.[31] The recitation of the names and notable deeds of previous civic dignitaries which one sees repeatedly in the Shows serves as only one example of this phenomenon, and aptly embodies the way, as Tittler puts it, 'locally situated collective memories . . . embrace . . . [a city's] own particular heroes and worthies'. As he concludes, in this respect civic culture 'served as the foundation for the local identity'.[32] Ian Archer too has written of the ways in which, as part of a civic 'theatre of memory' (which included the livery company halls as well as more obviously cultural forums), the 'theme of commemoration [of worthy deeds] as a spur to further charity struck a chord with the London reading public and theatre-goers', to whom one can add witnesses of Lord Mayors' Shows.[33] Even at the level of the banners and other paraphernalia carried during mayoral Shows a sense of both history and corporate identity was present, in the form of coats of arms and other heraldic emblems. All of these aspects of civic commemoration contain, in Archer's phrase, 'a very strong performative element' – the Lord Mayor's Show perhaps more than all the others, although Archer does not cite it in this regard.[34]

The rhetoric of the Shows, with its recurrent invocation of notable historical and mythical moments and figures, would have gained most of its effect from the audience's ability to relate what they were seeing and hearing to a collective narrative of the past. As Lawrence Manley puts it, 'in a traditional community like London, [the] customary "steps of the forefathers" could literally be followed along the routes and pathways where generations of calendrical reiteration has traced a pattern of civic precedents onto the urban space'.[35] Indeed, in important ways the Shows can be said to fashion or even create that sense of the past through what they include, what they highlight and what they omit (at times there is as much a collective forgetting as a collective remembering).[36] Mayoral pageantry was in itself a means by which civic traditions were preserved – history was very often their keynote – which in itself constitutes another reason why they deserve attention. The Shows therefore become an interesting series of examples of the presentation of what Middleton and Edwards call 'events and persons that are part of [the citizenry's] jointly acknowledged . . . cultural identity and common understanding'.[37]

The Shows were not relentlessly focused on the past, though: they often had contemporary significance, and could be made to serve various agendas. Although I would rebut Peter Lake's unhelpfully dismissive description of the Shows as 'inherently venal and self-serving' and containing 'celebratory rant', at the same time one should not understate the *latently* coercive elements of civic entertainments, at least in terms of the kind of community they routinely invoked.[38] Richard Halpern writes that 'the power of sovereignty works primarily by making itself *visible*; it promulgates and extends itself through public progresses, entertainments, and propaganda, on the one hand, and overt force or threats of force, on the other'.[39] The Shows were prime examples of the former. An informed contemporary witness, Thomas Dekker, neatly stated in the prologue to his 1612 Show that through pageantry 'the Gazer may be drawne to more obedience and admiration' (*Troia-Noua triumphans*, sig. A3v). However, although ample evidence survives of such 'admiration', the 'obedience' Dekker invokes was not necessarily forthcoming. Withington has argued that 'what was prescribed or initiated from "the summit" was not necessarily accepted and absorbed "on the ground"'.[40] It's worth bearing in mind that civic festivity of the kind that included the Lord Mayor's Show was not spontaneous, but rather a managed representation of collective virtues and priorities (which some of the citizenry may well not have shared). As Catherine Patterson puts it, within the rhetoric of civic ceremonial 'it is as if acting and speaking as though harmony exists . . . will help to bring it about in reality'.[41]

The Show itself was a decisive moment in the City's ritual year in which tradition loomed large. Hardin argues that the 'invocation of . . . historical origins and customs' integral to the Shows was largely a response to a 'suspicion of development and innovation' on the part of the City.[42] Furthermore, the Lord Mayor's progress through the City, Sheila Lindenbaum notes, 'was a powerful symbolic gesture [where] the mayor affirmed his territorial interests . . . The visual splendor of the mayor's "riding" enforced his claim to the civic terrain.'[43] The necessity of the physical presence of the Lord Mayor and his cohorts on the streets of the City is further demonstrated by the fact that there were no Shows between 1666 and 1671 in the aftermath of the Great Fire: during this period the streets were in no fit state to host the display. As with royal progresses, the passing of the Lord Mayor through the City worked as a literally visible assertion of his authority over this domain. Ian Munro writes that 'by tracing a time-honoured route through the ceremonial heart of the city, the shows sought to enact an urban space in which the power of the civic authorities was not only calendrically visible but . . . installed in the physical space of the city'.[44]

Indeed, the staging sites and other stopping points of the Show were meaningful landmarks, ranging from the sacred (St Paul's) to the mercantile (Cheapside). As this suggests, the time-honoured route to and from Westminster and then back through the heart of the City was structured around locations that had ceremonial or ritual significance. Manley has adeptly explored the 'symbolically climactic' status of the run along London's principal street towards its cathedral church within both specifically civic as well as royal pageantry (traditions which otherwise followed quite different routes): he writes that 'on ceremonial occasions . . . the customary processional route helped to link the city's open, outdoor public spaces, forming a single interior of contiguous ritual zones'.[45] Even down to the siting of the individual pageant stations, a meaning was thereby being transmitted to the onlookers. The use of public amenities like the Conduit on Cheapside as pageant stations, for example, edifices that were founded largely by endowments, pointed to the tangible impact on the City's inhabitants of the benevolence of the civic hierarchy.[46] As an instance, in Middleton's *Triumphs of truth*, the figures in one of the pageants at Paul's Churchyard both refer to and physically gesture towards that 'faire temple', the cathedral (sig. C1v). Geography and symbolism are thereby combined. One can imagine that such a tactic would have had a particular impact on those onlookers nearest the place in question when the King of the Moors directed their attention to it. The printed texts, a more permanent although ambiguous record of the event, also embody what Daryl Palmer has called a 'vision of hospitable practices tied to particular localities . . . [and] a kind of cartography of civil obedience'.[47]

R. G. Lang has emphasised the relatively self-contained nature of civic identity, arguing that London's merchant class 'were deeply bound to the city . . . most of all by the respect, prestige, and honour that attended success in the city and which could not be translated, like so much capital, to another social milieu'.[48] The interest of the civic hierarchy is an important consideration, for naturally the City and its constituent companies did not put on these Shows simply out of an altruistic desire to entertain the populace. The Shows were a striking aspect of the legitimation and dignification of civic rule in this period, and one for which (as we'll see further below), the City's livery companies were prepared to expend considerable sums. Malcolm Smuts has written that mayoral Shows 'articulated the hierarchical structure of the [civic] community's elite, while at the same time emphasizing the broad distinction between that elite and everyone else'.[49] This is not to assume, however, that the intended effects were always successful. The Shows were a complex, hybrid mixture of the 'popular' and the elite. They were first and foremost entertainments put on to foreground and celebrate the wealth and prestige of a civic oligarchy, but at the same time they encompassed elements that had been characteristic of 'popular' culture for centuries. Furthermore, as Smuts argues, and as we will see further in Chapter 3, 'the behaviour of the crowd of ordinary Londoners and people from up country' on these occasions was not as 'passive and deferential' as the authorities may have intended.[50]

The people who created, witnessed and participated in civic

pageantry – from the Lord Mayor himself, to the writers and artificers, to those who fired the cannons on the waterside – are therefore at the heart of this book. It's my argument here that if we want to comprehend the role of cultural forms in the lives of early modern Londoners, as well as to recuperate the *agency* of those responsible for producing and consuming such culture, we have to try to gain an understanding of what Wells, Burgess and Wymer call 'the alien world of assumptions, attitudes and values that circumscribe the range of meanings' available to these producers and consumers of culture.[51] Using the correct terminology is a start. No one in this period called the secular livery companies 'guilds', despite the way so many modern commentators treat these terms as interchangeable or even prefer the older word.[52] The term 'guild' refers to the quasi-religious fraternities which were the ancestors of many of the livery companies of the sixteenth century onwards; the companies themselves never used the term. In addition, as we will see further below, it is inaccurate to call the Lord Mayor's Show in its entirety a 'pageant'.[53] This is not just pedantry. If we are, as Peter Meredith puts it, to restore the 'human dimension' of 'theatrical activity or entertainment' 'it seems . . . to be important to tell the stories, to draw together the characters where they can be drawn together, [and] to set them against what background there is'.[54] Maureen Quilligan has also recently argued that

> if we ask what . . . objects and the material practices associated with them might look like if we didn't insist that they mark early modernity, but *remain embedded in a particular moment in time*, we might be in a better position to understand how historically deracinated our sense of the 'early modern' subject has become.[55]

Julian Yates calls the renewed attention to materiality 'a variously Marxist counternarrative', and I agree that it is important not to assume that such materialist criticism is invariably a form of conservative antiquarianism, denuded of politics, as some commentators have recently done.[56] My focus on material culture is also closely associated with the way in which much recent criticism has sought to temper the over-generalised, over-argued tendencies within New Historicism and its followers. Back in 1991 Halpern was arguing that 'new historicism has tended to avoid the materiality of the economic in order to focus on political or sovereign models of power'. The answer, however, as he points out, is 'not to argue that *everything* is an economy', as in Greenblatt's 'circulation of social energy' model, with its potential to 'obliterate the

specificity of the economic' within 'a sort of specious metaphor'.[57]
Loading up early modern culture with massive, epochal significance
is not only often unsustainable in itself, it also runs the risk of
erasing the small, local meanings – what Quilligan calls 'specify-
ing histories' – that might have had the most valency in that actual
space and time. My argument, following the helpful formulations
just cited, is that we can attempt to bring back those lost 'meanings', or, in Smuts's useful formulation, 'the cultural frame' of civic
pageantry, by paying suitable attention to the cultural events, and
the contexts in which they took place, that were significant to early
modern people, and not just to us, some four hundred years later.
To gain a comprehensive understanding of civic pageantry and the
ways in which it was appreciated (in both senses) by its contemporaries, as Smuts writes, 'we will need to examine both the symbolism of the [pageantry] itself *and* the responses and expectations of
those who watched it'.[58]

There is, therefore, a revisionist tenor to this book. Early modern
criticism across the range of literature and history has been increasingly concerned in recent years with material culture, and historical
studies in particular have moved away from large-scale explanatory
narratives. As Smuts argues, 'the "history" in which "literature" is
embedded invariably consists, not only of large ideological move-
ments and social trends, but a host of highly specific circumstances
that we can only hope to unravel through focused research'.[59] This
book's focus on the material aspects and the lived experience of
the Lord Mayor's Show therefore sits within more current critical
trends, and its approach will eschew the pseudo-historical gener-
alisations upon which so much historicist criticism of the last two
decades has rested. In terms of methodology, I have refrained from
interpreting the Shows anthropologically, as a form of predeter-
mined and fixed ritual, with predictable effects on a monolithic and,
crucially, passive audience. My account is rather more interested in
contingency – 'the inevitable and thwarting element of chance', as
Alice Hunt neatly puts it.[60] This book is also concerned with the
perceptions and experiences of the 'consumers' of the Shows as
much as with those of the producers and sponsors. With the benefit
of hindsight, we might think we can perceive clear ideological patterns in civic pageantry but that does not guarantee that this is how
they came across to contemporary audiences and readers. Hence,
perhaps, the surprising neglect of eyewitness accounts of the Shows
as a medium that may provide just such a perspective, which I
discuss at greater length in Chapter 3.

In this vein, Gary Taylor has posed the question as to whether one of Middleton's mayoral Shows should be considered to be 'news or art', thereby foregrounding the currency and ephemerality of the text versus its aesthetic qualities in a way that might have registered with a contemporary spectator or reader.[61] Although the input of the writers was, of course, intrinsic to the creation of mayoral Shows, Smuts has rightly suggested that to treat such entertainments as exclusively literary is both 'limiting and fundamentally misleading'; pageantry, he argues, 'derived instead from social and religious conventions deeply embedded within English culture'.[62] These writers and artificers had therefore to work within existing cultural parameters, such as with highly traditional material, with only a limited autonomy to invent. Perhaps the Shows' consistent emphasis upon the livery companies' 'ethics of community over individualism', as Andrew McRae puts it, is one of the reasons why they seem to be antithetical to modern commentators, given the sway of individualism in western culture after the early modern period.[63] It is my view that one should attempt to interpret the mayoral Shows, and the texts which they generated, in their own terms, as far as this is possible.

With that approach in mind, the Lord Mayors' Shows – especially when studied en masse, as here – can offer us access to a rich range of the symbolic meanings available to an inhabitant of, or visitor to, early modern London. Civic pageantry, after all, was derived from numerous cultural and historical traditions. Few forms of culture in this period, indeed, are so multi-faceted. There has also been considerable scholarly interest in recent years in the history and culture of cities per se, which makes the sustained attention I propose here to the celebratory culture of London, the chief city of England, all the more timely.[64] As J. R. Mulryne notes, there has been 'an increasing focus among academic commentators on the place of the city in the initiation and maintenance of a common culture'.[65] This book is a contribution to that enterprise. Within that wider context, foregrounding the Shows acts as a useful corrective to the focus on monarchical and governmental power that one often encounters in writing about this period. The presumption tends to be that court and/or aristocratic culture was the model. There is, however, an alternative approach, as outlined by Tittler: 'a number of aspects of civic culture, including . . . civic ceremony, emerged . . . from indigenous traditions of urban life, and to suit urban requirements, with far less need to be appropriated from elsewhere than has commonly been recognised'.[66] Relatedly, Paul

Griffiths has asserted that London's 'self-image' in the early modern period manifested itself in 'decidedly civic rhetoric for civic concerns', which did not always mesh with 'attempts by Stuart kings to turn London into a gleaming capital city that would outshine rivals on mainland Europe'.[67] Indeed, Manley argues that civic pageantry 'called attention to the urban wealth and security on which . . . courtly splendor depended'.[68] Like it or not – and as the seventeenth century progressed the relationship grew more strained – these two bodies, the City and the Crown, were forged into a mutual interdependence.

It seems perverse, then, that when he comes to discuss civic entertainments Chambers should prioritise the very occasional coronation entry over the annual Lord Mayor's Show in the chapter on 'pageantry' in his voluminous *The Elizabethan Stage*. Indeed, Chambers is so monarch-centric that he asserts that 'the opportunities for spectacular display, which provincial towns enjoyed during a [royal] progress, fell to London *chiefly* at the time of a coronation'.[69] By the time he eventually gets round to discussing what he disparagingly calls 'municipal pageantry' the damage has been done, and the message that entertainments for the monarch and his or her family (or even for some minor courtier) are inherently the most important, regardless of their size and significance, has been made. The brief account of the mayoral Shows that he does provide is prefaced with a grudging 'Even in the absence of the sovereign . . .'. The little he does have to say about the Shows is laced with haughty disdain: 'there were personages mounted on strange beasts. Speeches and dialogues afforded opportunities for laudation of the Lord Mayor and his brethren. There was generally some theme bearing on the history of the company or the industry to which it was related.'[70]

As I have shown above, Chambers's approach and its inherent prejudices have tended to linger in critical discourse. The mayoral Show cannot fairly be likened to a 'municipal' entity like a public toilet, however. For the Companies this was a day when they and their chiefs were in the limelight and, crucially, within their own domain, and being celebrated as such. David Cannadine has argued that 'politics and ceremonial are not separate subjects . . . [and] ritual is not the mask of force, but is in itself a type of power'.[71] Power – or rather, the projection of power – was indeed a central dimension of the Shows. Alexandra Johnston writes that

> the overwhelming sense one receives . . . is that . . . 'solemne pomps' were essentially about power – how to get it, display it, share it,

and retain it . . . [R]enaissance cities, though powerful communities
jealous of their own jurisdiction, were constantly negotiating their
relationships with other secular and religious authorities.[72]

The 'display' of power that Johnston cites, in particular, is central
to what the Shows were all about, and in London's case the 'secular
authority' with which it was the most engaged, in various ways,
was the Crown. At the height of its power and influence the City
of London, as an entity itself and in its constituent parts – the
livery companies and trading companies such as the Merchant
Adventurers – dominated England's greatest city. And London
in turn dominated the country. As the monarch's alternative in
extremis the Lord Mayor was, after all, the most important com-
moner in the country: in Jonson's words, 'for his yeere, [he] hath
Senior place of the rest'.[73] Orazio Busino, a seventeenth-century
Venetian eyewitness of one of the Shows (of whom more in Chapter
3), offers an outsider's perspective, calling the Lord Mayor 'a chief
for the government of the city itself, which may rather be styled a
sort of republic of wholesale merchants than anything else'. For the
Show itself, Busino commented that 'the cost incurred exceeded the
means of a petty or medium duke'.[74] Explicit reference to the Lord
Mayor's standing in relation to the monarch occurs in quite a few
of the Shows, such as Munday's 1611 Show *Chruso-thriambos*,
where advantage is taken of the coincidence of celebrating a mayor,
James Pemberton, who shared the King's name.[75] Munday takes
this opportunity to highlight the authority of the Lord Mayor that
derived from his role as the monarch's substitute.

Indeed, the zenith of the mayoral Shows in the early seventeenth
century came about partly because of a decline in royal civic entertainments under James I and his successor. The Lord Mayor's
status as monarchical 'surrogate' was thereby realised, in practice,
as mayoral pageantry increasingly eclipsed that of the king. In the
context of mayoral Shows, the new incumbent of the role demonstrates what David Bergeron calls 'office charisma', analogous to
that embodied in the monarch during royal entries, progresses and
the like.[76] In these events, the Lord Mayor *became* London. The
presence of the new Lord Mayor at the performance – and many
pageant speeches address him directly – is an important aspect of
these events. The Lord Mayor himself, processing in all his civic
regalia, was as much a part of the spectacle as the pageants. As
Hardin has commented, 'people expected to see their leaders . . .
[and] to witness the mayor hearing [the pageant] speeches . . . His

visibility in ceremonies of election provided the populace with a source of power.' Such visibility, he continues, 'served the interests of the status quo because it illustrated at least the illusion of openness and accountability'.[77]

The central presence of the Lord Mayor in the Shows demonstrates the ways in which there were parallels as well as significant differences between the mayoral Shows and monarchical entertainments, and, in some instances, with the court masque. For one thing, the civic elite performed an important ceremonial role during the royal entry as well as contributing large sums towards these events.[78] Although triumphal *arches* appear to have been the exclusive preserve of royal events, the printed texts of the Lord Mayors' Shows themselves underscored the parallels by repeatedly calling the mayoral Shows 'Triumphs', the term that points directly to classical, especially Roman, precedent. However, Manley writes, 'the lord mayor's shows were modeled formally on the Roman republican *prosessus consularis* and the military "triumph"', not on the imperial Roman triumph as were the royal entries.[79] Accordingly, twenty-two of the existing thirty-one printed Shows mention 'Triumphs' in some fashion on their title pages.[80] There are also analogies at the level of content. For instance, where Mulryne argues that in Renaissance triumphs 'records of past greatness were harnessed to create, or shore up, modern reputations. Henri IV or Maximilian I became (it was hoped) new and greater monarchs by association with figures from the history of pre-Christian Rome', one thinks of the ways in which previous and famed Lord Mayors (such as William Walworth) function in very similar ways to cast reflected glory on the new incumbent.[81] As James I is represented as London's 'bridegroom' in his royal entry of 1604, so is John Leman, the new Lord Mayor, for Anthony Munday's Show in 1616.[82] Furthermore, as we will see further elsewhere, in many of the Shows the new Lord Mayor – and, by implication, all those who watched the entertainment – are reminded that the former is the monarch's 'lieutenant', with all the consequent political undertones. Although it was understood that the monarch had the power over the Lord Mayor as over all his or her subjects, and this point was affirmed through the act by which the monarch's representatives had conferred the Lord Mayor's authority upon him at the start of the inaugural day at Westminster, the absence of the monarch during the main part of the day within the City itself would make the Lord Mayor the sole figure of authority.[83]

At a thematic level, as in the royal entry with the relative positions of monarch and people, the mayoral inauguration was sometimes likened to a marriage between the Lord Mayor and the City. Indeed, in terms of their gendering of the relationship between ruler and ruled there is little difference between the two genres. For Munday's *Chrysanaleia* (as I have discussed elsewhere) the City is John Leman's bride, as she is for Middleton, more briefly, in *The triumphs of loue and antiquity*. In the last speech of the latter text 'Loue' declares that the Lord Mayor is 'the Cities Bride-groome'. As her husband, he is told to be, 'according to your Morning-Vowes,/ A Carefull Husband, to a Louing Spouse' (sig. D1r).[84] More generally, there is in this period a use of gendered language to represent civic government. Hardin writes that 'the "feminization" of civic space was conducive to building ideologies of social domination and control'.[85] Indeed, Gail Kern Paster notes that 'because the city is walled for most of its history, it is early associated with the female principle . . . As a forti- fied place subject to siege and assault, this personified city becomes associated with sexual possession'.[86] Middleton, true to form, takes his own idiosyncratic approach in *The triumphs of truth*, where, in contrast to the norm, London, who gives the first speech, is the new Lord Mayor's mother. Her status as a representation of the City overrides the lack of propriety of a woman speaking: 'esteeme [not] / My words the lesse, because I a Woman speake, / A womans coun- sell is not alwayes weake', she says (sig. A4r). As we will see further below, the Shows repeatedly used gendered figures in the pageantry, usually inflected by the standard misogyny that underlines so much early modern culture. For Middleton in *The triumphs of truth*, the ultimately triumphant figure of Zeal is male, and the tempting but eventually defeated figure of Error, female.

Despite the likenesses between the various forms of ceremonial entertainment, a number of critics have tended to see the courtly and civic varieties as antithetical, if not openly at odds. Some time ago Wickham established the view of a rivalry between the court masque, in particular, and the Lord Mayor's Show. Paster sub- sequently followed Wickham in arguing that mayoral pageantry developed as an attempt to 'emulate' court entertainments, as part of an 'unofficial dramatic rivalry between court and city'.[87] This position has been slightly qualified more recently by Bergeron, who writes that 'perhaps [the Lord Mayors' Shows] rival the court masque . . . [although] I am uncertain that the mood becomes as sinister as Wickham implies'.[88] Even someone as expert on the Shows as Sheila Williams, however, is prone to the view that Bergeron is sceptical about. In her account of why John Taylor rather than Heywood wrote the 1634 Show, breaking the latter's ubiquity in this decade, she writes that 'one possible explanation lies in Heywood's defection [to the masque] . . . Thus having risen from bourgeois to Court spectacle, Heywood may have declined to divide his energies.'[89] Her use of the term 'defection' shows that the notion of competition or rivalry between the Lord Mayor's Show and the court masque underlies her interpretation. The word 'risen' also, probably unthinkingly, replicates the elite priority usually given to court entertainments. In fact, as Williams concedes, there is another – and more plausible – reason why Heywood may not have received (or even contested) the commission for that year, for Garret Christmas, Heywood's influential collaborator and the one of the pair who had increasingly handled their business, had recently died, and Heywood may well have felt unable to take on the responsibility without him.

Rather than being the 'rival' of court culture, then, one can at times see the Shows as a way of presenting a displacement of monarchical authority. To illustrate the point, Kipling's interpretation of the underlying meaning of royal entries can be applied without undue misrepresentation to the mayoral processions. He writes that 'because [royal entries] celebrate the first advent of the new king, they necessarily focus sharply on a single ruler [who] must enter the city . . . making . . . his first manifestation as king'.[90] Replace the word 'king' with 'mayor', and this acts as a succinct summary of the purpose of the Lord Mayor's inaugural celebrations too. Only the emphasis on 'a single ruler' should be qualified by an acknowledgement of the importance of the Lord Mayor's livery company as the corporate entity to which he belongs and the one which sponsors the Show. In the civic arena 'self-fashioning' was on the whole more collective than individual. The presence of notable dignitaries in the Shows was thus significant inasmuch as it was representative of general civic virtues, and the individual qualities mentioned tended to be foregrounded as exemplary. For example, in the brief printed text of Peele's 1585 Show Wolstan Dixie, the new Lord Mayor, is mentioned by name within the text only once (although he is elsewhere addressed more impersonally as 'your honour').[91] With some provisos (further explored in due course), Lord Mayors' Shows also tended to be more uniform, in terms of funding and political emphasis, than other triumphs, and their predictable regularity acts as another marker of difference with the more ad hoc royal entertainments. The mayoral entry into his City can be seen, in a useful phrase used by Edward Muir, as 'an urban rite of passage', a shift from the rule of the preceding Lord Mayor (only mentioned if a member of the same Company, of course, and not always then) in favour of London's (temporary) new ruler.[92] The Shows therefore had to negotiate both continuity and transition at the same time, a difficult ideological position.

The preceding discussion has, I hope, shown how the importance and complexity of mayoral pageantry makes it ripe for reappraisal. It is certainly the case that materialist and historicist criticism has some ground to make up here. As I have already suggested, such criticism has been largely indifferent to civic pageantry, preferring to tackle the theatre, the royal entry, or the court masque. This trend Bergeron calls the '"Whitehall syndrome", [one] which focuses exclusively on the court at the expense of understanding other sites of power'.[93] The neglect the Lord Mayor's Show has largely experienced, Bergeron comments, is deliberate: 'we do not lack evidence about the importance of pageants', he writes, ' we lack the scholarly will to explore them . . . [T]he benign neglect of pageants . . . marks a failure of scholarship'.[94] As with Chambers back in the 1920s, even Wickham's magisterial *Early English Stages* privileges the royal entry and royal progress over the Lord Mayor's Show as exemplars of civic pageantry; indeed, he excludes the Shows entirely from the volume covering the period of their dominance.

Of course, this is not to say that the Shows have been entirely overlooked. Bergeron has produced on his own a sizeable proportion of the extant scholarship and criticism on these works and their contexts. My work is greatly indebted to his, as it is to the careful scholarship of Jean Robertson and D. J. Gordon in the livery company archives, as well as to pioneers like Manley, whose *Literature and Culture in Early Modern London* offers an exemplary reading of civic pageantry. In addition, as Sullivan has more recently observed, there has at last been 'a move away from new historicism's court based narrative [resulting in] a growing interest in alternative social capitals' – literally so, in the case of London.[95] My intention here to bring this essential groundwork up to date and to explore some of the assumptions that have yet to be fully critiqued. One of these is the place of the Shows within literary history. In his thoughtful introduction to the revised edition of *English Civic Pageantry* Bergeron remarks that 'most of the major dramatists of the period, *excepting Shakespeare*, [wrote] civic pageants'.[96] He does not take the point very far, however, and his argument is somewhat undermined by the fact that almost the only stage plays he mentions in relation to the Lord Mayors' Shows are by Shakespeare rather than those writers with a keen interest in pageantry, such as Middleton or Heywood. In fact, it is very likely that Shakespeare's absence from the civic scene is one of the main reasons why the Shows (and other forms of civic pageantry, to an extent) have so often been overlooked.[97] The Shows were significant cultural productions and they employed some of the most talented and high profile writers of the day. It is an overlooked significance of these productions that the role of the 'poet' should, by and large, be so celebrated by the printed texts they generated, unlike the usual case with royal triumphs and entertainments, a large number of which were published anonymously.[98]

In themselves these writers constitute one of the most significant connections between the mayoral Shows and other cultural forms in this period. Although it seems obvious when one thinks about it, it has hardly ever been remarked upon that the zenith of the mayoral Shows was virtually the same as that of the professional early modern stage, i.e. from the late sixteenth century through to the outbreak of the first civil war. This is not a coincidence, and there is a case to be made that the one led to the other. Dutton asserts that 'given that many of the principal Jacobean dramatists . . . wrote for the civic pageants, it is hardly surprising that [the] influence [of the latter] should be perceived in plays written for the theatre'. As he comments, what is 'more surprising [is that] . . . this influence has been largely overlooked or ignored'.[99] The seemingly unlimited appetite of early modern Londoners for visual and aural entertainment underlies the success of both cultural forms in this period. These writers were very aware of the status of various forms of cultural production, and especially of the high profile of the Lord Mayor's Show, which is surely one reason why they undertook these commissions. Indeed, Heather Easterling has recently proposed that 'by far Middleton's greatest *contemporary* fame derived from his long career as the author of [these] annual pageants'.[100] The consequence of such 'fame', as Angela Stock argues, was that a writer involved in the production of mayoral Shows did so under the pressure 'of acquitting himself creditably as an impresario competing with other London writers and other forms of civic drama, knowing full well that his inventions would be noted by the satirical eyes and parodic quills of his colleagues'.[101] The parallels are, after all, numerous: these writers were engaged in a collaborative dramatic enterprise in both arenas.

However, despite the undoubted links between the theatre and civic pageantry, and although one would have thought that studying mayoral Shows would be of obvious value to critics of the works of Middleton, Heywood, Dekker and Webster (and even, to an extent, Jonson), critics have, in the main, neglected to tackle the full range of texts produced by these writers. One consequence of this is that they can have only a partial sense of these writers' oeuvres. Over the last two decades or so, for instance, neither Jacqueline Pearson's *Tragedy and Tragicomedy in the Plays of John Webster* nor Rowlie Wymer's *Webster and Ford* mentions Webster's Lord Mayor's Show; more significantly still, given his importance for the genre, Swapan Chakravorty entirely overlooks all of Middleton's numerous Shows in *Society and Politics in the Plays of Thomas Middleton*.[102] For Dekker and Heywood, the story is often the same: for example, McLuskie's *Dekker and Heywood* does not discuss the mayoral Shows written by either of her protagonists.[103] Jean Howard's more recent *Theater of a City*, which, as its title suggests, focuses extensively on Dekker, Heywood and Middleton as London writers, at the same time disregards their mayoral Shows completely in favour of the plays. Furthermore, she does not mention Munday – surely a key figure in any study of urban writing – in any regard whatsoever.

Partly, no doubt, the separation within so much criticism of the two closely related spheres of pageantry and playwrighting is due to the persistence of the old story of wholesale civic opposition to the stage, which is gradually being chipped away but still largely retains its status as orthodoxy.[104] In fact, as Hirschfeld points out, 'players, dramatists, and other professionals affiliated with the theater were not simply surrounded by civic companies but were intimately involved with them'; the livery company structure was as a consequence 'a palpable context for the playwrights' work'.[105] Not only were the professional dramatists more linked to civic entertainments than most commentators are prepared to admit, the dramatists themselves could make a good living from such commissions, which tended to be better remunerated than writing for the stage. Bergeron also points out that 'patronage by the guilds reached a wider array of artists than did that of the court'.[106] Furthermore, as Hirschfeld reminds us, such work was not necessarily sought for purely monetary reasons, but can be seen to have 'deriv[ed] from professional, political, and emotional as well as financial desires' – especially when, as we'll see further below, the writers had other forms of investment in civic employments.[107]

The all-too-frequent exclusion of their civic cultural productions from the analysis of these writers' works has led to a partial view on a wider scale, too. As Stock argues, 'the intertextual relations between early modern civic pageantry and London drama are a mine of material that has been neglected'.[108] There are so many missed opportunities to bring canonical and non-canonical together, whether within the corpus of one writer or across a range of contemporaries. As an indicative instance of the latter, consider what critics of *Othello* might make of Middleton's 'King of the Moores', his Queen and entourage in *The triumphs of truth* some ten years later.[109] Even within that one mayoral text, one can see fascinating – and until quite recently unexplored – verbal and conceptual parallels with other Middleton works written for the theatre, demonstrating another form of intertextuality worth considering. For example, *The Changeling*'s repeated insistence on the connection between sight and desire is echoed in *The triumphs of truth*, where one of the characters, Truth's Angel, says of the Lord Mayor 'I haue within mine Eye my blessed Charge' (sig. B1v). In addition, the similar phrases 'sweet-fac'd devils' and 'fair-fac'd saints' occur, respectively, in the mayoral Show and the play.[110] Such congruence does not apply solely to Middleton: the dialogue between Vulcan and Jove in Dekker's *Londons Tempe*, for instance, recalls that between Simon Eyre and his workers in *The Shoemaker's Holiday* by the same writer.

The use of emblems, in particular, shows how widespread was the cross-fertilisation between civic pageantry and other theatrical forms of culture in this period. Frederick Kiefer's *Shakespeare's Visual Theatre* has valuably juxtaposed plays to pageantry to show how certain cultural tropes worked across genres.[111] The Oxford Middleton project, and, yet to come, an equivalent complete works of Heywood, have also broken some of the ground to which this book contributes. More widely, given the paucity of evidence about the experience of theatregoing in this period, those contemporary eyewitness accounts which have survived to retell the experience of watching the Lord Mayor's Show should surely be prized, not neglected. I will demonstrate below how significant the Shows are in terms of our understanding of early modern performance technology, too. The writers and artificers took full advantage of the general munificence associated with the making of the Shows, and they produced prodigious spectacles.

Of course, this is not to say that mayoral Shows are all unfairly neglected works of genius. They are, as one would imagine given the constraints on their production, of varying quality and sometimes repetitive. But one has to bear in mind that the writers and artificers were working to commissions and had to please a committee of city bureaucrats who inspected proceedings as they went on. It's also salutary to remember that in early modern culture imitation tended to be more prized than originality. The Shows were hybrid productions in any case, drawing upon varying and perhaps competing traditions. For one thing, they were composed of both procession and spectacle, a combination that does not lend itself to the kind of artistic coherence usually valued by literary critics. The concept of 'unity', as Bergeron states, 'raises the wrong expectation for these pageants'.[112] In addition, Williams argues that 'the mayoral pageant-poets were engaged in the difficult task of trying to use in an unlearned commercial context the apparatus of classical myth and allegory which an aristocratic Renaissance culture had made more or less obligatory in public festivities'.[113] She goes on to illustrate how Taylor's work is 'an example of the pageant-poets' disregard for the decorous keeping apart of materials usually considered incongruous'.[114] As well as having issues of genre and form to deal with, the writers and artificers were increasingly responsible for overseeing the whole production and they often had very little time: Munday was contracted to produce his 1618 Show with less than three weeks' notice, for instance.[115] Commonly, the sub-committee for planning the Show was established only at the beginning of October; at the earliest, the detailed preparations did not generally commence until late September, for the Lord Mayor was elected on Michaelmas Day, 29 September. Only in 1613 did the production team appear to have had much time to prepare the entertainment (Munday had already submitted a proposal to the Grocers' Company in February of that year). In contrast, as Mulryne points out, more 'elaborate and memorable festivals', where the spectacle usually excelled that of mayoral Shows, 'must have entailed exceedingly time-consuming and expert conception and management'.[116]

There certainly was competition between writers and artificers for the job of producing the Shows, as discussed further below. There is therefore no evidence that I am aware of to back up Wickham's assertion that pageant-writing commissions were 'probably more keenly sought after to stave off a visit to the debtors' prison than for artistic satisfaction comparable with that derived from plays written for a Public Theatre'.[117] Paster corrects this view when she argues that 'the professional writers of the city were delighted enough with pageant commissions to compete eagerly for them'.[118] Despite his assertion elsewhere that one should not disparage 'the distinguished company of dramatists who devised [civic shows]', Wickham appears to have started from an assumption about the cultural superiority of the professional stage and then generalised across from Dekker's particular situation, though there is nothing to show that even the indebted Dekker wrote his Lord Mayor's Shows purely out of impecuniousness.[119] In the same vein, David Horne asserts that 'it is unlikely that [George] Peele himself was enthusiastic about [the Shows] but it was a way of earning a livelihood'. Peele's feelings about his pageant productions have not survived: Horne has imposed his own prejudices about the Shows' 'pedestrian' qualities and lack of 'originality of form' on to their maker.[120] Especially for those writers who were also members of the livery companies (which is surprisingly many), getting the job to write such a high profile, one-off entertainment must have been substantial incentive on its own. Neither Middleton nor Heywood was likely to have been that short of funds (unlike Dekker and, probably, Munday), and of course Jonson, who was keenly aware of the relative statuses of various kinds of literary production, was involved in at least one Lord Mayor's Show.[121]

It is surely more productive to see these two important traditions of urban culture as complementary rather than antithetical, for it is no coincidence that mayoral Shows reached their zenith of imaginative and dramatic power at pretty much the same time as the professional stage, for they shared many protagonists as well, naturally, as an audience. One should therefore see civic pageantry as an aspect of a culture full of confidence in its creative abilities, both on the street and on the stage. It should hardly need restating, as Margot Heinemann argued some thirty years ago, that the 'lavish expenditure on shows, entertainment and dressing-up should in itself qualify some of our simpler conventional notions about the City fathers as a set of kill-joys who objected in principle to "fictions", disguisings or spending money on enjoyment'.[122] Old critical habits die hard, though. Hardin, for instance, finds an imagined incongruity in the livery companies' employment of dramatists and actors, and is compelled to argue for a wider separation between theatre and civic pageantry than was the case.[123] The theatricality of the Shows is highly evident, in fact, as one might expect with the central input of professional dramatists. Indeed, one can imagine that the dramatists relished the theatrical opportunities offered by the lavish expenditure conferred on the Shows by the livery companies. Dekker's first Show, *Troia-Noua triumphans*, as an example, includes both dialogue and action that would not have been at all out of place on the stages of Bankside or Shoreditch; in the printed text the scenes are even set out like those from a play, complete with stage directions. Indeed, the room for 'special effects' was even greater than that offered by the playhouses: in the latter Show Envy and Virtue debate their relative superiority in speeches accompanied by spectacular rockets and fireworks. Plenty of audience response to the Shows has survived, too. Artefacts like Abram Booth's sketches of the 1629 Show and the lavish images produced for the 1616 Show are of tremendous value and would doubtless have been much more discussed had the disparagement suffered by the Lord Mayor's Show not excluded them from the view of so many. Indeed, these images are more illuminating of seventeenth-century dramatic practices than the much-reproduced and second-hand 'de Witt' picture of the Swan theatre, or the Longleat drawing of what may be a performance of *Titus Andronicus* at the Rose.

Civic culture is inherently multi-faceted and benefits from an interdisciplinary approach. As Mulryne has commented, 'festival is pre-eminently a composite topic of study . . . Music, choreography, visual design and script are as crucial to the presentation and interpretation of festival as political intent and economic supply.'[124] This book therefore attempts what Smuts has called 'a deeper and more thoroughgoing kind of interdisciplinarity'.[125] The chapters of this book deal with these aspects in turn, building to present a wholesale account of these important entertainments. The theoretical and conceptual issues outlined above underpin the book in its entirety. The approach of each ensuing chapter is then, to an extent, modelled by its subject matter. Archival sources are the key focus of much of Chapter 2, whereas bibliographical concerns dominate Chapter 4. Chapter 5 is where I focus most on the *content* of the Shows and their contemporary significance. As in Chapter 2, Chapter 3 also mines the livery company records, alongside the printed books, for information about the performance of the Shows, and foregrounds eyewitness accounts of these too. I start, however, with a discussion of the antecedents of the Shows, and of the forces that lead to their rise to prominence in the later sixteenth century.

'In Those Home-spun Times': the historical antecedents of the Shows

Although in many ways they were a distinct cultural phenomenon, the Shows did not emerge from nowhere, fully formed, in the 1580s when they began regularly to appear in print. Forms of pageantry were employed by guilds and livery companies from the medieval period onwards on many occasions and for a variety of purposes. Performances (often by professional players) were central to the livery companies' collective celebrations from at least the fifteenth century.[126] As forms of public pageantry, the mayoral Shows' roots can be traced to these antecedents. Their 'back story', however, is far from transparent. Any exploration of the early days of civic pageantry is inhibited by a lack of certainty as to when pageantry on Lord Mayor's Day began to be established practice, although the Shows' continuities with existing traditions were, on the whole, numerous.[127] Some kind of celebration was held prior to the 1580s to mark a mayoral inauguration, even if it was simply a feast.[128] By 1635 (the City's inveterate tendency to claim great antiquity for its customs notwithstanding), the Ironmongers' Company felt able to refer to the day's events as deriving from 'ancient custome'.[129] In a related sense, Heywood refers in *Londini status pacatus* of 1639 to the 'Annual argument' outlining the venerability of the City's offices and inaugurations (sig. A3r). Even at the relatively early dates of 1601 and 1604 the Haberdashers were requesting arrangements for the Show 'according as it hath bene done in former yeres'.[130] Tittler argues that 'the attribute of antiquity . . . conferred precedence, seniority, and virtue', which we will see to be aspects of the lexicon of mayoral pageantry as well as other forms of civic culture.[131] Rhetoric aside, there is some truth in these claims of antiquity, of course. On the basis of three different eyewitness accounts spanning some 70 years (Henry Machyn, Lupold von Wedel and Abram Booth), one can see considerable continuity in the practice of the livery companies on these occasions. As Robert Lublin comments, 'this is not to suggest that the ceremony was performed in exactly the same way year after year, but that it is *understood* by those involved to be unchangeable'.[132] The Lord Mayor himself may (in almost all cases) have been a different individual from year to year, but as with sovereign power the continuity of tradition in itself demonstrated that the role was uninterrupted.

This is not to say that civic ceremonies and entertainments proceeded wholly unchanged since time immemorial. Civic drama as a genre reflected changing times, and the livery companies themselves had experienced considerable upheaval in the run-up to the mid-sixteenth century. Although a number of the livery companies derived from religious fraternities (such as the Fraternity of St John the Baptist, from which emerged the Merchant Taylors' Company), as Ian Gadd and Patrick Wallis write, 'by the reformation, they had become sufficiently distinct from these that, for the most part, they survived the Edwardian legislation that annihilated religious guilds'.[133] In London, there was a consequent secularisation of civic ritual, resulting in an emphasis on celebrating the Lord Mayor, his Company, and the City of London: as Tittler writes, 'the thrust of a good number of these transformations was to place the mayor and his brethren in the limelight once occupied by the pantheon of biblical and other religious figures'.[134]

As far as continuities are concerned, from the fourteenth century onwards the guilds had had the responsibility for urban processions and plays. The Lord Mayors' Shows thus had connections with precursors such as the Midsummer Watch, guild plays and mummings held on religious festivals such as Twelfth Night, and other quasi-religious processions. Guild members performed roles in as well as watched these entertainments. Even in the early fifteenth century, over a hundred years before the Reformation, religious entertainments had a distinctly civic focus. One consistent theme of royal entries from the fourteenth century to the mid-sixteenth century, for instance, was the personification of London as a New Jerusalem.[135] Such forms of adaptation, as we'll see further below, became a consistent feature of the Shows too in due course. Indeed, Clare Sponsler asserts that 'the liturgical message of Epiphany could readily be appropriated within the context of a guildhall performance to reaffirm structures of authority and patterns of obligation linking mayor and merchants'.[136] Another context for the rise of the Shows, paradoxically, is the relative decline in the economic hegemony of the livery companies in the sixteenth and seventeenth centuries, in the light of which the high profile of the Shows at this juncture seems defiant rather than celebratory. Munro has noted that 'the Lord Mayor's show rose to civic prominence at the same time that London first began to noticeably suffer from the negative effects . . . [of] its rapid population growth . . . The presentation of the ideal community of the shows was in response to the perceived loss of urban significance and clarity.'[137] Although the companies still dominated the urban scene in this period, their survival was never absolutely guaranteed: Gadd and Wallis comment that 'the derivative processions, ceremonies, fur-and-velvet pomp and circumstance that even the newest companies adopted were . . . driven by [a] sense of insecurity'.[138]

As well as early forms of dramatic entertainment specific to the guilds, one of the main predecessors of the Lord Mayor's Show in London was the Midsummer Watch, held overnight on the eve of St John the Baptist's Day, 23–24 June, and St Peter and St Paul's

Day, 28–29 June. Henry III, according to Stow, established the Watch in 1253; however, the earliest surviving records for London are from 1504.[139] The Watch took two forms, the Standing Watch and the Marching Watch; the former, in Penelope Hunting's words, entailed 'lining the streets from 11pm to 2am so that the Marching Watch of some 2,000 soldiers could parade, thereby assuring the citizens that their City was secure and would remain so during the forthcoming year'.[140] As one might expect, the livery companies were expected to play their part, especially the Company of which the new Lord Mayor was a member. Indeed, Hunting writes that they 'vied with each other to present an impressive show of strength and the grand military muster was accompanied by torch bearers, trumpets, morris dancers [and] sometimes pageants'.[141] The general consensus is that pageantry became part of the Watch in the course of the fifteenth century.[142] The Watch was temporarily halted by the King in 1539 and then revived, briefly, about ten years later.[143]

Williams posits an implicitly competitive relationship between the two forms of street pageantry, asserting that 'London civic pageantry was principally represented from about 1500 to 1540 by the Midsummer Show, whose splendours possibly delayed the development of the Lord Mayor's Show'.[144] There was apparently an attempt to reinstate the Watch in 1583, a date very close to the date of the beginnings of *printed* Lord Mayors' Shows in 1585. Watches took place in 1567, 1568 and 1571, but with no pageantry to accompany them. Ian Doolittle writes that when the Watch took place in 1568 'it was no more than a brief resuscitation of a dying tradition . . . [for] the real hub of the City's ceremonial year was now the Lord Mayor's Show'.[145] Certainly, its principal features were inherited by the increasingly spectacular and important celebrations on Lord Mayor's Day, as one can see from Hunting's description of the Watch: 'the time, effort and expense involved in the presentation of [its] pageants was phenomenal. The frame or stage had to be specially constructed by carpenters and painters, children were hired and clothed to act in the drama; drums, flutes and harps played, giants and dragons appeared.'[146] The resemblance to the Lord Mayor's Show is striking.

There were, therefore, continuities as well as divergences between the two civic traditions. Although sometimes there was music, dancing and the ubiquitous giant, there were not always pageants, as such, as part of the Watch. In those instances where there *were* pageants for the Watch and other processions they were sometimes adapted for mayoral inaugurations, such as in 1539, when the King cancelled the Midsummer Watch, and the pageants were then used for the Lord Mayor's procession.[147] Other similarities include the way the Midsummer Watch pageants 'referred to' the Mayor's name (a popular trope, as we'll see). Another overlap with the Shows is the ways in which the Watch contained aspects of trade symbolism as a way of gesturing towards the Company of which the Lord Mayor was a member. Local symbolism of this kind was common, and London was in some ways a privileged space for the creation of such iconography. As Daniel Woolf has argued, 'in London, more than in any other place, a wide assortment of tales had sprung up concerning men and sometimes women . . . who figured in the mythology both of the city itself and also of its sub-communities, such as the guilds'.[148] We will see in due course how these 'tales' figured in mayoral pageantry.

As with the Lord Mayor's Show, the pageantry of the Midsummer Watch utilised figures and tropes extracted from biblical and classical history and mythology, often in the form of allegory.[149] However, in contrast to the Lord Mayor's Show, partly owing to its post-Reformation context, myth featured less often in the Watch than biblical and other religious images and stories. Despite its roots in religious drama and pageantry, and although it preserved some of the moral themes of its predecessors, the Lord Mayor's Show took on a more secular note. To demonstrate the point, Elizabeth McGrath instances the camels which occasionally featured in pageantry, which would have had their roots in 'the sumptuous retinue of the Biblical Three Kings'; likewise, the Grocers' 'Spice Islands . . . are but the descendants of the exotic Paradise Garden of the East'. For the mayoral Shows, she states, the livery companies 'all bent their best efforts towards the invention of happily "decorous" subjects', with 'classical mythology [being] predictably a well-favoured source'.[150] The Shows also became more theatrical, in terms of the use of dramatic speeches, than their predecessors – the Watch seems rarely, if ever, to have had speeches.[151]

This medieval ancestry could pose problems in the post-Reformation period. The Reformation had presented a severe challenge to pre-existing forms of civic memory and culture, many of which were manifested in religious or quasi-religious modes. 'With the iconoclastic destruction of the material elements of the old faith', Tittler writes, 'many longstanding and central elements of the civic heritage, and much of the sense of the local past [were] erased.'[152] In this light, one can see the inception of mayoral Shows in the immediate Reformation period as, implicitly at least, a means by which local history and memory could be celebrated outside of the aegis of a now-deposed faith. One should not overstate the displacement of religious traditions, however. As McGrath argues, and as we'll see further below, the companies' patron saints were 'determinedly adhered to by many loyal guilds [and] would appear even where the context meant that they would have to strike up some rather unlikely relationships with their new pageant companions'. St Katherine, the patron saint of the Haberdashers, a figure who appears with considerable consistency in the early modern Shows, McGrath comments, 'must have looked a bit out of place riding in a scalloped sea-chariot she had borrowed from Amphitrite'.[153]

The impact of the Reformation made itself felt in other aspects of the Companies' practice, too. For instance, the statue of John the Baptist that had been displayed at the Merchant Taylors' Hall was taken down, although the image of the saint was still used in the Company's pageantry in the 1550s, as Machyn's description of Thomas White's 1553 inauguration makes clear.[154] Although he was a Catholic, White's fame, as far as the City was concerned, stemmed from his role in preventing Wyatt's attempt to put Lady Jane Grey on the throne in preference to Mary and for the fact that he founded St John's College in Oxford.[155] Symbols and traditions did persist, even in altered forms. It was not until 1586 that the Merchant Taylors' coat of arms was denuded of its religious imagery of Our Lady and Child with St John, which was replaced, incongruously, by the camels that were to feature shortly in the pageantry of the Shows; the lamb was replaced with a lion, and the 'crest of the Virgin Mary' disappeared.[156] By 1637 Heywood was able to recast St Katherine as 'a Martyr . . . of the Church militant', showing her as entirely appropriated into Protestantism, and Protestantism of a radical flavour to boot (*Londini speculum*, sig. C4v).

The celebration of the Lord Mayor's inauguration itself, which traditionally took place on the day after the feast of St Simon and St Jude, can thus in general terms be traced back to the early medieval period (the first procession took place in 1215). It has even more historically remote links with the triumphal entries and processions of classical Roman times. Indeed, many pageant writers made explicit reference to the Roman triumph as a prototype for the London mayoral Show (Dekker repeatedly refers to the Lord Mayor as a 'Praetor', for instance).[157] It was, however, during the sixteenth century that the Shows took on the shape and format that was to dominate the next hundred years or so, the period when the Shows came into their own as a cultural and political force.[158] Nevertheless, as we will see again and again, the emphasis, as always in civic culture, was on continuity and tradition. Middleton describes the Lord Mayor's prayers at St Paul's after the main entertainment was over as 'those yearely Ceremoniall Rites, which Antient and Graue Order hath determined' (*The triumphs of truth*, sig. D1r). His words bear out Helen Watanabe-O'Kelly's statement that ceremonies of this kind 'are repeated according to a pre-ordained pattern of words and gestures, often enshrined in official documents but always sanctioned by usage and custom'.[159] Heywood, as was his wont, was keen to stress the classical antecedents (and by implication, authority) of the City's governing elite. In the second dedication of *Londons ius honorarium* he informed the Sheriffs that their role demonstrated 'how neere the Dignities of this Citty, come neere to these in Rome, when it was most flourishing'; the text proper commences 'When Rome was erected . . .' (sigs A3v–A4r). Paster writes that 'for Middleton, the presence of mythological figures in civic entertainments and the comparison of civic officials to their ancient Roman counterparts are ways of magnifying the men and the entertainments'.[160] Her statement applies, in fact, to most of the pageant writers of this period, who repeatedly accentuated the long lineage of the traditions to which they contributed.

The series of events of the mayoral inauguration itself evolved over time. Originally, the Lord Mayor rode to Westminster to take his oath of office before the Barons of the Exchequer, the official representatives of the sovereign, rather than travelling by barge as became the norm. According to Hunting, 'the Wardens' Accounts of the Drapers' Company for 1423–4 tell of fifteen minstrels in attendance on the Mayor's Riding of October 1423'.[161] On this occasion there were also banners, made of blue buckram. Middleton's *The sunne in Aries* (following Stow, in an uncommon error) claims that John Norman, mayor in 1453, was 'the first that was rowed in Barge to Westmynster with Siluer Oares, at his owne cost and charges' (sig. B1v). Munday started this trend in 1614, ascribing Norman's legendary deed to a concern for impoverished watermen (*Himatia-Poleos*, sig. B2v), Middleton then repeated the assertion in *The triumphs of health and prosperity* and Heywood made the same claim later still in *Porta pietatis*.[162] Hunting asserts, however, that it was in 1389 that it was 'agreed that the Sheriffs should not have a Riding but go [to Westminster] by water', an innovation then first taken up for the Lord Mayor's journey to Westminster in 1422.[163] Indeed, Dekker writes more accurately in *Londons tempe* that 'in the reigne of Henry 7. Sr. John Shaw Goldsmith, being Lord Maior, caused the Alderman to ride from the Guild-hall to the water-side, when he went to take his Oath at Westminster (where before they Rode by land thither)' (sigs A3v–A4r).[164] It does seem to be the case that Norman's inauguration was the first time when a livery company (in this case, the Drapers) had its own barge built, rather than hiring one.[165] Munday is therefore partly correct when he states in *Himatia-Poleos* that Norman 'at his owne cost and charge . . . made a very goodly Barge for himselfe and his Brethren, to be rowed therein by water to Westminster'. 'It was a costly Barge', Munday adds, 'and the Oares are said to be couered with siluer' (sig. B2v). Confusion persists, however, for Munday has Norman himself claim that 'I was the first Maior, that was presented to the Barons, [*sic*] of the Exchecquer' (sig. B3r).

As the preceding discussion reveals, even in the early modern period dating the stages of the development of the Lord Mayor's Show precisely was tricky, and it remains so. Its elements emerged gradually and in a piecemeal fashion. The livery company records for the period prior to the 1550s, for instance, indicate that music was part of the procession even if speeches were a later development. There is a specific reference in the Drapers' records to 'a pageaunt of thassimpcion boren before the mayre' in 1540, which cites as a precedent the pageantry associated with the inauguration of John Allen, a Mercer, in 1535.[166] This event has almost invariably been regarded by scholars as the first such instance of pageantry taking place within the mayoral inauguration. Thus 1535 has become by repetition and general consensus an epochal date in the history of mayoral pageantry.[167] However, Anne Lancashire points out that on careful reading of the civic archives it is clear that the Mercers were referring specifically to a precedent relating to the Lord Mayor's procession to *the Tower*, not to Westminster. For various reasons (often plague) the oath of fealty was sometimes taken at the Tower, with only limited associated ceremonial, as was the case in both 1592 and 1593, which were plague years.[168] The existence of pageants within the latter type of occasion would therefore have been particularly unusual, and it does not tell us anything about the usual Guildhall–Westminster inaugural route, as many scholars have presumed. There are no references to mayoral pageants in livery company records before 1528, although Lancashire cautions that 'from silence nothing can with certainty be inferred': Company records do not always survive, and those that do are not necessarily comprehensive.[169]

With this caveat, however, the Drapers' records do show signs of pageantry having been employed in conventional mayoral processions to Westminster in both 1528 and 1533, although one must be aware of the frequent vagueness of the term 'pageant' in livery company archives. Owing to this ambiguity, and also to a lack of many relevant livery company records for much of the 1540s, 'it is only when we reach 1553', Lancashire writes, 'that the known records definitely indicate substantial pageant structures'.[170] As I will discuss further below, Henry Machyn's 'diary' does demonstrate that speeches accompanied the pageantry in the Shows at least as far back as 1553.[171] In the light of these uncertainties, Lancashire carefully summarises what little we can know about the growth and development of the Shows in the pre-1553 period as follows:

> 'pageants' [may have come] into existence in the 1470s to 1480, [been] prohibited [by the Corporation] in 1481, reintroduced . . . in the 1520s or 1530s for reasons of Company (and/or individual mayoral) interest in and/or rivalry over visual display, and . . . [have] become elaborate constructions by at least 1553 because of a combination of factors including perhaps evolving custom and political/religious necessity and/or opportunism.[172]

Indeed, Manley argues with some justice that 1568 is more of a marker for the establishment of the mayoral Shows than 1535. Along with a 'fully fledged pageant' for Thomas Rowe fortuitously preserved in the Merchant Taylors' records, 1568, as Manley points out, saw 'the appearance of the first printed calendar . . . of London's civic holidays' which constituted part of what he calls 'a concerted effort by London's leaders at about this time to revive and transform London's civic memory'.[173]

As well as having historical antecedents, the Shows had synchronic relations with other forms of ceremonial, for the City of London had a complex variety of such ritual events, all of which contributed to its sense of itself as a political body founded on elective principles. As we have seen, and as Phythian-Adams remarks, a 'sequence of oath-taking ceremonies . . . regularly punctuated the life cycle of the successful citizen'.[174] For instance, ceremony was associated with the inception of a new Lord Mayor at the point of his election, which took place at Michaelmas (29 September), a month before the actual inauguration.[175] When Richard Dobbis, a Skinner, was elected Lord Mayor in 1551 the Company records indicate that Dobbis was accompanied by a retinue of civic dignitaries to be presented to the current Lord Mayor 'accordinge to the custome', and after said 'solemnytie' he was escorted back to his house.[176] The Recorder of London made a formal speech at the hustings for the election just as he did for the oath-taking part of the inauguration itself.[177] The Lord Mayor was also formally presented by the Recorder on two other occasions: once to the Lord Keeper in early October when the purpose was to 'make [his] election known' to the monarch, and, usually, to the sovereign himself or herself midway through the year of mayoral office.[178] For Dobbis's actual Lord Mayor's Day in 1551 the Company requested the usual 'squibbes for the wilde menne' and a 'greate boate or foyst'. A painter, George Cabell, was to make a 'luzerne' (lynx) and furnish the wild men with clubs. Although the word 'pageant' is not used on this occasion, there are tantalising signs that theatrical-style entertainments were planned: three players were required to 'apparell and trime themselves with redd dubbelats of sarsenet and redd hose lynede with blewe'.[179] It is notable too that even as far back as 1551 the Skinners referred to the celebrations surrounding Dobbis's inauguration as being held 'accordynge to the aunciente custome'.[180]

Another parallel form of civic festivity was the celebration of the election of a livery company's new master and wardens, which featured entertainments (sometimes over two days) and a feast.[181] As with the Lord Mayor's Shows, boy singers and actors from schools, such as Paul's or Westminster school, at times performed before the members of the Companies. The Tallowchandlers' Company records show a payment of 13s 4d to the children of Paul's and 5s to 'Maister Philippes' for overseeing the boys' performance.[182] The election of the sheriffs in June was another ritual moment of the governance of the City, and, here again, the Recorder made a formal speech. Alongside the Midsummer Watch, guild drama and the election of various civic officials, mayoral pageantry was also part of a wider annual cycle of civic ritual and entertainment, usually tied to feast days and other religious ceremonies, such as the annual St Mary Spital sermons after Easter, where the Lord Mayor and Aldermen processed formally (accompanied by children from Christ's Hospital in their blue coats) in a similar fashion to the inaugural Show.[183] These ceremonies were numerous and of long standing in most cases, and had for a considerable time been both recorded and regulated by the City in customals like the *Liber Albus*. As the sixteenth century progressed, as part of the increasingly self-conscious attitude to civic ceremony, printed calendars of civic ritual and pageantry were produced by the City.[184]

Returning to the roots of the Shows themselves, prior to the period covered by this book there are recurrent references to pageants in livery company records; indeed, the Haberdashers' records imply that the inclusion of 'the pageant' in the triumphal day was standard practice in the 1580s. The terminology is persistent, indifferent to change and often ambiguous, and may in its conventionality disguise shifts in the form and content of the Shows through this period. Even as late as 1617, the Grocers' accounts tell of payments for '*the* pageant and *other* showes', although elsewhere in the same accounts where they list the separate devices it is not clear which is which.[185] The printed texts tend not to distinguish between the two terms; indeed, their titles habitually prefer 'triumph'. Even when we get towards the end of the sixteenth century uncertainties remain. A frustratingly throwaway comment in the Haberdashers' Company minutes is all that remains of the pageantry which would have accompanied George Barne in 1586, the year after the first surviving printed text of a Lord Mayor's Show: 'And as for the pageant and such like it is ordered that the same shalbe done in comely order for the honor of the Citie and worshipps of this companie according to form.'[186] The terminology used in the Court minutes on this occasion – 'according to form' – indicates that previous precedents for such pageantry might have included Haberdashers' Shows in 1579 and 1582.

The speeches for Thomas Offley, Lord Mayor in 1556, a Merchant Taylor, were probably written by Nicholas Grimald; the company records for this occasion show a lot of detail in terms of the content of the show and those who participated in making it.[187] Livery company archives from 1561 and 1568 also indicate speeches, and the Ironmongers' records from 1609 refer back to speeches written by James Peele for the 1566 inauguration.[188] The speeches for 1568 (and quite probably 1561 too) were written by Richard Mulcaster, the first headmaster of the Merchant Taylors' School, who is likely to have composed speeches in English and Latin for Elizabeth I's coronation entry into the City a few years previously, as well as acting in the same capacity for King James's entry in 1604.[189] The pageantry for the 1568 Show was explicitly framed to 'suit' Mulcaster's speeches, making 1568 one of the earliest years when the Show begins to sound more like those which dominated the scene some forty years later.[190] The actual speeches for both 1561 and 1568, as well as for 1553, unusually, were reproduced in the Merchant Taylors' records.[191] In 1587 the Haberdashers' Court of Assistants ordered 'a pageant, a ffiost, and all other things' for Lord Mayor's Day, although even at this relatively late date nothing more is known about the pageantry and there is no reference to a writer or artificer.[192]

Although individuals like Grimald and Mulcaster were bought in to write the speeches for Lord Mayor's Day in the 1550s and 1560s, there does not seem to be the 'writer and artificer' arrangement that dominated most of the post-1585 period. Mayoral entertainments of this earlier period seem more to resemble the occasional events put on for members of the royal family, with the use of conventional 'morality' emblems, speeches written by schoolmasters and given by children, and the usual sideshows such as fireworks.[193] Indeed, chief among the enabling factors of the Shows proper was the extant dramatic tradition of 'the medieval cycle drama' usually sponsored by guilds, from which the resultant livery companies developed the habit of sponsoring entertainments, together with schools (some of which were also connected to the Companies) able to provide writers and performers for civic entertainments. The Merchant Taylors' records for 1556 leave the job of devising the pageant and arranging the participants, the music and apparel to those members of the Company appointed to oversee the event. The Company appointed 'p[er]sons to be devisors surveyors & overseers of all suche bussynes & doynge as shall conserne A Pageant . . . and to devise other conceyte as woodwarde [the wild man] & other pastymes to be had'.[194] With these demands in mind, it is quite understandable that as the pageantry got more elaborate professionals were bought in and given the task of organising the content of the Show whilst the Bachelors, the association of freemen whose responsibility the Show became, maintained an overview. As we will see further below, it is certainly the case that the ostentation and complexity of the pageantry increased over this period, in terms of the number of individual pageants and the sophistication of their content. Later still, the title cover of the first Show of the Restoration period (politically entitled *The royal oake*) boasts that it contains 'twice as many Pageants and Speeches as have been formerly showen', which did not stop Pepys describing the former as 'many . . . but poor and absurd'.[195]

As I have already indicated, there were also consanguinities between the Shows and related entertainments like the royal entry and other ad hoc events sponsored by the livery companies and/ or the Corporation of London, such as those held to celebrate the investiture of the Princes of Wales, Henry and Charles, in 1610 and 1616, and the ceremony that marked the opening of the New

River in 1613. They were all forms of 'occasional drama', and, as
with the Shows, royal entry pageants were located at particular
places on the sovereign's route (in some cases the same pageant
locations, such as conduits, were used); the livery companies
were expected to contribute towards these entertainments too.[196]
Kipling notes that 'the introduction of pageantry . . . transformed
the civic triumph decisively in the direction of drama'.[197] The
Shows echoed the development of royal entries in this regard too.
One should not overstate the similarities between entertainments
put on for the monarchy or aristocracy and the Lord Mayor's
Show, however. Wickham emphasises that civic pageants 'were
essentially bourgeois activities [where] responsibility for their
devising and enactment [lay] with the municipality'.[198] In civic
entertainments for the monarch, in contrast, as McGee writes,
'the balance between local concerns and causes and those of the
centre tipped in favour of the latter'.[199] Although the two genres
are sometimes juxtaposed, and their titles can resemble each other,
mayoral Shows share relatively little with the court masque.[200] As
Roze Hentschell points out, the masque took place 'in an enclosed
architectural space . . . in front of a limited and largely aristocratic
audience invited to view the display', and in its celebration of the
monarch and aristocracy the masque can be seen as 'antithetical'
to the mayoral Show.[201] In its form, content and purpose, the
masque therefore differs significantly from Lord Mayors' Shows,
which were performed on the open streets of London in front of
an audience of all comers.

Although they shared some characteristics with royal entries in
terms of imagery and the placement of pageant stations, the Shows
did present a specifically civic version of the inaugural entrance into
the City of the new sovereign, an occasion when, as Caroline Barron
puts it, 'the culture of the court met London culture directly'.[202]
Kipling highlights the 'inaugural function' of the royal entry,
writing that 'civic triumphs marked the king's first advent; they celebrated his coming to his kingdom'.[203] On a smaller scale, the same
can be said of the Lord Mayor's Show: here too a new ruler is welcomed into his territory after swearing an oath of office. There were
important differences too. As we have seen, civic entertainments did
not attempt to replicate the courtly, chivalric tenor of spectacles like
tournaments, but rather chose 'religious' and 'didactic' topics. The
triumphal arch was reserved for royalty, and London Bridge was
not a venue for pageantry during mayoral inaugurations as it often
was for royal entries.[204] The latter phenomenon demonstrated the

way in which monarchs, dukes and the like entered the City via the boundary of the bridge as provisional visitors; the Lord Mayor was not a visitor but rather the leader of the City itself.[205] An additional difference between specifically civic pageantry and entertainments, entries, progresses and so on put on for members of the court, as Barron points out, was the involvement of (elite) women in the latter alone. As she writes, 'the civic processions expressed the need to defend the City and to rule it, and women had no role to play in either task . . . In this respect the Londoners appear to have eschewed chivalric attitudes.'[206]

The Lord Mayor's Show of the early modern period therefore had various models, ancestors and analogues, some direct and some more tangential. It had the strongest roots in guild plays, the Midsummer Watch and other forms of civic festivity. What chiefly linked these entertainments to the mayoral Shows was the extensive involvement of the livery companies, to which the next chapter turns.

Notes

1 The Lord Mayor's Show still takes place, although the date, route and political significance have all changed since the early modern period. The term 'Lord Mayor', although not an official title, is of considerable antiquity. The City of London itself dates the usage of 'Lord Mair' back to 1414, and Felicity Heal states that it was 'routinely used from the 1530s' (*Hospitality*, p. 310). Accordingly, this book consistently refers to the 'Lord Mayor'.

2 It is a rather different story regarding continental triumphs, however, where an extensive body of scholarship exists (for a summary, see McGowan, 'The Renaissance triumph', p. 43 n. 1).

3 Wickham, *Early English Stages*, vol. I, 1980, p. 111. Fennor's *Cornu-Copiae* testifies to the variety of spectacles available to Londoners: the 'dainty fare' of the City's 'gallant crue' include 'Plaies, Pageants, and the tilting day' (sig. I3r).

4 Taylor, *Buying Whiteness*, p. 125. Kiefer makes the point that mayoral Shows 'must have been seen by many of the same people who frequented the London theatres' (*Shakespeare's Visual Theatre*, p. 133). The masque took place in a self-contained courtly world when compared to the Shows.

5 *Jacobean Civic Pageants*, p. 7. Dale Randall concurs that 'we will fare better in the long run if we know something about [mayoral Shows]' (although I would dispute his description of them as 'only marginally dramatic') (*Winter Fruit*, p. 141).

6 'The ages of man', p. 74.

7 Chambers, *The English Stage*, vol. I, p. 138. Middleton's relatively
   slight 1613 entertainment to celebrate the opening of the New River,
   in contrast, Chambers calls 'quite exceptional' (p. 137).

8 Sullivan, 'London's early modern creative industrialists', p. 314. As
   we'll see further in Chapter 2, working for the Companies was treated
   not in fact as hack work but rather as 'service'.

9 Parry, *The Golden Age*, p. 3. Middleton's contribution does not merit
   a mention here.

10 Lobanov-Rostovsky, 'The Triumphes of Golde', pp. 879–80 (see also
   my *Anthony Munday*, p. 80). Most have followed Bergeron's line on
   the relative quality of the Shows. For Stock, Middleton's 1613 Show
   can be considered 'the most sophisticated' of its kind ('Something
   done in honour', p. 126); for Hutchings and Bromham it is a given
   that this is Middleton's 'finest' mayoral Show (*Middleton and His
   Contemporaries*, pp. 12 and 39; see also Dutton, *Jacobean Civic
   Pageants*, pp. 8 and 137).

11 Lobanov-Rostovsky, 'The Triumphes of Golde', p. 893 n. 2.

12 Osteen and Woodmansee, 'Taking account of the New Economic
   Criticism', p. 7.

13 See Gasper, *The Dragon and the Dove*, pp. 1–2 and 12–14 (for the
   same argument in relation to Munday, see Hill, *Anthony Munday*,
   pp. 1–5; see Capp, *The World of John Taylor*, pp. 189–90, for an
   account of Taylor's literary standing). Howard calls Heywood both
   'naïve and often-scorned', which, it seems to me, is having it both ways
   (obviously his Cambridge days didn't knock the naivety out of him)
   (*Theater of a City*, p. 16).

14 Sullivan, 'London's early modern creative industrialists', p. 314.

15 Osteen and Woodmansee, 'Taking account of the New Economic
   Criticism', p. 6.

16 See, for example, Osteen and Woodmansee, eds, *The New Economic
   Criticism*, and Woodbridge, ed., *Money and the Age of Shakespeare*.

17 Guillory, 'A new subject for criticism', p. 224.

18 See Osteen and Woodmansee, 'Taking account of the New Economic
   Criticism', p. 40.

19 Middleton and Edwards, *Collective Remembering*, p. 4. Unfortunately,
   Laura Stevenson's pioneering study, *Praise and Paradox*, does not
   address the Shows because of her focus on printed, mass-market
   'popular' works alongside 'plays that were accessible to large theatre
   audiences' (p. 14): the exclusion of mayoral Shows from the latter category is a missed opportunity, although she does state that Dekker and
   Heywood were among the writers 'most concerned with merchants
   and craftsmen' (p. 49). The continued and deliberate exclusion of
   mayoral Shows (usually yoked together with masques and university
   drama) from bibliographical studies, in particular, is infuriating.

20 *The Rhetoric of Credit*, p. 11.

21 'Conceiving cities', p. 19.
22 Withington, 'Urban political culture', p. 251.
23 *Ibid.*, p. 252.
24 'Ceremony and the citizen', p. 61.
25 Withington includes 'the built environment [and] also civic regalia, civic mythology, civic portraiture, local historical writing, and drama, ritual, and ceremony' ('Urban political culture', p. 254).
26 Fumerton, 'Introduction: a new New Historicism', p. 5.
27 *Table-talk*, p. 93.
28 Manley, *Literature and Culture in Early Modern London*, p. 260.
29 Fletcher, 'Playing and staying together', p. 20. David Cressy, inexplicably, asserts that 'civic occasions, such as entries, triumphs and pageants . . . had an ad hoc quality and enjoyed no fixed periodicity' – perhaps he forgot about the Lord Mayors' Shows (*Bonfires and Bells*, p. xii). He elsewhere usefully discusses the ways in which people's lives were structured by various calendars, legal and agricultural as well as civic.
30 See Middleton and Edwards, *Collective Remembering, passim.*
31 Tittler, 'The Cookes and the Brookes', pp. 67–8.
32 *Ibid.*, p. 68.
33 Archer, 'The arts and acts of memoralization', p. 90.
34 *Ibid.*, p. 105.
35 Manley, 'Civic drama', p. 299.
36 See Middleton and Edwards, *Collective Remembering*, p. 5. I am grateful to Chris Ivic for the development of this point, and for his advice on this chapter as a whole.
37 Middleton and Edwards, *Collective Remembering*, p. 8.
38 Lake, 'From Troynovant to Heliogabulus's Rome', p. 221.
39 Halpern, *The Poetics of Primitive Accumulation*, p. 3.
40 Withington, 'Urban political culture', p. 250.
41 Patterson, 'Married to the town', p. 171.
42 Hardin, 'Spectacular Constructions', p. 10.
43 Lindenbaum, 'Ceremony and oligarchy', pp. 175–6.
44 Munro, *The Figure of the Crowd*, p. 56.
45 Manley, *Literature and Culture in Early Modern London*, pp. 225 and 240.
46 Recorder Finch's speech at the Exchequer when Peter Proby took his oath celebrates Proby's predecessor, Edward Barkham, for his acts of civic altruism such as endowing a new water conduit and contributing towards the building of a new City church (BL Add. MS 18016, fol. 166r). A different attitude towards public amenities is indicated by the case of Sara Guy, who was accused of having '"sundry tymes" "beast-lye" pissed in' the Cheapside conduit (Griffiths, *Lost Londons*, p. 47).
47 Palmer, *Hospitable Performances*, p. 123.
48 Lang, 'Social origins and social aspirations', p. 47.
49 Smuts, 'Public ceremony', p. 72.

50 *Ibid.*, p. 74.
51 Wells *et al.*, *Neo-historicism*, p. 21.
52 For instance, in the Oxford Middleton, Middleton's own use of the perfectly correct term 'companies' is glossed by the editor as 'guilds' (*Middleton: The Collected Works*, p. 974).
53 For clarity, in this book, 'Show' or 'Triumph' (the latter term being the most ubiquitous in the printed texts) should be taken to refer to the entire event, whereas 'pageant' means one of the specific scenes or tableaux that formed part of the entertainment. I have retained the term 'pageantry' for the overall mode of these events.
54 Meredith, 'Fun, disorder, and good government', pp. 52–3.
55 Quilligan, 'Renaissance materialities', p. 427; my emphasis.
56 Yates, *Error Misuse Failure*, p. 4. Hugh Grady's recent survey of the field is an example of what I mean: he argues that 'in this newer materialism . . . cultural and critical theory is largely assumed and undiscussed, and a political relevance to the present is undefined' ('Shakespeare Studies', p. 110).
57 Halpern, *The Poetics of Primitive Accumulation*, p. 14.
58 Smuts, 'Public ceremony', p. 68; my emphasis.
59 'Occasional events', p. 198.
60 *The Drama of Coronation*, p. 9.
61 Taylor, 'Making meaning', p. 63.
62 Smuts, 'Public ceremony', p. 68.
63 McRae, 'The peripatetic muse', p. 43.
64 Notable recent publications in this area include: Dillon, *Theatre, Court and City*; Gadd and Gillespie, *John Stow*; Gadd and Wallis, *Guilds, Society and Economy*; Gordon and Klein, *Literature, Mapping, and the Politics of Space*; Griffiths, *Lost Londons*; Griffiths and Jenner, *Londinopolis*; Harding, *The Dead and the Living in Paris and London*; Howard, *Theater of a City*; Lancashire, *London Civic Theatre*; Merritt, *Imagining Early Modern London* and *The Social World of Early Modern Westminster*; Munro, *The Figure of the Crowd*; Newman, *Cultural Capitals*; Orlin, *Material London*; Turner, ed., *The Culture of Capital*; Twyning, *London Dispossessed*; Withington, *The Politics of Commonwealth*.
65 Mulryne, 'Introduction', p. 1.
66 Tittler, 'The Cookes and the Brookes', p. 58.
67 Griffiths, 'Building Bridewell', pp. 228–9.
68 Manley, 'Civic drama', p. 294.
69 Chambers, *The Elizabethan Stage*, vol. I, p. 131; my emphasis. This volume of Chambers's work is subtitled 'The Court', reflecting his overall approach.
70 *Ibid.*, pp. 135 and 138. In contrast, Chambers offers considerable detail about royal entertainments, including, for example, the menu for an Elizabethan progress in 1602 (see p. 118).

71 Cannadine, 'Introduction', *Rituals of Royalty*, p. 19.
72 Johnston, 'Introduction', *Civic Ritual and Drama*, p. 7. I am grateful to Alan Marshall for the development of this point.
73 Jonson, B. *Ion: his part*, sig. B4r.
74 *CSP Venetian*, vol. 15, pp. 58–9.
75 Munday, *Chruso-thriambos*, sig. C3v.
76 Bergeron, 'King James's civic pageant', p. 214.
77 Hardin, 'Spectacular Constructions', p. 154 (he elides the mayoral *inauguration*, for which the Shows were produced, with the *election* of the Lord Mayor, which took place a month before: the events were quite distinct).
78 'One side of the processional route was reserved for them. Each guild assembled at its appointed place in ceremonial livery, beneath heraldic banners bearing its coat of arms and behind rails draped in blue cloth . . . The Mayor, Recorder, and aldermen of London also waited along the route, in crimson robes of office' (*Middleton: The Collected Works*, p. 220).
79 Manley, 'Civic drama', p. 306.
80 For more on the Shows' use of republican Roman terms such as 'senator', see Hill, *Anthony Munday*, pp. 154–5, Hardin, 'Spectacular Constructions', pp. 146–7, and Paster, *The Idea of the City*, pp. 127–8 and 142–7.
81 See Munday's *Chrysanaleia*, for instance. I explore the notion of the Lord Mayor as the monarch's substitute in more detail in Chapter 5.
82 See Dekker, *The magnificent entertainment*, and Munday, *Chrysanaleia* (for commentary, see my *Anthony Munday*, pp. 24–5, and Bergeron, 'King James's civic pageant', p. 227).
83 Hentschell's claim that the monarch actually participated in the mayoral Show and 'gave the Lord Mayor a sword or scepter to carry in front of the sovereign throughout the [inaugural] procession', as well as the argument she then goes on to make about the relative roles of the Lord Mayor and monarch on the day, is based on a misreading of Manley, who makes it clear that this symbolic handover took place within the *royal entry*, not the Lord Mayor's Show (*The Culture of Cloth*, p. 170; see Manley, *Literature and Culture in Early Modern London*, p. 220).
84 Paster notes that 'the Romans, too, describe their most honored citizens as husbands of the city' ('The idea of London', p. 60).
85 'Conceiving cities', p. 32.
86 *The Idea of the City*, p. 4.
87 *Ibid.*, p. 124. Anthony Parr follows suit, positing a 'cultural rivalry between Whitehall and London in the early seventeenth century' (*Middleton: The Collected Works*, p. 1431).
88 Bergeron, 'Pageants, politics and patrons', p. 139.
89 Williams, 'A Lord Mayor's show by John Taylor', pp. 505–6.

90 Kipling, 'The King's advent transformed', p. 98.
91 Peele, *The deuice of the pageant*, sig. A2r–v.
92 Muir, 'The eye of the procession', p. 131.
93 Bergeron, *Practicing Renaissance Scholarship*, p. 9.
94 *Ibid.*, p. 17.
95 Sullivan, 'London's early modern creative industrialists', p. 313.
96 Bergeron, *English Civic Pageantry* (revised ed.), p. 4; my emphasis. Bergeron's comment here resembles Chambers's bizarre observation about the absence of Shakespeare's name in an account of the 1616 Accession Day tilt, to which the response must surely be – why should it appear in this context anyway? (see *The Elizabethan Stage*, vol. I, p. 148).
97 Paster's rather coercive statement that 'my reader *may* finally decide that Shakespeare is more profoundly responsive to the meaning of cities than either of his contemporaries or than any of his predecessors, known or unknown' not only confers an exaggerated sense of Shakespeare's very limited contribution to urban writing whilst giving her reader little choice but to concur with that exaggeration, but also traduces the important ways in which the pageant writers I focus on here dealt with their primary subject, London (*The Idea of the City*, p. 8; my emphasis). At the opposite end of the scale, Palmer rather cheekily suggests that through his work on the Shows 'Munday was to the streets, what Shakespeare was to the stage' ('Metropolitan resurrection', p. 373).
98 Chambers provides an extensive list of anonymously authored 'Receptions and Entertainments' (*The Elizabethan Stage*, vol. I, pp. 60–74).
99 *Jacobean Civic Pageants*, p. 13.
100 *Parsing the City*, p. 43; my emphasis.
101 'Something done in honour of the city', p. 127.
102 In contrast, Gasper's book on Dekker explicitly deals with 'every genre Dekker worked in', including civic pageantry (although she discusses only one of Dekker's three Shows) (*The Dragon and the Dove*, p. 15).
103 A long overdue study of the civic contexts of Heywood's works by Richard Rowland, *Heywood's Theatre*, was published in 2010.
104 See my *Anthony Munday*, chapter 4, for a more extended critique of this view. Michelle O'Callaghan takes a more measured line than many have done before, acknowledging that the civic authorities 'were developing their own interests in theatricality', notably through mayoral Shows, and that even Calvinists did not automatically regard 'fictional art as necessarily deluding' (*Thomas Middleton*, pp. 14 and 102).
105 *Joint Enterprises*, pp. 9 and 11. Curiously, she does not acknowledge that a number of these dramatists were actually members of livery companies.

106 Bergeron, *Practicing Renaissance Scholarship*, p. 46.

107 *Joint Enterprises*, p. 13.

108 'Something done in honour of the city', p. 127.

109 There is commentary of this kind – briefly – in Eldred Jones's *Othello's Countrymen* (pp. 34–5). Rebecca Bach discusses the colonial dimensions of mayoral Shows but not in relation to other works by the same writers (see *Colonial Transformations*, pp. 149–63, and, for further discussion of this topic, Chapter 5 below).

110 *The triumphs of truth*, sig. C1v, and *The changeling*, sig. I1v.

111 He writes, for instance, that Munday's *Chysanaleia* 'provides important clues to how the [Five] Senses may have looked in *Timon of Athens*' (*Shakespeare's Visual Theatre*, p. 133).

112 'Middleton and Munday', p. 470.

113 Williams, 'A Lord Mayor's Show', p. 514.

114 *Ibid.*, p. 527.

115 Munday also complains in *Londons loue* that his and the City Corporation's time to prepare the entertainment was 'verie short' (sig. A3v). Poor Thomas Churchyard was asked to prepare an entertainment for Queen Elizabeth later the same day, which compares starkly to the two years given over to planning Katherine of Aragon's extravagant coronation celebrations (see Wickham, *Early English Stages*, vol. I, p. 110, and Kipling, 'Anne Boleyn', p. 44).

116 Mulryne, 'Introduction', p. 9.

117 Wickham, *Early English Stages*, vol. I, p. 81.

118 Paster, *The Idea of the City*, p. 138. Heinemann states that Middleton gained 'a considerable part of his income, perhaps the greater part of it' from his civic employments (*Puritanism and Theatre*, p. 121).

119 Wickham, *Early English Stages*, vol. I, p. 111.

120 Horne, *The Life and Minor Works of George Peele*, p. 76.

121 As Dutton points out, Jonson went to some lengths to underplay his involvement in civic pageantry when his *Workes* were published in 1616 (*Jacobean Civic Pageants*, p. 24).

122 Heinemann, *Puritanism and Theatre*, p. 122.

123 Hardin, 'Spectacular Constructions', p. 142 (see also Chapter 2, below).

124 Mulryne, 'Introduction', p. 2.

125 Smuts, 'Occasional events', p. 198.

126 Lancashire writes that the Drapers' Company 'included play performances as a regular, expected part of its annual election feast celebrations over a period of about 112 years, from at least 1430 to 1541' ('Medieval to Renaissance', p. 310).

127 The Show did not always take place on 29 October in this period: when the date fell on a Sunday the Show was postponed to 30 October, as in 1609 and 1615, for instance. In 1665 and 1702 the Show took place on 9 November, prefiguring its permanent move to November, where

it has remained. The feast of St Simon and St Jude, 28 October, was one of those which survived the Reformation purge of saints' days. Although they are not the concern of this book, it is important to bear in mind that other major English towns, such as Norwich and York, celebrated the inauguration of their mayors (and other notable dates such as midsummer) with forms of pageantry, although one should also heed Tittler's warning that such were the differences between London and provincial towns that 'the two milieux are sometimes best considered apart' (*The Reformation and the Towns*, p. 337). Such celebrations, writes Heal, 'survived little altered in many English towns until at least the late eighteenth century' (*Hospitality*, p. 335). On the continent, trade guilds also produced civic entertainments.

128 The Stationers' Company records show that there was a mayoral feast in 1601 and 1602, dates for which little is known about the inauguration celebrations (Arber, *Transcript*, vol. III, p. 325). Conversely, even feasts were often curtailed in times of crisis: for instance, in 1573, a plague year, the Queen ordered that there be no entertainment at the Guildhall when the Grocer John Rivers came into office (see Heath, *Some Account of the Worshipful Company of Grocers*, pp. 252–3). The 1633 edition of Stow's *Survey* notes that in 1563 there was 'no Maior's Feast by reason of the Plague' (p. 586).

129 GH MS 16,967/4.

130 GH MS 15,842/1, fols 119r and 142r.

131 *The Reformation and the Towns*, p. 273.

132 'Costuming the Shakespearean stage', p. 206 n. 15; my emphasis. I am grateful to Dr Lublin for allowing me to quote from his unpublished PhD thesis.

133 Gadd and Wallis, *Guilds, Society and Economy*, p. 5. The connections between the fraternities then known as the guilds and various religious bodies came about because the guilds, 'having no common meeting house . . . commonly gathered in a neighbouring church, monastery or hospital, whose saint they adopted as patron' (see www.thedrapers.co.uk/History/1_Introduction.html). Clifford Davidson writes that cycle plays in towns and cities such as York and Coventry, which represent one of the roots of the Lord Mayor's Show, 'which proceeded at a frenetic pace prior to the third decade of the sixteenth century, came to a virtual stop after the [1534] Act of Supremacy' (*Technology*, p. 101 n. 5). Tittler notes that in London 'Corpus Christi festivities disappeared in the reign of Edward VI' (*The Reformation and the Towns*, p. 319).

134 *Ibid.*, p. 319.

135 See Kipling, 'Anne Boleyn', p. 52.

136 Sponsler, 'Alien nation', p. 235.

137 Munro, *The Figure of the Crowd*, p. 57. Grantley usefully relates the rise in prominence of civic pageantry in the late sixteenth century to the increase of 'theatrical renderings' of London, although his claim

that Peele's 1585 Show marks the 'beginning of the representation of London in eulogistic terms' overlooks the centuries of tradition that precede this date (*London in Early Modern English Drama*, p. 65).

138 Gadd and Wallis, *Guilds, Society and Economy*, p. 5. I explore the consequences of the Companies' changing realities at greater length in Chapter 5.

139 See Robertson and Gordon, *Collections* III, p. xiv. Street pageants also took place in various locations on 17 November, the anniversary of Elizabeth's accession.

140 Hunting, *A History of the Worshipful Company of Drapers*, p. 75; see also Manley, 'Civic drama', pp. 299–302, for a useful and concise account of civic religious ceremony in the pre-Reformation period.

141 Hunting, *A History of the Worshipful Company of Drapers*, pp. 75–6. Stow gives a colourful account of the Midsummer Watch, in the course of which he mentions how the pageantry was organised to reflect the City hierarchy: 'the Mayor had besides his Giant, three Pageants, [whereas] each of the Sheriffes had besides their Giantes but two Pageants' (*A suruay of London*, sig. F6v).

142 See Barron, 'Chivalry, pageantry and merchant culture', p. 229. Heal states that the Watch came to an end in 1539 'largely because of its cost' (*Hospitality*, p. 346); Ronald Hutton puts it down to concerns about immediate post-Reformation 'security', arguing that the official line about cost was an 'excuse' (*Merry England*, p. 76); for Manley, citing the 1538 injunctions against the use of images, the reasons were partly financial and partly religious ('Civic drama', p. 302). The Midsummer Watch continued a little longer in Coventry, until c.1565 (see Phythian-Adams, 'Ceremony and the citizen', p. 79).

143 See Cressy, *Bonfire and Bells*, p. 27, and Lancashire, 'Continuing civic ceremonies', p. 84.

144 Williams, 'A Lord Mayor's show', p. 502.

145 Doolittle, *The Mercers' Company*, p. 25; see also Griffiths, *Lost Londons*, p. 351.

146 Hunting, *A History of the Worshipful Company of Drapers*, p. 76. Manley writes that 'it appears that for a period of more than 30 years [from 1539 to 1568], coinciding with the period of the greatest religious instability in England, there was considerable uncertainty regarding the ceremonial priority of the Midsummer Watch and the mayoral inauguration' ('Civic drama', p. 303).

147 Lindenbaum, 'Ceremony and oligarchy', p. 182.

148 Woolf, *The Social Circulation of the Past*, p. 314. 'The more urban the community', he remarks, 'the likelier it was that an episode from the past . . . would find a variety of channels of expression' (p. 315).

149 See Cartwright, 'The Antwerp *Landjuweel*', for a discussion of the use of 'moral, religious, or political statement in the form of tableau or dumb show' in civic ceremony in the Low Countries.

150 McGrath, 'Rubens's Arch of the Mint', pp. 203–4.

151 Robertson and Gordon cite only one example, from 1541 (*Collections* III, p. xxii).

152 Tittler, 'The Cookes and the Brookes', pp. 68–9.

153 McGrath, 'Rubens's Arch of the Mint', p. 204. Walsh remarks that Heywood presents St Katherine as 'a thoroughly classical figure . . . rather than the medieval saint' ('St Martin in the City', p. 78 n. 12). He also notes in the post-Restoration Shows the 'still potently "Catholic" [livery company patron] saints were relegated to the status of heraldic emblems, chiefly of historical interest' (*ibid.*, p. 76).

154 Davies and Saunders, *History of the Merchant Taylors' Company*, p. 98.

155 Edmund Campion, better known as a Catholic martyr executed in 1581, presented White's funeral oration (see *ibid.*, p. 120). Manley describes White's 'lonely vigil' when he attempted to reintroduce the old traditions during his mayoralty ('Civic drama', p. 304). In *Monuments of honor* Webster gives quite a long account of how White came to found St John's College, in which he takes care to point out that the story of the elm tree which inspired White's action is 'in no way superstitiously giuen' (sig. B4v).

156 See Davies and Saunders, *History of the Merchant Taylors' Company*, p. 149. Cressy discusses the post-Reformation 'purging' of the festive calendar at length (see *Bonfires and Bells*, pp. 4–10).

157 Heywood provides a typically erudite account of the term in *Londons ius honorarium* (sig. A4v).

158 Mayoral inaugurations took a backward step in the late fourteenth century, when, as Barron explains, 'the "pantomime" additions to the [mayor's] riding [to Westminster] were thought to be getting out of hand', with the consequence that 'disguysyng' and 'pageoun[s]' were prohibited ('Chivalry, pageantry and merchant culture', p. 229). Thereafter, there is documented evidence of Shows from as far back as the 1520s, as well as an undated fragment of what may be a mayoral Show, held in Trinity College, Cambridge. Little is known for certain about this manuscript (see Withington, 'A note on "A fragment"' and Adams, 'A fragment of a Lord Mayor's pageant').

159 Watanabe-O'Kelly, 'Early modern European festivals', p. 15.

160 Paster, *The Idea of the City*, p. 142.

161 See Hunting, *A History of the Worshipful Company of Drapers*, p. 76. Sutton reproduces a contemporary account of a mayoral procession (on horseback) to and from Westminster in 1419 ('Civic livery', p. 22).

162 Despite the fact that it was corrected by subsequent scholarship some time ago (see Carr, 'Barge flags of the City livery companies', pp. 223–4), this erroneous assertion has been treated as accurate by generations of commentators (see, for example, Grupenhoff, 'The Lord Mayors' Shows', p. 16 and Sykes, 'Lord Mayor's Day', p. 80).

163 Hunting, *A History of the Worshipful Company of Drapers*, p. 79. The Lord Mayor in 1422 was William Walderne, a Mercer, and on this occasion the Company hired the barge (see Palmer, *Ceremonial Barges*, p. 5). In 1576, when the new Lord Mayor was a Goldsmith, the Clothworkers and Skinners shared a barge for Lord Mayor's Day (*ibid.*, p. 64).

164 Dekker states that Shaw was the first to introduce the feast at the Guildhall rather than at the Company Hall and he also claims that to facilitate the Guildhall feast, 'all the Kitchens, and other Offices there, [were] built by [Shaw]' (sig. A4r).

165 Palmer, *Ceremonial Barges*, p. 5. As Middleton makes clear, Norman paid for the barge himself; Kenneth Palmer comments that 'it is unclear whether or not the Drapers' Company was given the use of Norman's barge after 1453' (*ibid.*, p. 30). Company barges tended to be kept in barge houses in Lambeth and Vauxhall, on the southern side of the river.

166 Cited in Lancashire, 'Continuing civic ceremonies', p. 83.

167 See, for instance, Manley, *Literature and Culture*, p. 265.

168 The Vintners' records for 1592 show a payment to 'Mr Philipp', their waterman, for his charges 'although the Companie went neither to westm[inste]r nor to the Tower when Sir Willm Row tooke his oath at the Towergate' (GH MS 15,333/2, fol. 167). It was the same story the following year, when the Vintners again paid Mr Philipp 'for his charges although the Lo: Maior toke his oath at the Tower Hill' (GH MS 15,333/2, fol. 183). This must have been especially disappointing for the Vintners, for whom Buckle was only the second mayor in the entire sixteenth century (they weren't to have the honour again until the 1640s, when elaborate pageantry was not an option for other reasons). Compounding the misfortune, Buckle himself died in office and was succeeded by Richard Martin, a Goldsmith.

169 Lancashire, 'Continuing civic ceremonies', p. 85.

170 *Ibid.*, p. 91.

171 Wickham comments that speeches were a natural development within 'processional pageantry' (*Early English Stages*, vol. I, 1980, p. 54). McGee, for some reason, dates the use of 'pageants and other theatrical forms' in 'mayoral inaugurations' as taking place 'after 1578' ('Mysteries, musters and masque', pp. 106–7).

172 Lancashire, 'Continuing civic ceremonies', p. 98. Hentschell was therefore mistaken to follow Tumbleson's claim that 'the first Lord Mayor's show was performed in 1535 and the last in 1701' (*The Culture of Cloth*, p. 163 n.18).

173 'Civic drama', pp. 304–5.

174 'Ceremony and the citizen', p. 59.

175 The process could be truncated: in 1622, with the intervention of the Crown, Peter Proby translated from the Barber Surgeons to the Grocers only in June, took the oath as one of the Company assistants

in July, and was elected Lord Mayor shortly thereafter (see GH MS 11,588/3, fol. 205) I discuss Proby's mayoral inauguration at greater length in Chapter 5.

176 GH MS 30708/1, fol. 1r. Trumpeters and giants were also arranged.

177 Sir Heneage Finch's speech on the election of Edward Barkham in 1621 relates how he 'rose from the Chaire and went to the window where the Town clerk stood . . . [then] the Aldermen came one by one and gave their voices all for Ald. Barkham' (BL Add. MS 18016, fol. 141r).

178 For the former, see, for instance, BL Add. MS 18016, fol. 145v.

179 GH MS 30708/1, fol. 1v, and GH MS 34,048/10. The players, whose names were Robert Wayte, Thomas Furston and John Harte, received 41s 8d in 1602 for 'there paynes'. The identity of these three is unknown, although a 'Thomas Funston' acted in university drama some fifty years later (see www.shakespeareauthorship.com/bd/bio-f.htm).

180 GH MS 30708/1, fol. 2v.

181 See Benbow, 'Sixteenth-century dramatic performances', p. 129.

182 *Ibid.*, p. 130. In the early 1570s, these entertainments were curtailed by the City's Common Council (*ibid.*, p. 131). There were numerous other opportunities for a party, however, such as when in 1595 the Skinners' Court minutes 'ordeyned that the drinkinge on St Margaretes Daye shalbe contynued' (GH MS 30,708/2, fol. 228r).

183 The three Spital sermons were even more 'civic' occasions than the Good Friday sermon preached at Paul's Cross, for the Spital preachers were appointed by the Court of Aldermen. The religious significance of these events was matched by their secular status: charitable donations were expected towards the upkeep of the City's hospitals, and the sermons also acted as another opportunity for a display of civic cohesion and prestige. Stow gives an account of the 'honourable persons' attending the sermon: 'against the said pulpit . . . remaineth also one fayre builded house of two stories in height for the Mayor and other honorable persons, with the Aldermen and Sheriffes to sit in, there to heare the Sermons preached upon Easter holy dayes. In the loft ouer them, the Ladies and Aldermens wiues doe stand at a fayre window or sit at their pleasure . . . The Maior, with his brethren the Aldermen were accustomed to bee present . . . in their Scarlets at the Spittle in the Holidayes, except Wednesday in violet' (*A suruay of London* (1598), sig. K1r–v). The importance of ceremonial dress is echoed in the mayoral procession (see Chapter 3).

184 See Manley, *Literature and Culture in Early Modern England*, p. 263. Formal guidelines continued to exist for the conduct of Lord Mayors' Shows and other types of civic ceremonial (see, for example, the 1933 *Handbook of Ceremonials*).

185 GH MS 11,590, fol. 21; my emphases. The day of the Show was invariably called 'Lord Mayor's Day' by the Companies, and usually glossed

as 'the day that my Lord Maior shall take his oath at Westminster' or similar.

186 GH MS 15,842/1, fol. 27r. George Barne was Francis Walsingham's brother-in-law and had strong court connections.

187 Robertson and Gordon, *Collections* III, p. 39, and Sayle, *Lord Mayors' Pageants*, p. 21.

188 See GH MS 16,969/2.

189 Robertson and Gordon speculate that Mulcaster also wrote the speeches for the 1561 Show (*Collections* III, pp. xxxi and xxxiv). Mulcaster was commissioned to write his pamphlet by the City Corporation, and a copy of it was given to the new queen (for a full discussion of this complex work, see Hunt, *The Drama of Coronation*). One quite significant difference between this work and the Shows is that Mulcaster represents the Queen's reactions (or alleged reactions) to the pageantry she was presented with; she apparently also requested that the meanings be explained to her (see *ibid*, p. 170).

190 See McGee and Meagher, 'Preliminary checklist of Tudor and Stuart entertainments', p. 83.

191 See Robertson and Gordon, *Collections* III, p. 38. Those for 1561 and 1568 are reproduced in Sayle, *Lord Mayors' Pageants*, and in *Collections* III, pp. 42–3. Speeches for civic entertainments in other towns were sometimes preserved in civic archives (see McGee, 'Mysteries, musters and masque', p. 106 n. 6).

192 GH MS 15,842/1, fol. 32r. John Shute, a painter-stainer, was paid £12 'for making the Merchant Taylors' Company's pageant' in 1561, as was to become the norm.

193 For example, an entertainment for the Queen in Norwich in 1578 contained biblical-themed pageants, speeches given by boys and an oration by 'Stephan Limbert, publike Scholemaster' (*The Ioyfull receyuing of the Queenes most excellent Maiestie into hir Highnesse Citie of Norwich*, sig. Diiiv). Owing, one assumes, to their familiarity both with public speaking and with managing schoolboys, school masters were often called upon to write and/or deliver speeches: the magnificently named Hercules Rollock wrote Latin verses to celebrate Anna of Denmark's entry into Edinburgh in 1590.

194 Cited in Sayle, *Lord Mayors' Pageants*, p. 22.

195 Sayle, *Lord Mayors' Pageants*, p. 129. Tatham's text strikes a fervently revisionist royalist note, as one might expect in 1660: the Show is said to have taken place not in the first but rather 'in the 12th year of his Majesties most happy, happy Reign' (*The royal oake*, title page).

196 There is a discrete section in the Merchant Taylors' accounts, for example, for James's royal entry, where the individual Company members were assessed for their contributions (see GH MS 34,048/8).

197 Kipling, *Enter the King*, p. 28.

198 Wickham, *Early English Stages*, vol. I, p. 54.

199 McGee, 'Mysteries, musters and masque', p. 106.

200 The names of court masques from the 1630s include *Albion's Triumph* (1632) and *Britannia Triumphans* (1638).

201 Hentschell, *The Culture of Cloth*, pp. 163–4.

202 Barron, 'Chivalry, pageantry and merchant culture', p. 230.

203 Kipling, *Enter the King*, p. 39.

204 See Barron, 'Pageantry on London Bridge'; see also Stevenson, 'Occasional architecture' for more on triumphal arches. In Elizabeth's coronation entry the final pageant was placed outside of the City boundary, on Fleet Street.

205 'The bridge had a major role to play in ceremonies that presented the interaction of the City and the monarchy, but it was little used in civic ceremonies such as the midsummer watch or the Lord Mayor's riding, since these focused on the internal spaces of the City' (Harding, 'Pageantry on London Bridge', p. 114). This important distinction should temper Karen Newman's claim that the bridge 'was a place of ritual celebration and pageantry for Londoners' (*Cultural Capitals*, p. 56).

206 Barron, 'Chivalry, pageantry and merchant culture', p. 230. As she comments, women were not excluded from civic life entirely: 'they had a real role to play in the economy of the City'.

2

'Our devices for that solemne and Iouiall daye': the writers, the artificers and the livery companies

Planning the look and content of the Shows was a complex and expensive business. Such events, Mulryne has written, 'represent a remarkable coming-together of organisational and management skills . . . [including] the task of harnessing and co-ordinating the talents of writers, musicians, scenographers, choreographers', as well as performers.[1] In addition, being the creator of a Lord Mayor's Show was often (although not always) a contested position, where writers and artificers competed with each other for commissions. As well as exploring how the Show was financed and put together (a topic continued in Chapter 3), I will here, in adition, highlight the often-overlooked roles of the artificer and those other craftsmen who contributed so valuably to the day's entertainment.

The commissioning and organising of the Shows can in themselves tell us a great deal about civic culture in this period. The records demonstrate the relative degrees of importance that the Companies laid on certain aspects of the Shows. They tended to prioritise expenditure on the procession instead of the pageantry – clothing the 'poor men' as well as the mayoral party, for instance – and on forms of visual representations of their power and prestige such as decorated banners, streamers, ensigns and so on. Crucially, the livery company documents help to defamiliarise many preconceptions about authorship and collaboration in this period by revealing the ways in which civic pageantry was brought to life by writers working *alongside* the artificers and others about whom the printed works are often silent. In particular, as we will see, the apparently pedestrian and bureaucratic livery company records are not only full of human incident, but they sometimes provide the only remaining information about what took place on those occasions when either no printed text was produced or none has survived. My practice in this regard therefore echoes that of Kara Northway, who argues that cultural history should be characterised by a 'reading [of] nonliterary in addition to literary texts in order to elucidate the attention given to financial and political value in the production of Renaissance occasional drama'.[2] Such an approach is, after all, more in keeping with the ways in which these entertainments were planned and executed.

It must be stressed from the outset that the Lord Mayor's Show was first and foremost the concern of the Great Twelve livery companies from the ranks of one of which the Lord Mayor was elected, even if, to make this possible, he had transferred quite recently from one of the smaller companies. (See Appendix 2 for the organisation of the linear companies.) The City Corporation dealt only with pageantry, entertainments and hospitality relating to visits from members of the royal family and other non-civic dignitaries, although on those infrequent occasions the set-up was very similar to the approach taken over mayoral Shows.[3] The costs of the Shows fell to individual Company members, whose putative contribution was assessed: for example, in 1604 the highest rank of the Bachelors of the Haberdashers' Company who were going to be 'in foins' (wearing pine-marten fur) paid a charge of £3 6s each, those wearing the more lowly 'Budge' (lambs' wool) £2 10s, and the other members' various sums from £4 to a few shillings; by 1620 the cost to the Haberdasher's Company Bachelors in foins had risen to £5 each.[4] To fund these occasions considerable numbers of the Company in question were – voluntarily or not – elevated to the Bachelor rank of the Company. Those who tried to avoid the charge without good cause were fined, and errant members (as we'll see further below) could be pursued for outstanding contributions for years.

The Companies were assiduous at collecting contributions from their members because their main priority was to ensure that the Lord Mayor's Show was a suitably splendid reflection of the status of the role it inaugurated. The celebration of the glory reflected on the Company by a mayoral incumbent was often informed by a competitive awareness of what the other Great Twelve were capable of doing, so competition between the Companies also played a part in their preparations. Archer notes that 'companies tried to outbid each other in the sumptuousness of their display, and kept a jealous eye on the practice of the others'.[5] When the Merchant Taylors heard that the Goldsmiths had purchased an embroidered cloth for their barge, they decided to do the same.[6] The Haberdashers were equally concerned to match the new barge purchased by the Fishmongers in 1638. The civic pride manifested on these occasions prompted satire from other quarters. Jasper Mayne's 1639 court play *The citye match*, for instance, parodies such pride in the accoutrements of civic power via a conversation between Ware-house, a city merchant, and Plotwell, his nephew and heir. Ware-house describes his hope that his nephew would rise through the civic oligarchy to reach the 'Citie Senate' and take on 'th' sword and Cap of Maintenance'. Plotwell in turn mocks his uncle's desire that he will attend sermons in his 'Chaine and scarlet' and that 'Gates and Conduits will be dated from [his] yeare' (sig. C1v). Later on in the play another character says to Plotwell 'I lookt the next Lord Maiors day to see you o'th Livery, or one oth'Batchelour Whiflers' (sig. G1v).

Mockery aside, the Companies themselves, naturally, took the trappings of mayoral inaugurations – from the 'Cap of Maintenance' to the 'Batchelour Whiflers' – very seriously, and they devoted personnel as well as money to their realisation. As well as funding the day, the detailed arrangements for the Show were typically the responsibility of the Bachelors of the livery company in question, who delegated the work to a small committee (the Bachelors would previously have taken on this role for the Midsummer Watch).[7] In 1585, for instance, the Skinners gave the responsibility for organising Lord Mayor's Day to some of the Wardens of the Yeomanry; on this occasion, as was commonplace, they were enjoined to arrange things 'according as hath byn accustomid for . . . this Companye'.[8] The 'pageant' for Lord Mayor's Day in 1611 was, unusually, under the direction of the more important Wardens of the Goldsmiths' Company (perhaps this was due to the expected presence of the Queen).[9] Members of the Skinners' Lord Mayor's Day committee for 1628 were reimbursed for 'viewing' both the pageants and the galley foist, which shows, as was commonplace, that committee members kept a close eye on developments.[10]

This responsibility in itself could be contested. One gains a sense of tension over the negotiations over the 1616 Show, not, as one might expect, between putative candidates for the job of producing the event, but rather between different parts of the Fishmongers' Company themselves. Representatives of the Fishmongers' Yeomanry 'did chalendg to haue the managing of all that busynes to them selves', and it seems they had to convince the Wardens and Assistants to allow them the role, which had previously been the joint responsibility of both the Yeomanry and the Wardens of the Company. The Yeomanry cited the precedent of the way things had been recently handled by the Drapers' Company, from whose

ranks the last two Lord Mayors had been elected; this was rebuffed
by the starchy response that 'the presedents of this Companie were
quite contrarye'. The new arrangement was eventually assented to,
however, on the understanding that no financial call would be made
on the Wardens. Flexing their newly gained muscles, the Yeomanry
representatives then asked that they be allowed to 'prefer on Cley, a
carver and shipwright' the job of making the 'fishing busse' (fishing
boat) that the Company had already begun to negotiate with
Munday (i.e. that Munday be required to subcontract this work
to their candidate, Cley). Cley was ordered to present a 'plott' of
the ship to the Wardens for their approval.[11] (I will explore further
aspects of his particular commission below.)

The more common form of competition between potential writers
and artificers was not inevitable but was probably encouraged by the
Companies to ensure they got the best deal.[12] This perhaps was the
cause of the 'envy' mentioned in the printed texts of Shows by both
Middleton and Munday. In the dedication of *Sidero-Thriambos*
Munday states his hope that the Ironmongers appreciate his efforts
'in the despight of enuy, and calumnious imputations', suggesting
that someone had tried to impugn his reputation (sig. A3r). Sullivan
claims that the companies 'asked and paid for two or three sketches
[of the Show] . . . and withheld payment if the final performance
was not up to standard'.[13] She has slightly over-simplified the way
the business was carried on, however. There weren't unsuccessful parties on every occasion, for one thing. In 1629, for instance,
Dekker and Christmas were asked to present the Company with
their 'plot' in order to agree a fee. There is no sign of a competitor:
the Ironmongers seem to have settled on Dekker and Christmas as
early in the year as August and then negotiated the sums involved.
Much the same method seems to have applied in 1609, where again
the Ironmongers' Company simply requested 'to see a plott drawne
for the pageant' and 'the devise of the speeches'.[14] In addition, on
those rare occasions when their disappointment with what took
place on the day was considerable the Companies only ever withheld part of the fee. Middleton and Christmas, for instance, only
had their payment for some aspects of the production 'putt of' by
the Drapers in 1626 due to an 'ill performance'.[15]

Whatever the vagaries of the process, commissions of this kind
were evidently sought after, for the Companies paid quite hand-
somely (within limits, as we'll see below), and the Shows carried
considerable prestige. Where there had been a sizeable gap between
mayors for any particular Company those generally employed on

these occasions did not hesitate to make themselves known to the prospective employer. Writers and artificers presented 'plots', and those who undertook other roles made overtures to the Company.[16] For example, the keeper of Blackwell Hall (the City's main cloth market) was present at the Fishmongers' Court in October 1616, where he 'made the house acquaynted, that the use and manner is, that the pageants on the Lord Maior's day of tryumphe be sett there [i.e. in his Hall] . . . for which use of the house his usuall allowaunce is xls. which he desireth to have'.[17] Sometimes it is impossible now to tell what kind of competition and negotiation had gone on. In 1611, for instance, Munday simply appears as de facto 'poet' in the Goldsmiths' Court Minutes.[18] Similarly, and even more tantalisingly, when in September 1615 the Drapers established a sub-committee to 'take viewe and consideracon of suche plotts and shewes as are offered to be of service to this Companie', they were simply required to report back to the Court of Assistants.[19] Any evidence of the identity of the other candidates for the commission – and evidently there were some – along with the Drapers' deliberations which lead to Munday's selection, have left no trace in the records. This is not to say that the Companies made their selection, when a selection was to be made, on the basis of specifically aesthetic considerations, or at least the kind of aesthetic considerations valued by modern commentators. As Dutton remarks, 'visual effects and ingenious stagings seem eventually to have carried more weight with the [livery companies'] committees than the dramatists' "inventions"'. With the political imperatives inherent in the Shows, as he points out, 'the need to dazzle doubtless always ran ahead of calls for intellectual complexity'.[20]

'The need to dazzle' invariably resulted in a concomitant need to be *seen to* spend lavishly; no Company wanted it to look as it had stinted on the celebrations. At the same time, the companies were habitually concerned to demonstrate that their mayoral festivities were rooted in long-standing tradition, although, as we'll see below (in the context of a society which did not have our modern concept of 'inflation') this was sometimes a disguise for mere economy. Northway writes that 'the liveries "interpreted" remuneration by searching their own and other liveries' financial records to discover the original prices paid for work on drama and thus to restrict prices'.[21] This practice had the desired effect: as Palmer remarks, 'payments remained static often for years at a stretch'.[22] The year 1609, for example, was the year of the first Ironmonger Lord Mayor since the 1560s. The Company explicitly went back to inspect the 'charges of the pageant in former tymes whereout a computation may be had of the Charge present'. This search revealed that 'Mr Peele' (the elder) had in 1566 received 30s 'for his invention of speeches & paines' and that the making of the pageant cost £18.[23] The expense of the Show had increased considerably in almost fifty years so one wonders if the chief purpose of these earlier costings was simply to keep costs down.[24] In the event, Munday's agreement for 'the setting out of the pageant' and his other jobs came to £45, a reasonable although not munificent increase on 1566, and Grinkin received the same sum. More realistically, in 1619, after a gap of more than twenty years since their last Lord Mayor, the Skinners requested information from the Ironmongers on their expenses for the previous year's Show (the request was granted).[25] The Merchant Taylors paid 'Ricknor [a clerk?] for the Coppie of a [precedent] from the Haberdashers' in 1602, which may have been for the same purpose, as the two previous years' Lord Mayors had been Haberdashers.[26]

On those occasions when Companies were being unusually generous, they highlighted the fact in their minutes. In 1611 the Goldsmiths, for instance, recorded 'a more liberall benevolence than hath bene formerlie granted to any Lord Maior of this Companie' when they bestowed two hundred marks on James Pemberton towards his mayoral expenditure.[27] This generosity should be considered in the context of the great wealth of the Goldsmiths, of course, and the fact that they had only two mayoral inaugurations to fund in this period: Richard Martin in 1589 and James Pemberton in 1611. With these infrequent exceptions, the Companies clearly had an eye to expense as much as spectacle, for in both 1633 and 1635 Heywood and members of the Christmas family received commissions in preference to John Taylor and Robert Norman by underbidding the latter by just £10. As Northway comments, 'no flat rate existed for the dramatist'.[28] The year 1595 appears to be the first in which Company records show a writer making a suit for the commission. 'Mr Pele' (George Peele) was appointed by the Skinners, and it was agreed that there would be a 'lusarne' [lynx], a pageant and a 'moscovitor'.[29] The Skinners' Court minutes do not mention whether Peele had had any competitors for his 'sute'. In general terms, the preliminary stage of the process, it would seem, would be to request a 'plot' for the pageantry from the would-be producer(s) – this is certainly what happened both in 1609 and in 1619, when Munday vied with Middleton for the work – but that is not to say that at every juncture more than one plot was evaluated, at least as far as the Companies' archives can tell us. It is, however, certainly the case that writers and/or artificers (and sometimes other parties) were often offered money for unsuccessful bids.[30] 'Mr Taylor and the Poet' were given £5 by the Skinners in 1628 when they lost out to Dekker and Christmas, and the Grocers similarly reimbursed Munday and Dekker with 'benevolences' in 1613.[31] The latter accounts state that Munday was paid 'for his paines in drawing a project for this busynes which was offered to the Comyttees': Munday received £5 and Dekker £4 'for the like'. These are not inconsiderable sums, and suggest that both disappointed suitors had done a lot of work in anticipation of the commission. It is also testament to the kudos associated with the Shows that at least three professional writers should vie for the role.

Sullivan makes the useful point that 'payments [made] by a corporate body' (such as a livery company) were undertaken in a semi-public way and documented as such in the companies' records, making it more straightforward to determine the 'market rate' for cultural productions such as the Lord Mayor's Show. Indeed, as we'll see further below, if the Merchant Taylors had not kept such carefully itemised accounts we would know very little about their 1602 and 1610 Shows. Writers and artificers were also sometimes recompensed when the Show did not take place at all. In 1630, for instance, the Merchant Taylors' accounts state that 20s was 'given and paid by the consent of the Committees to Thomas Decker the Poett for his service offered to the Companie if any Pageants had been made'.[32] There was, however, the usual triumphal procession that year, as well as the city waits playing, cannons in barges, and so on, although the total outlay was considerably less than in other years.[33] Twenty shillings is not all that generous: back in 1569 James Peele and Peter Baker (a painter-stainer, possibly the son of Richard Baker who worked with Peele on the 1566 Show) received 26s 8d 'for the devise of a pageant, which tok none effecte'.[34]

The Companies' normal method of confining the detailed arrangements to a sub-committee means that little is generally recorded about the discussions relating to the commission, nor, in most cases, about the nature of the pageantry once the commission had been agreed (the Court of Assistants, whose deliberations were recorded, tended to concentrate almost exclusively on how to recoup the expense of the Show from Company members).[35] On infrequent occasions, though, the process was sufficiently transparent and recorded in enough detail for us to see the negotiations in action. In 1619 the Skinners' Company note that Middleton competed successfully with two other 'poets' for their Show: 'Anthonie Mondaie, Thomas Middleton and Richard Grimston poetts, all shewed to the table their severall plotts for devices for the shewes and pagentes against St Symon and St Judes tide and each desired to serve the Companie'. A decision was not made then and there on this occasion, but instead 'it was wholie referred to the Consideracon of the Committee formerlie Appointed for busines of the like nature and they are to make Choice of whome they shall best approve of'.[36] The Court of Assistants and the Wardens reserved the right to 'ratifie and allowe' the consequent decision but made it clear that they wanted no part in the process beyond this. One unfortunate consequence of the Skinners' arrangement at this juncture is that the subsequent planning – especially how the decision was arrived at to give the job to Middleton – is now lost to us. For cultural critics this is especially vexing: how interesting would it be to have seen how the Companies evaluated the various protagonists' aptitude for the role.

There are exceptions, fortunately. The Ironmongers' Company records are extraordinarily full. In 1609, for instance, its Court minutes list twenty-seven items for action of various members, and rather than simply stating that all should be done 'as is fit' in the usual manner, they actually explain the requirements. The level of detail is such that we can see exactly what the child actors' 'breakfast' was on the day, since the Company reproduced Munday's itemised bill.[37] More significantly, their records for 1629 and 1635 also give a more extensive flavour of the bidding process in action than those of the other Companies; indeed, they are detailed enough to allow us virtually to re-enact the negotiations. Some three weeks before the Show, at a meeting on 2 October 1635, Robert Norman and John Taylor presented their 'project of 5 pageantes for the Lord Maiors shewe for which they demanded 190^{li} and under that price they would not undertake it'. Their intransigence about their fee (feigned or not) did them no favours, however, as their competitors, Heywood and John Christmas, stepped in with 'their Invencion of 5 pageante for the said shewe . . . which Pageante they offered to make furnish well & sufficiently . . . for 180^{li}'.[38] As before, the unsuccessful candidates received compensation for their pains. Hard bargaining appears to be a feature of the commissioning process, for £180 is £20 less than Dekker and Christmas managed to extract from the Haberdashers seven years before. (£180, the sum often received by the writer and artificer in this period, is around £16,000 in modern terms.) On the other hand, the Ironmongers' Company generously offered Munday £3 more than his negotiated fee 'as a free guift' in 1618 owing to the 'good performance of his business undertaken and of the spoyling of his Pageant apparaile by the foule weather'.[39] Northway cites this as an instance of the Companies' tendency to treat payment or reimbursement as 'tips': she points out that the 'free guift' 'must have compensated for some of the income he lost from replacing damaged costumes and thus did not supplement his pay'.[40]

The beneficence demonstrated here compares interestingly with what happened to Munday nine years previously, where he was called into the same Ironmongers' Court to be rebuked for his failings. The charge was that 'the children weare not instructed their speeches . . . the Musick and singinge weare wanting, [and] the apparell [was] most of it old and borrowed'.[41] He was warned, ominously, that the matter would be dealt with on the return of 'Mr Leats', one of the Company wardens. Typically impervious to common sense, a few days later, in the presence of Mr Leats, Munday claimed a further £5 over his agreed fee of £45 on the basis that he had written additional speeches 'for the water [show]'. The Ironmongers responded by reminding him that 'he performed not his speeches on land, nor the rest of his contracted service', and refused to 'goe beyond their bargaine'.[42] The message seems to have been that Munday should consider himself lucky to get any payment at all, and one wonders how he thought he would get away with this request. At the same time, looking at the list of complicated devices he and his collaborators agreed to provide, including '2 persons upon a flyenge dragon and unicorne . . . [and] an Ocean about wherein shall moove Mermaides, Tritons & playeng on instrumentes and singing', it is perhaps unsurprising that he and Grinkin fell short, as the original brief may have been over-ambitious.[43] Munday, in particular, knowing that the fee was often negotiable, was an inveterate seeker after extra payments. When he made the same kind of request of the Fishmongers a few years later as repayment for 200 additional books and some damaged clothing he had to settle for a lesser amount than he had demanded.[44] Munday's behaviour illustrates Northway's comment that the writers 'signed contracts written in the livery language of favors and service and took advantage of the implications of this language regarding parting gifts'.[45] As Hirschfeld points out in connection to the professional stage, relations between the various protagonists can be described as 'companionship and collegiality . . . inflected with a distinctly commercial flavor'.[46] Such a trade-off between 'service' and monetary self-interest characterises the actions of all the parties when it came to the commissioning of the Shows.

The financial aspects of the Shows were never far from the surface, for the honour and prestige of the mayoralty came at a cost to the Companies, all the more so because of the expectations incumbent on them in terms of hospitality. As Heal writes, 'members of the oligarchy had to show an appropriate face to the outside world'; the lavish dinner held on Lord Mayor's Day was, she continues, an opportunity 'to articulate both collective reputation and the honour due to particular sectors of the society' and its 'main function' was 'the integration of the companies who formed the basis of the freeman body into the celebration [of the mayoral inauguration]'.[47] Corporate feasting was an important 'bonding' activity for the Companies. However, sometimes the face presented to the wider world was a brave one in the face of adversity. As Griffiths has argued, 'civic pageants and parades dazzled in times when London's prestige was said to have slumped to an all-time low, a counter-rhythm to doom and gloom'.[48] Admission to the rank of Bachelor was considered an honour, but one suspects that many of those elevated to that rank as a money-raising measure in the run-up to a mayoral inauguration, whose names are listed so proudly in Company minutes, were not always entirely willing. It is unsurprising, then, as Archer writes, that 'each time that a triumph was held there were difficulties in inducing men to serve as bachelors and pay the assessments that financed the costly celebrations . . . [O]ften defaulters had to be brought before the Mayor before their compliance was secured.'[49]

Considerable anxiety on this score emanates from the Skinners' Court minutes in the late sixteenth century, when the Company had three Lord Mayors in twelve years as well as substantial building works to pay for. Its minutes show that it was prepared to go to some lengths to ensure that its members paid their share of the expenses: in 1585 (and again in 1595) it was recorded that obstinate defaulters would 'forthwith . . . be committed to prisone' until they paid up.[50] Even in 1619 more overt concern is expressed by this Company than is generally the case over how 'money [is] to bee provided for the lord maiors shewes'.[51] Here again, with the prospect of 'great expenses and somes of money' to be paid out, it was twice ordered that all those eligible for the freedom of the Company should present themselves at the Hall or face the consequences.[52] In 1597 the Skinners, who were under particular financial pressure owing to the rebuilding of their hall, complained that 'dyvers menes sonnes and servants . . . doe not come into the said Company to be made free'.[53] This meant that they were suffering from a shortage of funds because of an under-supply of Bachelor freemen, who contributed the lion's share of the money required to stage a Show. Fines of £5 were proposed to 'encourage' members to enter their apprentices to the freedom. Almost two years after the 1619 Show the Skinners were still pursuing 'delinquents'.[54] Conversely, the Wardens of the Yeomanry of the Clothworkers had to wait almost a year to be reimbursed for £5 they spent in 1633 'towards the shewes and trymphes late done and performed on the day of the late Lord Mayor'.[55] The Skinners' Company's accounts for 1628 show that the Assistants paid the large sum of £50 each, the liverymen over £21 and some of the Bachelors £6 towards the cost of the celebrations.[56] One of the Clothworkers 'stubbornlie refused' to perform his role of bachelor in budge for the 1583 inauguration, and was sent to gaol for his intransigence.[57] Wealthier companies obviously found it less of a struggle to raise the funds. The Merchant Taylors, for example, managed to accumulate over £1000 for their third mayor in less than a decade.[58] In 1610 they received from their members 'threescore two poundes fyve shillinges and threepence' more than they spent for the Show.[59]

Even so, and although the Company members probably experienced reflected glory on these occasions, the claim in the Goldsmiths' Court minutes that some 50 members of the Company, as well as 'a great nomber of the yeomanry', 'gave an assured shew of their willingness' to pay their share for the 1611 Show gives one the sense of an official line.[60] A more realistic notion of the call on Companies' finances, perhaps, lies behind the decision by the City Corporation to exempt the Clothworkers from the precept assessing them for £55 10s to pay their part of the pageantry laid on for the King of Denmark's entry into the City in 1606, on the specific grounds that the Company was 'shortlie to be at greate chardges concerninge the new lo. maior'.[61] As well as reusing extant pageant devices, another common tactic to keep the costs under control was to set aside the same sum for a particular expense every time a mayoral Show came around, in the guise, naturally, of tradition instead of economy. Thus, for instance, in 1628 the Skinners budgeted £50 for the 'trymming up' of the new Lord Mayor's house 'according to an ancient order', just as it had over twenty years previously.[62] The rather less impecunious Merchant Taylors conferred 100 marks on William Craven on the basis that this sum had been given to two preceding mayors of its Company.[63] These instances temper Dekker's claim in *Brittannia's honor* that for mayoral inaugurations 'Faire, Spacious, and Pallacious Houses [are] Beautified, Painted, and Adorned' (sig. A4r). One should remember, too, that the mayoral role (as with the roles of alderman and sheriff) was 'an office of charge' where the incumbent would have had to make considerable financial outlay during his time in office.[64] Munday reminded James Pemberton in 1611 that although 'prodigality' is a 'crime', all the same, the role of Lord Mayor's 'forbids ye now to pinch or spare, / But to be liberall, franke, and free, / Such as beseemes a Maioraltie' (*Chruso-thriambos*, sig. C4r).[65] The Lord Mayor was supposed to hold virtually an open house during his term, which was sometimes a difficult balancing act. Bald, quoting John Chamberlain, states that Francis Jones, Lord Mayor in 1620, found the cost of bearing the mayoralty too great: 'to escape his creditors, he decamped on the night before his term of office expired, "conveying all of worth out of his house, and he and his wife into some secret corner of the countrie"'.[66] In so doing Jones had betrayed the trust laid on him during the Show that he would 'execute [his] charge' with 'honor'd care' (*Tes Irenes Trophaea*, sig. B4r). Somewhat unsurprisingly, Jones was subsequently to be absent – he was 'excused' owing to an apparent 'sudden infirmity' – when his successor, Edward Barkham, took his oath in 1621.[67] In contrast, Barkham's 'greate bounty and hospitallity . . . feastes and entertainments' were highlighted by the Recorder of London when he was presented to the Barons of the Exchequer on the latter occasion.[68]

Unexpected vicissitudes had to be dealt with at times too. The Bachelors of the Merchant Taylors' Company had to contribute more than usual in 1605, when Leonard Holliday's Show was repeated on All Saints Day in November owing to 'very wett and fowle weather'. Further costs on this occasion included 'repayring the Pageant, and the rest of the other shewes', rebuying the apparel for the child actors, purchasing coal for fires to dry out the pageants, and so on.[69] The Goldsmiths found themselves in a similarly difficult situation in 1611. They had already decided that the waterborne procession would contain only the barges and the usual galley foist and 'no extraordinarie shewes' but had to revisit the arrangement when it became 'certain' that Queen Anna 'in her royal person will . . . see those shewes and triumphes, aswell on the land as by water'. Various 'alien' and domestic goldsmiths saved the day by agreeing to contribute to the extra expenses.[70] This 'new devise for the shew on the water' was then hastily cobbled together and approved by the Company only four days before the Show.[71]

No hint of the Goldsmiths' discomfort made its way into Munday's text, however.

'Partners in the business': the collaborative commission

As these scenarios demonstrate, writers worked alongside artificers, and, once the role of the latter had become more significant, they usually contested and took on commissions as teams. There is ample evidence to disprove Richard Grupenhoff's assertion that 'from the start the playwright was the most important member of the creative team, for it was he who produced the script and set the tone of the show, while the artificer had only to mount it'.[72] Grupenhoff seems to be in thrall to the dominant post-Romantic attitude to literary production, which, as Osteen and Woodmansee write, 'downplays the social aspect of writing to foreground its individual aspects [and] figures it as essentially solitary and originary rather than collaborative'.[73] As Hirschfeld writes in relation to the masque, 'the relatively insignificant place of written or spoken text in comparison to scenic, musical, and costume display, should challenge any priority granted to the writer'.[74] Barbara Ravelhofer argues in a similar fashion that 'a lingering contempt for the "body" [i.e. the physical aspects of the entertainment] seems to have been passed on to masque scholarship', and, by extension, the scholarship associated with early modern performance more widely.[75] Her own research has demonstrated how impressive and important the 'architecture' of the masque was, and the same principle applies to the Shows. Henslowe's Diary and other contemporary documents demonstrate that those pageant writers who had personal experience of dramatic collaboration prior to their involvement in the Shows include Dekker, Munday, Middleton, Heywood and Webster: Hirschfeld calls Dekker, in particular, a 'veteran collaborator'.[76] In some cases they had worked with each other at the Rose and/or Fortune, as I discuss further below. In all these cases (bar that of Munday, whose involvement in mayoral pageantry began unusually early), writing Shows came late to the dramatists' careers. Working in tandem with non-dramatic collaborators was thus unlikely to have been all that unusual an experience for them; quite the reverse, in fact.

Dekker wrote in *Brittannia's honor* that 'it would puzzle a good memory to reckon vp all those Trades-men (with other extraordinary Professions which liue not in the City) who get money by this Action', by which he means from the making of the Shows (sigs A3v–4r). The livery company records bear out his claim, as well

as Inga-Stina Ewbank's argument that, compared to the role of the
'poet', the Companies 'would pay possibly even more attention to
the artificer who was to construct the edifices, chariots and strange
beasts'.[77] As Northway writes, it is important to 'acknowledge this
larger network, [as] we could [then] begin to trace in the archives
the names of less well known participants, such as painters, tailors,
and upholsterers who might have moved easily among the liveries
and the theaters'.[78] Exploring these 'concrete fields of production',
in Hirschfeld's useful phrase, helps us rediscover the role of what
she calls 'the material contexts as well as the personal interests
that structured the choices and chances' of those most involved
in the making of the Shows.[79] I'll return to the particular issue of
'personal interests' and the associated personal connections later in
this chapter. What is for sure is that the examination of any Great
Twelve livery company archive from this period demonstrates that
such collaboration was integral to the Shows. In 1611, for instance,
Grinkin, the painter-stainer, provided all of the numerous properties and 'devises' whilst Munday supplied apparel, produced 'fitt
and apt speeches', 'cause[d] 500 bookes . . . to be made and printed'
and had general responsibility for the whole event.[80] As Pafford
has commented, 'their functions overlapped . . . Munday's overall
"devising" was usually done with his partner Grinkin': one cannot
image the event taking place without the work of these two men
in tandem.[81] It is also important not to overstate the pre-eminence
of the apparently more 'glamorous' activity of the writers, at least
as far as the sponsoring Companies were concerned. After all, as
Northway asserts, 'the primary expenses from a pageant came
not from scripting, but from putting on the performance, such as
acquiring and feeding actors, providing props and costumes, and
building sets'.[82]

Henry Turner's analysis of the meanings of the word 'plot' in this
period is enlightening here. He comments that the near-synonyms
'design' and 'plot' (both of which were terms regularly used for the
plans for mayoral Shows) 'carried intellectual and mechanical connotations simultaneously'.[83] In other words, for civic entertainments
as much as for plays, the term 'plot' does not signify solely the 'literary' or 'artistic' content of the Show; rather, it incorporates both
elements needed to bring the design to life. Indeed, it is impossible
to separate them, as we see in the Shows from Peele onwards. The
latter referred to the 'Mechnicall or Liberall' aspects of the Show
being combined 'to honour London with [their] skill' (*The deuice*,
sig. Aiiv). There is also evidence of this dual approach in the 'plot'

cited below, which bears out Turner's conclusion that 'action is given form within the *material* attributes of both stage and page'.[84] Turner's interpretation compares interestingly to the view of one contemporary writer, Jonson, whose view tended to be that there was a hierarchical distinction between what could be called 'the body' of a staged performance, created by the artificer ('short-liu'd', as he puts it, and appealing to the senses) and its 'soul', created by the poet (designed to appeal to the understanding).[85] The former, more 'artisanal' part of the equation, also had connections to 'plat', 'the technical term for the schematic working drawings used by the mason, carpenter and surveyor'.[86] This highlights again the importance of physical construction in the realisation of the Shows. The artificer or other chief collaborator was often, for obvious reasons, a member of a trade relevant to the making of a Show: for instance, Robert Norman, who worked with John Taylor in 1634 and with Dekker and Garret Christmas in 1628, was free of the Painter-Stainers; the ubiquitous Garret Christmas was a carpenter.[87]

As time wore on, the term generally used by the Companies for the writer was the rather grand 'poet'.[88] There is an irony here, of course, given that at the same time Jonson was striving to establish a literary reputation for himself based on the grounds that *he* was a 'poet' whereas Middleton, for instance, was but a 'base fellow'. Although the Companies clearly saw things differently, in what Taylor calls Jonson's 'textual hierarchy', pageant writing did not qualify a writer to enter the exalted realm of the poet.[89] Robertson and Gordon draw an analogy between the author and artificer of the Show, and the author and designer of the masque, such as Jonson and Inigo Jones. Jonson's falling-out with his erstwhile collaborator demonstrates the potential tension in the relationship between poet and artificer, in Jonson's case anyway.[90] The lack of stable boundaries between the major protagonists' responsibilities is again demonstrated by the case of the 1623 Show, where Munday and Middleton collaborated, albeit, it seems, at a remove from each other: the Drapers' accounts record separate payments to the two writers, Munday for the 'Argoe' and Middleton for the 'shewes'.[91] Both were already known as 'poets', of course. Unlike those of some of his peers Munday's printed texts tend to have just 'Written by' on their title pages rather than 'Devised and written by', which gives some indication of the fluid categories at work within the context of these entertainments. David Norbrook cites an instance from 1613 where the writer of a celebratory text 'did not . . . devise the themes of the pageantry but merely wrote the description'.[92] The possibility of such a division of labour taking place in the context of mayoral Shows is always worth keeping in mind. The face that a single name appears on a printed work does not necessarily mean that uncomplicated authorship, or sole authorship, occurred.

On the evidence of the Companies' commissioning practices, the artificer's profile rose throughout this period. By the 1630s John and Matthias Christmas (the sons of Garret) received the commission and 'subcontracted' Heywood as the writer. Thus in both 1638 and 1639 the Christmas brothers were required by the Drapers to 'discharge Mr Thomas Hayward the Poet for writing the booke' out of their total remuneration.[93] For the 1635 Show, although the company records state that 'Thomas Haywood' subscribed his name with his collaborator, he did not actually sign the agreement with the Ironmongers, leaving that responsibility to the Christmas brothers. It is possible that Heywood was not even present at Ironmongers' Hall when the contract was agreed. Similarly, Garret Christmas was paid £200 by the Haberdashers for 'pageants and shewes' in 1627; as with Heywood, Dekker's name does not appear in the Company accounts in this instance.[94] The Clothworkers negotiated directly with 'Mr Christmas Carver towchinge the providinge of such pageants as shalbe on the day of the Lord Mayor elect his presentm^t at Westm' in 1633; their accounts show charges for dinner following a 'meeting and conference . . . with Mr Christmas towchinge the shewes and triumphes'.[95] Again, Heywood is not mentioned.

However, both Dekker and Garret Christmas are listed as being in attendance at a meeting at the house of one of the Ironmongers' Company officials on 17 September 1629. They were also mentioned in the minutes of, although apparently not present at, an earlier Court of Wardens' meeting in August, where they were granted the commission for that year's Show. It's worth pausing here, for on the later occasion the Ironmongers' characteristically comprehensive records allow us to see the negotiations over the contents and cost of a Show in process.[96] The negotiations of September 1629 put some flesh on the bones of Heywood's passing remark in *Londini emporia* that in the early planning stages the Company perused his 'then unperfect' papers and made suggestions about how the 'plot' might be realised. Thus, much as a dramatist may have offered a theatre company an outline of their proposed play – such an outline was also, one should note, called a 'plot' by Henslowe, for one – Dekker and Christmas are reported to have presented the assembled citizens with

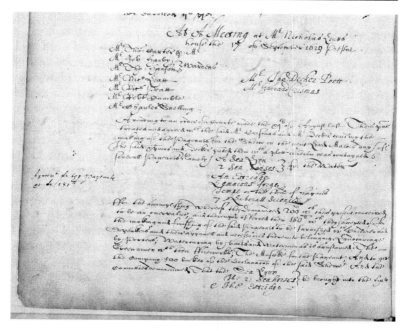

2 Extract from the Ironmongers' Company records (1629):
the commissioning process

a plott wherein was contayned 6 seuerall pageantes Namely A Sea
Lyon
  2 Sea Horses
  An Estridge
  Lemnions forge
  Tempe or the Field of hapiness
  7 Liberall Sciences.

The first two items are bracketed together (appropriately enough, given the kind of animals mentioned) as 'for the Water', i.e. to form part of the pageantry to accompany the barges down-river (see Figure 2). Although 'wherein was contained' does not disclose all that much about the way in which this 'plott' was presented, it seems most likely that it would have been simply a summary outline of the nature of the various pageants, albeit one written in sufficient detail for the Company to be able to make a judgement about it. The speeches themselves (the content of which is hardly ever mentioned in the Companies' records, giving further weight to my theory) often would have required some research into topics

like the history of the Company and were as a result unlikely to
have been written before the bid was accepted; furthermore, a
writer might have been wasting their time had they produced such
advanced content for a purely speculative bid. In this account of
the 1629 negotiations a side note states that the pageants had been
agreed for the sum of £180, although the minutes themselves disclose that some haggling had taken place: 'for the accomplyshing
thereof' the pair had 'demaunded 200 which theis present conceived
to be an overvalue and thereupon offered them 180ˡⁱ'. The payment
was to include, *inter alia*, organising children and their apparel for
the speeches, the 'Greenmen', fireworks, porters for both land and
water-shows, and 'to give the Company 500 bookes of the decla-
ration of the said Shewe'.[97] The Company further demanded that
the sealion, seahorses and ostrich be 'brought into the Hall (after
the Solemnity)'; Christmas requested that he be allowed to keep the
seahorses for himself, which was agreed. (These animal figures,
as can be seen further in Chapter 3, and as on this occasion, were
almost invariably models, often made of wood: 'Sea Horses' refers
to the mythical beasts that accompanied marine deities, not to the
actual creatures we know as seahorses: see Booth's drawing of the
1629 water show, Figure 12.) Four men were also appointed to help
Christmas transport the pageant properties to the Company Hall.
The quasi-legal, binding nature of this discussion is emphasised
by the fact that both Dekker and Christmas signed the minutes to
confirm their agreement (see Figure 3).[98] Christmas appears once
again in the Ironmongers' Court minutes later in October 1629 to
request an additional 'allowance' for 'theis thinges following as is
usually allowed by other Companies', including '8 guides for the
pageants . . . for the lighting of the Shewes from Paules 4 [dozen] of
Torches . . . [and] 2 scarfes for himselfe and his sonne'.[99]

Apart from that, the finer details of the actual pageantry were
left to Dekker and Christmas to bring to fruition. For the rest of
September and October the Company's attention then turned primarily to which roles were to be performed by its members on the
day, from the wearing of budge and foins to the entertaining of
guests. This is not to say that the Company washed its hands of the
Show once Dekker and Christmas were commissioned, however: it
appeared to take the whole business very seriously, meeting regularly throughout October (as the month drew on, sometimes more
than once a day) to discuss various matters. Indeed, it was still
finishing off its business into the following January, when various
absentee Bachelor members were fined for their non-appearance. As

3 Extract from the Ironmongers' Company records (1629): the commissioning process

usual, the Company retained the responsibility for practical matters
to do with marshals, whifflers (attendants employed to keep the
way clear), porters to carry the banners, and so on, as well as for
drummers, fife-players, ensign bearers, and other participants in the
procession who were not strictly part of the pageantry. Individuals
'from the Artillery Garden' were appointed to deal with this aspect
of the day's entertainment.[100] Company members themselves had
a variety of roles to perform, from forming the procession in foins
and budge, through to acting as stewards and whifflers or welcoming and serving the guests at the feast. Indeed, going by the relative
levels of expenditure devoted to each facet of the inauguration, it
appears that for the Companies the procession of civic dignitaries
was the most important part of Lord Mayor's Day; theatrical pageantry comes across generally as rather ancillary. Their accounts
demonstrate that assessing their members for the contributions
required to participate in the procession, and spending large sums
on fabric for those processing (from the mayoral party to the 'poor
men'), were their two major preoccupations (I return to this subject
in Chapter 3).

These multi-faceted enterprises were often organised surprisingly
quickly. As we have already seen, the general pattern was to start
arranging the celebrations only a few weeks before Lord Mayor's
Day, owing to the fact that the new Lord Mayor was elected on
29 September (although these elections were generally a formality,
since it was the senior alderman who had not passed the chair who
was elected). ('Below' or 'beneath' the chair refers to a City alderman who had not yet served as Lord Mayor; one who had 'passed
the chair' had served as Lord Mayor.) Middleton praised Garret
Christmas's skill at putting together 'the Fabricke or Structure of
the whole Tryumph, in so short a time' in *The triumphs of health
and prosperity* (sig. B4r). Unusually, however, the Grocers started
making arrangements for the 1613 Show as early as February,
although there was a disingenuous pretence for some months
that these arrangements were merely preparatory for whenever a
member of the Company was next elected Lord Mayor. The Grocers
would, nevertheless, have been fairly sure that one of their members
was to be given the honour; they even had the ceiling and wainscot
of the Hall painted 'just in case'. In February the Wardens and
Assistants were instructed to consider the necessary arrangements
and report back to the Court, and the committee was accordingly
established in March.[101] The preparations were especially elaborate
and prolonged: the Grocers were still nominating sub-committees

and appointing a treasurer months later. Munday, ever alert to an opportunity, clearly tried to get a head start, as he had already offered the Company a 'Devise or proiect' by February.[102] He had to share the eventual commission with Middleton, however.

The Goldsmiths, too, began their planning early in 1611. In April of that year orders were made that the Company banners be repainted and trimmed, and by July Richard Kemby, painter-stainer, had agreed to supply various pavises (large shields), trumpet banners and the like.[103] John Lowin was asked to liaise with Munday over the part of 'Leofstane', which implies that the speeches, at least, as Pafford points out, were available to be consulted on 3 September, when Lowin was present at Goldsmiths' Hall.[104] On this occasion Munday was more successful than in 1613, having prepared the ground with a presentation of a copy of his *Briefe chronicle*, which was rewarded by a generous gratuity from the Goldsmiths on the grounds that he had 'remembered the worthie antiquity of the Companye'.[105] Indirectly, one can suppose, this also furthered his cause when it came to gaining the commission for Pemberton's Show, although Munday's tactics in this regard did not always work. Despite the fact that he 'name-checks' both of the high-profile aldermen John Swinnerton and Thomas Middleton in *Chruso-thriambos* as 'most worthy Gentlemen', he was not commissioned to write either of the next two Shows on their behalf.[106]

As the preceding discussion has demonstrated, the Company records are an under-used source of information. For one thing, it is sometimes possible to reconstruct aspects of a Show from livery company records where the printed text of the entertainment has not survived. For the early years such testimony is vital. All we know about Cuthbert Buckle's inauguration in 1593, for instance, is that there was evidently at least a procession to the Tower (as it was a plague year the usual journey to Westminster was curtailed, a fact alluded to by the Recorder of London when the oath-taking at the Exchequer was revived the following year).[107] The Vintners itemised their expenditure, which included banners with silk fringes (one for the Lord Mayor and one for the Company), the hire of five dozen javelins, numerous blue coats and gowns, other fabric and ten dozen torches.[108] No mention is made of actual pageantry in the Company accounts for that year. The Lord Mayor himself received £300 'towardes his charges'.[109] Less comprehensive, but still revealing, are the Clothworkers' accounts for 1606, another year with no printed Show. There was evidently some limited pageantry ordered for this occasion, including 'beasts' such as a seahorse and 'seawatte' (a play on the Lord Mayor's name, John Watts).[110] We do know, however, from payments in the Clothworkers' accounts that the Lord Mayor and his entourage were taken up-river to Westminster by barge in the usual manner and enjoyed the traditional feast at the Guildhall.[111]

We have Edmund Howe's assurance that the 1610 Show was both 'pleasant' and extraordinary', and the Merchant Taylors themselves give a fuller sense of the spectacle.[112] For example, along with the usual outlay on banners and so on, their accounts provide the detail that one of the water-borne pageants featured 'kings that sate in the Rock, on the Thames', and that this pageant carried 'nyne lardg pendents'.[113] The person who 'represented . . . Merlyn in the Rock' is also mentioned, though it's not clear if Merlin sat alongside the kings (unusually, this actor, although unnamed, seems to have been paid direct by the Company rather than via an intermediary like Munday). The land-borne 'Chariott' – there appear to have been only two actual pageants, one on water and one on land – was composed of the Merchant Taylors' traditional heraldic animals, lions, unicorns and a camel, along with 'two gyants'. Munday supplied apparel for 'all the children' and was, as in 1604, responsible for arranging the printing of the books. The 'Shipp' contained a boy trumpeter, fireworks and 120 'brasse Chambers', which were double-discharged on the day, and an 'Ancient' (standard bearer) 'went on the Companies bardg'.[114] Other conventional elements of the 1610 celebrations included the six 'greenemen' with fireworks who accompanied the procession, along with streamer bearers, thirty-two trumpeters, numerous men with lances, javelins, staves and torches, and the ubiquitous blue-coated poor men.[115] The City Waits were employed to provide music, as were drummers and fifers; as a side-show, sixteen men fought with hand-swords. Large numbers of men were required to attend the procession, which was in itself composed of hundreds of Company members.[116] The Ironmongers' characteristically lengthy minutes serve to supplement the only surviving copy of Munday's 1609 text, *Camp-bell*, which is missing its first few pages. From the Company records we can tell that as well as 'A bell field carried in A Chariott . . . drawne by ii Estriges with Children upon them', evidence of which does survive in what is left of the text, the Show also featured 'a flynege dragon and unicorne with their speeches'.[117] This part of the Show must have been described in the section of *Camp-bell* which is lost. Only the speeches by 'Saint Andrew' and 'Saint George' survive, although it appears from the Company minutes that there were others (*Camp-bell*, sigs B3r–B4r).

Similar insight into the spectacle can to a lesser extent be gleaned from the Haberdashers' Accounts and Minutes for 1627, a year which marked Dekker's return to civic pageantry after his time in prison. Although they are fairly brief, these accounts do reveal some aspects of a production for which, in the absence of a printed text, we have no other evidence. The usual galley foist, trumpeters, streamers, torches and so on are present and correct. The terse record, 'paid to Mr Christmas for the pageants and shewes – [£]200', however, is all the Haberdashers thought it necessary to say about the actual pageantry, which would of course have formed the bulk of any printed text. The sum of £200, which is in keeping with the usual sum conferred on the writer and artificer in the period, certainly suggests that the full gamut of pageantry was employed on this occasion, although the Haberdashers did not see fit to record it in any detail. (Such a lack of detail about the more theatrical dimensions of the Show in the Companies' formal records is not uncommon, as we have seen elsewhere in this book.) Their accounts for 1627 do not list any payment for books, either: perhaps on this occasion there were none, for the Haberdashers did record the cost of £2 for the printing of 300 copies of the book that accompanied their 1631 Show, Heywood's *Londons ius honorarium*.

The Company records also disclose a great deal about the various makers of the Shows. Garret Christmas, who features so extensively in many Companies' plans, was highly regarded and much sought after as a craftsman, by both City and court. He comes in for great commendation from his collaborators. Heywood is particularly effusive, writing in *Londini artium* that Christmas was 'the Artist, the Moddellor and Composer of these seuerall Peeces'. Indeed, Christmas's achievement is likened to that of Roman architects (high praise from Heywood the classicist): rather like the emperor Augustus turning Rome from brick to marble, Heywood wrote that Christmas 'found these Pageants and showes of Wicker and Paper' and gave them 'sollidity and substance' (sig. C2r–v). According to Adam White, 'in 1620–21 [Christmas] is known to have worked on a masque performed before the king at Whitehall Palace by the gentlemen of the Middle Temple; presumably he did for the theatre largely what he did for the pageants'.[118] He was also employed on Charles I's abortive royal entry and is said to have produced a bas-relief of King James on horseback on Aldersgate. John Grinkin, Munday's usual collaborator, was likewise in great demand as an artificer, being involved in at least nine mayoral Shows.[119] Like Christmas, Grinkin had received commissions from wealthy and

powerful men from within and outside City circles. He worked for
Lord William Howard, and a self-portrait of him was, apparently,
in Charles I's collection.[120] As well as continuing their father's work
on the Shows, Garret Christmas's sons John and Matthias were
employed as master carvers; they were collaborators with Heywood
in the construction of emblematic decorations to the King's new
ship *The Sovereign of the Seas*, launched at Woolwich in 1637.[121]
The input of those others who made substantive contributions to
the Show, such as the artificer, painter, carpenters, and the printers
and publishers, should therefore not be sidelined.[122] The artificer
had a particular responsibility to construct the most impressive
spectacle, as it was unlikely that the speeches would have been
heard at all well by most of the onlookers, as we will see further
below.[123] Hence, in part, the emphasis in the Shows upon easily
recognisable symbolism. As the involvement of John Lowin in the
1611 Show – Lowin was an actor from the King's Men with connections with Munday – and of Lowin and Burbage in Munday's
1610 *Londons loue* suggests, the writers were generally responsible
for arranging the actors, be they children or adults.[124]

Gordon's assertion that 'we know little about the figure of the
designer in connexion with the pageants' is not really sustainable.[125]
We certainly do know what they were employed to do, often in considerable detail. Given how central the visual impact of the Shows
was, it is hardly surprising that the complex role of the artificer
should be so foregrounded. L. J. Morrissey writes that 'whether or
not the playwrights credited the devisers, civic ridings were dramas
of symbolic material objects'. What he calls the 'physical properties
of the event' were of crucial, perhaps primary importance to the
overall effect.[126] Most of the writers were keen to credit the work
of those who made their devices a reality, and they often represent
the relationship between poet and artificer as a reciprocal one.[127]
After all, as Kiefer reminds us, the concept of the 'device' was in
itself inherently visual and related to the emblem, with its pictorial qualities; indeed, the word was sometimes used as a synonym
for 'emblem', 'impresa' or 'hieroglyph'. A device was therefore
designed, in the fullest sense of the word; in the words of one contemporary, it functioned as 'a delightfull object to the sight'.[128] As
O'Callaghan argues, 'the devices are absolutely integral to the allegory and its success; machinery and poetry work in harmony'.[129]

To illustrate the point, in *The tryumphs of honor and industry*
Middleton, a generous acknowledger of others' contributions (on
the whole), thanks not only Rowland Bucket but also 'Master

Henry Wilde, and Master Jacob Challoner, partners in the business' (sig. C2r).[130] In *The sunne in Aries* Middleton concludes with an acknowledgement of Garret Christmas's talent and reliability. The latter quality was clearly appreciated as Middleton regularly praises it. With only three to four weeks to bring the Show to fruition reliability is understandably a prized quality in a collaborator. Christmas is here described as 'a Man excellent in his Art, and faithfull in his Performances', and the 'credit' 'for the Frame-worke of the whole Triumph . . . iustly appertaines' to him (sig. B4v).[131] In most cases Middleton was evidently prepared to foreground the teamwork involved in producing a Show: that subsequent scholars have so often more or less erased the contribution of those who enacted the physical spectacle is unfortunate and quite misleading. For instance, Wickham claims that in 1617 'Middleton received £282 for his labours', when in actuality Middleton was paid this sum 'for the ordering overseeing and writing of the whole devyse . . . tryming the shipp . . . and for all the Carpenters work . . . and for all the portage and carryage' and so on, which makes it clear that much of the money was intended only to reimburse Middleton for 'subcontracting' various aspects of the work.[132] Pafford states that Grinkin, for one, worked with Munday 'on a footing of equality'.[133] Robertson goes even further, claiming that the Clothworkers' archives from the 1630s 'illustrate the subservience of the poet to the artist-craftsman'.[134]

Like some seventeenth-century Oscar acceptance speech, Dekker's *Magnificent entertainment* goes to the lengths of acknowledging everyone, from the sixteen committees elected by the Corporation to manage the entertainment to the seventy labourers who worked on it.[135] Munday's part in the Show that generated the work entitled *The triumphs of truth* is, in contrast, rather more briefly credited by Middleton after he has thanked John Grinkin, the painter/artificer (who was the artificer with whom Munday, in fact, had the closest working relationship), and Humphrey Nichols, the firework maker. Middleton simply records Munday's role as 'those furnished with Apparell and Porters by Anthony Munday, Gentleman' (sig. D3r).[136] This incident should temper O'Callaghan's assertion that Middleton is 'always careful to acknowledge the work of his fellow artisans in devising the pageant', for Middleton does Munday a disservice.[137] The Company accounts show that the latter, who appears first in the accounts, received £149 'for the devyse of the Pageant and other shewes' as well as for more functional matters like supplying apparel, actors and porters. For his work on the production

4 Extract from the Grocers' Company accounts (1613): payments to
Munday and Middleton

Middleton got only £40 (see Figure 4).[138] The payment to both is
dwarfed by the £310 which Grinkin received (see Figure 5)

> for the making of the Pageant, Senate Howse, Shipp, errors and truths
> Chariott, withall the severall beasts which drew the five Ilandes, and
> for all carpenters worke, paynting, guilding, & garnishing of them
> . . . and also in full for the greenemen, divells & fyre workes.[139]

On this evidence it would seem most likely that Middleton had the
governing role in terms of the coherence of the Show – the 'ordering

5 Extract from the Grocers' Company accounts (1613): payment to John Grinkin

overseeing and wryting of the whole device' – but that Munday's total responsibilities were greater.[140] In this, his first mayoral work, Middleton does appear to be reluctant to admit to sharing the responsibility for the more artistic dimensions of the Show. Anyone whose understanding of the event was based solely on the printed text with its terse little acknowledgement would probably miss Munday's contribution altogether – and some critics have done.[141] Indeed, the Drapers' records reveal that Middleton and Munday also worked together to produce the 1621 Show, although this time around Middleton does not acknowledge Munday's input at all in the printed text.

In *The triumphs of fame and honour*, however, Taylor makes it plain that he and Norman were true collaborators. Indeed, he usefully pinpoints which of them was responsible for which part of the production:

> to giue desert her due . . . it were shamefull impudence in mee to affirme the inuention of these Structures and Architectures to my selfe, they being busines which I neuer was inured in, or acquainted with all, there being little of my directions in these shewes; onely the Speeches, and Illustrations which are here printed I doe justly challenge as mine owne, all the rest of the Composures and Fabricks were formed and framed by the Ingenious and Industrious Mr Robert Norman Citizen and Painter of London, who was indeed the prime inventor prosecutor and finisher of these works.[142] (sig. B4r)

Here Taylor admits to being a tyro in civic entertainments (either modestly or disingenuously, as he had in fact written a celebration of the marriage of Princess Elizabeth and Duke Frederick in 1613, *Heauens blessing, and earths ioy*). He emphasises that the speeches for which he was responsible would have been as nothing without their physical embodiment in Norman's 'Composures and Fabricks'. Perhaps because of Taylor's inexperience, Norman's involvement was such, as Williams has pointed out, that he appears to have invented at least some of the Show's themes, a job normally reserved for the 'poet'.[143] She rightly states that 'to refer to the devices of [*The Triumphes of*] *Fame and Honour* as Taylor's is more a matter of convenience than of accuracy', and it belies Taylor's conscientious efforts to confer praise where praise is due.[144] Conversely, in *The triumphs of the Golden Fleece* Munday seems reluctant to accept any praise for the achievements on display on the Thames, writing that 'whatsouer credit or commendation (if any at all) may attend on the Artefull performance of this poore de[v]ice: it belongeth to the Arts-Maisters, Richard Simpson, and Nicholas Sotherne' (sig. A4v). Perhaps he is passing the buck for a weak production in what was, after all, his last year of involvement in civic pageantry.

Apart from the fairly common acknowledgements by the writers of the expertise of the artificer, and although the printed texts invariably highlight the 'cost and charges' of the Companies, the writers, perhaps to retain the dignity of the occasion, only infrequently defamiliarise the commissioning process by discussing it overtly. Working for the livery companies, as Northway has shown, tended to be treated not as waged employment but as 'service', with all its connotations of moral value transcending bare payment.[145] This practice also, implicitly, reveals the relative positions of the protagonists. Fleetingly, Munday states in *Chrysanaleia* that the description he provides in the text relates only to those parts of the Show for which he was responsible, those aspects which 'apperteineth to my charge and place', as he puts it, referring simultaneously to both parts of the equation (sig. B4r). There are exceptions to this norm, however, and when the writers do engage with the process it reveals a lot about the varied relationships between the pageant poets and the Company officers with whom they dealt so closely. Heywood interrupts the speeches in *Londons ius honorarium* to inform the reader of what took place behind the scenes. In the process he gives the impression of a relatively interventionist approach, albeit benignly so, on the part of the Company. He writes:

> I cannot heare forget that in the presentment of my papers to the Master, Wardens and Committees of this Right Worshipfull Company of Haberdashers . . . nothing here deuised or expressed was any way forraigne vnto them, but at all these my conceptions, they were as able to Iudge, as ready to Heare, and to direct as well as to Censure; nether was there auy [*sic*] dificulty which needed a comment, but as soone known as showne, and apprehended as read.[146] (sig. C3v)

Heywood's experience seems to have been uniformly positive – or at least, he was keen to represent it as such, perhaps in the interests of further commissions, despite a disclaimer that he wishes to avoid 'the imputation of flattery' – for a couple of years later he again praises the discrimination shown by the Company (in this case, the Clothworkers), this time at even greater length. Heywood concludes *Londoni emporia* by acknowledging not only Garret Christmas, as was the norm, but also the input of the Clothworkers'

sub-committee. As well as trying to strike the appropriate balance
between 'vaine glory' and 'parsimony' by emphasising that neither
'incouragement' nor 'bounty' were lacking, he also presents a personal testimony of his experience as follows:

> I cannot without iust taxation of ingratitude, omit to speake some-
> thing of this Worshipfull company of the Cloath-Workers . . . for
> the Master the Wardens and the Committi, chosen to see all things
> accommodated for this busines then in motion, I cannot but much
> commend both for their affability and courtesie, especially vnto my
> selfe being at that time to them all a meere stranger, who when I read
> my (then vnperfect) Papers, were as able to iudge of them, as atten-
> tiuely to heare them, and rather iudicially considering all things, then
> meerly carping at any thing. (sig. C1r–v)

In the preface to his only Show, Webster refers in an apparently
similar fashion to the practical arrangements that enabled his work
to take place by praising

> the great care and alacrity of the Right Worshipful the Master and
> Wardens, and the rest of the selected and Industrious Committees;
> both for the curious and iudging election of the subject; and next
> that the working or mechanicke part of it might be answerable to the
> Invention. (*Monuments of Honor*, sig. A3r–v)

This provides a further insight into how the commissioning process
was perceived by one of its beneficiaries. It also suggests that,
like Jonson, Webster may have perceived a subordination of the
'working or mechanicke part' of the Show, for which the artificer
was responsible, to the poet's more cerebral 'Invention'. Webster
clearly found the experience of being 'iudged' by a bureaucratic
committee unusual, although it is hard to tell if he also found it
unpalatable, as this would hardly be the right place to air such a
misgiving. He does state in the dedication that his 'indeuours . . .
haue receiued grace, and alowance' from the Company (sig. A2v).
He also indicates that the Merchant Taylors took a particular interest in the realisation of the Show in relation to the 'Invention' they
had accepted. Indeed, it is possible that Webster's artificer was
chosen for him. As we have seen, he stresses that the Company committees took care that the 'working' dimension of the Show should
be 'answerable to the Invention' and the text lacks the usual thanks
to the artificer. The Show as a genre does not appear to have suited
Webster all that well, for he complains in the preface that 'both my
Pen, and ability . . . are confin'd in too narrow a Circle'. As a result,
he has insufficient space to do justice to 'the Original and cause of

all Tryumphes'. 'So short a Volume', he continues, permits him 'to expresse onely with rough lines, and a faint shadow . . . the great care and alacrity' of the Company's committees (sig. A3r). Dutton has speculated that Webster's complaints about being 'confin'd' may mean that the Company 'may have imposed some limits' on his invention.[147] This is possible, for even Munday, by 1614 quite an old hand at mayoral pageantry, alludes somewhat huffily to constraints he experienced in the planning of the Show that was printed as *Himatia-Poleos*. 'As meane additions', he writes, 'to giue some small luster to the Showe, because ouer many were thought inconuenient, we make vse of a golden pelleted Lyon . . . and with these fewe slender deuices, we vsher his Honors way towards Guilde-Haule' (sig. B4v). 'Meane', 'small', 'fewe' and 'slender': a disgruntled air comes across quite strongly in his words, and although he does not identify those who thought his proposals 'inconuenient', he still manages to make it clear that the decision was not one he agreed with.[148] He appears to have had a more agreeable experience in 1616, when in *Chrysanaleia* he praises the 'discreete and well aduised iudgement of the Gentlemen, thereto chosen and deputed' to agree the devices for that year's Show, which *'were and are* accordingly proportioned' (sig. B1r; my emphasis).

Webster is therefore not alone in at times differentiating his artistic desires from the forces of economy or indifference. In the face of such a collective endeavour he consistently tries to emphasise his own personal contribution. His description of the various pageants is notable for its use of the first person pronoun – for Webster, it is always 'I present', 'I fashioned', and so on. He also, perhaps indelicately, draws attention to the role of the Company officials as 'supervisors of the costs of these Tryumphs' (sig. A2v).[149] In *Monuments of Honor*, as Bergeron has noted, 'Webster as writer sketches the space in which he works'.[150] Indeed, as Dutton argues, Webster's text is notable for (or 'marred by', in Dutton's view) the author's 'repeated assertion that he would [as a 'learned poet'], given the opportunity, have produced a more impressive volume than this'.[151] Whether it was the genre or brevity of the mayoral Show (or both) that caused the problem, or simply that the Shows did not suit the slow, painstaking way he preferred to work, it is not altogether surprising that Webster wrote only one of these entertainments, despite the fact that he flags his availability for further civic employments in the dedication to *Monuments of Honor*. Nevertheless, however things may have worked out for Webster, the Company were obviously pleased with the production as they

awarded the team 'by way of Gratuity' an additional £10.[152] In
contrast, Middleton's account of his dealings with the Grocers'
Company takes a more familiar, and less complicatedly deferential
tone. Unlike Dekker, who tries to square the circle of generosity
versus thrift, Middleton praises the Grocers' indifference to cost. 'It
hath beene twice my fortune in short time to haue imploiment for
this Noble Societye', he begins *The tryumphs of honor and industry*, 'where I haue alwayes mette with men of much vnderstanding,
and no lesse bounty, to whom cost appears but as a shadow, so
there be fulnesse of content in the performance of the solemnity'
(sig. A4r). Webster was unusually explicit about his role and that of
others, perhaps because he was less familiar with the process than
some of his peers and thus noticed its peculiarities.

   In some (early) cases, however, it can be quite difficult to determine the extent of the involvement of any given writer or other
contributor to the content of the Show. The earliest reference to a
named author, according to Robertson and Gordon, was one 'Mr
Grimbold' (probably Nicholas Grimald) in 1556.[153] Subsequently,
the role and prestige of the 'poet' seems to have increased during
the latter half of the sixteenth century. In 1566 James Peele (father
of George), who also wrote the (unperformed) Show for 1569,
received only 30s whilst the fee for Richard Baker, the painter-
stainer, was £16 with the offer of a further 40s 'if it fortune him to
be a loser at that price'.[154] However, the rise of the writer was not at
the expense of the artificer, whose responsibilities were considerable
once lavish pageantry had become the expected form of the day.
Indeed, in some ways the role was amplified. In 1609, for instance,
Grinkin agreed to make and paint a dragon, unicorn, two ostriches,
some trees, a fountain, a golden field, an ocean complete with
'Mermaids and Tritons artificiallie mooving', 'a maiesticall throne'
and 'iii maiesticall diadems'. For all these substantial labours he was
granted £45.[155] Munday too received £45 for his work that year,
which included furnishing and clothing the child actors for the pageants, writing the speeches, and providing the Company with 500
copies of the book; it is also implied that he shared the design of
the pageants with Grinkin.[156] Only a few years later the Merchant
Taylors paid Dekker and Heminges 'one hundreth fourescore and
seventeene pounds' for the device of their land shows, and for printing the books and clothing the actors.[157] One of the perks of the job,
it would appear, is that the poet and artificer could sometimes join
the procession, for in 1610 both Munday and Grinkin were given
money for their 'cullors [colours]' by the Merchant Taylors in the

same way as were those 'that did beare streamers'; Munday was also given eight dozen ribbons in the Company colours to wear.[158] With Munday's allegiance to all things civic this must have been a proud moment for him.

The various roles were, perhaps of necessity, fluid, and the protagonists would have been expected to be versatile. In 1605, alongside his work as the 'poet' Munday was reimbursed 10s for the cost of providing 'one dozen of staff torches, which he used in bringing the Pageant and other shewes into Carter Lane'.[159] In 1602 he was paid 30s 'for prynting the bookes of speeches in the pageant'.[160] Munday may not have actually *written* the speeches he arranged to have printed on this occasion. William Haynes, the schoolmaster of the Merchant Taylors' School, is recorded in the Company's accounts for 1602 as receiving a fee in the following terms: 'Mr Heynes the Companies schoolem[r] at their schoole at St Lawrence Pountneis for the Chardge of p'paring a wagon, and appeling ten schollers, wch did represent the nyne muses and the god Apollo, before my Lord Maior in Cheapside'.[161] It is not known for sure whether Haynes or Munday wrote the children's speeches; they may even have collaborated. Sayle asserts that 'without any doubt [Munday was] the author of the speeches', evidencing that Munday's remuneration was 'somewhat excessive [for printing the speeches alone] and . . . probably included his fee for writing the speeches besides the repayment for having them printed'.[162] Even if he only printed the speeches Munday certainly supplied apparel for the 1602 Show, for which he also received payment. Haynes is still a candidate for the authorship of the speeches, however, as he was required to write a speech for one of his pupils to deliver before King James at his coronation celebrations in 1604. On this occasion, in addition, there was an explicit reference back to what must have been the recent mayoral inauguration, when, it is recorded, Haynes was paid for 'preparing his schollers, to make a shew and speeche in Cheapsyde, on the day my Lord Maior went to Westmynster'.[163] As the answer seems to hinge on the meaning of 'preparing' in this context, it remains the case that there is no conclusive evidence either way.

As is evident, it is not always clear who was being recompensed for what. From the early days (as with George Peele, for instance), it would appear from the scant extant evidence that the writer was sometimes required to 'oversee' the whole production. Conversely, in his only recorded foray into mayoral pageantry Jonson received £12 from the Haberdashers in 1604 for 'his device, and speech for the children'. The Haberdashers' Court Minutes for that year give merely a perfunctory insight into what the device may have consisted of, as they requested only 'a faire Pageant Chariat and a Lion'.[164] Munday was allocated £2 'for his paines', and a person unknown £1 for 'printing the booke of the device'. The implication here by the repetition of the word 'device' is that it was Jonson's work which was printed, although no publication from that year has survived; indeed, Dutton's view is that 'Jonson did not choose to preserve [this work] in print'.[165] Other examples of writers and/ or artificers being rewarded 'for their pains' suggest that on this occasion Munday either did not manage to make a substantial contribution to the Show or his role was very much that of an assistant. The word 'device' is also that which was used in relation to Peele's even earlier productions, so in the absence of a printed text or much other evidence it seems sensible to assume that the 1604 show was of the same minimalist nature as Peele's.

Robertson and Gordon remark in passing that 'Munday may have written those [Shows] for 1597, 1598, 1600, and 1601', but they do not supply any evidence for this supposition.[166] In fact, a transitory moment in the livery company records appears to have been overlooked by their otherwise diligent scholarship, for there *is* evidence in the Skinners' Company Court minutes for Munday's involvement in some capacity in the 1597 Show, along with 'Mr Kendall', whom I take to be Thomas Kendall, the Haberdasher who supplied the apparel for the 1604 Show.[167] Just above a payment to 'the bargman', the Court minutes record that 'Mr Sturman shall paye unto Mr Kendall and Mr Mondaye in benevolence xs but that it shalbe noe peyment hereafter'.[168] This suggests to me four possibilities: Munday and Kendall had supplied apparel for the Show and were being paid an additional sum for their labours; Munday (and Kendall?) had bid for the Show but not been chosen, and 10s was their compensation; they had indeed undertaken work on the entertainment and this payment was a kind of extra bonus (as, for instance, Munday received from the Ironmongers in 1618 and Dekker and Christmas from the Skinners themselves in 1628); or the Show was commissioned but did not take place.[169]

On balance, given that 10s is a small sum and that its description as a 'benevolence' indicates an optional payment rather than a reimbursement for something specific, I think the first is the most likely scenario, in part because if they had received the commission they would probably have featured elsewhere in the Skinners' records for this year, and they do not, as far as I have found. All in all this probably indicates only a small-scale role for the pair; even so, this demonstrates that Munday's civic pageantry work can indeed be dated back before 1602, as has been speculated. It also adds to the case that Munday had sufficient visibility in the world of civic entertainments by the time Jonson chose to satirise him as the 'Pageant Poet to the City of Millaine . . . when a worse cannot be had' in the 1609 edition of his play *The case is alterd* (which, incidentally, was first performed in 1597).[170] In addition, any prospect of a collaboration in this context between Kendall and Munday, who regularly supplied apparel for Shows, is intriguing.

Inconclusive though they may sometimes be, these earlier records do preserve some sense of how the various tasks were allocated. By the 1620s the artificer often received the total payment and it is not often possible to tell how the responsibility was spread, if at all. A person unknown was paid £2 in 1631 for 'printing 300 books of the shew': this may have been Raworth (the printer), Heywood, or someone else entirely, although the syntax of the entry both here and the following year does imply a direct payment from the Company to the printer.[171] Similarly, the trend towards appointing a sub-committee to oversee the arrangements lead to a kind of shorthand in the Companies' minutes, where those delegated the responsibility for the Show are often simply asked to ensure that the triumph, pageant(s), galley foist, banners, streamers and so on are in order.[172] For example, the Ironmongers' Court of Wardens appointed a committee 'for the Maior daye' in the September of 1618. At a later meeting on 30 September responsibility for the 'pageant', 'gallies' and barges was appointed; on 5 October the usual arrangements were made to assess the Bachelors in foins and in budge. Explicit reference back to the precedents established in previous years is also common, and appears to have given certain conventions a degree of authority as far as the Companies are concerned: the phrase 'as in former years' comes across as a kind of trump card.[173]

As I have already suggested, artificers and painter-stainers were well remunerated. In 1631 the sum of £200 was paid to Garret Christmas 'for pageants and shewes'; Heywood's name does not appear in the Haberdashers' records for that year, nor for the following year, where again it was only Christmas who received payment.[174] 'Mr Scarlett' and 'Mr Hearne', painters, received considerable sums from the Merchant Taylors in both 1602 and 1605 for decorating the banners, staves and the actual pageants.[175] Indeed, Hearne's responsibility was like that of an artificer in 1602, when he made as well as painted the pageant beasts. Careful scrutiny of the livery company records shows that the responsibility for the Show was often more complex than might appear from the text alone. Middleton's name may be on the title page of *The triumphs of truth* (indeed, this is his best-known mayoral text) but Munday is listed first in the Grocers' accounts and, as we have seen, his payment was the greatest. From this evidence, in contrast to that of the text, it appears that the two had at least equal roles: as far as it is possible to tell, Munday may have produced the ideas (he was, after all, a noted 'plotter') and Middleton may have then carried them out and written them up.

If the experience of those who produced the 1988 re-enactment of part of Middleton's *Triumphs of truth* is anything to go by, the artificers (and those others whose names have not been recorded) earned their fees. In the programme written to accompany this event, Sue Mallett records 'the feat of structural engineering' required to bring the spectacle to reality. Indeed, this event provides an interesting retrospective insight into the practical issues inherent in staging the Shows, such as the need for the costumes to be 'visible from the river banks and bridges . . . sturdy enough to withstand the weather, and practical for moving on and off the barges'.[176] What was a challenge in the 1980s must have been an extraordinary achievement some four hundred years earlier. The artificer's role, in particular, was obviously a crucial one, and, in order to understand these events in their own terms, we must try to lose the writer-centric view that the printed text is the most important part of the Lord Mayor's Show rather than being an ancillary component which has sometimes not survived. Munday and the artificer Grinkin clearly shared the work for the 1610 Show: indeed, from the Merchant Taylors' accounts it would seem that the latter had the more 'creative' role, being recompensed for 'making, painting, and gilding the Pageant, Charriott, Three Lyons, two Unicornes, a Camell, Two Gyantes [and] new painting the Shipp'. Munday's responsibility extended to 'providing Apparell, for all the Children, and . . . printing the booke'. The pair received a joint fee of £126.[177] The making of the Shows should rightly be assigned to the team: thus, in 1621 the Show was produced by Middleton, Munday and Christmas.[178] Indeed, the Company accounts usually make this clear: in 1622 the Grocers, for instance, paid £220 to 'Thomas Middleton gent and Garrett Christmas carver for orderinge overseeing and wrytinge of the whole device', including the printing of 500 books and all the necessary porterage.[179]

Certain teams dominated for periods of time, such as Munday and Grinkin's near hegemony between 1602 and 1618, Middleton and Garret Christmas's thereafter, and Heywood and the Christmas family's in the 1630s. John Squire's artificer in 1620 was Francis Tipsley, a member of the Haberdashers who also worked in some capacity (chiefly as a painter-stainer, it seems) on all the other Haberdashers' Shows in this period.[180] Squire thanked his collaborator thus: 'the credit of this workmanship (curiously exceeding many former shewes, and far more ritch then any, in regard no mettall was used to adorne it but gold and siluer) I impose on Francis Tipsley Cittizen and Haberdasher of London' (*Tes Irenes Trophaea*, sig. C2r).[181] Expenditure on the Shows was fairly lavish, but Squire's claim that only gold and silver metals were used 'to adorne' the pageants strikes me as an exaggeration. Indeed, had gold and silver been used to decorate the devices of this Show the Haberdashers would have been disregarding a royal proclamation of the previous year which stipulated that gold was only to be used for 'Armons, or Weapons, or in Armes or Ensignes of honour, at funerals, or Monuments of the dead'.[182] Gold and silver may have been used for gilding, but the livery company committees, after all, were composed of tough-minded businessmen, and the commissioning process did sometimes involve haggling. As we have seen, Dekker and Christmas's initial request for £200 for the Show for James Campbell in 1629 was negotiated down to £180, including all props, transport, music and the cost of 500 copies of the books.[183] The haggling could work both ways, though: for the same Show, the trumpeters desired a price rise of £2 and refused an increase of £1 from the Ironmongers from their previous Show over ten years previously.[184]

Dekker himself attempted to represent the correct balance between ostentation and economy in *Troia-Nova triumphans*. He begins the text, somewhat unpromisingly, by drawing a distinction between 'the Rich and Glorious Fires of Bounty, State and Magnificence' on the one hand, as opposed to ephemeral triumphs which are 'but a debt payd to Time and Custome'. The Lord Mayor's Show, he controversially claims, is in the latter category, whereas rich, glorious bounty is preserved for 'the courts of Kings'. He goes on to explain, though, that the Merchant Taylors' approach to the Show encompasses the best of both worlds, demonstrating

a sumptuous Thriftinesse in these Ciuil Ceremonies . . . for it were not laudable, in a City (so rarely gouerned and tempered) superfluously to exceed. As contrariwise it is much honor to her (when the Day of spending comes) not to be sparing in any thing. (sig. A3r)

Dekker's use of the oxymoron 'sumptuous Thriftinesse' may point to an uneasy awareness of the compromises that had to be made on these occasions, or perhaps to a sense that such ostentation was not really in keeping with the civic virtues of prudence and economy.[185] In *Chruso-thriambos* Munday grapples with the same problem when reminding the new Lord Mayor of the financial commitment implicit in his role:

> your former care
> Forbids ye now to pinch or spare,
> But to keepe good Hospitality,
> Such as beseemes a Maioraltie,
> Yet far from prodigiality.
> To be too lauish, is like crime
> As being too frugall in this time.

(sig. C4r)

In general, the Companies can sometimes be seen to struggle to reconcile the prosaic matter of affording the entertainment with the desire to appear to be indifferent to the cost. Although the Companies' accounts and minutes are, of course, full of records of payment, at the same time, as Northway argues, they can be seen to demonstrate a kind of denial that the financial relationship between the various parties is the crucial one. Northway writes that the Companies 'depict the worker not as working, but performing favors, [and] they also portray themselves not as paying prede-termined wages, but as awarding gifts'.[186] The lexicon of 'pains', 'rewards' and 'benevolences' therefore acts as a mystification of the true nature of the business in hand and represents the power as being in the hands of the giver, not the receiver.

'Your poore louing Brother': forms of association in the making of the Shows

In the context of a competitive environment, it is instructive to explore the reasons why one team was preferred to another. At times, as we have seen, the successful bidders simply undercut their competitors, but in other cases different reasons come into play. Personal networks and contacts in the City were important, if some-times underestimated, factors and there were often connections between the writers and the livery companies, such as membership of the Company. For instance, it is probable that George Peele was commissioned to write the Shows for 1585 and 1591 as a direct consequence of his father's employment in the same business in 1566. There were also familial connections between the Lord Mayors: two daughters of the Lord Mayor on the latter occasion (1566), Christopher Draper, married Wolstan Dixie and William Webbe, who were mayors in 1585 and 1591 respectively.[187] Like the Peeles, father and son, Webbe was a Salter.[188] Some two years before his first Lord Mayor's Show Peele may have worked in some capacity in dramatic productions at Oxford, which, in Horne's words, 'involved the devising and presentation of special stage effects' and thus would have acted as a direct precursor to his civic pageantry productions.[189] The writers and artificers were also required to know something of the new Lord Mayor – his personal background, notable civic achievements and so on – in order to incorporate such facts into the Show to tailor the entertainment to its recipient.

Rather missing the point, his analysis side-tracked by the mistaken belief that the theatre was uniformly 'abhorred' by the City oligarchy, Hardin claims that it is 'ironic . . . that [the livery companies] employed both dramatists and actors' for mayoral Shows.[190] It seems 'ironic' only if a wholesale split between these two worlds is posited. In fact, the Companies were doubtless well aware of the theatrical careers of those they commissioned. Indeed, this factor probably played a large part in the commissioning process itself, as it would have been unwise to have given this role to someone with no experience of writing dramatic-style entertainments. As Lancashire has shown, some of the livery companies had been employing players since at least the fifteenth century; in some cases, these were members of professional troupes such as the (sixteenth-century) King's Players.[191] Overall, in terms of both participants and creators, there were considerably more overlaps between the professional stage and mayoral Shows in the post-Peele period than there were between the latter and forms of *courtly* pageantry. Furthermore, in the small world of London culture the dramatists, in particular, tended to know each other and in many cases they had worked together in the theatre. Munday, for instance, had collaborated on plays for the Admiral's Men with Webster, Dekker and Middleton, and Middleton co-wrote with Dekker in the genres of both drama and prose; indeed, Dutton makes the reasonable speculation that it may have been the prior collaboration with Dekker that paved the way for Middleton's first mayoral

Show in 1613.[192] Both Taylor and Webster produced congratulatory verses for their 'friend' Heywood's *Apology for actors* in
1612.[193] Likewise, marking out their future territory, both Dekker
and Webster produced prefatory odes for Harrison's *Arch's of
triumph.*[194] Middleton's foray into civic pageantry began with a
small-scale contribution (one speech) for the same event, James's
royal entry in 1604, in which Dekker, of course, had a more extensive part to play.[195]

Such connections were not always amicable. On occasion
Middleton attempts to create an artistic identity for himself by criti-
cising the flaws of his contemporaries. He begins *The triumphs of
loue and antiquity* with the desire that the 'Cleare Art and her gracefull properties' contained within his work will be appreciated by the
spectators as well as by the Lord Mayor and his Company. As far
as the former constituency is concerned, however, Middleton is not
altogether sure that they are sufficiently discriminating to appreciate the difference. His work, he claims, 'takes delight to present it
selfe' despite the fact that 'common fauor . . . is often cast vpon the
undeseruer, through the distresse and miserie of Iudgement' (sig.
A4r). The same note is struck in *The triumphs of truth*, where he
launches another, even more direct attack on some unnamed contemporary. The title page foregrounds the antagonistic element of
this work, stating that the Show has been 'directed, written, and
redeemed into Forme from the Ignorance of some former times,
and their Common Writer'. Middleton expands on the theme at
greater length in the prefatory section following the dedication,
where he criticises the failings of 'the impudent common Writer' for
whom he feels both 'pitty and sorrow'. 'It would heartily grieue any
vnderstanding spirit', he goes on, 'to behold many times so glorious
a fire in bounty and goodnesse' – by which he means the patronage
of the Lord Mayor – 'offering to match it selfe with freezing Art,
sitting in darknesse, with the candle out, looking like the picture of
Blacke Monday' (sigs A3r–v). Because of the reference to 'Blacke
Monday', and with his track record of prompting hostility from
his contemporaries, most commentators have (understandably)
claimed the object of Middleton's scorn to be Munday. However, as
Bergeron pointed out when he revisited this issue, one must remember that Munday and Middleton collaborated in the making of the
1613 Show (as they had on the lost play *Caesar's Fall* more than
ten years previously).[196] This is not to presume that all writers were
great friends with their collaborators, but to explore more critically
the assumption that Munday must be the target. Furthermore, if,

as Middleton's prose suggests, he is directing the criticism towards his immediate predecessor in the writing of mayoral Shows, then the target may in fact have been Dekker rather than Munday, for Dekker wrote the 1612 Show and bid unsuccessfully for the job in the following year.[197] In the dedication of his 1612 Show *Troia-Noua triumphans* Dekker claims that triumphs are 'the Rich and Glorious Fires of Bounty, State and Magnificence' (sig. A3r). Unless it's just a coincidence, or he was simply consciously or unconsciously plagiarising, it may be that Middleton picked up on the phrase 'Glorious Fires of Bounty' and turned it into a way of impugning the artistic ability of its originator.

For that 1612 Show Dekker worked with John Heminges, who is now, of course, remembered chiefly for his co-editorship of the first Shakespearean folio. Dekker was called 'the Poet' by the Merchant Taylors, which implies that Heminges's role was that of the artificer or impresario. Certainly, the two are named by the Company as jointly responsible for the production of the 'devices'. Although they were both free of major livery companies it is perhaps most likely that Heminges became acquainted with Dekker through the theatre, despite the fact that at that date Dekker was writing mostly for one of Heminges's competitors, the Queen's Majesty's Company at the Red Bull. Heminges, who had been made free of the Grocers' Company in 1587 and became a liveryman in 1621, had by 1612 already established a theatrical career for himself, initially as an actor and then as a manager (he was manager first of the Chamberlain's Men, then the King's Men, for over thirty years). Both roles would have served him well when it came to civic pageantry. Mary Edmonds writes that 'in court records [Heminges] is constantly referred to as "presenter" of plays for command performances: in consultation with the master of the revels he would presumably have made the arrangements about places, times, dates, rehearsals, temporary seating in palaces, and transport'.[198] Such experience would have made him eminently well placed to be co-producer of a mayoral Show; indeed, it is rather surprising that he appears only to have done so once.

Family connections came into play too. As we have seen, George Peele succeeded his father James, and Munday's son Richard was a painter-stainer and worked on Shows (decorating banners and the like) regularly from at least 1613 onwards.[199] John Webster the younger would quite probably have attended his father's Company's school, which itself had connections with mayoral Shows – providing child actors and speech-writers – at least as

far back as Richard Mulcaster in the 1560s.[200] In 1620, William
Squire and Francis Squire (who may have been relations of John
Squire, that year's poet) received various payments although the
Haberdashers' records do not say what for.[201] Others who worked
to bring the Show to life were employed repeatedly, and in many
cases for a number of years, often regardless of which Company
was paying for the Show. Thomas Jones, for instance, was a fencer
who is mentioned in the Drapers' accounts for every one of their
Shows between 1621 and 1639; Tilbury Strange, a waterman who
provided the galley foist, was just as ubiquitous. Connections did
not always benefit the writers, though. When Dekker was arrested
for debt in late 1612 and then gaoled in the King's Bench prison, in
one of those haunting coincidences that demonstrates what a nexus
London was, one of his creditors was John Webster senior, the playwright's father, who was regularly involved in supplying wagons
and horses for mayoral pageantry; another was Nicholas Okes, the
printer of that year's Show.[202] Bradbrook states that *Troia-Noua
triumphans* 'ruined' Dekker: if, as seems plausible, his debts were
indeed accrued as a result of his commission for the Show, it looks
like he may not have given the printer and coach-maker their share
of the payment.[203]

The overall range of connections that come into play in the
context of the mayoral Shows exemplify Bradbrook's comment
that 'Londoners were self-conscious and intensely organised'.[204]
Indeed, almost all the pageant writers in this period, from Peele
to Middleton, were Londoners born and bred, as were the artificers, the Christmas family. This in itself marks a major difference
between mayoral inaugurations and civic entertainments for the
monarchy where writers with connections at court, such as Thomas
Churchyard, rather than local poets or playwrights, were preferred.[205] George Peele, as we will see below, had both court and
civic links; the writers chosen thereafter, however, were predominantly not of courtly provenance. Consequently, their treatment
of the City and its Lord Mayor tended to focus on the reigning
monarch to a lesser extent than Peele had done in 1585 and 1592.
Heywood, somewhat surprisingly for a writer who, David Kathman
notes, 'had been a booster of apprentices and tradesmen since his
earliest plays', was originally from provincial Lincolnshire and
came to London via Cambridge.[206] Although he only mentions
his own connection with the county in passing, Heywood makes
a great deal out of Nicholas Rainton's Lincolnshire origins in his
1632 Show, as well as those of other important men from that

county, including a number of Lord Mayors: 'not so many [Lord Mayors] hauing attained to the same Dignity [were] bred in any one County', he claims (*Londini artium*, sig. A2r). Heywood had been living and working in the city for over three decades before his first Show in 1631, however, and his allegiance to London is unquestionable: Howard rightly calls him 'that tireless apologist for the city'.[207]

John Taylor, who was from Gloucestershire, was another exception, but by the time he produced his Show in 1634 he was very well established in the Watermen's Company (indeed, he was notably active in the Company in 1634) and he too had been living in London for around forty years.[208] The Watermen's Company was not one of the Great Twelve, of course, but it was probably the largest of the companies. Bernard Capp points out that, from his profession as waterman, 'Taylor's links with the Bankside theatres included actors, writers, and spectators with court connections', as well as, no doubt, many bargemen.[209] Specifically, Taylor appears to have known Dekker, Heywood and Jonson, and he also wrote an account of the celebrations of the marriage of Princess Elizabeth in 1613, which would have served as a useful precursor to his Lord Mayor's Show some twenty years later.[210] Capp asserts that Heywood helped Taylor gain a lucrative post at the Tower. Given the former's ubiquity in terms of pageant-writing in the 1630s it is possible that he may have recommended Taylor to the Clothworkers for their 1634 Show (1634 was the only year in the 1630s, apart from 1636 when no full Show took place, when Heywood did not write the Show); the two men certainly seem to have had a connection over many years.[211] It is a reasonable supposition that Taylor may have gained the commission in 1634 in preference to Heywood because Garret Christmas, Heywood's long-standing collaborator, had recently died, which may have impacted on Heywood's ability to bid for that year's Show, and perhaps even on his credibility without the estimable Christmas alongside him. Taylor did have the right kind of experience, as well as useful contacts. Amongst his other varied activities, he also acted occasionally as a kind of promoter and impresario for ad hoc entertainments in London and elsewhere, not all with himself as a protagonist (Capp calls him a 'showman'), which in itself drew on some of the talents required for mayoral Shows.[212] His ability to write fast under pressure would doubtless have served him well too. Indeed, as is the case with Taylor, pageant writers tended to be versatile and productive, and to work across genres:

Munday's career was notable for its variety, Jonson seems to have co-written at least one mayoral Show as well as plays, masques and other entertainments put on at court, and Heywood wrote plays, an elegy on the death of King James and a wide range of prose works too.

The commissioning of royal civic entertainments, however, did not work in quite the same way as it did with the mayoral Shows. As Kipling remarks, before their employment on Anne Boleyn's coronation entry neither John Leland nor Nicholas Udall 'had any significant prior – or subsequent – association with the City'.[213] In contrast, despite his later court connections, George Peele had been brought up and educated in Christ's Hospital, under the aegis of the City Corporation; his father James had been the Clerk of the Hospital.[214] To compound the interconnections, both Dixie and Webbe, the Lord Mayors for whose inaugurations George Peele was employed, were Governors of Christ's Hospital. Thomas Nelson, who like Squire and Webster seems to have written only one Show, was probably a Londoner too: he was a bookseller and ballad maker, and a member of the Stationers' Company. He also wrote a handful of quasi-political texts, including, the year after his Show, *The blessed state of England. Declaring the sundrie dangers which by God's assistance, the queen's maiestie hath escaped*, and an epitaph for Francis Walsingham in 1590.

Corporate identity, too, was evidently significant when it came to the mayoral Shows. As well as having a proven track record in play-wrighting, the majority of the pageant poets were members of one of the Great Twelve companies (even Jonson was free of the minor company the Tylers and Bricklayers), and companies do seem to have employed their own members from time to time.[215] The artificers, painter-stainers and others who made substantial contributions were also, naturally, members of the relevant trades. John Lowin, the King's Men actor, appeared in the Goldsmiths' Court minutes as a 'brother' of the Company when he was required by the Wardens to perform the role of Leofstane in the 1611 Show.[216] Lowin's membership of the Company evidently came into play explicitly here. However, although it may have been taken as read, I have not discovered any tangible evidence that the companies deliberately, let alone invariably, took *writers*' company membership into consideration when determining commissions. In the absence of such evidence, Charles Forker's claim that the Merchant Taylors 'would not have paid an outsider to do what one of their own number [Webster] had already proved he could do so well' remains unsubstantiated.[217] Equally, Hardin asserts that the Drapers commissioned Munday to write their 1614 and 1615 Shows for the 'strategic' reason of wanting to have 'a yeoman [of their Company] speaking for the livery'.[218] He thus appears to assume that Munday was specifically selected by the Drapers, rather than winning a commission. However, nothing in the Drapers' records leads one to that conclusion, nor do the texts reveal any such selection process beyond Munday's own undoubted pride in writing for his Company. At the same time, membership of one of the Great Twelve Companies gave the writers access, in a limited fashion, to the inner workings of these organisations. It is possible therefore, in some instances, that they had prior acquaintance with those who commissioned their Shows. From the beginning of this period, writers were regularly members of livery companies. Both the Peeles, father and son, were members of the Salters' Company (James probably by redemption; George by patrimony).[219] Middleton was free of the Drapers by redemption (his father had been a member of the Tylers and Bricklayers and his stepfather was a Grocer). Munday was also a Draper, by patrimony. Webster was, as *Monuments of Honor* claims, 'borne free' of the Merchant Taylors (his coachmaker father John supplied 'horses and Charrett' for the 1602 Show for that Company).[220] Webster's only Lord Mayor's Show was therefore written for his own Company; indeed, the text foregrounds the poet's membership on its title page as well as elsewhere in the text, notably in the dedication, where he implies to the Company that he ought to be considered for that reason for future preferment.[221] Dekker and Heminges may have won the commission for the Show in 1612, in preference to Munday or Middleton, in part because Dekker was a member of the Merchant Taylors. Indeed, some contemporary owner or reader of the text has written 'Marchantailor' next to Dekker's name on the title page of one copy of this Show.[222] Sayle speculates, in addition, that Dekker may have been chosen to write the 1612 Show because of its proximity to the festivities surrounding the marriage of Princess Elizabeth to the Elector Palatine and Dekker's past involvement in James's accession royal entry, although Taylor might be considered even more appropriate on the first score.[223]

Dekker himself was unable to bid for the Show in the year after *Troia-Noua triumphans* as he was in a debtor's prison in 1613, where he remained for the next seven years. He was back in the frame, though, after Middleton's death in 1627, which ended the latter's predominance from c.1617 to the mid-1620s.[224] Dekker himself, in the dedication to the Lord Mayor, Sir Hugh Hammersley, in his 1628 work *Warres, Warre[s], Warres*, reveals that he had been involved in Hammersley's mayoral Show the previous year, although Dekker's name does not feature in the Company's accounts (Christmas's payment of £200 'for the pageants and shewes' was probably shared between them).[225] As Dekker puts it, 'it was some ioy to me, to bee imployed in the Praesentation of your Triumphs, on the day of your Lordships Inauguration' (*Warres, Warre[s], Warres*, sig. A2v). Munday was getting on in years by 1627, Middleton had just died and Heywood had yet to come on to the scene, so perhaps Dekker was the only likely candidate. Indeed, had Dekker's pageants been used in 1630 (when a full-blown Show did not take place) he would have dominated the scene for four consecutive years. Middleton, in turn, was unlikely to have been in the frame to write the 1624 Show – which became Webster's sole commission – because of the controversy provoked by the former's *Game at Chesse* the previous year.

As we have seen in relation to Webster, the writers themselves often flagged up their citizenship. As a Draper, Munday approached the task of writing Shows for his own company with considerable enthusiasm and pride. Indeed, regardless of which Company sponsored them, all his printed Shows proclaim his identity as 'Citizen and Draper of London'.[226] In contrast, with the exception of his first, *The triumphs of truth*, all Middleton's printed Shows call him 'Thomas Middleton Gent.'. Even though by 1626, the year of his last Show, Middleton had actually become a member of the Drapers, his affiliation is not cited in the text despite the fact that Cuthbert Hacket, the new Lord Mayor, was himself a Draper. Nevertheless, Taylor speculates that Middleton's 'family link' to the Grocers' Company, of which his stepfather was a member, 'might have helped him secure' the commission for his first Show, written for a Grocer Lord Mayor.[227] Like Munday, Webster highlighted the fact that he was a Merchant Taylor (there are two references in *Monuments of Honor* to 'our Company', for instance).[228] Forker even argues, somewhat implausibly, that by choosing to claim his freedom by patrimony in 1615 Webster was 'positioning himself as a candidate to write the Lord Mayor's pageant next time a brother of the guild should be honoured by election'.[229] There were, of course, other contenders for that role, and in any case Webster had to wait almost a decade for his sole turn. Membership of one of the Great Twelve Companies, after all, conferred more advantages than the faint prospect of a commission to write a Show. One writer who we can be fairly sure had such ulterior motives was, of course, Munday, who via judicious use of dedications and gifts of his books actively endeavoured to make himself the likely candidate for such work.[230]

Writers who were, for whatever reason, in favour with the Corporation and/or individual Companies sometimes received other, related civic commissions at around the same time as a Show. In Middleton's case, this happened at least twice: he produced an entertainment to celebrate the opening of the New River in 1613, the year of his *Triumphs of truth*, and his *Honorable entertainments* was printed in 1621, the same year as his mayoral Show *The sunne in Aries*. Only on the latter occasion was Middleton the City Chronologer, and thus an obvious choice for such work; indeed, Bald asserts that Middleton's ubiquity at this juncture (including his contribution to some of the various entertainments contained in *Honourable entertainments*) 'helped him to win the office [of City Chronologer]'.[231] In the latter text Middleton does refer to the Mayor, Aldermen and Sheriffs as 'all of them . . . his Worthy and Honorable Patrons' (sig. A2r). It is Heinemann's view that Middleton's 'Puritan' leanings enhanced his connections with some of those in the City of like mind, especially in the Grocers' and Haberdashers' Companies.[232] The post of City Chronologer in the 1620s would have increased his profile in civic circles even more. Taylor calls Middleton at this point civic pageantry's 'dominant, and most inventive, practitioner'.[233]

Munday too was commissioned to write another ad hoc entertainment, *Londons loue*, an account of the civic celebrations held to celebrate the investiture of Prince Henry as Prince of Wales. Chronologically, as with Middleton, this work was both preceded and succeeded by Munday's mayoral Shows. Relatedly, as we have seen, Heywood wrote both a mayoral Show and a description of the King's new flagship, the *Sovereign of the Seas*, in 1637. Indeed, in his mayoral Show of the following year he takes the opportunity to plug his other publication (which must have been successful, as it went to two editions). 'Concerning Ships and Nauigation', Heywood writes,

> with the honour and benefits thence accrewing. I haue lately delivered my selfe so amply in a Book published the last Summer of his Majesties great Shippe, called the Soueraigne of the Seas, that to any, who desire to be better certified concerning such things, I referre them to that Tractate, from which they may receive full & plenteous satisfaction. (*Porta pietatis*, sigs B3v–B4r)

Only John Squire's commission to write the 1620 Show looks especially anomalous, for he had no major civic or court connections,
being a sermon-writer and preacher at St Leonard's, Shoreditch.[234]
Were it not for the fact that the dedication to the 1620 Show is signed
'Io. Squire' it would be hard to credit Squire as the mayoral poet for
that year. Indeed, apart from this name, the only evidence seems to
be that Squire (the cleric) had sermons published at around the same
time as the Show. The sole pretext for choosing Squire to write this
Show might have been that he also preached the inaugural sermon for
the Lord Mayor, Sir Francis Jones.[235] By the time of Thomas Jordan
in the 1670s–80s, however, the job of writing the Show went to 'the
poet of the Corporation of London', an established post (Jordan,
who followed Tatham, was succeeded by Matthew Taubman, and
the latter by Elkanah Settle, the City laureate from 1691).[236] The
institutionalisation of the role of pageant poet in the later seventeenth
century shows how far things had moved on from the days when 'Mr
Pele' was offered a handful of shillings to write a few verses.

Notes

1 Mulryne, 'Introduction', p. 9.
2 Northway, 'I desyre to be paid', p. 406.
3 For instance, in July 1606 Sir Stephen Soame and Sir John Garrard
   were ordered by the Court of Aldermen to 'joine with the committye
   lately appoynted for preparation of the pageantes showes and other
   servyces at the Royall passage of the Kings most excellent majestie and King of Denmark through this Cittye' (Court of Aldermen
   Repertories, vol. 27, fol. 248v). The City Corporation records do not
   typically mention the Lord Mayor's Show, even in times of crisis such
   as outbreaks of plague when the full pageantry was suspended.
4 GH MS 15,869, fols 3–7; GH MS 15,869, fol. 10r–v. I discuss attire
   within the Shows in more detail in the next chapter.
5 Archer, *A History of the Haberdashers' Company*, p. 138.
6 See Sayle, *Lord Mayors' Pageants*, pp. 60–1.
7 The Bachelors or Yeomanry were those members of the Company who
   had yet to be elevated to the Livery.
8 GH MS 30,708/2, fol. 120r. The Merchant Taylors too note in a
   memorandum in their accounts that 'the charge of the barge ... which
   in former yeres was paid out by the yongest Renter Warden ... was
   this yere [1602] paid by the Bachelors Company' (GH MS 38,078/8,
   fol. 220).
9 Goldsmiths MSS vol. 14a, fol. 4v.
10 GH MS 30,708/6, fol. 361. For more on the galley foist see Chapter
   3. The money spent whilst viewing pageants was probably for the

'severall dinners' for which they billed the Company over £23 (livery company officers seem as assiduous as any modern politician at claiming expenses). The children participating in the Merchant Taylors' pageant for 1602 rehearsed their performance before the Master and Wardens of the Company, and received 'a smale banquet' for their pains (GH MS 34,048/8).

11 GH MS 5570/2, fols 183–4.

12 For fifteenth-century royal entries, in contrast, it looks as if the pageantry was designed according to a pre-set 'ordinance, or specification' (Barron, 'Pageantry on London Bridge', p. 94).

13 Sullivan, 'London's early modern creative industrialists', p. 381. The Ironmongers' minutes are particularly likely to preserve evidence of their displeasure when things did not go according to plan, such as when Munday was rebuked for using 'old and borrowed' clothing in 1609, and when a bargeman was 'complained of' in 1629.

14 GH MS 16,969/2, fol. 225r.

15 Drapers MS III, fol. 202r. O'Callaghan erroneously claims that Middleton received no payment at all in this year; the Drapers' accounts, however, make it clear that he was rewarded for at least some of his work (*Thomas Middleton*, p. 15).

16 As Ravelhofer comments, presenting draft summaries to commissioning bodies also took place as a matter of routine within the court masque in this period, although without the competitive element of the Shows (*The Early Stuart Masque*, p. 188).

17 GH MS 5570/2, fol. 193. Note the emphasis on custom and practice. The last Fishmonger mayor had been John Allot in 1590, and the Company seems to have been short of funds in 1616: it admitted that it hadn't 'trimmed' Leman's house as was customary, and could confer only £100 on him, plus the loan of plate and pewter for entertaining (GH MS 5570/2, fol. 194). As with the Skinners in 1597, the Fishmongers pursued errant members' payments for weeks after the Show.

18 See Goldsmiths MSS vol. 14a, fol. 8r.

19 Drapers MS III, fol. 165r. This seems to have been the Drapers' usual practice, for in 1623 too it was stated that 'fowre Mr Wardens shall take present course for the fittinge providinge and compoundinge for of [*sic*] all things as shalbe fitt and necessarie for or touching the said showes and triumphes' (Drapers MS III, fol. 182v).

20 *Jacobean Civic Pageants*, p. 10.

21 Northway, 'I desyre to be paid', p. 406.

22 Palmer, 'Music in the barges', p. 174. The Clothworkers gave Ralph Freeman the same benevolence for 'beautifynge' his house, £25, as they had given John Spencer forty years previously (Clothworkers' accounts, 1633–34, fol. 12r). All the same, some Lord Mayors were extremely wealthy: it has been estimated that James Campbell, Ralph

Freeman and Robert Ducy left estates of at least £50,000 (see Lang, 'Social origins', p. 30).

23 GH MS 16,969/2, fol. 216v. £18 is around £3000 in modern values.

24 Northway remarks that 'instead of estimating a new price comparable to former prices plus inflation, the former prices became the prices to beat' ('I desyre to be paid', p. 409).

25 See Robertson and Gordon, *Collections* III, p. 99. The Drapers conferred a benevolence of £40 on Martin Calthorpe, the Lord Mayor elect in 1588 'accordinge to an order taken the first daye of October 1578' (Drapers MS I, fol. 327).

26 GH MS 34,048/8. This incident exemplifies Woolf's comment that 'in London and in provincial towns, documents were borrowed and sent from place to place with a freedom that would make a modern archivist swoon' (*The Social Construction of the Past*, p. 283).

27 Goldsmiths MSS vol. 14a, fol. 15r. A mark was worth 13s 3d. As Julia Merritt has shown, the Companies contributed to the refurbishment of many City churches, although they expected their generosity to be made evident in stained glass and the like ('Puritans, Laudians', pp. 945–6).

28 Northway, 'I desyre to be paid', p. 411.

29 GH MS 30,708/2, fols 229v–30r. 'A pageant and a luserne' were also ordered for 1597 (see GH MS 30,708/2, fol. 252r).

30 In 1632 one 'Widdowe Walker' was paid by order of the Haberdashers' Court the sum of £5, 'her husband having made suite to make the pageants' (GH MS 15,869, fol. 31r). It is not possible to tell if her husband's 'suite' failed due to his demise or for other reasons, nor is it clear what is meant by 'making' the pageants: perhaps he was a carpenter.

31 GH MS 30,708/6, fol. 359 and GH MS 11,590, fol. 15.

32 GH MS 34,048/15; my emphasis. The Company accounts for 1630 list only 200 members assessed for their contribution to Lord Mayor's Day rather than the 320–360 of previous years, and the sums required of the members were smaller than had been the norm for this Company (around 50s for the Bachelors in budge; in contrast, in 1613 the Grocers assessed their Bachelors for individual sums as high as £8 (GH MS 11,590, fol. 1v)). As a result, the total sum received by the Merchant Taylors was less than £500, whereas in 1624 the Company accumulated more than twice this amount, and in 1613 the Grocers received nearly £500 from the Bachelors' liverymen alone (total receipts for that year came to nearly £1300 – about £127,000 in modern terms) – perhaps times were hard in 1630 even for the Merchant Taylors. Richard Wunderli has calculated that there was a pronounced 'spike' in the number of aldermen being fined out of office in the later 1620s, showing that the City's funds were tight ('Evasion of the office of Alderman', pp. 5–8). For an account of how

the financial pressure of civic office was lessened by statute in the later seventeenth century, see Stow ed. Strype, *A survey of the cities of London and Westminster*, p. 246.

33 GH MS 34,048/15. John Terry, the painter-stainer who worked with Webster in 1624, was once again employed to paint and gild various banners, pavises and targets.

34 Robertson and Gordon, *Collections* III, p. 50.

35 The Haberdashers' Court minutes for 1627 – where it seems pretty certain that Dekker wrote the Show – exemplify this convention: they tell us nothing but how members were to be assessed for their contribution and who was responsible for collecting this money (see GH MS 15,842/1, fol. 248r–v).

36 GH MS 30,708/2, fol. 33v (I have been unable to identify Richard Grimston, unfortunately). The following April 'Thomas Middleton poett' was granted 23s: the Skinners' minutes do not say what for, but it is likely to be an additional payment following his Show the autumn before (GH MS 30,708/3, fol. 42r). Despite the Skinners' concerns about how they were to afford it, the total cost of the 1619 Show was over £725 (see GH MS 30,727/6, fol. 47r).

37 GH MS 16,969/2, fol. 248v (they ate mutton and rabbit).

38 GH MS 16,967/4. Two weeks later Christmas was granted an additional 40s for providing '2 great horses' and two men in white armour for the Show.

39 *Ibid.*

40 Northway, 'I desyre to be paid', p. 408.

41 GH MS 16,967/2, fol. 66v. John Grinkin, the artificer, was paid his £45 in full with no complaints. Pafford claims that Munday 'was also a keeper and apparently a hirer-out of clothing and properties used in pageants' (*Chruso-thriambos*, ed. Pafford, p. 45).

42 GH MS 16,967/2, fol. 68r.

43 GH MS 16,969/2, fol. 223v. See Chapter 3 for more on 'special effects' of this kind.

44 GH MS 5770/2, fols 201–2; see also Hill, *Anthony Munday*, pp. 82–3. On the same day Kemby, a painter-stainer, had his 'unreasonable' bill reduced (this is probably 'Richard Kimby', the arms painter mentioned in the Painter-Stainers' records for 1620: see Englefield, *The History of the Painter-Stainers Company*, p. 92). Munday had made similar 'newe demands' from the Goldsmiths in 1611, but there is no indication in the Company records if a further sum was conferred (see Goldsmiths MSS vol. 14a, fol. 20r). Kemby worked with Munday on both the 1611 and 1616 Shows.

45 Northway, 'I desyre to be paid', p. 419.

46 Hirschfeld, *Joint Enterprises*, p. 95.

47 Heal, *Hospitality*, pp. 301–2 and 326.

48 Griffiths, 'Building Bridewell', p. 230.

49 Archer, *A History of the Haberdashers' Company*, p. 122.
50 GH MS 30,708/2, fol. 122r.
51 GH MS 30,708/3, fol. 33r.
52 *Ibid.*, fols 35v–36v.
53 GH MS 30,708/2, fol. 253r.
54 GH MS 30,708/3, fol. 53r. Another miscreant was brought before the Court in 1622 to pay a 40s fine relating to this Show (*ibid.*, fol. 63r). The Grocers fined John Smyth £25 for 'not performing his Stewardshipp on the Lo. Maiors day' in 1622 (GH MS 11,88/3, fol. 222).
55 Clothworkers' Court Orders, July 1634, fol. 150r.
56 GH MS 30,727/6, fols 358 and 366.
57 Clothworkers' Orders of Courts, October 1583, fol. 30r.
58 GH MS 34,048/10. A total of 320 Company members contributed on this occasion. The expense of Webster's Show in 1624 was such, at over £1000, that even the Merchant Taylors gained only 'eight pounds fifteene shillings [and] one penny' from their contributions in excess of the cost of the Show (GH MS 34,048/13). One should bear in mind, however, that royal entertainments were considerably more expensive than mayoral Shows: Smuts states that the cost of Princess Elizabeth's marriage in 1613 totalled over £90,000 ('Public ceremony', p. 89).
59 GH MS 34,048/10. The excess, where there was one, tended to be given to the Warden of the Company, who was then billed for it in due course (see, for instance, GH MS 34,048/13).
60 Goldsmiths MSS vol. 14, fols 726–7.
61 Clothworkers' Court Orders, July 1606, fol. 9v.
62 Dekker, once again, gives a sense of how widespread and well-known the practices associated with mayoral inaugurations were: in *The guls horne-booke* the 'cherry lippes' of the would-be fashionable gull are 'open like the new painted gates of a Lord Maiors house' (sig. C3v). Nashe uses much the same image in *Pierce Penilesse* (1592).
63 GH MS 30,708/3, fol. 36v and GH MS 34,048/10. As well as the conventional £40 for the new mayor, the Grocers also conferred £30 on one of their Sheriffs elect in 1622 'towards the beautifyinge of his house' (GH MS 11,588/3, fol. 217). In 1611 James Pemberton himself requested additional plate from the Goldsmiths for his mayoralty (Goldsmiths MSS vol. 14a, fol. 4r; the Court Minutes list the inventory too, as one might expect of this particular Company, and also note that the plate was returned the year later). Owing to a relative scarcity of 'great houses' in London, Lang writes, 'succeeding generations of Lord Mayors and Sheriffs tended to occupy the same houses', and in some cases the livery companies owned the houses, which were leased out ('Social origins', pp. 40–1). Lang has calculated that, even

for those men with suitable houses for the roles, the offices of sheriff and mayor could cost their incumbents between £2000 and £4000 for the year; for those who had to buy or lease a house the cost was higher still (*ibid.*, p. 45).

64 See Wunderli, 'Evasion of the office of Alderman', p. 4, and Heal, *Hospitality*, p. 310.

65 Palmer makes the interesting suggestion that this passage 'may quote the Geneva Bible's translation of Psalm 112.9', which also uses the words 'pinch' and 'liberal' ('Metropolitan resurrection', p. 378).

66 Middleton, ed. Bald, *Honourable Entertainments*, p. vii. Parr calls Jones 'fiscally unreliable' and 'an altogether less impressive man' than Cockayne, his predecessor (*Middleton: The Collected Works*, p. 1434). The Lord Mayor was also sometimes instructed to provide accommodation for visiting diplomats.

67 BL Add. MS 18016, fol. 152r. There may be a deliberate irony in Finch's remark that Jones had 'willingly' laid down the burden of office (fol. 150r) and also in his ambiguous comment that Jones 'cannot give a greater testimony of him[self] than his meane estimation of him selfe' (*ibid.*). In 1622 Barkham was given a valedictory testimonial by Finch in which it was stated that – unlike his predecessor, Jones – he performed the role with 'dilligence from the first [day] of the [mayoral] yeare to the last' (fol. 165v).

68 *Ibid.*, fol. 166r.

69 GH MS 34,048/9. Some thirty men, according to the Company accounts, worked through two nights and a day and a half to make it possible to restage the Show (and the Company clerk charged 10s for once again entering the accounts). Pepys and Tatham testify to inclement weather for the Show in 1664.

70 Goldsmiths MSS vol. 14a, fol. 19r.

71 *Ibid.*, fol. 20v.

72 Grupenhoff, 'The Lord Mayors' Shows', p. 20. In the same vein, Munro calls the Londinium arch for James I's coronation entry 'Jonson's creation', overlooking Stephen Harrison's essential contribution (*The Figure of the Crowd*, p. 51).

73 Osteen and Woodmansee, 'Taking account of the New Economic Criticism', p. 9. Bergeron comments that such an approach to early modern culture is grounded in 'a romantic cult of the proprietary single author . . . who dismisses [and] erases competitors' ('Middleton and Munday', p. 477).

74 *Joint Enterprises*, p. 63.

75 Ravelhofer, *The Early Stuart Masque*, p. 5.

76 *Joint Enterprises*, p. 34.

77 Ewbank, 'Masques and pageants', p. 110.

78 Northway, 'I desyre to be paid', pp. 419–20.

79 Hirschfeld, *Joint Enterprises*, p. 5.

80 Goldsmiths MS vol. 14a, fols 9v–10r. Grinkin was paid £75 and Munday £80.

81 Munday, ed. Pafford, *Chruso-Thriambos*, pp. 12 and 48.

82 Northway, 'I desyre to be paid', pp. 415–16.

83 Turner, 'Plotting early modernity', p. 87). 'Plot', as used in livery company records, is obviously also related to the kind of 'plot', sum-marising the play's action, which was hung up on the back of the stage in professional theatres.

84 *Ibid.*, p. 95; my emphasis.

85 Jonson sets out the distinction in his preface to his masque *Hymenaei*. Turner notes that Jonson often uses 'plot' 'in this restricted and quasi-mechanical sense' (*ibid.*, p. 88).

86 *Ibid.*, p. 91.

87 Heinemann notes that Christmas also held the position of woodcarver to the Navy, a post to which he had been appointed by the Earl of Nottingham, the Lord Admiral. As she points out, this may stand as another personal connection, for Middleton began his theatrical career writing for the Admiral's Men at the Rose (*Puritanism and Theatre*, p. 122 n. 3).

88 Thus, the Ironmongers refer to Dekker as 'Mr Tho: Decker the Poett'; Garret Christmas is simply a 'workeman' (GH MS 16,967/4). On this occasion (1629) Dekker and Christmas were commissioned in August, relatively early; the usual pattern was restored in 1635, when Heywood and John Christmas won the commission on 2 October.

89 *Companion*, pp. 45–6. Jonson's collaborator George Chapman was of the same mind, disparaging Middleton as 'a poore Chronicler of a Lord Maiors naked Truth (that peraduenture will last his yeare)', which is perhaps a jibe directed specifically at *The triumphs of truth*, given the 1614 date of Chapman's attack, and the way in which Truth is depicted as 'thin and naked' in the Show (*Homer's Odysses*, sig. A4v). As Bergeron points out, 'ironically, Chapman helps confer per-manence on Middleton's [Show] by this very reference' (*Middleton: The Collected Works*, p. 963).

90 See Robertson and Gordon, *Collections* III, p. xliii.

91 Drapers' Bachelors Accounts, fols 36–7.

92 'The Masque of Truth', p. 106 n. 15. Williams states that 'it was very unusual to employ one person to devise spectacles and another to describe them' ('A Lord Mayor's Show by John Taylor', p. 530).

93 Robertson and Gordon, *Collections* III, pp. 127 and 129.

94 GH MS 15,869, fol. 21v.

95 Clothworkers' Court Orders, September 1633, fol. 140r; Clothworkers' accounts, 1633–34, fol. 11v. In 1634 on at least two occasions the Wardens of the Yeomanry met Zachary Taylor and Robert Norman, the artificers, not John Taylor, the poet (unless he was one of the

'others' mentioned, although not by name) (Clothworkers' accounts, 1634–35, fol. 11r–v).

96 Watanabe-O'Kelly has aptly noted 'the mania of early modern . . . bureaucracy for recording everything' ('Early modern European festivals', p. 19). The almost neurotic level of detail in the Ironmongers' minutes is such that we even learn that some of the trumpeters absented themselves for part of the day.

97 The Ironmongers' Registers for 1629 say: 'paid Thomas Decker Poett and Garrett Chrismas workeman for 6 [several] Pageants which with the Contracte is particularly entred in Court Booke' (Robertson and Gordon, *Collections* III, p. 119). The word 'particularly' reveals that the Company was aware that this was not usual practice.

98 GH MS 16,967/4. Perhaps because the clerk and/or the Company was especially interested in these matters, the Ironmongers' records for 1629 also contain 'The explanacion of the Shewe on the Lord Maiors day', which describes Dekker and Christmas's proposed pageants in some detail. I will discuss how these 'explanations' compare to the printed text, *Londons Tempe*, in Chapter 4.

99 GH MS 16,967/4.

100 The Artillery Garden often supplied drummers and fifers, and payments to them appear regularly in Company records (there are references to 'Captaines' and sergeants in the Merchant Taylors' accounts for 1624, for instance). In *Porta pietatis* Heywood singles out 'two eminent Gardens of Exercise . . . [one] Artillery' as notable features of the City (sig. A3v).

101 See GH MS 11,588/2, fols 733 and 740. The related 'Triumphs Accounts' for this Show run from October 1613 to April 1614 (these beautifully presented accounts emanate excitement and pride). At a total cost of well over £1000 it was a very expensive production: Sullivan comments that its overall cost was around the same as for the building of the second Globe theatre ('Summer 1613', p. 168). The lavishness is understandable if the Grocers' two preceding inaugurations in this period (1598 and 1608) were, as it seems, somewhat curtailed; as a comparator, the Haberdashers' total expenditure on the 1620 Show was just over £750. Another parallel for the level of expenditure is aristocratic funerals: the cost of the Duke of Norfolk's funeral in 1524 was £1300 (Loach, 'The function of ceremonial', p. 60).

102 The Grocers' forthcoming Show must have been an open secret for some time, for in July two watermen petitioned to supply the galley foist (GH MS 11,588/2, fol. 770). In the same way, the Fishmongers were approached by 'one Hynxman' offering to sell them 'Redd Capps' for the procession in early July 1616 (GH MS 5570/2, fol. 178).

103 Goldsmiths MSS vol. 14, fols 710 and 721.

104 Munday, ed. Pafford, *Chruso-Thriambos*, p. 13.

105 Goldsmiths MSS vol. 14, fol. 722. The Goldsmiths also rewarded
    Munday in 1617 for a copy of his *Survay*, which he had explicitly
    presented for 'recompence' (vol. 14a, fol. 162r). Munday wrote
    Pemberton's epitaph, too: another spin-off from his earlier employ-
    ments with the Goldsmiths (see my *Anthony Munday*, p. 157, and
    Munday, ed. Pafford, *Chruso-Thriambos*, pp. 55–7).

106 Munday, *Chruso-thriambos*, sig. C3r. Munday had also dedicated two
    religious works to Swinnerton in 1602, the year he became alderman
    (see my *Anthony Munday*, pp. 90–1).

107 He stated 'it is full three years past . . . that by occasion of God's pun-
    ishment, the Cittizens of London have been constrayned to forbear
    their comeing to this honourable place' (Nichols, *The Progresses and
    Public Processions of Queen Elizabeth*, p. 254).

108 GH MS 15,333/2, fols 184–5.

109 The Vintners were not the wealthiest of Companies: Anne Crawford
    states that this 'total sum [was] almost equivalent to an entire year's
    income for the Company' (*A History of the Vintners' Company*, p.
    94). £300 was only a contribution to the likely costs: for more on the
    considerable personal expense involved in the mayoralty, see Tittler,
    Architecture and Power, pp. 106–7.

110 Clothworkers' Accounts, 1606–1607, fol. 11r. As 1606 was a plague
    year, the street procession and shows were called off 'by reason of the
    sicknes then increasinge in this Cittie' (Clothworkers Court Orders
    (1621), fol. 245r).

111 Clothworkers' Court Orders, 1606, fol. 13r.

112 Cited in Sayle, *Lord Mayors' Pageants*, p. 86.

113 GH MS 34,048/10. The Grocers evidently held a procession and feast
    in 1608, another year when records are scant; there is, however, no
    reference in the Company minutes to any pageantry (see GH MS
    11,588/2, fols 512–15). The Grocers didn't hold the Warden's elec-
    tion dinner in July of that year either, 'in respect of the dearenes of the
    tyme' (GH MS 11,588/2 fol. 495), and the Company's 'garner' was
    called upon, suggesting a time of dearth (fols 516–17).

114 In 1624 the number of cannons had been increased to 140 (see GH MS
    34,048/13).

115 A 'gilded head of Iron, cutt through' was hired for 'the cheif Ensigne'
    (GH MS 34,048/10).

116 GH MS 34,048/10. In 1612 the Merchant Taylors employed
    'Threescore and eight gentlemen ushers'. The Grocers hired 130
    javelins and 29 dozen staves for whifflers for their 1613 Show, which
    probably indicates the numbers involved (GH MS 11,590, fols 4v–5r).
    They really pushed the boat out in 1613, spending over £36 on 47
    dozen torches alone (*ibid.*, fol. 5r).

117 GH MS 16,969/2, fol. 225r.

118 *Oxford DNB*, 'Christmas family'. I have preferred 'Garret' for

'Gerard', as he is sometimes called (as in the *DNB*), because that is what his collaborators called him.

119 Pafford notes that 'payments to Grinkin are always among the highest' (Munday, ed. Pafford, *Chruso-Thriambos*, p. 52).

120 *Ibid.*, p. 53.

121 As discussed below, Heywood mentions this work, *A true description of His Majesties royall ship*, in *Londini speculum*, sig. C4v. He praises the Christmas brothers' artistry in the latter text too (see sig. G4r).

122 As well as the painter-stainers, armourers and wax and tallow-chandlers benefited from civic ceremony, as did musicians (see Palmer, *Ceremonial Barges*, p. 130). 'Mr Ridg Armorer' got 30s 'for the hyer of the Javelyns' in 1602 (GH MS 34,048/9).

123 GH MS 16,967/2, fol. 66v.

124 See the Merchant Taylors' accounts (GH MS 34,048/10) for their outlay on the latter occasion.

125 Gordon, 'Poet and architect', p. 177.

126 Morrissey, 'English pageant-wagons', p. 354.

127 Post-1640s mayoral texts did the same: for instance, although for some reason the artificer 'desired to have his Name concealed', Tatham did thank the painters, joiner and carver employed in the making of the 1659 Show (*London's Tryumph*, sig. C4r).

128 Quoted in Kiefer, *Shakespeare's Visual Theatre*, p. 16.

129 *Thomas Middleton*, p. 99.

130 *The triumphs of truth* was the first mayoral text where the writer thanked his collaborators. Henry Wilde, mentioned in 1617, was a painter-stainer who worked on a number of Shows, decorating 'targets' and the like; Challoner collaborated with Richard Munday on the 1613 Show, too (see GH MS 11,590, fol. 6v). The Companies' accounts often record recompense paid to individuals for their 'greate and extraordynary paynes', as the Merchant Taylors put it (GH MS 34,048/10). The Company emphasised in 1624 that such ex gratia payments were 'not hereafter to be a president [precedent]', however (GH MS 34,048/13).

131 Masque texts often bore similar acknowledgements of the work of designers and the like (see, for example, Jonson's *Masque of Queenes* (1609)).

132 Wickham, *Early English Stages*, vol. I, p. 110; Robertson and Gordon, *Collections* III, p. 92. It is perhaps this lack of knowledge about the range and subtleties of the roles behind the Shows that leads Kathman to call one Christopher Beck 'an actor in Lord Mayor's shows' when the livery company records actually indicate that he (and a colleague called Hugh Watts) was often called upon either to find 'woodmen' or to take on such a role himself: the word 'actor' is somewhat misleading in this context (*Bibliographical Index of English Drama*).

133 Munday, ed. Pafford, *Chruso-Thriambos*, p. 54.

134 Robertson and Gordon, *Collections* III, p. 5.

135 See Dekker, *The whole magnificent entertainment*, sigs I3v–I4r.

136 Grinkin himself received £46 from the Haberdashers in 1604 'for the pageant, lion, mermaides, chariott & other things' (GH MS 15,869, fol. 7v).

137 *Thomas Middleton*, p. 99.

138 GH MS 11,590, fol. 6r (see also Munday, ed. Pafford, *Chruso-Thriambos*, p. 47: Pafford's discussion of Munday's larger role in the 1613 Show appears to have passed most commentators by). The Grocers make a point of calling both writers 'Gent'.

139 GH MS 11,590, fol. 6. The 1611 court entertainment *Oberon* won Jonson £40 and Inigo Jones, as the equivalent of the artificer, at least £390 (*Middleton: The Collected Works*, p. 1255). £310 converts to around £30,000 in modern prices.

140 GH MS 11,590, fol. 6.

141 Donna Hamilton's argument that Munday's alleged crypto-Catholicism resulted in the properly Protestant Middleton being chosen to write the 1613 Show is fatally damaged by the fact (of which she seems unaware) that the two were actually collaborators that year (*Anthony Munday and the Catholics*, pp. 159–60).

142 Taylor also thanks Zachary Taylor, 'a quaint and well knowne curious Carvar' (*The triumphs of fame and honour*, sig. B4r).

143 Williams, 'A Lord Mayor's show by John Taylor', pp. 507–8.

144 Williams, *ibid.*, p. 509. Even Ceri Sullivan, a scholar more attuned to the pragmatics of literary production than most, claims the commissions were contested by 'dramatists', which disregards both the artificers and those pageant writers – like Squire and Taylor – who were not dramatists ('London's early modern creative industrialists', p. 381).

145 'I desyre to be paid', p. 405.

146 Dekker offers a similar account of the making of the 1604 royal entry: 'for more exact and formall managing of [the] Businesse, a Select number both of Aldermen and Commoners . . . were . . . chosen forth, to whose discretion, on the Charge, Contriuings, Proiects, and all other Dependences, owing to so troublesome a worke, was intirely, and Iudicially committed' (*The magnificent entertainment*, sig. B2v).

147 *Jacobean Civic Pageants*, p. 175 n. 2.

148 He strikes a similar note more briefly in *Sidero-Thriambos*, referring to the defects of a performance designed 'in so slender a compasse' (sigs A4v–B1r).

149 There is no evidence in the Merchant Taylors' accounts whether or not Webster or his collaborators, the painter John Terry, William Patten and George Lovett, arranged for the printing of the books, as was usual. We do know that the sub-committee met at least twenty-one times to 'confer concerning the provision of shewes' because they

charged the Company for the expenses of that many dinners (GH MS 34,048/13).

150 Bergeron, *Textual Patronage*, p. 71.

151 *Jacobean Civic Pageants*, p. 170.

152 GH MS 34,048/13.

153 Robertson and Gordon, *Collections* III, p. xxxiii.

154 GH MS 16,967/1, fol. 53v. It seems that Baker acted as an artificer on this occasion as his role extended to making 'the pageant', and it was noted that Baker's role did not extend to providing the children and their apparel: John Tailor from Westminster School undertook this.

155 GH MS 16,969/2, fol. 225.

156 In a rather loose use of the term, Hardin claims that Munday acted 'as artificer for later Lord Mayor's shows written by others' and he instances the supply of cloth to back up this view ('Spectacular Constructions', p. 77). The role of artificer, however, cannot be defined simply by supplying cloth, and Hardin's understanding of Munday's civic career is a little garbled.

157 GH MS 34,048/10.

158 *Ibid*. Bradbrook states that Webster too participated in the procession of his own Show, in 1624, although he is not present in the list of members in the Company records for that year: perhaps he did not process as a member, or alternatively Bradbrook may have confused John Webster with Edward Webster, who did join the procession (see *John Webster*, p. 166). She also speculates that Milton, a student at Paul's School in 1624, may have either acted in or marched in the procession accompanying Webster's Show ('The politics of pageantry', p. 74).

159 GH MS 34,048/9. Munday was also reimbursed nearly £4 by the Grocers in 1613 for 'the cleareing of all Chardges for the standing of the Pageant etc at the bell in Carter lane' (GH MS 11,590, fol. 6r). Carter Lane runs parallel to the southern edge of Paul's Churchyard and is thus just off the route back from Paul's Stairs; it features in a number of the Companies' accounts. It was blocked off to traffic with a chain when the cathedral was being used, as in mayoral Shows: hence 'Paul's Chain'.

160 GH MS 38,048/8.

161 *Ibid*.

162 Sayle, *Lord Mayors' Pageants*, p. 71.

163 *Ibid*., p. 72.

164 GH MS 15,842/1, fol. 142r.

165 GH MS 15,869, fol. 7v; *Jacobean Civic Pageants*, p. 24. Jonson did allow other suitably courtly works of pageantry to be printed, however, such as the entertainments he wrote for the new royal family for performance at Althorp and at Highgate in 1603–4, as well as his 'part' of *The magnificent entertainment*.

166 Robertson and Gordon, *Collections* III, p. xxxv.

167 For some reason, there are quite a few details relating to Skinners' Shows not transcribed by Robertson and Gordon, and there are also a number of relevant items in the Clothworkers' accounts for 1594–95 (John Spencer's inauguration) which they omitted to record.

168 GH MS 30,708/2, fol. 254v.

169 In 1628 Dekker was given an additional £3 and Christmas £10 'in benevolence' and 'over and above the severall somes agreed' (GH MS 30,708/3, fol. 119r). The Skinners were evidently very pleased with the production: even the boy drummer was granted an extra 20s.

170 Jonson, *The case is alterd*, sig. A2r; see also Hill, *Anthony Munday*, p. 75.

171 GH MS 15,869, fol. 26r.

172 The Grocers' Court minutes for 1617 are exemplary in this respect: a committee of wardens was appointed in July (again, relatively early) 'generally for to doe and order all matters of triumphes and shewes', reporting back to the Court of Assistants when required (GH MS 11,588/3, fol. 48).

173 The use of St Peter's Church on Cheapside as a venue for the city waits to perform is an example of this trend: one can imagine Company officials telling the churchwarden 'but we've always done it this way . . .'. Of course, those affected by these traditions were generally compensated for their trouble too.

174 GH MS 15,869, fols 26r and 31r.

175 GH MS 34/048/8 and 34,048/9. Richard Scarlett and George Hearne were senior members of the Painter-Stainers in 1605 (see Englefield, *The History of the Painter-Stainers Company*, p. 64 n. 5); Scarlett, who decorated 'targettes' in 1602, also worked on the 1610 Show alongside Rowland Vaughan. Large quantities of banners and the like were used: even the trumpeters had banners on their instruments.

176 *The Mayor of London's Jacobean Thames Pageant*, p. 9; see also *Middleton: The Collected Works*, p. 966.

177 GH MS 34,048/10.

178 The artificers in 1624 were John Terry, William Patten and George Lovett.

179 GH MS 11,590, fol. 21.

180 'Francis Tipslie and Mr Squire' were paid £180 for the 'pageants' for the 1620 Show. In 1604 Tipsley was paid £5 for painting two banners (see GH MS 15,869, fol. 8r). For the 1631 Show he got £56 'for painting & guilding the streamers and banners' (fol. 26r), and in 1632, over £20 for 'work done about the streamers' (fol. 31r). The case of Thomas Kendall also indicates that the Haberdashers' Company seems to have been prone to employ its own members.

181 Although Tipsley was the main co-producer with Squire, Grinkin

was still involved, receiving over £54 for 'the silke workes' (GH MS 15,869, fol. 16r).

182 Quoted in Wortham, 'Sovereign counterfeits', p. 345.

183 Financially cautious they may have been, but Company officials were not soulless bureaucrats: the Drapers record a payment of 2s 6d to a boy 'who should have been a drumer but was disaponited' (Robertson and Gordon, *Collections* III, p. 105), and in 1602 the Merchant Taylors paid someone sixpence 'for carying one of the Children home' (GH MS 34,048/8).

184 See *Collections* III, p. 116. Palmer comments that it was 'common for musicians . . . to demand what Companies regarded as too high a fee, requiring negotiation' ('Music in the barges', p. 174).

185 Gasper argues that Dekker may also have been motivated by a political desire to distinguish civic entertainments from what he may have regarded as 'the pointless extravagance and display of Whitehall' (*The Dragon and the Dove*, p. 130).

186 Northway, 'I desyre to be paid', p. 408.

187 Such family connections were legion: two of James Campbell's daughters married men who eventually become Lord Mayors, and the 1613 Lord Mayor Sir Thomas Middleton's first wife was the daughter of the Lord Mayor of 1597, Richard Saltonstall. Munday understates the situation for rhetorical impact when in *Sidero-Thriambos* he claims that Campbell's mayoralty, following that of his father, 'is no commo[n] thing' (sig. B4v). Many of these families also had long-standing involvement in trading companies like the Merchant Adventurers and East India Company, an issue I explore further in Chapter 5 (see Brenner, *Merchants and Revolution*, p. 90, for an account of the marital connections between the Campbell, Clitheroe and Garway families).

188 Horne, *George Peele*, pp. 71–2.

189 *Ibid.*, p. 73. On the basis of a passing reference in the posthumous *Merry Conceited Jests of George Peele* (1607) to Peele having 'had all the ouersight of the pagiants', Horne concludes that 'Peele had acquired sufficient prominence and experience to be regarded as a man who might be called upon to produce the pageant as well as write the device for it' (*ibid.*).

190 Hardin, 'Spectacular Constructions', p. 142.

191 See 'Medieval to Renaissance', pp. 306–8; she concludes that from 1516 the Drapers' Court minutes 'show that the players . . . are almost invariably well-known professionals with court/aristocratic patronage' (p. 310).

192 *Jacobean Civic Pageants*, p. 137.

193 See Heywood, *An apology for actors*, sigs A2r–A4r.

194 See Harrison, *The arch's of triumph*, sig. Bv.

195 Heinemann claims that Middleton may have gained the commission for his first Show in 1613 through the offices of Sir Thomas

Middleton, that year's Lord Mayor, but she provides no evidence for this (*Puritanism and Theatre*, p. 125).

196 Middleton speaks highly of Munday's work on the water show in 1623, calling it 'Glorious and Apt' (*The triumphs of integrity*, sig. A3v).

197 As Bergeron points out, J. P. Collier made this connection many years ago, but no one subsequently pursued it ('Middleton and Munday', p. 466; see also my *Anthony Munday*, pp. 77–9). Bergeron provides a painstaking account of the lineage of the alleged Middleton/Munday rift which I do not need to rehearse here. Times have changed: in his introduction to *The triumphs of truth* in the *Middleton Collected Works* Bergeron does not mention Munday at all in this regard.

198 Edmonds, 'Heminges, John', *Oxford DNB*. 'Heminges had been employed by the Merchant Taylors several years before [his Show with Dekker] in training his apprentice John Rice to deliver a speech at the Merchant Taylors' dinner for royalty' (Bentley, *The Profession of Player*, p. 61). Neither Heminges's *DNB* entry nor Andrew Gurr's potted biography of him in *The Shakespeare Company* (see p. 230) mentions his work for the Shows. The cultured alderman John Swinnerton (Lord Mayor in 1612) acted as a kind of producer for the entertainment given on the occasion of this visit by the King and Prince Henry to Merchant Taylors' Hall, when the latter was conferred the freedom of that Company: Swinnerton's responsibilities included liaising with Jonson over the speech and organising the boy actors (for a full discussion of this event and its wider implications, see Perry, *The Making of Jacobean Culture*, pp. 193–8).

199 GH MS 11,590, fol. 7r. In 1613 Richard Munday received £14 for 'working silvering guilding and paynting of one long streamer of 14 yards long, with the image of St Anthony', plus other work, the cost of which is not recorded. By 1639 he had risen to be Upper Warden of the Painter-Stainers and his own arms appeared in the windows of the Company Hall: his father would have been very proud, no doubt, had he survived that long (Englefield, *History of the Painter-Stainers Company*, pp. 92 and 109 n. 3).

200 See Bradbrook, *John Webster*, p. 20. Admittedly building speculation upon speculation, it is just possible that Webster himself may have performed in civic entertainments in the mid-1580s to early 1590s.

201 GH MS 15,869, fols 16r–17r. William Squire was at that point the Beadle of the Yeomanry of the Haberdashers, and doubtless assisted them in that capacity (see Archer, *The Haberdashers' Company*, pp. 53–4).

202 See Forker, *Skull Beneath the Skin*, p. 20. Dekker apparently owed Webster £40 for the cost of the pageant wagons from the previous year's Show (see Bradbrook, *John Webster*, p. 180), although Gasper is sceptical about this claim (*The Dragon and the Dove*, p. 132).

Yet another creditor was Ralph Savage, the manager of the Red Bull theatre, who may have lent Dekker money.

203 'The politics of pageantry', p. 68.

204 *Ibid.*, p. 10. For a useful illustration of how familial and social networks operated in sixteenth-century London, see Harding, 'Citizen and mercer', pp. 32–3.

205 One of the writers for the Queen's 1578 entertainment in Norwich is identified as 'Citizen of London' in the printed text.

206 Kathman, 'Heywood, Thomas', *Oxford DNB*.

207 Howard, *Theater of a City*, p. 28.

208 See Capp, 'Taylor, John', *Oxford DNB*, and *The World of John Taylor*, p. 8. Capp does not mention Taylor's Lord Mayor's Show in his *DNB* entry, and merely dismisses it as having 'very little literary or dramatic merit' in *The World of John Taylor* (p. 33). Tessa Watt remarks that 'Taylor's corpus does seem to occupy an ambiguous place . . . probably coming into some degree of contact with both the highest and the lowest levels of literate society' (*Cheap Print*, p. 293). Two years before his mayoral Show Taylor won a case for slander at the Guildhall so he would have been known to City leaders (Capp, *ibid.*, p. 32).

209 Capp, *Oxford DNB*, 'Taylor, John'.

210 He knew Munday, too, at least by reputation: we have Taylor to thank for the anecdote that 'Mr. Anthony Munday (sometimes a Writer to the City of London) would run from the Table at the sight of a forequarter of Lambe roasted' (*Taylors feast*, sig. E4v). The (posthumous) identification of Munday as a City writer is notable here. If his late work *The hierarchie of the blessed angells* is anything to go by, Heywood knew a considerable number of his contemporaries, ranging chronologically from Peele to Ford (Webster, apparently, was known as 'Jacke' rather than John, and Middleton and Dekker were both 'Tom') (sig. S1v).

211 Capp, *The World of John Taylor*, pp. 43–4. Williams comes to the same conclusion as I do ('A Lord Mayor's show', p. 506). Taylor included a work by Dekker in a 1615 collection of verses (Capp, *ibid.*, p. 44).

212 Capp, *The World of John Taylor*, pp. 57–8.

213 The two were chosen because of their court connections (see Kipling, 'Anne Boleyn', p. 50, and, for Udall, Streitberger, *Court Revels*).

214 Unlike some of the later writers, both of Peele's Shows celebrate the fact that he was 'Master of Arts in Oxford', not that he was a citizen and Salter.

215 If membership of a livery company, especially one of the Great Twelve, came into play for other roles in mayoral Shows too, then it is possible that John Wilson, a theatre musician who was free of the Grocers and also a member of the City Waits, may have participated in post-1622 Shows (see Kathman, 'Grocers, Goldsmiths and Drapers', p. 9).

216 Goldsmiths MSS vol. 14s, fol. 8r. Gurr suggests that Lowin's
    Goldsmiths' Company membership was the sole reason for his
    employment on this occasion (*The Shakespeare Company*, p. 233).
    Robert Armin was also free of the Goldsmiths.

217 Forker, *Skull Beneath the Skin*, p. 9. The Merchant Taylors did at
    one point choose a writer, but for his specific expertise rather than
    company membership: their account of commissioning Jonson to
    write a speech to welcome the King to their Hall prefers the drama-
    tist to the 'Scholemaster and Schollers' of their school because the
    latter 'be not acquainted with suche kind of Entertagnements' (see
    Hirschfeld, *Joint Enterprises*, p. 66). It's notable that in the forty
    years or so since Mulcaster wrote civic pageantry the Merchant
    Taylors' school had lost its reputation for writing and performing
    speeches.

218 Hardin, 'Spectacular Constructions', p. 78.

219 See Horne, *George Peele*, p. 10. Horne speculates that James and
    George Peele may have been descended from Sir John Piel, Lord
    Mayor in 1372 (*ibid.*, pp. 11, 132 and 139). Bradbrook asserts that
    Webster's membership of the powerful Merchant Taylors was 'the
    most important fact about [his] origins' (*John Webster*, p. 11).

220 GH MS 34,048/8.

221 For instance, he refers to 'our Hall' when discussing the Company in
    the time of Edward III (sig. B1r). Gasper speculates that Webster may
    have been present at Dekker's 1612 Show (*The Dragon and the Dove*,
    p. 131). Webster was not made free of the Merchant Taylors until
    1615, however, so if he did attend the Show it would have been merely
    as a spectator. One 'Edward Webster' is assessed for a contribution to
    the 1624 Show (see GH MS 34,048/13).

222 See the copy held in the British Library, sig. A1r (the title page is repro-
    duced in Sayle, *Lord Mayors' Pageants*).

223 Sayle, *Lord Mayors' Pageants*, p. 97.

224 Dekker continued to write during his time in prison – chiefly about
    his experience of imprisonment – although he would not have been
    able to bid for a mayoral Show. Perhaps not knowing that Dekker
    was in prison at this time, Lobanov-Rostovsky prefers to see Dekker's
    absence from the scene during these years as a reflection of the livery
    companies' distaste for his alleged unwillingness to take on an 'exclu-
    sively celebratory tone' in *Troia-Noua triumphans* ('The Triumphes of
    Golde', p. 885).

225 GH MS 15,869, fol. 21v.

226 See Hill, *Anthony Munday*, pp. 171–4. The copy of Munday's
    Triumphes of re-united Britania held in the Bodleian has 'Champion
    for the Cittie or the Citys Champion' written in a contemporary hand
    on its title page.

227 *Buying Whiteness*, p. 140. Taylor also claims that Middleton 'could

hardly have avoided thinking about his Grocer-stepfather when writing *The triumphs of truth*' (*ibid.*). This, of course, we can never substantiate.

228 Webster, *Monuments of Honor*, sigs B2r and B3v; see also sigs A1r and A2v.

229 Forker, *Skull Beneath the Skin*, p. 9. Forker (who does not seem to know that Dekker too was a Merchant Taylor) rather hyperbolically calls Webster 'the official poet of the [Merchant] Taylors' and their 'laureate'. With three Shows for this Company Munday, in fact, had a better claim to such a status.

230 See Hill, *Anthony Munday*, pp. 81–91.

231 Middleton, ed. Bald, *Honourable Entertainments*, p. vi.

232 Heinemann, *Puritanism and Theatre*, p. 126. I think she overstates the case that Middleton was 'a protégé of Parliamentary Puritans among the City oligarchs', however (*ibid.*); Taylor disputes her views too, arguing that Middleton is more accurately seen as a Calvinist (*Oxford DNB*, 'Middleton, Thomas').

233 Taylor, *Oxford DNB*, 'Middleton, Thomas'. Middleton received 'gifts from £6 to £20 yearly' for his role as City Chronologer; Hirschfeld calls him 'a thoroughly civic professional' (*Joint Enterprises*, p. 101).

234 According to the title pages of his other publications (all of which are religious works), Squire had a Master of Arts from Jesus College, Cambridge.

235 See Heinemann, *Puritanism and Theatre*, pp. 122–3. For Heinemann, Squire is an example of the appointment by the Haberdashers of 'Puritans' to jobs in their gift.

236 Jordan was a poet, playwright and actor who was responsible for thirteen mayoral shows.

3

'A day of well Compos'd Variety of Speach and shew': bringing the Shows to life

Given their predominantly visual appeal to the original audiences it is perhaps surprising that relatively little attention has yet been paid within literary and historical scholarship to how the visual and aural spectacle of the Lord Mayors' Shows would have been experienced on the day of the performance. This is partly down to the general dominance within literary scholarship of printed texts, and it is also, of course, due to the elusive nature of pageantry, which would seem hard for critics to reconstruct. David Cannadine argues that 'the invisible and the ephemeral are, by definition, not the easiest of subjects for scholars to study. But this conceals, more than it indicates, their real importance [and is] . . . no justification for failing to try.'[1] Smuts writes in a similar vein that 'modern scholarship has . . . [treated] language and visual iconography as central . . . while largely ignoring . . . elements of spectacle that must often have dominated the impressions of contemporary spectators'.[2] Even though some of the more fleeting aspects of the Shows have left no record, we must still acknowledge their existence in their own moment. Putting the printed texts to one side it is salutary to remember that, like masques, the Shows were composed of various elements, most of which were non-verbal: alongside the speeches (some in verse, others prose) there were costumes, music and dance, as well as special effects such as fireworks. Indeed, some of their more spectacular qualities far exceeded those that the playhouses were able to stage.

Despite these apparent obstacles there are, in fact, various ways to retrieve some sense of the vanished spectacle and to reconstruct aspects of the lived experience of these multi-faceted events. This chapter will therefore discuss, *inter alia*, the actors' roles, the props, music and costumes used during the Show and how the pageantry was staged; it will also look at how important emblems and imagery were to these productions. The overall intention, following

Ravelhofer's approach to the masque, is, as she writes, to 'arrive at a fuller grasp of the . . . experience [by trying to] balance . . . various aspects of performance and textual record against each other, and compare the sartorial, kinetic, iconic, and verbal languages of the event'.[3] One should therefore give due attention to what Davidson calls the 'technology' of these events. Not all such aspects were under the control of the makers of the Shows, who also had to deal with a number of practical constraints and challenges, starting with the early darkness and often-inclement weather of late October.[4] It is thus important to address some of those moments when things went wrong. One must also remember, as Paster comments, that, unlike masques, Shows were not presented in entirely appropriate venues: 'with all the visual and acoustical difficulties of an open-air procession', she writes, 'the pageant poet faced severe handicaps'.[5] The dimensions and acoustics of the locations of the pageant stations varied too, from open spaces like Paul's Churchyard to narrow streets like Soper Lane, off Cheapside, to cramped conditions like the river banks. Pageant writers and artificers took advantage of the space available to them just as dramatists did on the professional stage (in many cases, of course, they were the same people). In *The triumphs of truth*, for instance, Middleton uses the relatively capacious South yard of St Paul's as the setting for a battle between Error (in a chariot) and Envy (on a rhinoceros) with Truth in her chariot, accompanied by Zeal, whereas at the crowded riverside at Barnard's Castle only two figures appear, both on horseback rather than on an unwieldy pageant wagon or chariot.

'To dazle and amaze the common Eye': eyewitnesses of the Shows

The Lord Mayor's Show was a renowned spectacle that drew a vast audience from home and abroad. As Dekker puts it in *Brittannia's honor*, 'What Deputie to his Soraigne [*sic*] goes along to such Triumphes? To behold them, Kings, Queenes, Princes and Embassadors (from all parts of the World) haue with Admiration, reioyced' (sig. A3v). As Dekker suggests, visitors to London often included the Show in their itinerary, and as a result there are a number of recorded experiences from across virtually our whole period. Indeed, to make the written texts come alive, those eyewitness accounts of the Shows that have survived are essential evidence for the impressions of contemporary spectators, together with the few extant drawings and other illustrations of the Shows. These are more important than the limited attention they have received implies, for there are more eyewitness descriptions of watching a mayoral Show than there are of watching a stage-play, and, as I will demonstrate, they can be very enlightening.

Chief among these are the sketches that accompany the written descriptions of the 1629 Show made in his journal by Abram Booth, secretary to the delegation of the Dutch East India Company, of which James Campbell, the new Lord Mayor, was also a member.[6] Booth's account is particularly valuable because it gives visual as well as prose evidence. The images in his 'Journael' have been sketched out in pencil then over-drawn in ink, suggesting that Booth took the original impression from life; the 'Journael' itself is small enough to have been carried around and used as a notebook. Indeed, such is the detail contained in Booth's journal that it is somewhat puzzling that he mentions no speeches, music or songs. Fifteen years previously another visitor, Michael van Meer, included in his 'Album Amicorum' some exquisite miniature images depicting a procession of the Lord Mayor, aldermen and sheriffs coming out of church on a 'Veestdagen [feast day]' in 1614: going by the participants in the procession and their ceremonial attire this was *probably* the mayoral inauguration.[7] Georg von Holtzschuler recorded part of the 1624 procession in his album.[8] (Relatedly, a contemporary witness of James I's London royal entry preserved on a copy of Dekker's text for this occasion his or her impression of the day in a sketch that may show aspects of the staging of the Londinium arch, along with some of the captions used on the arches.)[9] As well as eyewitness illustrations, in 1635 a series of engraved images representing the conventional 'Ages of Man' transition were published, accompanied by mildly satirical verses. The images standing in for the four ages (Childhood, Youth, Manhood and Old Age) appear to have been based on some of the traditional participants in the Shows like the whiffler, although, as Astington points out, one should treat these with a degree of caution, as the satiric purpose may have dominated over the desire to reproduce elements of the Shows accurately.[10]

A number of the spectators who have left records of their experiences of mayoral Shows were overseas emissaries, like Booth, Orazio Busino (the Venetian ambassador's chaplain, who attended the 1617 Show), Abraham Scultetus (the German court chaplain, who was present at the 1612 Show), and Aleksei Zuizin (the Russian ambassador, who saw the 1613 Show). Lupold von Wedel, who was in London for the 1585 Show, was simply a curious traveller.[11] They were not always voluntary spectators: Zuizin's report relates that the Russian party were given no choice in the matter, being ordered to attend the Show by King James despite their repeated protestations that protocol demanded they meet the King first.[12] Regardless of the particular circumstances, however, all these witnesses can offer an insight into what Munro has usefully called 'the framing action of the onlookers'.[13] What they share is their 'foreignness'. Indeed, Steward and Cowan argue that 'much of the evidence relating to early modern cities has come from outsiders, sensitive to material and cultural differences and eager to make comparisons . . . Travellers commented above all on what was to be seen.'[14] Given the relative frequency of such observers it is curious, as Ravelhofer argues in relation to the masque, that 'few critics have put themselves into the place of [an overseas visitor], trying to imagine the masque stage from the point of view of a puzzled observer'.[15] Middleton offers a typically caustic take on this subject, arguing in *The triumphs of loue and antiquity* that

> if Forreine Nations haue beene struck with admiration at the Forme, State and Splendour of some yearly Triumphs, wherein Art hath bene but weakly imitated, and most beggarly worded, there is faire hope that things where Inuention flourishes, Cleare Art and her gracefull proprieties, should receiue fauour and encouragement from the content of the Spectator. (sig. A4r)

In his idiosyncratic way, Middleton here implies both that the other pageant writers' productions are artistically inadequate (as he did in *The triumphs of truth*) and also that 'Forreine Nations' are ignorant enough to be impressed with such poor fare. To reinforce the point he repeated the statement a few years later, in *The tryumphs of honor and industry*.

Of course, not all observers *were* from overseas. Other eyewitnesses were indigenous inhabitants of the city, although these inhabitants could not be relied upon to preserve their impressions. As Astington writes, 'there is relatively little native English information about these remarkable annual events'.[16] Paul Seaver comments of Nehemiah Wallington, a godly citizen of early modern London, that he 'must have witnessed some of these events . . . but he has left no record of any such occasion or of his feelings about such displays'.[17] John Greene of Lincoln's Inn (whose birthday it was on 28 October) either did not attend or chose not to write about the 1635 Show in his diary.[18] A Londoner who did write about the Show was William Smith, a Haberdasher who included in his 'A Breeff Description of the Famous Cittie of London' an account of the 1575 inauguration of Ambrose Nicholas, a Merchant Taylor.[19]

Previous to that, we have Henry Machyn's 'diary', with its descriptions of some of the Shows in the 1550s and early 1560s. Indeed, Machyn (of whom more below) is our only source of eyewitness information about the pageantry employed in this early period.[20] Machyn's manuscript, Ian Mortimer has stressed, has value not only for its descriptions of a period of civic pageantry about which relatively little is known but also, as Mortimer asserts, for its status as 'probably the earliest instance in England of a poorly educated man consciously taking responsibility for systematically recording the history of his own times'. His work, Mortimer writes, testifies to 'the beginnings of the written expression of identity by the emerging urban middle class'.[21] Furthermore, Mortimer argues that it is possible that 'Machyn wrote with an awareness of a wider [later] historical readership' for a text which he himself called a 'chronicle'.[22] Machyn's vantage point, then, can provide a useful contrast to that of overseas visitors and dignitaries.

Their differences notwithstanding, what can be gained from all these diverse eyewitness records – and from nowhere else – is a taste of the incidental, impromptu aspects of the Shows, those which pertain exclusively to the day itself and which are by definition very ephemeral.[23] As Lusardi and Gras point out in connection to Abram Booth's eyewitness account, 'things don't always go according to script [and] . . . Booth introduces authentic detail that was certainly not scripted'.[24] Their comments are borne out by a moment recounted by Busino in 1617. One of Middleton's pageants featured a man playing a Spaniard, who according to Busino 'kept kissing his hands, right and left, but especially to the Spanish ambassador, who was a short distance from us, in such wise as to elicit roars of laughter from the multitude'.[25] Although one has to factor in Busino's eye to his home readership in terms of the way he chose to inflect his experiences (the same applies to Zuizin, who stressed the subordination of the City and its Show to the Crown), it remains the case that neither this actor's stage business nor the reaction of the audience would have survived the transitory moment had Busino not included them in his report. Middleton's text is not concerned with preserving such detail, which would doubtless have been improvised. Indeed, if his text had been printed before the Show, he would not have known about it. *The tryumphs of honor and industry* simply provides the Spaniard's speech, in both Spanish and English. Conversely, possibly because of language difficulties, like both Booth and Zuizin, Busino does not mention the speeches to which the printed text devotes so much space.

6 Abram Booth's drawing of the 1629 Show: Lemnion's forge and 'London's Tempe' pageants

Booth's descriptions, written and pictorial, of Dekker and Christmas's pageants for *Londons tempe* (1629) bear some interesting discrepancies from the printed text. Whereas Dekker states that the 'Londons tempe' pageant comprised 'an arbor, supported by 4 Great Termes: On the 4 Angles, or corners ouer the Termes, are placed 4 pendants with armes in them' (sig. B4v), Booth records the pageant in the following manner: it contained, he writes, 'a tree in the four seasons, crowned by Angels, richly decorated'.[26] His accompanying drawing also shows the pageant without any supported and decorated arbour, as in Dekker's text but rather topped by flying angels bearing a crown (see Figure 6). Booth also appears to have followed the text rather than the evidence of his eyes when he states that 'on top of all [stood] a lion's head, belonging to the Mayor's coat of arms': the drawing actually omits the lion's head.[27] Perhaps, if he was relying on the text to prompt his memory, Booth misread 'Angles' for 'angels' and hence invented the latter, which do not feature in the printed work. Dekker's version is certainly more

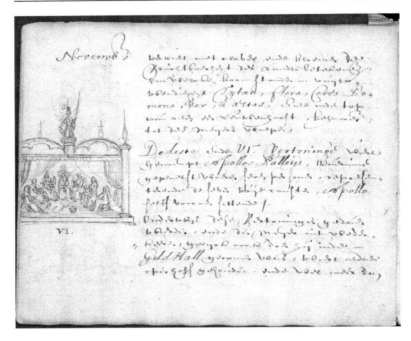

7 Abram Booth's drawing of the 1629 Show: Apollo's palace pageant

practical: as Robertson remarks, Booth's 'angels' have 'little visible
means of support'.[28] However, Booth's drawing of the 'Apollo's
Palace' pageant correctly shows seven figures (see Figure 7). There
are other minor differences. The Indian boy on the ostrich is said
by Dekker to be wearing 'attire proper to the Country', whereas
in Booth's drawing the boy does not appear to be wearing anything (unlike the turbaned and robed figures he is accompanied
by) (see Figure 8). Moreover, *Londons tempe* states that there are
four figures alongside the platform on which the boy and ostrich
are placed, 'a Turke and a Persian' – as Booth shows – and also 'a
pikeman & a Musketeere', which do not appear in the drawing. The
'12 siluer Columnes [and] foure golden Columnes' cited by Dekker
as part of the structure called 'Apollo's Palace' are not drawn by
Booth, who has substituted a more prosaic-looking stage with four
columns, perhaps because it was easier to draw – or because the
sixteen gold and silver columns did not materialise (see Figure 7).
Neither does he depict the 'Embosd antique head of an Emperour'
Dekker claims to have appeared at the top of this pageant. Lusardi

8 Abram Booth's drawing of the 1629 Show:
Indian boy and ostrich device

and Gras comment, 'did Dekker's ambition outstrip his resources
. . . or is Booth being careless?'[29] It is not necessarily the case that
Booth simply could not see the precise design of the pageants and
thus made mistakes. There is so much other 'authenticating detail',
as Lusardi and Gras put it, in the drawings, such as the helmeted
statue with shield and lance at the top of Apollo's Palace, and the
globe and compass lying at the feet of those impersonating the seven
liberal sciences, none of which is mentioned in *Londons tempe*, that
the likeliest interpretation is that what Booth did depict what he
could see to the best of his ability. His journal thus may reveal to
us the eventual results of necessary compromises in the realisation
of the Show that Dekker's text does not disclose, or could not have
disclosed. For the 1629 Show we are therefore privileged to have
access to a threefold insight into the events, all aspects of which
reveal the crucial role of contingency in the making of the Shows,
and which taken together offer a full and lively account of the event:
Booth's eyewitness descriptions and sketches, the printed text itself

and (as we'll see further below), remarkably revealing Ironmongers' records.

There may well be actual connections between some of these facets of this Show, for elsewhere in his journal Booth's account of the pageants is so close to Dekker's descriptions that it is possible that he had a copy of Dekker's text to hand. As a member of an important party guesting at the Show and banquet he was likely to have had access to a copy of the text, assuming, as seems plausible, that the work was available on the day and distributed to visiting dignitaries. The fact that he provides the names of the individual pageants, such as 'the Lemnian Forge' as well as the names of the actual figures contained in them, underlines this possibility, since these are unlikely to have been available to onlookers without the text unless placards were used to set the scene, of which there is no evidence in the printed text – Dekker being Dekker he would undoubtedly have mentioned them.[30] Booth also follows the wording of the printed text quite closely when describing the second water pageant showing the sealion representing Campbell's various trading roles. *Londons tempe* states that 'his Lordship is Maior of the Staple, Gouernour of the French Company, and free of the East-land Company' (sig. B1v); Booth writes that Campbell is 'mayor or dean of the staple of Cloth, Governor of the french and Freeman of the Eastland Company'.[31]

Zuizin, for his part, and apparently without the assistance of an explanatory pamphlet, was clearly trying to make sense of a spectacle that was foreign to him in more than one way. Of the pageantry performed during the 1613 Show he writes somewhat vaguely that there were men 'who carried on themselves wooden [models of] towns, worked and painted'. His account continues:

> And in the [model] towns were churches and on the towers and along the wall were constructed guns, and on the steeples of the churches and on the city ladder sat old and young people and boys and girls in bright dresses. And on them were masks like human faces and like all sorts of animals.

Unless these are pageant devices not mentioned by Middleton's text, it seems that Zuizin is relating the alien devices he saw to things he was familiar with, such as towns, churches and towers (Busino too likens the spectacle to those he knew back in Venice).[32] After all, one can hardly expect Zuizin to have recognised Middleton's 'Chariot of Error', for instance. Given that his account starts with the departure of the mayoral party up-river to Westminster it's doubtful that he would have witnessed the speech by 'London' at the very beginning of the day, which appears to be the only part of the pageantry on this occasion where 'a modell of Steeples and Turrets' is used, and even then to quite different effect. His description of the physical layout of the pageant cars, however, is more reminiscent of others', and also of those given in the printed texts: 'on all sides, above, and below, sat small girls and boys and here they carried a variety of great beasts: elephants, and unicorns, and lions and camels, and boars, and other animals'.[33] Where Middleton describes 'a little Vessel' bearing the King and Queen of the Moors and their attendants (*The triumphs of truth*, sig. B4v), Zuizin recalls something similar, 'a small decorated ship'.

As we can see, the printed text and eyewitness accounts both gain in credibility when they offer consistent descriptions of the Show. The account of Abraham Scultetus, as Hans Werner states, 'follows Dekker's [1612] text exactly, even down to the "Speech of Fame"'.[34] As well as duplicating it, personal recollections could also supplement the printed text where the latter gave relatively little information about the visual look of the Show. Von Wedel recounts that in the 1585 Show 'some men [carried] a representation in the shape of a house with a pointed roof painted in blue and golden colours and ornamented with garlands, on which sat some young girls in fine apparel'.[35] Von Wedel's likening of the pageant to a 'house' suggests that the structure he saw had similarities to the sixteenth-century pageant wagons described in David Rogers's *Breviary*, which states that 'these pagiantes or cariage was [*sic*] a highe place made like a howse with 2 roomes beinge open on the tope'.[36] As we will see below, mayoral pageant cars did use multiple tiers. Furthermore, Peele's very short printed text supplies only the speeches made by these girls, who are there called 'nymphs'. Unlike von Wedel's description, Peele's text tells us nothing about the way in which the pageant was shaped and coloured, the look of which would have been quite lost had the German traveller not chosen to recount it. Eyewitness accounts also offer insights into the way the Show was realised, the order of the procession and so on, relatively prosaic but still important matters which the printed texts did not usually focus on.[37] Zuizin, for instance, stresses a number of times that the new Lord Mayor was accompanied by his immediate predecessor, John Swinnerton. Swinnerton's Show itself was witnessed by the Elector Palatine and his entourage, who were in town for the latter's marriage to Princess Elizabeth. We have Scultetus to thank

for the detail that the Archbishop of Canterbury accompanied the
Elector Palatine in a coach following the aldermen in the procession.[38] The Goldsmiths' Company had an expectation that Queen
Anna was 'certainly' to attend the 1611 Show, although on this
occasion there is no specific reference to the royal viewer in the text
beyond Leofstane's fleeting reference to 'Guests of great State and
Honour' (*Chruso-thriambos*, sig. C1r) and, probably, Munday's
somewhat forced comparison between the new Lord Mayor's
name, James Pemberton, and that of the King.[39]

Those instances where eyewitnesses did write down their perceptions emphasise that when exploring civic triumphs it is wise to
keep, in Mulryne's cogent formulation, 'an alert sense of fact as well
as intent'.[40] Indeed, putting such eyewitness descriptions alongside
the sometimes extremely detailed livery company records shows
the printed texts, on the whole, and perhaps contrary to expectations, to be a rather formal and static account of the proceedings.
As Watanabe-O'Kelly argues, the printed texts 'present the festival
already pre-packaged, already interpreted. The iconography is
spelled out for us, the political pretensions of the ruler are under-
lined'.[41] Munro writes that although the printed book may represent
'a textual progress of quiet contemplation . . . the performed scene
of the shows remains inherently mixed and contradictory'.[42] For
one thing, as Paster comments, 'for the civic entertainments there
were audiences within audiences', requiring a 'sophisticated awareness' on the part of these audiences. In the Shows a larger group
of spectators were watching a smaller one, the Lord Mayor and
his entourage, being addressed by the performers. Even that larger
audience was implicitly playing a role as part of the 'symbolic social
entity', in Paster's phrase, repeatedly conjured up by the Shows.[43]
One should not assume, however, that the desired effect on the
audience ensued, and due attention should be paid to what Mulryne
calls 'immediate events, human motivation and accident'.[44]

On the basis that they are likely to be at least generally accurate,
the printed texts of the Shows themselves, naturally, do provide
valuable information in terms of their description of what took
place on the day, although there are provisos here, which I will
discuss more fully in the next chapter. Suffice it to say at this stage,
as Mulryne argues, that

> however sumptuous and perfect the official records make festival
> appear, the reality . . . may be very different. Inclement weather,
> lack of preparation and sheer incompetence could turn formality
> into chaos . . . [and] adverse circumstances could serve as ironic

counterpoint to the claims of competence and authority embedded in performance.[45]

Examples of all three of these contingencies have survived and will be discussed in due course. Nevertheless, we can look to Dekker's account of James's royal entry for at least a sense of the lived experience. Here Dekker is describing – or at least representing – an entertainment which bore many resemblances to the Shows and shared their impact on the city's population. He conjures up a rich image:

> the Streetes seemde to bee paude with men; Stalles insteed of rich wares were set out with children, open Casements fild up with women. All Glasse-windowes taken downe, but in their places, sparkeled so many eies, that had it not bene the daye, the light which reflected from them, was sufficient to haue made one. (*The magnificent entertainment*, sigs B3v–B4r)

In *Troia-Noua triumphans* Dekker numbers the witnesses of the Show as 'at least twenty thousand', which may be realistic (sig. A4r). Heywood also has the figure of London refer to 'all places . . . with people covered, as If, Tyl'd with faces' (*Londons ius honorarium*, sig. A4r). John Taylor even more hyperbolically claimed that there were 'innumerable' spectators of Charles I's procession into London in 1641: 'the bankes hedges, highwayes, streets, stalls, and windowes were all embroydered with millions of people, of all sorts and fashions', he writes (*Englands comfort, and Londons ioy*, sig. A2r). Exaggerations notwithstanding, various eyewitnesses echo the stress we find in all of these texts on the number and diversity of spectators. Heinemann writes that Show was 'essentially . . . a popular holiday', designed 'to impress and entertain not only the Lord Mayor and his eminent guests . . . but also the crowds out for the day'.[46] Contemporary witnesses bear her out. Zuizin, the Russian ambassador, reported that 'many people, men, women and children – the whole City – watched this ceremony'.[47] For Busino, as for Dekker, the sight of the citizens of London celebrating formed part of the entertainment. Conversely, Busino's testimony indicates that watching noble audience members' reactions to the Show could sometimes provide the ordinary Londoners with entertainment.

Busino watched the 1617 procession from the vantage point of a house on Goldsmiths' Row, Cheapside.[48] His colourful account is worth quoting at length. Like Dekker, he recounts how the windows

> were all crowded with the sweetest faces, looking like so many pretty pictures . . . On looking into the street we saw a surging mass of

people, moving in search of some resting place which a fresh mass
of sightseers grouped higgledy piggledy rendered impossible. It was a
fine medley: there were old men in their dotage, insolent youths and
boys, especially . . . apprentices . . . painted wenches and women of
the lower classes carrying their children, all anxious to see the show.[49]

In the 1580s Lupold von Wedel too was obviously struck by the
large number of onlookers, and especially the presence of women,
which was clearly not the convention on the continent. Indeed, he
is relatively indifferent to the pageantry itself, being more preoccupied with the procession and general order of events; in particular,
perhaps because of linguistic difficulties, he entirely disregards the
speeches, which, in contrast, form the totality of Peele's printed
text.[50] With the exaggeration we have seen in other accounts of the
Shows, von Wedel writes that 'the whole population' followed the
mayoral procession, 'men as well as women, for the English women
want to be present on all such occasions'. 'Fine-looking women'
were spotted among the multitude, which for von Wedel 'was
wonderful to be seen'. Von Wedel also describes the way in which
the crowd was controlled, which was never likely to have been a
concern of Peele's text (although one can imagine Dekker being
unable to resist mentioning it): 'there are some fire-engines ornamented with garlands, out of which they throw water on the crowd,
forcing it to give way, for the streets are quite filled with people'.[51]
    Eyewitness accounts convey the visual and auditory impact of
the day very well. After the 1553 Show Machyn recounted a dizzy-
ing combination of music (the City Waits were generally employed
and the instruments included trumpets, flutes and drums), cannons,
coloured banners, traditional mumming-style figures such as the
devil and fireworks.[52] *The excellent and renowned history of the
famous Sir Richard Whittington* has a woodcut image of one of
Whittington's inaugural processions that clearly shows onlookers wielding fireworks (see Figure 9). As one can imagine, noise
featured strongly in the experience of the event.[53] Accordingly,
Machyn's impressions were primarily of colour and noise:

then cam [one] [with a] drume and a flutt playng, and a-nodur with a
gret f[ife?] . . . and then cam xvj trumpeters blohyng, and then cam in
[blue] gownes, and capes and hosse and blue sylke slevys, and evere
man havyng a target and a gayffelyn [javelin] to the nombur of lxx
. . . and then cam a duyllyll [devil] and after cam the bachelars all in
a leveray, and skar lett hods; and then cam the pagant of sant John
Baptyst gorgyusly, with goodly speches; and then cam all the kynges

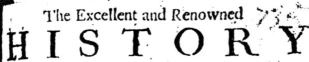

9 Woodcut of Dick Whittington's mayoral procession showing onlookers
with fireworks, from *The excellent and renowned history of the famous
Sir Richard Whittington* (sig. A1r)

> trumpeters blowhyng, and evere trumpeter havyng skarlet capes,
> and the wetes capes and godly banars, and then the craftes, and then
> the wettes playhyng, ... and after dener to Powlles . . . with all the
> trumpets and wettes blowhyng thrugh Powlles, thrugh rondabowt
> the qwer and the body of the chyrche blowhyng.[54]

Machyn is at pains to record decorated streamers, banners and
the like, probably because his work as an undertaker involved the
supply of similar accoutrements for funerals. As Machyn witnessed
Shows with only limited pageantry – he does mention the pageant
of John the Baptist on more than one occasion, but only in passing
– his account focuses primarily on the procession of Company
members and various entertainers. Indeed, the very syntax of his
recollections mimics the actual procession, repeating the phrase
'and then cam . . . and then cam' throughout. Machyn's impressions
of the day bear out Randall's argument that mayoral Shows had a
'mingled nature of tableau and processional': as we have seen, contemporary witnesses are useful sources of information about how
both aspects were experienced.[55]

The printed texts of Lord Mayors' Shows do little to convey
the audience's reaction to the Show as such, so here eyewitness
accounts are especially valuable.[56] At the same time, here and there
the printed texts do self-consciously foreground the large number
of spectators regularly attracted by the Show. This occurs especially
when the Shows' speeches focus on how 'the outside world' might
perceive the city and its celebrations. Dekker's repeated recourse to
metatheatricality provides some interesting instances of this trope.
In *Troia-Noua triumphans* the figure of Neptune draws the attention *of* the watching crowd *to* the watching crowd by a series of
rhetorical questions:

> . . . what does beget
> These Thronges? this Confluence? Why do voyces beate
> The Ayre with acclamations of applause,
> Good wishes, Loue, and Praises? What is't drawes
> All Faces this way?
>
> (sig. B1r)

Heywood adapts this tactic when in *Londons ius honorarium* he
has the figure of London herself ventriloquise the amazed reaction of her 'sister Cittyes' ('Westminster, Yorke, Bristoll, Oxford,
Lincolne, Exeter, &c'):

> Is it to see my numerous Children round
> Incompasse me? So that no place is found.

In all my large streets empty? My issue spred
In number more then stones whereon they tread.

(sig. B4r)

Similarly, in *The triumphs of truth* Middleton has the King of the
Moors express surprise at being the object of amazed scrutiny by
'so many Christian Eyes' (sig. B4v). This is often a crafty way of
highlighting the delights of the Show, of course, and Munday's
treatment of the theme in *Himatia-Poleos* accordingly has a self-
conscious air. The Shepherd also begins his speech with questions:

> Why gaze yee so vpon me? Am I not a man, flesh, bloud, and bone, as
> you are? Or in these silken sattin Townes, are poore plaine meaning
> Sheepheards woondred at, like Comets or blazing Starres? Or is it
> this goodly beast by me, that fills your eyes with admiration? (sig
> B3v–B4r)

Here the usual dichotomy of urban sophistication versus untu-
tored rustic credulity is turned on its head. For Munday's
Shepherd, it is in 'silken sattin Townes' that 'Comets and blazing
Starres' are 'woondred at', rather than the rural setting in which
one might find a 'poore plaine meaning Sheepheard', who in this
instance has a better understanding of the spectacle than the
urban audience are alleged to. (The 'goodly beast' which they
are supposed to so admire, by the way, is a sheep: the beast with
which, according to Heywood's *Porta pietatis*, no other animal
can compare).

As we can see, at times the onlookers themselves are described,
and not only the mayoral party and other dignitaries. Dekker's
words in *Brittannia's honor* echo those of Busino and other
writers I have quoted (including Dekker's own earlier text of *The
magnificent entertainment*) on the subject of the audience. One of
the pageant cars in *Brittannia's honor* bears a Russian prince and
princess, of whom Dekker writes:

> How amazde they look, to see streetes throng'd, and windowes glaz'd
> With beauties, from whose eyes such beames are sent,
> Here moues a second starry Firmament.
> Much, on them, startling admiration winnes,
> To see these Braue, Graue, Noble Citizens
> So stream'd in multitudes, yet flowing in State,
> For all their Orders are Proportionate.

(sig. B3v)

The experience of such a throng was clearly so memorable and had
become such a byword that it turns up in other contemporary works.

William Fennor's *Cornu-copiae* says of the crowd, 'What multitudes of people thither sway, / Thrusting so hard, that many haue miscaried . . . / How mighty and tumultuous is that presse' (sig. H1r). Similarly, it is exclaimed in the epilogue of *Eastward hoe*: 'See, if the streets and Fronts of the Houses, be not stucke with People, and the Windows fild with Ladies, as on the solemne day of the Pageant!'[57] Many of the contemporary sources agree that women tended to watch the Show from buildings rather than the streets; such a good vantage point would have been in great demand, despite the fact that it would doubtless have made the speeches almost impossible to hear. Many spectators would also have thronged the river banks to watch the lavishly decorated barges and galley foist, and the river itself would have been full of smaller vessels bearing sightseers.[58] One can understand why the Companies needed large numbers of 'whifflers' to control such crowds, despite Dekker's claim that the 'multitudes' were kept orderly and 'proportionate'.[59]

'With much care, cost and curiosity are they brought forth': the realisation of the Shows

This takes us on to the practical aspects of the staging of Lord Mayor's Day. The carefully planned arrangements began early in the day. The Haberdashers' accounts from 1632, for instance, detail the way in which the Company members were ordered to assemble at 6am at the Company Hall, in the traditional reverse order of seniority (the youngest and least important went first), in order to accompany the Lord Mayor to the Three Cranes landing stage where the party embarked on boats to go up river to Westminster. The thirty trumpeters were specifically instructed to be silent until the Lord Mayor emerged from his house, at which point they were to sound. The Company members then formed lines through which the Lord Mayor and his retinue passed.[60]

Once the mayoral party had arrived at Westminster for the oath-taking, one of the chief ritual cruxes of the day, further formalities ensued. The new Lord Mayor, accompanied by the outgoing incumbent, took his oath of office at the Exchequer before dignitaries of the Crown and of the City. The latter body was represented, as well as by the two Lord Mayors, by the Recorder of London, who made a speech tailored to the occasion in which the rights and responsibilities of the City and its officers were laid out (this is an inversion of the traditional practice for royal entries into the City, where the Recorder would address the visitors on behalf of the City). The

Lord Chief Baron and the Lord Treasurer then responded in a like manner with speeches. These rituals are fairly well documented, and the rhetoric employed on these occasions bears scrutiny, for it reveals much about the relative positions of power between the City and the Crown, and it can, if read carefully, expose some of the latent tensions in their relationship.

Recorder Thomas Fleming's speech for the oath-taking ceremony in 1594 is typical in many respects. As was conventional (although, as we will see, the reality was increasingly a point of contention into the Stuart period), the Recorder's speech began with a summary of the 'many excellent and princely grants, liberties, and priviledges' which pertain to 'we the Cittizens of London, seperatlie by ourselves'.[61] (As with the other Recorders, Fleming's use of personal pronouns indicates his position of spokesman for the City.) The right of the citizens to *elect* their chief magistrate rather than having one 'emposed' on them was very emphatically cited in all the Recorders' speeches (and as we will see, in the rhetoric of the Shows themselves) as a particularly significant privilege which marked out the City's degree of governmental autonomy from the Crown. Indeed, the oath-taking ceremony itself embodies the delicate balance implicit on the occasion between civic independence on the one hand and the simultaneous need to have their choice of Lord Mayor sanctioned by the monarch on the other. To emphasise the former point, an account was given later in this Recorder's speech of how John Spencer's election took place. The remainder of Fleming's speech comprised a delineation of the virtues and characteristics required of the Lord Mayor, such as 'integrity, prudence, moderation, and innocency'.[62] Recorder Heneage Finch also devoted considerable space in his mayoral oath-taking speeches in the 1620s to highlighting the City's rights and privileges. In 1621, for instance, he began his speech at the Exchequer by stating that to 'number the priviledges and prerogatives which the grace and goodnesse of so many kings and princes for so many ages past . . . hath conferred upon this noble and famous Citty of London' would 'consume the day'. From the City's perspective, one should note, nameless 'kings and princes' may come and go, but the City's rights persist. Using what seems to have been the traditional phraseology, Finch stated that the City not only was 'trusted' to choose its own governor but was 'allowed and appointed' so to do.[63]

I shall move on now to 1602, a year for which the exchanges on both sides have been preserved in John Manningham's diary. Here too there is evidence of how the respective roles were negotiated.

Manningham begins by describing the way in which the Recorder, John Croke, stood formally 'at the barr betweene the twoe Maiors, the succeeding on his right hand, and the resigning on his left'.[64] The relative positions of the protagonists clearly had ritual significance, with the new Lord Mayor as the Recorder's 'right-hand man'. Croke's speech appears to have taken a fairly predictable line, expressing sentiments that one finds repeated in the pageantry that ensued on all these occasions, such as the need for good governance during the mayoral term, 'in regard', as Manningham has him put it, 'of the prayse or shame that attends such men for their tyme well or ill imployed'. This emphasis on the longer-term reputation of the Lord Mayor once his time of office has expired, along with exhortations about standards of governance one finds displayed consistently and at greater length (as we'll see further below) in the speeches written for the pageants. 'Then', Manningham recalls, Croke 'remembered manie hir Majesties fauours to the Citie, their greate and beneficiall priviledges, their ornaments and ensignes of autoritie, [and] their choise out of their owne Companies'. Here, as with Recorder Fleming, we find the key aspects of the City's independence economically outlined and, implicitly, defended, albeit with a prefatory note acknowledging the Crown's 'manie fauours' and a statement of gratitude to the Queen for her 'great, and exceeding great . . . goodnes to this City'.[65] Again, there is a parallel here with the rhetoric of the pageant speeches, and, especially, with the ways in which the printed texts of the Shows so often begin with an account of the City's autonomy and privileges. Croke concluded his address by commending the performance of the outgoing Lord Mayor, John Garrard, and by presenting the new incumbent, Robert Lee, to the Court of the Exchequer.

For their part, the agents of the Crown – the Lord Chief Baron and the Treasurer, Thomas Sackville – responded with two speeches, the subtexts of which were rather more overt than those of the Recorder. The Lord Chief Baron began by stressing – as if such stress were needed – 'hir Majesties singular benefits' which should receive the City's 'thankefull consideracions'. His speech then moved directly on to a rather pointed 'admonishment' that the City establish 'monethly strict searche' for those bogeys of late Elizabethan policy, 'idle persons and maisterles men . . . the very scumme of England, and the sinke of iniquitie', of whom, he claimed, there were some thirty thousand currently in London, an exaggerated number for sure.[66] His colleague, the Treasurer, then 'spake sharpely and earnestly', as Manningham puts it, cutting

straight to the chase by announcing that 'of his certaine knowledge there were two thinges hir Majestie [was] desyrous should be
amended'. If Manningham's account is accurate, Sackville issued
no conciliatory preamble as did the Lord Chief Baron, but simply
made the stark statement that 'there hath bin warning given often
tymes, yet the commaundement [is] still neglected'. Sackville's
speech appears to have been designed to make it eminently clear to
the City's representatives that no excuses for further inaction would
be tolerated by the Crown. The new Lord Mayor is warned that
'while [the City's] fault sleepes in the bosome of hir Majesties clem-
ency' there is a limited opportunity – not to be repeated – 'to amend
their neglect'. The two areas to be addressed were the provision and
storage of corn (a major concern after the dearths of the 1590s) and
'the erecting and furnishing [of] hospitals'. The two areas which the
City is chastised for neglecting are, ironically, exactly the kind of
acts of municipal altruism so celebrated by the Shows themselves.
The Treasurer's speech concluded on an ambiguous note: much as
'he honour[s] the Cytie in his privat person', he cautioned that he
would not hesitate to 'call them to accompt' should they not comply
with instructions.[67] One is left with a sense of a headmasterly scold-
ing received in silence (there is no evidence in Manningham's diary
or any other source that either the old or the new Lord Mayor
actually spoke during the ceremony), accompanied by fairly explicit
threats of punitive action if the sovereign's demands were not met.
It must have been quite a relief for the mayoral party to retreat back
to their area of jurisdiction, where they would hear much more in
the way of unrestrained praise for the remainder of the day, and
where their power in their own domain could be celebrated.

Once safely back within the City, then, in ordinary circumstances
the pageantry proper commenced on the Lord Mayor's disembar-
kation from the trip up-river to Westminster. Unusually, the 1613
Show (a particularly lavish production) featured pageantry from the
outset of the day. In *The triumphs of truth*, having noted that the
procession began 'earlier then some of former yeares', Middleton
first describes at Soper Lane 'a Senate-house . . . vpon which
Musitians sit playing'. The Lord Mayor is there greeted with a song.
Upon his appearance from the Guildhall on the way to embark on
the barge for Westminster a trumpet sounds from a scaffold, and
a speech of greeting is heard, performed by a 'Graue Foeminine
Shape . . . representing London'. She is 'attired like a reuerend
Mother, a long white haire naturally flowing on either side of her:
on her head a modell of Steeples and Turrets'. Because she stands

for the City she wears a 'habite [of] Crimson silke' to be 'neere to
the Honourable garment of the Citty' and she holds 'a Key of gold'
(sigs A3v–A4r).

The celebrations extended right through the day to the evening.
After the banquet at Guildhall and the service at St Paul's, the procession escorted the new mayor back to his house, which was traditionally 'trimmed' and sometimes redecorated for his mayoralty.[68]
The other Companies which were not actually in the limelight that
year still regularly hosted dinners and banquets at their Halls on
the day of celebration.[69] The Fishmongers' Court Ledger records
the menu for their Lord Mayor's Day feast in 1595, which included
'Brawne and mustard, Rosted Beeof, Rosted [and boiled] Capon',
and a leg of mutton (they were also to have mutton for breakfast).[70]
One can see why Vanessa Harding notes that 'collective celebration,
including commemorative dinners, remained an important function
[of the Companies], and the social side of company membership
must have been one of its most valued aspects'.[71] The feast at the
Guildhall was another key concern of the Companies, who habitually spent large sums on the hire of plate for the banquet, as well
as on all the food and drink. The menus that survive show that
they did not stint themselves. Indeed, the Companies devoted considerable attention to the aftermath of the street pageantry. Their
records reveal that it was customary for the pageants to be set up
in the relevant Company Hall after the mayoral Shows.[72] In 1613
the Grocers took the opportunity to request 'pictures of famous
and worthy Magistrates and benefactors of this Companie to be
made and plated in most fitt and convenyent plates in this Hall (as
in the Haberdashers Hall)'.[73] Beautifying the Hall in this fashion
was another feature of the culmination of a day of celebration: the
Goldsmiths ordered ten gilded leopards' heads for the windows of
their Hall in 1611.[74] Borrowings included the hire of pewter utensils
from the Pewterers' Company for the Lord Mayor's feast, and, in
1610 and 1612, the hire of 'the kings picture, and a velvett chaire'
(for the Lord Mayor, one would guess).[75]

The main substance of the triumph itself, however, took place
on the Lord Mayor's return from Westminster; the journey down
to Three Cranes was usually more of a preamble to the main event.
During this focal part of the day the performers were usually, but
not always, children, and girls may have performed some female
roles, for many of the symbolic figures were gendered female. As
well as the ubiquitous classical goddesses such as Venus, other
candidates for female performers would include *The triumphs*

of truth's Envy, 'with her left pap bare' (sig. B2r), and possibly Munday's 'housewifely virgin' in *Metropolis coronata* (sig. B2v). Machyn states that 'chylderyn' appeared in the pageant for 1561; von Wedel's eyewitness account of Peele's 1585 Show refers to both boys and girls taking part, as does Zuizin's description of the 1613 Show.[76] The caption on one of the drawings related to *Chrysanaleia* includes the statement that 'five children' are to sit 'at the foote of the [lemon] tree representing the five senses'.[77] The use of children as actors is demonstrated by the note of a payment in 1604 to Thomas Kendall (himself a Haberdasher) for 'furnishing the children with apparrel and other thinges needfull for the shewe'.[78] Child actors were used so often because they were practically more useful: the pageant stations were sometimes tiered, child actors were obviously lighter than adult performers, and, as Harold Hillebrand comments, they also 'would be more in proportion to the scale of the construction'.[79] Indeed, one of the images from the Fishmongers' Show for 1616 – the pageant of Richard II and the Royal Virtues – shows smaller figures who were probably children (see Figure 10). The Ironmongers' minutes for 1609 reveal that the pageants on this occasion bore at least nine or ten costumed children each, and the main pageant in *Tes Irenes Trophaea* would have carried a minimum of twenty-one, if the text is accurate: St Katherine, twelve maids of honour, a shepherd and at least seven servants (sig. B3r).[80] 'Londons Genius' in *Chrysanaleia* is called a 'comely Youth' (sig. B3r), and the Grocers' Shows traditionally featured a boy, in Rees's words 'gorgeously attired in an Indian robe of divers colours', scattering spices, fruit and nuts to the onlookers.[81] On the occasion of their 1617 Show the Grocers bought 'Nutmegges, Gynger, almondes in the shell, and sugar loves [*sic*]' to be 'throwen abowt the streetes by those which sate on the Gryffyns and Camells'.[82] In his account of this Show, Busino accordingly recalls 'bales from which the lads took sundry confections, sugar, nutmegs, dates and ginger, throwing them among the populace'.[83] One of the 1616 illustrations shows the King of the Moors throwing what appear to be coins (see Figure 11). Munday suggests (as does the illustration of this pageant) that live fish were also 'bestowe[d] bountifully among the people' (*Chrysanaleia*, sig. B1v). (These 'gifts' to the onlookers represented another facet of the Company's munificence, of course.) One of the pageants in that Show also featured, according to Busino, 'children in Indian costume . . . [who] danced all the while with much grace and great variety of gesture'.[84] In this instance Middleton's text bears Busino out: 'these Indians

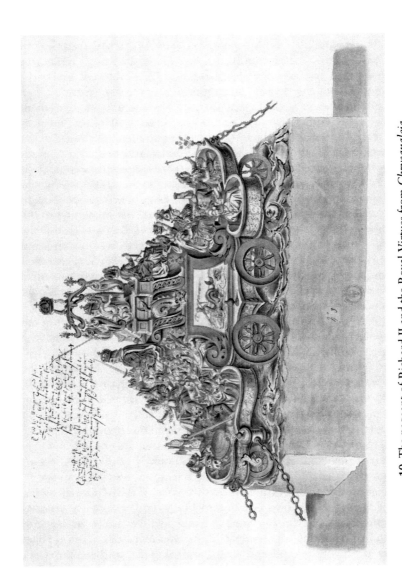

10 The pageant of Richard II and the Royal Virtues from *Chrysanaleia*

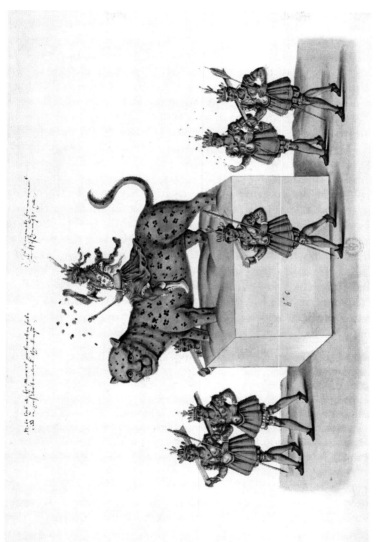

11 The pageant of the King of the Moors from *Chrysanaleia*

are al actiue youths, who ceasing in their labours, dance about the trees' (*The tryumphs of honor and industry*, sig. A4v). 'Indians' appear mostly in Shows written for the Grocers' Company, but not exclusively so: in his 1623 water show for the Drapers Munday stipulates that 'Sixe Tributarie Indian Kings . . . rowe the Argoe, all of them wearing their Tributarie Crownes, and Antickely attired in rich habiliments' (*The triumphs of the Golden Fleece*, sig. A4v).[85]

Despite the convenience of their size, there were also disadvantages in using child performers for, as Lublin comments, they may 'have been audible when performing at the indoor theatres in front of 500 or fewer people [b]ut surrounded by many thousands in the street . . . the children were unlikely to be heard even by the Lord Mayor himself'.[86] Although it seems likely that the preferred style for the pageant speeches, with a regular if plodding rhythm and rather simplistic rhyming couplets, was employed chiefly for clarity (for if the audience heard one line they were better placed to be able to at least guess at its rhyming accompaniment), the evidence shows that at times all tactics failed. In *Camp-bell* Munday – unsuccessfully, as it turned out – tried to circumvent this potential problem by having two adult actors ('men of action and audible voices', as he calls them) impersonating St Andrew and St George to make speeches 'to acquaint the Lord Maior, with the relation and meaning of both [the] devices'. With some exaggeration of the limitations within which he and his collaborators were operating, he explains the rationale for this overview as being twofold:

> the rather haue we yeelded to this kinde of deliuery, because the time for preparation hath beene so short, as neuer was the like vndertaken by any before, nor matter of such moment so expeditiously performed. Besides, the weake voyces of so many children, which such shewes as this doe vrgently require, for personating each deuice, in a crowde of such noyse and unciuill turmoyle, are not in any way able to be vnderstood, neither their capacities to reach the full height of euery intention, in so short a limitation for study, practice and instruction. (sigs B2v–B3r)

Munday's candour reveals some of the compromises inherent in street pageantry. Children are both 'urgently require[d]' *and* inaudible and under-rehearsed, although his disclaimers may have been retrospective, for this is the very year when the Company was displeased with the poor audibility and preparedness of the children. It is made clear by the use of adult performers to 'explain' the meanings of the pageants that for Munday the children are chiefly in place for visual purposes: hence the emphasis one finds in all of his productions on conventional emblems which one would hope would be readily interpreted by the onlookers. As with the use of animals and porters, as we will see, there were risks involved in the employment of child actors and singers. Munday was reprimanded by the Ironmongers for various 'defects' in relation to the 1609 Show, including that 'the children weare not instructed their speeches which was a spetiall iudgement of the consideration, [and] that the Musick and singinge weare wanting'.[87] As we have seen, in the printed text – true to form – he defends himself, blaming instead the unruly crowd and the lack of time for preparation for the children's shortcomings. Indeed, he steers very close to the wind by virtually blaming the Ironmongers for being too small and not wealthy enough a Company to produce a suitable spectacle. He articulates the problems in the final speech of the day, addressed directly to the Lord Mayor by St George: 'And let me tell you', St George exclaims, 'did [the Ironmongers'] numbers hold leuell with other Societies, or carry correspondencie in the best helping manner, their bountie should hardly haue gone behinde the best'. Although his intention may have been to praise the Company's efforts despite their shortcomings, and although he adds that the Company 'come now but little short of precedent examples', the effect is still that *they* (along with their under-rehearsed children) 'come short' – not Munday himself (sig. B4r).

Regardless of their evident disadvantages, the use of children as performers goes back to the early days of mayoral pageantry, when there were closer links with City schools, such as the Merchant Taylors', Christ's Hospital and St Paul's School, than became the usual mode once the poet and artificer pattern had become established. As we have already seen, William Haynes from the Merchant Taylors' School may have co-written part of the 1602 Show, and children from Westminster School took part in the 1561 and 1566 Shows, accompanied by their choirmaster, John Tailor.[88] Later into the Jacobean period children from choir schools were still being employed. In *Himatia-Poleos* Munday states that 'diuers sweet singing youths, belonging to the maister that enstructeth the yong Quiristers of Pauls' gave 'a most sweet dittie' as the barge carrying the figure of 'Sir John Norman' returned from Westminster (sig. B3r–v). One wonders if it was a young boy, an adult male actor or perhaps a female performer who was called on to act the part of the lascivious Medea in *Metropolis coronata*, who 'sitteth playing with [Jason's] loue-lockes, and wantoning with him in all pleasing daliance'; or indeed who played the 'diuers comely Eunuches' who rowed the Argoe (sig. A4r). Less frequently, performers from the children's acting companies were also called upon to participate in civic pageantry. *The magnificent entertainment* (in which there were only two speaking parts) featured 'one of the children of her Maiesties Reuels' in the role of 'Thamesis' and other choirboys sang to accompany the speeches.[89]

Occasionally adult actors participated in civic pageantry, such as Alleyn's role as the Genius of the City and William Bourne of King Henry's Men as Zeal in *The magnificent entertainment*, as well as Burbage's performance as Amphion in Munday's *Londons loue* alongside John Rice (who also had also given a speech written by Jonson before the King, Queen and Prince Henry at the Merchant Taylors' Hall in 1607).[90] As far as mayoral Shows are concerned, an adult actor of some experience is surely Munday's referent in *Metropolis coronata* when he writes that 'another man, of no meane sufficiency, both for knowledge and exquisite use of action' appeared in two devices and also delivered the speech of Time to the Lord Mayor (sig. B3v). Apart from the regularly cited example of John Lowin performing the part of Leofstane in *Chruso-thriambos* (1611), there are only sporadic explicit references in livery company records to professional players (whether members of livery companies or not – Lowin was a Goldsmith) taking part in mayoral Shows, although they probably did so more often than we imagine. References to 'players' occur occasionally. For example, in 1613 the Grocers reimbursed 'the players for boots, gloves and other thinges, and for the singing boye and also mr Godfrey whoe did sing at Sop[er] lane end'.[91] Thomas Rowley, the (probable) brother of the playwright William and better-known writer and actor Samuel, and a member of the Admiral's Men in 1602, performed as a giant in Munday's *Triumphs of re-united Britania*.[92] It is interesting to see on this occasion that the professional actor did not take on the role of one of the *pageant* actors giving speeches, as one might have expected, but rather was chosen to perform what would have undoubtedly been a non-speaking role. William Hall, another player (probably of the King's Revels Company at the time), was paid by the Drapers for 'his music and actions in Cheapside' in 1639.[93] Bentley concludes that 'it seems likely that the various sharers in the major [theatrical] companies made a little money on the side by helping in the pageantry for Lord Mayors' shows and other City occasions'.[94]

Peter Fryer speculates that, in addition to members of the various

theatre companies and city schools, some of those who played
roles may have been black performers. Middleton does refer in *The
triumphs of honor and vertue* to a 'blacke personage representing
India' (sig. B1v). Pictorial images of the pageantry offer more clues
still. Although the illustrations for *Chrysanaleia*, as Fryer concedes,
shows the King of the Moors as white, one of Booth's drawings of the
1629 Show does appear to depict a black boy playing (in Dekker's
words) 'the Indian boy, holding in one hand a long Tobacco pipe, in
the other a dart [whose] attire is proper to the Country' seated on an
ostrich (*Londons tempe*, sig. B2r).[95] The presence of a tobacco pipe
and dart signal that by 'Indian' the Americas are meant. In Booth's
drawing the figure is deliberately cross-hatched to show black skin,
unlike all the other figures in his illustrations (see Figure 8). As
we'll see below, the 1609 Show may have featured a 'Blackamore'.
However, the word 'negro', which does not feature in the Shows
in our period, *was* in use in the early seventeenth century, and the
fact that in the 1660s and later it was invariably used for black
performers in mayoral Shows does throw some doubt on the accuracy of this interpretation of Booth's drawing. The characters were
undoubtedly intended to represent 'Moors' or 'Indians'; the question is whether they were performed by white actors in black face, as
with Queen Anna and her ladies in Jonson's *Masque of Blackness*,
or actually embodied by black actors. Booth's drawing does suggest
that the black skin was not confined to the boy's face. The livery
company records for the year of *Londons tempe*, unfortunately, give
no corroborating evidence, and Busino, who saw similar 'Indian'
characters in 1617, merely says they were in 'Indian costume', but it
remains an intriguing possibility.

Being written in the main by dramatists, the printed texts naturally included stage directions and other pointers as to how the
action was realised. The livery company records make it clear that
the performers were rehearsed, probably under the supervision of
the writer himself in some cases. They were evidently called to *act* as
well as to represent symbolic figures in a purely static way, for not
all of the pageants were merely tableaux: some necessitated a fair
degree of movement, dialogue and so on. Even where there were no
speeches, the performers were often required to react to each other
and/or to various properties, or indeed to the audience themselves
(as we have seen, not always following a script), to emphasise the
meanings presented to the onlookers. Munday is especially keen to
include stage directions, and also regularly cites the use of musical
instruments to punctuate proceedings and add emphasis. The end

result is that it is relatively easy to envisage how his pageantry was played out. Thus in *Chrysanaleia* Walworth is raised from slumber by London's Genius, accompanied by 'Surden Trumpets': a marginal note in the text instructs that 'Here the Genius strikes on him with his wand, whereat he begins to stir, and comming off the Tombe, looks strangely about him'. The performer playing Walworth then stands before the tomb, 'doing reuerence to the Genius'. Whilst he speaks 'he doth reuerence to' the mayoral party (sigs B4v–C1r). To aid still more the audience's comprehension of the names of 'many famous Magistrates, / From the Fishmongers ancient name' cited in his speech, he points 'to the Scutchio[n]s of Armes as they hang in order on the Bower' (sig. C1v).

As well as the performers themselves, the pageant cars on which they were placed often moved around. However, there is a question as to how the individual pageants were staged, as well as whether the separate pageant stations around which each Show was created were fixed in certain places on the route or moved around the City, following the procession. Even the waterborne procession did not always start from and arrive at the same place, owing to the vagaries of the tidal Thames.[96] The general consensus is that the pageants were peripatetic, joining the procession at its end once their function as venues for tableaux and speeches was concluded. They also look to have been used on both land and water: Munday's 'Fishmongers' Esperanza', the fishing boat, moved on land from the river, and the five islands which the Lord Mayor first encountered in the river in the 1613 Show later reappeared at Paul's Churchyard. Furthermore, to raise 'greater astonishment', Middleton has a 'strange Ship' with 'neither Saylor nor Pilot' make towards these five islands (*The triumphs of truth*, sig. B4v). Busino confirms that the ships carried 'highly ornamented stages with several devices, which subsequently served for the land pageant, for triumphal cars, when passing through the principal street', suggesting that the pageant devices moved from river to street.[97] If Rogers's account of earlier sixteenth-century pageant wagons is accurate, the use of peripatetic devices went back some time: he records that 'when the[y] had donne with one cariage in one place theie wheled the same from one streete to another'.[98]

Dekker's *Troia-Noua triumphans* is especially up-front about the practicalities. Most of his individual pageants, it is clear, follow each other once their moment has passed. The first show on land, Neptune's chariot, not only provides a link with the water show in its use of sea-imagery and characters but is then superseded by 'the second Land-Triumph' waiting in Paul's Churchyard. 'The former Chariot of Neptune', Dekker informs his readership, 'with the Ship [from the water show], beeing conueyed into Cheap-side, this other takes the place' (sig. B2r). The same happens in turn to this second device, the 'Chariot or Throne of Virtue', which 'is then set forward, and followes that of Neptune, this taking place iust before the Lord Maior' (sig. B4r). With no apparent regard for the integrity of the theatrical impression (my view, as discussed below, is that the texts often used the original brief without much amendment), Dekker helpfully explains that later on in the procession the same device 'passeth along vntill it come to the Crosse in Cheape, where the presentation of another Triumph attends to welcome the Lord Maior in his passage, the Chariot of Virtue is drawne then along, this other that followes taking her place' (sig. C1r). Only the pageant of the Forlorn Castle stayed at its station, at the Little Conduit on Cheapside, to be used for 'further pageantry' when the Lord Mayor returned from the Guildhall to St Paul's for the religious service after the banquet (sig. B4v). 'All the former conceits', as Munday calls the devices in *Himatia-Poleos*, are 'gracefully borne before' the Lord Mayor as he proceeds to the cathedral (sig. C2r). It was conventional for the last pageant car to wait until after the sermon at Paul's and then escort the Lord Mayor to his house. The majority of the texts conclude with a speech 'at my Lords Gate' (in 1613, the Lord Mayor's house was 'neere Leadenhall', quite a distance from the processional route). In *Chruso-thriambos*, for instance, Munday has Faringdon explain that, 'as custome wils it so . . . Till you returne, heere will we stay, / And usher then a gladsome guiding, / Home to the place of your abiding' (sig. C2v).

Munday too states explicitly that in the 1616 Show Walworth's 'goodly Bower . . . is appointed *first* to stand in Paules Church-yard: And at such a place as is thought most conuenient' (*Chrysanaleia*, sig. B2v; my emphasis). This reveals a few things about the practicalities of that year's Show: first, that this particular pageant moved on from Paul's Churchyard, its original location, and, second, that discretion could be exercised as to its precise location there. In its contingency, Munday's text thereby gives the impression of being based, at least in part, on the provisional 'plot' offered to the Fishmongers that year. Later on, Munday explains, as if in the context of a pitch to the Company rather than as required by the printed text, that 'in the afternoone, when the Lord Mayor returneth to Paules, all the Deuices . . . [are] aptly placed in order neere to the little Conduit' (sig. C2v). Walworth's bower in *Chrysanaleia*, he explains, 'was appointed first to stand in Paules Church-yard'; the bower and tomb are then 'borne along before him' (sigs B2v–B3r). Always a bit of a grumbler, Munday seems especially aware of and especially willing to complain about the limitations of performances in his texts: he provides plenty of apologies and disclaimers along the lines of 'this is the best we could do in the circumstances'. In *Metropolis coronata*, clearly produced after the event, he sounds rather aggrieved at how things worked out. The preparations, he states, which 'require[d] much decencie in order: [were] yet much abused by neglect in marshalling, and hurried away with too impudent hastinesse'. It would appear that those responsible for clearing the way and for ensuring that the pageant cars appeared in good order had fallen short, for 'nothing but meere wilfulnesse', he complains, can have ruined plans which were 'so aduisedly set downe in proiect' (sig. B2r). More apologetically, he comments in *Chrysanaleia* that the depiction of Walworth's famous deed at Smithfield is done 'according to our compasse of performance', although he admits that 'it is all but a shaddow' of 'the magnificent forme [in] which it was [originally] done' (sig. B3v). A similar note is struck more briefly in *The triumphs of the Golden Fleece*, 'which might haue beene more, had time so fauoured' (sig. A2r).

There were also, at times, additional pageants (some of which were static) that did not participate in the Show's main narrative. These were often based on the traditional tropes, motifs and symbolic animals of the Company in question, such as the dolphin Munday and his artificer designed for *Chrysanaleia*, which, the text makes clear, started out as part of the entertainment on the river. Munday writes that 'the Fishing-Busse, Dolphine, Mer-man and Mer-mayd [appeared] vpon the water first, and [were] afterward marshalled in such forme as you haue heard on land' (sig. B4r). According to Wickham, in the medieval period (and for royal entries throughout the early modern period too) the use of architectural features of the City such as the city gates, standards and water conduits as 'stages' resulted in a series of static tableaux, where 'for a change of scene, the procession had to move along the street to the next major monument converted for the occasion into another stage'.[99] He points out that those onlookers located near one of the fixed pageant stations would not necessarily have been able to witness every one of the individual pageants.

The early modern Show was more mobile, though, and in broad terms the route of the procession followed much the same pattern across the period, beginning and ending at the Guildhall via St Paul's (see Figure 1). More often than not, as we've seen, the individual pageants and devices joined the procession once the speeches had been given. The words 'borne before' in the titles of two of Peele's printed Shows – *The deuice of the pageant borne before Woolstone Dixi* and the lost Show for 1588, probably called 'The device of the Pageant borne before the Righte Honorable Martyn Calthrop' – reveal that, even in the early days when there was only one such pageant, it too was peripatetic. From the evidence of Machyn's diary it seems that the mayoral party landed at Paul's Wharf or Barnard's Castle on their return from Westminster, and the sole pageant presented in that period appears to have been located in Paul's Churchyard. By 1660 Tatham referred a number of times to pageantry occurring at 'the accustomed place', and the procession, by his account, took 'the accustomed way' down to Three Cranes to embark on the barges (*The royal oake*, sig. B3r). He also provides a breakdown of the path taken by the procession, which few earlier pageant-writers did systematically. Pafford, however, does attempt to reconstruct the route of Munday's 1611 Show. The pageantry began at Barnard's Castle, where the Lord Mayor and his entourage disembarked from the trip up-river to Westminster. Pafford writes that

> the procession then went, perhaps by Upper Thames Street, Garlick Hill and Bow Lane, to Lawrence Lane, and gave the second and main pageant – the Orferie – probably where the Lane joins Gresham Street (then Catte Street) near the Guildhall, and finally, in the evening, held the last show outside Camden House which was in the western part of what is now Gresham Street, close to Goldsmiths' Hall.[100]

As Pafford's account shows, it is possible to recreate at least part of the route from Munday's text. *Chruso-thriambos* discloses that the characters who featured in the water show joined the land procession in a chariot. Later on, Time and Faringdon followed the mayoral entourage to Paul's, 'as custome wils it so', as Munday puts it. Accordingly, Leofstane's final speech, as was the convention, was given 'at my Lords Gate'. Middleton too embeds some of the City's main landmarks into the pageantry. In *The triumphs of truth* the figure of Time gestures towards Paul's Cross (the location is named in a marginal note for the reader's benefit), saying to the Lord Mayor, 'Seest thou yon place, thether Ile weekely bring thee, / Where Truths coelestiall Harmony Thou shalt heare'. Immediately afterwards, the procession moves along Cheapside where it halts beside the Little Conduit, used as a venue for the occasion for 'a Mount Triumphant', albeit one 'ouer-spred with a thicke Sulphurous Darknesse', the fog created by Error (sig. C2r).

As before, although he says little about the speeches, Busino provides vital evidence of how the pageants moved through the streets to supplement what the texts can tell us. His account clearly describes peripatetic pageants drawn by horses disguised in various ways. The first ones, he writes, were 'harnessed to griffins ridden by lads in silk liveries. Others followed drawn by lions and camels and other large animals . . . The animals which drew these cars were all yoked with silken cords.'[101] One of the pageants in the 1609 Show, 'the Chariot of the Bellfield', was according to the Ironmongers' Company to be drawn by 'two Estriches of silver'.[102] The performer playing Walworth in *Chrysanaleia*, according to the handwritten note on the image as well as the printed text, followed the procession on horseback. As we can see, here and there individual performers were seated on horseback, as also was the case with the figures of 'Truth's Angel' and 'Zeal' in *The triumphs of truth*. The pageants and shows were generally performed on wagons or cars, however, a feature of the Lord Mayor's Show that resembled the court masque as well as the Shows' medieval predecessors. Nancy Wright draws an analogy between the vehicle for the pageants and 'the stage car used in Jonson's *Masque of Queens*, [where] characters at the apex of the pageant car sat above actors personating "famous scholars and poets of this our kingdom"'.[103] The 'stage car' she describes does seem to have a considerable resemblance to those used for the Shows, especially if the illustration of the pageant chariot of Richard II and the Royal Virtues in *Chrysanaleia* is anything to go by. For Munday their ancestry could be traced even further back: the 'beautiful Chariot drawne by two golden pelleted Lyons and two Golden Wooolues' in *Metropolis coronata* is said to be designed 'after the manner of the triumphall Chariots of the Romaine Emperours' (sig. B1v). As far as the dimensions of the pageant cars are concerned, Morrissey concludes that 'eight feet by fourteen feet . . . was the average size for London pageant wagons'.[104] He points out that the height and breadth of any peripatetic pageant wagons were determined by the breadth of the streets and lanes through which they had to pass, although the livery company records do show that shop fronts and the like were sometimes taken down to allow the procession through.[105] One of the pageant writers bears him out: Heywood comments in *Londini speculum* that the skill of the artificers, Matthias and John Christmas, was such that 'in proportioning their Workes according to the limits of the gates through which they were to pass', the pageants did not 'exceede one Inch, either height or breadth' (sig. C4v).

This could have been a difficult task, for the textual (and, in the case of *Chrysanaleia*, visual) evidence makes it clear that many of the pageants had two or more tiers. The illustrations for the 1616 Show, for instance, reveal that the pageant of Richard II and the Royal Virtues bore at least seventeen figures distributed over at least three levels (see Figure 10).[106] In *The triumphs of re-united Britania* Munday states that the 'seuerall children' in the Britain pageant speak according to their 'degrees of seating', indicating the same kind of staggered arrangement (sig. B2v). Following the conventional height differential between figures of varying degrees of authority, in *The triumphs of truth* Middleton's 'Triumphant Mount' appears to have been built in stages too, with the 'evil' characters at the foot, London 'sitting in greatest Honour' above them, whilst 'next aboue her in the most eminent place, sits Religion' (sig. C2v). Dekker also stresses the significance of height differential, and in the process underlines the large number of protagonists required by some of the individual pageants (at least twelve, in this case). In *Troia-Noua triumphans*'s second land show, 'Vertue' takes the 'most eminent place' whilst 'beneath Her, in distinct places, sit the Seauen liberall Sciences'; in addition, 'at the backe of this Chariot sit foure Cupids' (sig. B2r–v). Zuizin clearly saw a similar arrangement the following year, for he describes 'a dais, or platform, with high decorated steps on four sides and on the top and on the places sat one person in each place'.[107]

Moving these substantial structures around must also have posed some logistical problems. Unlike in royal entries (where, owing to their size and complexity, the triumphal arches and devices were static) but as with the Watch and the court masque, the mayoral pageants and other devices were usually carried around by porters (as many as 100 porters for five pageants in some Shows, such as in 1611).[108] The Merchant Taylors spent £8 employing twenty porters 'for carrying the pageant shipp and beaste' in 1602, and used an even more extravagant 'fowrescore and eight porters, for carying of the Pageant, Shipp, and the other shewes' when the Show was repeated because of bad weather in November 1605.[109] Zuizin's eyewitness account of the 1613 Show refers to pageant structures carried by men.[110] McGrath points out that the construction of the pageants could be as much practical as spectacular. She comments that mountains and the like, descending to the ground, could usefully 'help to mask a mechanism of wheels, or even to hide the human shunters essential to its movement'.[111] Indeed, what she calls 'the process of trundling around' may have, in part, determined the way the pageant was fashioned. On the basis of the practice in continental Europe, Fairholt speculates that, when the pageants were moved around on wheels, the mechanism was hidden from the onlookers' view by painted cloth 'curtains'; the lower section of the pageant station or car was also used to hide the performers until they were needed.[112] In *Metropolis coronata* Munday does state that the chariot car 'runneth on seuen wheeles [and] is drawne by two Lyons and two Horses of the Sea' (sig. B4r). In one of his earliest works (and in a telling prefiguration of his later career) Munday has Zelauto recount to his friend Astraepho his experience of witnessing a 'braue and excellent deuice' of Apollo and 'his heauenly crew of Musique' performed as part of a tournament for Queen Elizabeth. This device, Zelauto explains, 'went on wheeles without the helpe of any man', indicating some disguised form of movement (*Zelauto*, sig. Eiir). Likewise, one of the illustrations to *Chrysanaleia* bears a caption that states that the mermen and mermaids 'went afore the pagent Charriot-wyse', i.e. that their part of the pageant drew the 'great pageant' on its car with Richard II at the top.[113] Munday's text is likewise quite explicit about how the pageant cars were conveyed, stating that 'our Pageant chariot, is drawne by two Mare-men, & two Mare-maids . . . In the highest seate of eminence, sits the triumphing Angell . . . King Richard sitting a degree beneath her' (*Chrysanaleia*, sig. B3v).

The means of transportation were therefore various. In 1604 the Haberdashers hired horses 'to drawe the chariott', and paid men to ride the horses in armour.[114] 'Seuerall beasts' were used to draw the pageant cars in the 1617 Show, but neither the Grocers' accounts nor Middleton's text reveal what manner of beasts these were.[115] The 'Chariot of Loue' in *The triumphs of loue and antiquity* is drawn by '2 Luzarns' (lynxes) (sig. C4r). Dekker wrote in *Troia-Noua triumphans* that he and Heminges had designed the pageants to be drawn by horses 'queintly disguised like the natural fishes, of purpose to auoyd the trouble and pestering of Porters, who with much noyse and litle comlinesse are euery yeare most unnecessarily imployed' (sig. B1r).[116] Indeed, Dekker stresses the lengths that were gone to to give the impression that Neptune's chariot was really drawn by 'liuing beasts'. The construction, he remarks, is not 'begotten of painted cloath, and browne paper' as it may have been in the primitive days of what he calls 'the old procreation' (*ibid.*). The horses disguised as fish may have been hung with painted cloths to create the effect. Like Dekker, Webster states that one of his pageants, 'a rich and very spacious Pauillion', was 'drawne with fower horses, (for Porters would haue made it moue tottering and Improperly)' (*Monuments of Honor*, sig. B2v).[117] Given that it is notoriously unwise to work with children and animals, and despite Dutton's remark that 'Webster clearly wanted something [more] stately than porters', one might wonder how replacing human porters with 'liuing beasts' would have improved things.[118] Dekker's reference to the noise and uncomeliness of the porters offers another insight into the lived experience of the day, as he implies that the porters sometimes took advantage of being in the limelight. Webster also indicates that porters could struggle with the weight of the pageant. The Goldsmiths allocated the task of oversee-ing the porters to certain members of the Company, who were also to 'comand them to do theire dueties', suggesting that the porters, at least in 1611, were not trusted not to do their job properly.[119]

Many other people were employed to help the event run smoothly, for apart from their essential if implicit role as the audi-ence (and occasional acts of over-excitement), there were other forms of impact on the locality. Care was taken to minimise the inconvenience both to the onlookers and to the traders and resi-dents of the City. There are numerous references in livery company records of payments to carpenters for preventative measures to enable the Show to pass through the narrow streets, and to citi-zens being reimbursed for damage to their property. In 1602, for instance, the Merchant Taylors' Company paid 2s 6d for 'break-ing pte of a shopp for the pageant to passe out of Chrystchurch', and in the same year the churchwardens of St Peter's in Cheapside received compensation from the Merchant Taylors for the City Waits 'standing on their Leades of the Church'.[120] The Merchant Taylors' records from 1612 refer to the 'taking up and setting downe [of] the postes at Paules gate, as in former yeres hath byn accustomed'.[121] This would have been to allow the pageant cars and the spectators to pass. In 1624 the City Carpenter was paid to take down and afterwards put back up 'xxiii signes, 12 signe postes, and six Taverne Bushes, in diverse streets where the Pageants were to passe'.[122] In the narrow city streets large pageant cars and the volume of onlookers would doubtless have damaged any overhang-ing signs and the like.

It was not only buildings that were in danger of being damaged, especially when one considers the chaotic crowds and the potential perils of the ordnance, fireworks and so on. It would have required some skill to fire off cannons across the river and not hit any of the spectators, and those who operated the cannons themselves did not always escape unscathed. The Skinners paid one William Adames 20s in 1585 'towardes his releife because he was maymed at Baynardes Castle on Symon and Iudes daye aboute the Companynes Busynes'.[123] Richard Lambert was even unluckier: in December 1619 his widow Alice was granted a weekly pension by the Skinners in recompense for the loss of her husband, a gunner 'who was slaine on the banck side by the breaking of one of the chambers on the daie of triumph'.[124] Another fatal incident was also recorded by the Vintners in 1593: 9s (a paltry sum, in the circumstances) was paid to 'Singwills wyfe the Auncient [ensign] bearer whose husband died flourishinge the Auncient in the Hall'.[125]

Despite such unfortunate accidents, the Companies did try to ensure that the procession was orderly and dignified, although, as we'll see, not always successfully. They employed numerous whifflers and ushers armed with staves and swords to control the crowds, as well as costumed figures like the greenmen and giants. As Astington comments, 'the difficulties of coordinating and moving the show through crowded and frequently unruly streets must have been considerable'.[126] Busino records the appearance of 'the City Marshal on horseback' as well as the use of 'lusty youths and men armed with long fencing swords' to clear the path of the procession, although he also recounts an outbreak of disorderly behaviour from the onlookers.[127] In 1624 'the Porter of the gate at the Heralds yard' (i.e. the College of Arms, between the river and St Paul's) was paid to call and 'sett in order' the names of the Bachelors as the Lord Mayor returned from Westminster and the former joined the procession going towards St Paul's.[128] In 1608, the Grocers' Court minutes give a list of the Company members for the procession which shows that they marched in pairs in order of seniority, starting with the Wardens: the names are 'redd and marshaled accordinge to theire ancienties'.[129] Thought also had to be given to how the onlookers would be able to see the latter stages of the day's events. To that end, a large number of tall staff torches was needed (the Merchant Taylors paid for eight dozen in 1612), partly for dramatic effect, no doubt, but mainly because the final events of the day would have taken place in autumnal darkness, a fact sometimes integrated into the speeches which took place at the end of the day. As Munday puts it in the farewell speech of *Chrysanaleia*, 'And now are spred. / The sable Curtaines of the night . . . The twinkling Tapers of the Skie / Are turn'd to Torches' (sig. C4r).[130]

'With Barges, Ensignes; Trumpets, Fyfe and Drum': the water show

Returning to the earlier part of the day, once the mayoral party had left the Guildhall in the morning, the pageantry proper generally began with the 'Seruice . . . performed upon the Water', as Munday puts it in *The triumphs of the Golden Fleece* (sig. A4v). The role the river Thames played in the Shows is another aspect that has, in the main, lost its original significance for modern commentators, although it is clear that the Companies considered the barge, galley foist and entertainments accompanying the Lord Mayor along the river to be at least as important as the pageantry on land. Indeed, Palmer argues that 'the use of ceremonial barges gradually developed into the most visually spectacular part of the triumphal day. Barges allowed much more scope for lavish splendour with such items as banners, streamers, musicians, water-borne pageants, fireworks, and cannon fire from the shore'.[131] The river would have been packed with craft ranging from large, highly decorated state barges to smaller boats manned by ordinary citizens. In 1555 Machyn recalled that 'ther wher ij goodly pennes [pinnaces] deckyd with gones and flages and stremars, and a m. penselles, the penes pentyd, on whyt and bluw, and the thodur yelow and red, and the oars and gowne [guns] lyke coler'.[132] Some sixty years later Zuizin recounted a similar picture:

> before the [Lord Mayor's] ship and behind and on the sides, over the whole river, sailed on many boats, the King's gentlemen, and knights, and aldermen, and merchants, and traders, and the bodyguard of the King's court, and all sorts of people of the land in bright costume.[133]

Heywood presents a quite nationalistic account, differentiating the 'strong', masculine, Protestant English barge from the 'wanton', Catholic Venetian gondola. The single most marvellous aspect of London, he claims in *Londini artium*, is that its magistrate is

> not waited on by Boats made of the Trunks
> Of Canes, or hollowed Trees, or petty Iunks,
> Or wanton Gondelaes: but Barges, strong,
> And richly deckt.
>
> (sig. B2r).

The livery companies took the barges as seriously as did Heywood. The Company barge, in particular, was often ordered well before the detailed content of the Show was even considered. The

Companies also usually paid out for the hire or purchase of barges (plus watermen) for other Companies' Shows. Hunting provides a detailed account of the state barge used for the Shows, as well as for other events such as coronations and so on.[134] Each barge, she writes,

> was built along similar lines, being basically an elongated, more elegant version of the Thames wherry [the boat used for passenger traffic]. The length of a state barge was between 60 and 80 feet, nine oars a side was the norm, and the cabin increased in size as time went on. Musicians, an essential part of the enjoyment, sat in a well or cockpit and the Bargemaster perched in the stern. The most luxurious state barges were richly carved and painted with the Company's coat of arms on the stern.[135]

Von Wedel's recollections of the 1585 Show, when taken alongside evidence of expenditure from the livery companies' accounts and the testimony of Zuizin quoted above, confirms that the barges were highly decorated. The Lord Mayor's barge, von Wedel says, was festooned with the City's colours, red and white, in taffeta, and the Company barges flew flags to indicate their corporate allegiance. Zuizin notes that 'as is the case with a straight [sided] ship, the lower decks had windows and in these windows were rowers on both sides'.[136] Von Wedel also states that there was 'a very large barge, painted black and white, which was called the apprentices' barge'.[137] The water procession was an important part of the day's events, and one for which the companies were prepared to dig deep. The Drapers invested in a new barge upon the election of Thomas Hayes in 1614, as did the Salters in 1633, for which John Hartwell, their usual supplier, was paid £4.[138] Where the Companies did not own barges they were borrowed or hired: the King's bargemaster supplied two barges, the galley foist and a galley to the Fishmongers in 1616.[139]

In 1638 members of the Drapers' Company incited its bargemen to out-row and thereby overtake the Lord Mayor's barge, suggesting, as Williams says, that the 'order of precedence was sometimes taken unexpectedly lightly'.[140] The Drapers' Company seems to have been especially pleased with its feat, as there is quite a long entry in their accounts to record the reward of drink received by the bargeman and his colleagues. The accounts rather gloatingly comment that the Company barge landed at Westminster 'before the Lo. Maior and Aldermen were landed (the Lo. Maiors barge being allmost out of sight rowing towards Westminster before

our Company barge tooke water)'.[141] Indeed, Dekker, with his
usual endearing frankness, states at the end of *Londons tempe* that
'this yeere, giues one Remarkeable Note to after times, that all the
Barges followed one another (euery Company in their degree) in a
Stately and Maiesticall order' (sig. C2v). Other records show that
the coming and going of the barges at Westminster could be 'disor-
derlie': there was an attempt to marshal the barges in better order,
although Dekker's comment indicates that this may not have been
wholly successful in most years.[142] Beyond that, relatively little is
known about the mechanics of the water show compared to the
shows on land. One of the few texts to mention the practicalities of
how the river was used, Heywood's *Londini emporia*, has a side-
note from which it appears that on the river there were 'sun[dry]
water-[en]gines', the function of which is unclear (sig. A4v).[143]

Another aspect of the water show that has often not been
properly understood is the nature and function of the galley foist.
Carnegie has corrected a longstanding and widespread misconc-
ception about what the galley foist was. Rather than the ornate
barge in which the mayor travelled down river to Westminster, he
explains that it was actually 'a small escorting war-ship famous for
its incessant gunfire'.[144] The Ironmongers' minutes record it as '60
Foote longe well rigged and furnished with 16 bases & 10 small
shott' as well as 'powder and fireworkes'.[145] That the galley foist
was a distinctive accompaniment to the city barges is made apparent by the ways in which contemporary writers used it, often as a
metaphor, and often gendered female. As Carnegie comments, the
galley foist's ubiquity as a point of reference in the drama of this
period demonstrates that it 'was an enormously popular annual
attraction'.[146] In Dekker's *Match mee in London*, a character likens
the King's mistress, 'a Citizens wife' to 'a Pinnace [which] (Was
mann'd out first by th'City,) [and] is come to th'Court, New rigg'd,
a very painted Gally foist' (sig. F2r). In *The Honest Whore*, too,
Mistress Horsleach, a woman of low virtue, is likened to a showy
'Gally-foist' (sig. H5v). Even Jonson deigned to pay it attention: in
Epicoene, he refers to 'sonnes of noise and tumult' 'begot' on an
auspicious day such as 'ill May-day', or 'when the Gally-foist is
a-floate to Westminster' (sig. I3r).

One of the main functions of the galley foist was simply to make
a tremendous racket. The foist, which was probably wider than
the barges which it accompanied, as Carnegie comments 'invokes
far more noise than even trumpets and drums'.[147] Contemporary
descriptions of the Shows do highlight the noise, size, smoke and

overall impact of the galley foist and the other river traffic. Busino, for instance, relates how

> a dense fleet of vessels hove in sight, accompanied by swarms of small boats . . . The ships were beautifully decorated with balustrades and various paintings. They carried immense banners and countless pennons. Salutes were fired, and a number of persons bravely attired played on trumpets, fifes and other instruments . . . the discharges of the salutes were incessant.[148]

The noise of the gun salute, Busino wrote, 'made a great echo' which was 'repeated even more loudly when my Lord Mayor landed at the water stairs near the court of Parliament'.[149] Once again, other sources bear him out. Sharpham's *The fleire* refers to 'all the Gunners' that fire off 'at Lambeth, whe[n] the Maior and Aldermen land at Westminster' (sig. F4r). The eyewitness Zuizin concurs: 'they fired a great salute from the ship in which the Lord Mayor sailed and from other ships which were there and from big boats and from the City wall. And from all the small boats there was a great shooting of muskets'.[150] The 'salute' they both mention would probably be the 'Noble Volley[s] at his Lordships landing' mentioned by Middleton in his 1619 Show (*The triumphs of loue and antiquity*, sig. B1v). The pageant writers and artificers may understandably have felt that their elaborate land-based tableaux were in danger of being eclipsed by the more unsubtle appeal of the non-stop gunfire from cannon and musket, and the drums and other instruments carried on this ship. Indeed, Dekker admits as much in *Troia-Noua triumphans*, writing that 'their thunder (according to the old Gally-foyst-fashion) was too lowd for any of the Nine muses to be bidden to it' (sig. D1v); in a more positive light, he also has Neptune refer to 'this warlike thunder of lowd drummes, / (Clarions and Trumpets)' (sig. B1r). For Munday, 'the seuerall peales of Ordinance . . . can make better report in the aire, then they can be expressed by pen' (*Metropolis coronata*, sig. B3v). The Companies' records show the care that went into this aspect of the preparations. In 1635 the Ironmongers instructed Tilbury Strange, a Waterman, to prepare the galley foist with '10 peeces of ordinances' and numerous other armaments.[151] For the Drapers' Show in 1621, seventy cannon 'were placed against Westminster [and] 50 against Paules Wharfe'.[152] According to the Merchant Taylors' accounts, 'chambers [cannon]' were 'dischardged doble at two places viz Lambeth and the bankesyde'.[153] The Companies also invested further large sums in making the galley foist ready for Lord

Mayor's Day; the foist, like the barges, was painted and decorated with banners, shields and the like. Back in 1556, the Merchant Taylors requested that 'a foyst . . . be well appoynted with ordnaunce and shott' (it had twenty cannons), which shows that the gun and cannon-fire were important aspects of the use of the foist from early on.[154]

Although (with the exception of Munday's *Triumphs of the Golden Fleece*) the water show was never the main focus of attention, the printed texts do mention the galley foist and other aspects of the water-borne part of the entertainment in passing. Heywood's 1635 text has the marginal 'stage direction' of 'A Peece goes off' alongside a speech by Mars; later on Heywood comments, 'the speech being ended, the Ordnance goeth off from the Castle' (*Londini sinus salutis*, sigs A8r and Br). Webster too refers to the 'peale of Sea-thunder' from Bankside that accompanied the entourage back on shore after the trip to Westminster (*Monuments of Honor*, sig. A4r). In *The triumphs of truth* Middleton presents the water show in more detail than is often the case, describing 'the Riuer deck't in the richest glory . . . [with] fiue Islands art-fully garnished with all manner of Indian Fruite-Trees, Drugges, Spiceries; and the like, the middle Island with a faire Castle especially beautified' (sig. B1r). All this evidence makes it hard to understand why the water shows have been so relatively neglected by critics, who invariably focus on the street pageantry.

Munday dealt with the water show in unusual depth in his mayoral Shows, which taken alongside other texts such as *Londons loue* suggests that this was an aspect of civic pageantry in which he took an particular interest. He was especially prone to use ships, in various guises, within the pageantry he devised. This interest went as far back as *Zelauto* in 1580, where the protagonist recalls within a triumph 'a braue and comely Shippe . . . wherein were certaine of [the Queen's] noble Lordes'. This device 'ran upon a Rock, and was disployled' (sig. Eiir). *Zelauto* emphasises the importance of the ship device with a full-page illustration. Once Munday embarked on creating mayoral Shows his predilection for ships was given even fuller rein. *Chruso-thriambos* begins with a description of 'sundry Ships, Frigots, and Gallies', one of which bears 'Chiorison the Golden King, with Tumanama his peerlesse Queene'. 'Diuers Sea-fights and skirmishes' take place on the journey to Westminster and back again, and the Indian king and queen then become part of the land procession, there 'beeing mounted on two Golden Leopardes, that draw a goodly triumphall Chariot' (sig. A3v). *Metropolis coronata* has two ships, Jason's Argoe and the 'Ioell', and the first speech of the Show takes place on the water, whilst the Lord Mayor and his party are embarking on the barges for Westminster. Indeed, *Metropolis coronata* demonstrates that the water show featured pageantry at least as elaborate as that on land. Fitz-Alwin's speech to John Jolles is delivered from a tiered sea-chariot upon which also sit the 'eight Royall Vertues' and the figures of Fame and Time, along with numerous painted heraldic shields (sig. A4r–v). Even 'the Shewes appointed for seruice on Land' in this work have a nautical aspect. After the appearance of the 'Ioell', which bears Neptune and Thamesis, another pageant appears: 'in stead of Neptunes Whale on the water, commeth another Sea-deuice, tearmed *The Chariot of Mans life*' (sig. B2v). The water show, these sources demonstrate, went beyond the use of barges and other vessels to include elaborate water-borne devices like the five islands created for the 1613 Show. The writers and artificers had the Thames to hand, so to speak, and were understandably keen to exploit its potential as a venue for pageantry.[155]

'The true morality of this deuice': emblems and symbols in the Shows

The stages, wagons, chariots, barges and so on were used to convey pageantry composed of elaborate, often highly symbolic content. Before moving on to discuss the nature of the emblems and symbols used in the Shows, however, I should point out that the term 'pageant' often seems to be distinguished from the other 'shewes' and 'devices' employed on these occasions. For instance, in 1611 the pageant featured, as the Goldsmiths put it, 'leopards unicorns and mermaides' and was placed in the gallery of Goldsmiths' Hall after the Show; the entertainment on the river is called a 'shew', as are Munday and Grinkin's set pieces accompanied by speeches. The Merchant Taylors' accounts invariably separate pageants from shows, too. In Cooke's *Greenes Tu quoque* the character Spendall aspires to become Lord Mayor, 'and haue three Pageants carried before me, *besides* a Shippe and an Unicorne' (sig. C2r; my emphasis). This suggests a generally understood separate identity for the pageants, perhaps indicating that the practice within religious civic drama and the Midsummer Watch of having traditional freestanding 'pageants' like the Mercer's Maid still had currency. Indeed, in 1607, during a period when the Shows seem to have been in abeyance to some extent, the Mercers required the use only of 'the maid', their traditional emblem.[156] The distinction between pageant and show thus persisted, as far as the Companies were concerned, for in 1612 Dekker and Heminges were paid for 'land shewes' and at least two pageants.[157] For the 1613 Show, the Grocers' accounts even more carefully differentiate between the two terms. As we have seen, Middleton was paid £40 for 'the ordering overseeing and wryting of the whole Devyse and alsoe for the appareling [of] the p[er]sonage in the Pageant', whereas Munday received £149 'for the devyse of the Pageant and other shewes, and for the appareling and fynding of all the p[er]sonages in the sayd shewes (excepting the Pageant)'.[158] The 'Pageant' itself comprised a 'senate howse, Shipp, 2 Chariotte, the 5 Ilande with all the severall beaste'.[159] Ships are almost always singled out; indeed, the Companies' minutes often bracket these off separately. Generally speaking, the Shows were more fragmented than one might have assumed from the coherence attempted by the printed works.

Their content, too, was often eclectic. Munday manages to combine Jason, Medea and the argonauts, Neptune and Thamesis, the river gods, Fitz-Alwin, the first Lord Mayor, and Robin Hood and the rest of his merry men in the course of one single Show; indeed, the pageant of 'Metropolis Coronata', the apparent focus of the Show (going by the name of the printed text) barely features at all.[160] Heywood is very given to using stories and characters from classical mythology – he himself calls this an expression of 'grave History' – the significance of which, beyond showcasing his erudition, is sometimes quite hard to fathom.[161] *Londini sinus salutis*, for instance, includes a device featuring 'the twelue Caelestiall signes' (sig. A5v). Although Heywood goes to some lengths to expound on their provenance and various meanings, he does little to signal why they are in any way relevant to the matter in hand – they are, it transpires, used to stand in for the Great Twelve livery companies, although Heywood never makes this explicit. This is despite his claim that they 'were for our example made' (sig. A8r). Relatedly, he refrains from embarking in the usual, and probably expected, account of 'the commodiousnesse of Iron and Steele' (this is an Ironmongers' Show) on the basis that the onlookers and/or readers can see this for themselves. As this indicates, Heywood does seem to have a lack of interest in purely civic imagery when compared to contemporaries such as Munday or Dekker. The slightly disengaged quality to some of his Shows is exemplified in *Londini sinus salutis*, where the final speech at the Lord Mayor's gate is prefaced by the remark that this is 'onely a Summary, or reiteration of the former Showes' (sig. B3r).

The emblems employed in the Shows were thus taken from a range of places. Civic histories and archives and related texts like John Stow's *Suruay of London* were utilised in the writing of the Shows, as were other, wider sources. The *Suruay* would naturally have been one of the first places of resort for information about the history of the various civic roles and of their notable incumbents.[162] For Munday, that would have been a task very close to home given his work on the 1618 edition of Stow's text.[163] Eclectic or not, Munday's cited authorities for his foray into the non-metropolitan past in the quasi-historical account of 'Britain' in *The triumphes of re-united Britania* include Bale, Camden, Leland and Geoffrey of Monmouth, who constitute pretty much the full panoply of chroniclers used in this period, with the notable exception of Stow (who does feature in a marginal note in *Chruso-thriambos*).[164] *Chrysanaleia* commences in characteristic Munday style with an invocation of historical authorities. 'I finde it faithfully recorded in Authors of reuerend Antiquity', Munday begins, before going on to trace the antiquity of the Fishmongers' Company back to the time of the Crusades (sig. A4r). Where the image requires it, other notable writers are marshalled: for his explication of the meanings of the female pelican in the same work, Aristotle and Pliny are the 'cited Authors' used to 'variously affirm' that Munday's account is correct (sig. B2r). In the same work Munday's opportunistic use of the image of the lemon tree to celebrate John Leman brings in the five senses of which this tree is an 'admirable preservative': here his classical authorities ('Iulius Solinas Polyhistor, Dioscorides, Pomponius Mela, Petrus Mexius and Antonius Verdierus') are even more 'various' and certainly more obscure (sig. B2v). As Kate Levin observes (ironically enough, given Jonson's view of his contemporary), Munday's mayoral texts 'teem with scholarly justifications and marginal glosses, as if aspiring to the solidity and profundity of a Jonsonian entertainment'.[165]

As previously indicated, pageantry had been a feature of mayoral inaugurations for some considerable time. For 1554, Machyn describes 'a goodly pagant, a gryffen with a chyld lying in harnes, and sant John Baptyst with a lyon'.[166] William Smith's account of the 1575 Show gives an even fuller sense of how those entertainments that preceded the Shows of the later period looked. They contained most of the elements of the later, more complex pageantry in embryo. Smith tells how the procession included 'the pageant of Tryumphe rychly decked, whereuppon by certayne fygures and wrytinges, (partly towchinge the name of the said mayor), some matter

towchinge justice, and the office of a maiestrate is represented'.[167]
'Towchinge the name of the said mayor' was quite a tradition. Back
in 1561, for example, the pageant produced for William Harper, a
Merchant Taylor, contained many references to famous harpers of
antiquity. Earlier still, in 1431, according to Lydgate, the pageantry
for John Wells was 'devised notably indede / For to accordyne with
the Maiers name'.[168] Middleton presents a rather obvious (he calls it
'fit', of course) use of William Cockayne's name in the figure of 'yon
Bird of State, the vigilant Cocke . . . at whose shrill Crow the very
Lyon trembles' (*The tryumphs of honor and industry*, sig. B3r).[169]
For *The sunne in Aries* Middleton uses the synonym 'bark' for boat
as a way of exploiting the Lord Mayor's surname, Barkham. The
ship that Munday invents for John Jolles in 1615 is neatly called the
'Ioell', 'stiled by the Lord Maiors name', as he puts it (*Metropolis
coronata*, sig. B2v). As well as trading on the possibilities of the
specific Lord Mayor's name, other common elements in the Shows
(as we'll see further in Chapter 5) were the symbolic representation
of aspects of the office of a magistrate, with the emphasis on giving
advice on how best to govern the City.

Symbolic meanings were put across to the onlookers in part by
the extensive use of properties. Animals were quite ubiquitous, for
they had multiple symbolic functions and were (usually) recognisable. They also feature repeatedly in eyewitness and other contemporary accounts of the Shows, such as *Cornu-Copiae*, which refers
to 'Elephants and Vnicornes pass[ing] by' (sig. H1r). Where they
were not performed by masked actors, as sometimes appeared to
have been the case, most of the animal figures in the Shows were
made of lath and plaster or wood. Dekker helpfully states that the
'sea Lyon' on which Tethys rides in *Londons tempe* was 'cut out
of wood to the life'; the 'Estridge' on which the Indian boy sits
is likewise 'cut out of timber to the life' (sigs B1v–B2r).[170] This
seems entirely likely, as Garret Christmas, the artificer, was, after
all, a very celebrated wood carver; indeed, if Booth's drawings of
the ostrich and Tethys's lion are accurate, the phrase 'to the life'
seems justified (see Figures 8 and 12).[171] For obvious reasons the
Companies' traditional beasts, symbols and imagery played a large
part in the content of the Shows as well as in their titles, on occasion
(*The triumphs of the Golden Fleece* for the Drapers, for example).
These iconographic traditions are part of what Kiefer calls 'a rich
fund of symbolism' drawn upon by the writers and artificers, and
he makes the point that although the inclusion of such figures may
appear 'contrived, conventional, or even archaic', they 'had long

12 Abram Booth's drawing of the 1629 Show: the water show

been a feature of English culture' and were as a result less likely
to seem strange or inappropriate to a contemporary audience.[172]
Ironmongers' pageants usually featured ostriches, and in 1556 the
Merchant Taylors hired a camel – a real one, it seems, sweetened
with rose water – which was, Sayle states, ridden 'by a man and as
many children as it could probably carry'.[173] In September 1601
the Haberdashers' Court of Assistants stipulated 'that there shalbe
a faire pageant, an Ounce [leopard] & a lyon, a Castle [,] foist
. . . banners streamers and all other things provided', singling the
Company's heraldic animals out for inclusion.[174]

    As these examples suggest, animal symbolism was as prevalent in
the Shows as elsewhere in early modern culture: witness Middleton
and Grinkin's use of 'an Eagle, a Hart, a Spider, an Ape and a
Dogge' as the 'proper Emblemes' to represent the five senses in *The
triumphs of truth* (sig. B4v). Webster adorns the figure of Prince
Henry in *Monuments of Honor* with a veritable zoo of symbolic

creatures to emphasise the greatness of the dead heir. His 'Circklet
. . . [is] charged with foure Holy Lambes', there is 'a Bee Hiue, to
expresse his Grauety in Youth' and 'a Dromedary shewing his speed
and alacrety in gratifying his Followers'; ants are used to signify
'his forward inclination to all Noble exercise', Chastity's unicorn
is 'a guide to all other vertues', Obedience's elephant is 'the strongest Beast, but most obseruant to man of any Creature', and finally
there is 'a Serpent wreath'd about [a pillar] to expect his height of
minde' (sigs C1v–C2r).[175] Although they were usually conventional,
such images were not always used in the same way. Whereas for
Heywood in *Porta pietatis* the 'Rinoceros', a 'harmlesse and gentle'
creature, stood as the 'enemy of all beasts of rapine and prey' (sigs
B2v–B3r), for Middleton's *Triumphs of truth* this animal is a sinister beast, the bearer of Envy, one of the threats faced by the new
Lord Mayor. Envy herself, however, is depicted in *The triumphs
of truth* in a way that would have been instantly recognisable to
anyone familiar with her conventional emblematic appearance (see
Figure 13). Middleton's text describes her as 'attired in red silk . . .
[with] her left Pap bare, where a Snake fastens, her Armes halfe
Naked, holding in her right hand a Dart tincted in blood' (sig. B2r).

Munro comments that the extensive use of allegory and symbolism in the Shows represents 'a constant looking-backward to a
supposed time when sign and referent did cohere, [and] significance
was stable'.[176] In these terms the conventional imagery of the Shows
can be seen to exhibit the same kind of 'nostalgia' that many commentators have ascribed to Stow. The Shows' symbolism provides
further evidence of a general concern for tradition and antiquity
within the Companies. As Gadd writes, 'antiquity . . . was the
highest compliment that could be paid to any institution in early-
modern England . . . [and] it also provided a fundamental basis
upon which customary and legal rights could be justified'.[177] The
emphasis on 'trade symbolism' is a case in point, as by the period
in question the Great Twelve Companies were no longer exclusively
concerned with the trades that they had been set up to protect and
oversee. Lord Mayors' Shows were not simply backward looking,
however: on occasion, as I'll demonstrate in Chapter 5, they could
engage with contemporary matters, some quite controversial. As we
have seen, emblems often in themselves bore didactic or even critical meanings. As Bergeron argues of John Taylor's use of Fame in
his 1634 Show, 'Fame teaches partly through citing notable people
of the past' whose estimable deeds the new Lord Mayor is thereby
encouraged to aspire to.[178]

94

Inuidiæ defcriptio.

Ad Rd. W.

Inuidiam Ouid.
defcribit 2. Me-
tamorph.

W H A T hideous hagge with vifage fterne appeares?
Whofe feeble limmes, can fcarce the bodie ftaie:
This, Enuie is: leane, pale, and full of yeares,
Who with the bliffe of other pines awaie.
And what declares, her eating vipers broode?
That poyfoned thoughtes, bee euermore her foode.

Lucret. 3.
*Macerat Inuidia ante
oculos illi effe poteſtem,
Illum afpectari, claro
qui incedit honore:
Ipſi ſe in tenebris volui,
carnoque queruntur.*

What meanes her eies? fo bleared, fore, and redd:
Her mourninge ftill, to fee an others gaine.
And what is mente by fnakes vpon her head?
The fruite that fpringes, of fuch a venomed braine.
But whie, her harte fhee rentes within her breft?
It fhewes her felfe, doth worke her owne vnreft.

Whie lookes fhee wronge? bicaufe fhee woulde not fee,
An happie wight, which is to her a hell:
What other partes within this furie bee?
Her harte, with gall: her tonge, with ftinges doth fwell.
And lafte of all, her ftaffe with prickes aboundes:
Which fhowes her wordes, wherewith the good fhee woundes.

Ouid. lib. 1. De
Arte Amandi.

*Fertilior feges eft alienis femper in agris,
Vicinumq; pecus grandius vber habet.*

De In-

13 'Envy' emblem from Geffrey Whitney, *A choice of emblemes* (sig. M3v)

Originality was not a prized virtue in mayoral pageantry, on the whole, although Heywood explicitly praises himself in *Londini speculum* for the novelty of having St Katherine, patron saint of the Haberdashers, form part of the water show. She tells the Lord Mayor and aldermen

Oft have I on a passant Lyon sate,
And through your populous streets been borne in state:
Oft have I grac't your Triumphes on the shore,
But on the Waters was not seene before.

(sig. B3v)

Opportunistic use of mythological figures was commonplace: for example, Vulcan and Lemnion's forge invariably features in Shows put on for the Ironmongers. As with most aspects of the Shows, these conventional images can be dated back to earlier times. Kipling notes, for instance, that 'London trade-symbol pageants almost always [took] the form of portable structures carried in procession . . . [here] the pageant serves as an identifying totem, a mascot, for the guild'.[179] Busino, the Venetian ambassador's chaplain, emphasised this aspect of the Show, writing that the Lord Mayor, George Bolles, 'arranged his installation with the greatest pomp, but always with allusion to his trade of grocer'.[180] Equally, it had long been the tradition to refer to the individual being celebrated in a civic triumph – be they monarch or mayor – as London's bridegroom, an analogy Munday uses to rather peculiar effect in 1616. The Merchant Taylors' records for 1602 make it clear that the Company was insistent that the content of the Show should be 'appropriate'. They state that the ship, lion and camel, long-standing symbols of the Merchant Taylors, 'doe properly belong unto our Companie, and are very fitt and answerable for this tyme . . . the Lyon being parte of the Companie's Armes, and the Cammell the Companie's supporters'.[181] Even Nelson's 1590 Show, which appeared to comprise only one pageant, featured William Walworth, as Fishmongers' Shows tended to do henceforth. Munday's 1616 Show for the Fishmongers incorporated emblems associated with the Goldsmiths, traditional allies of the former Company, as his text explains. Such 'swapping' was unusual, however, as Heywood's concern to explain the potentially contentious nature of his usage of animal symbolism in Garway's 1639 Show demonstrates:

> though the pelleted Lyons might have serv'd more properly to this place, as being supporters of the Armes belonging to the Right Worshipful Company of the Drapers; yet these [camels] are as genuine to the purpose: to show his Lord-ships generall negotiation in all kinds of Merchandise whatsoever. (*Londini status pacatus*, sig. B4v)

Unfortunately, Heywood's excuse is itself rather problematic, as it hinges on an overt reference to the ways in which drapery, the original concern of the Company, has been subsumed by involvement in 'all kinds of Merchandise whatsoever' (a topic to which I shall return). In addition, camels were traditionally associated with the Merchant Taylors, not the Drapers.

The Shows also used properties and/or costuming that was conventionally associated with figures outside of the Companies' specific iconography, such as the greenman, or figures from classical and other forms of mythology, such as Munday's 'fiue Sences' in *Chrysanaleia*.[182] Squire's four figures for the '4 parts of the World, Asia, Africa, America, and Europa', all with their proper garments and accessories, would doubtless have resembled the ways in which these continents were represented in other texts of the time. 'America', for instance, is 'a tawny Moore' wearing 'a crowne of feathers, and bases of the same; at her backe, a quiuer of shafts, and in her hand a Parthian bow'; the less exotic 'Europa' is dressed in 'a robe of Crymson taffaty, on her head an imperiall crowne conferred on her by the other three as Empresse of the earth, and holding in her hand a cluster of grapes' (sig. A3v). Other pageant texts demonstrate that certain figures were not the exclusive property of the livery companies. Neptune in his sea-chariot drawn by seahorses features in mayoral Shows – Dekker's 1612 Show, for instance – as well as, reportedly, being part of the 'tilt and tourney' held in Heidelberg in 1613 to honour Palsgrave and his wife.[183]

'What the others had I forget': (mis)understanding the Shows

It is important to consider how these symbolic meanings were experienced as much as how they were conveyed. In *A contention for honour and riches* Shirley refers, no doubt ironically, to 'understanders on Cheapside' watching the Shows, and both the printed texts and other sources reveal many aspects of how this 'understanding' – or lack of it – manifested itself. Once again, eyewitness accounts come into their own. Although Smith and Machyn experienced Shows that were not printed, so to a large extent we only have their word for it, Busino's account of the 1617 Lord Mayor's Day, in contrast, can fruitfully be placed alongside Middleton's text, *The tryumphs of honor and industry*. It is rare for eyewitness descriptions to be read against the printed texts of Shows, although as Palmer points out, 'no dramatic genre presents the critic with more subtle – and less studied – complications of mediation'.[184] In some ways, the two accounts of the 1617 Show complement each other. Busino spends more time on the look and sound of the Show, whilst Middleton, naturally, emphasises the symbolic content and the speeches. However, it appears that Middleton's efforts to invest the pageantry with significant meaning were largely lost on the ambassador's chaplain, who refers to the Show's 'symbols of commerce' very much in passing. Busino's experience here bears out Smuts's argument that unlike viewing a performance, 'reading [a printed text] facilitates reflection and systematic comparison, making it easier to discern complex intellectual meanings'.[185] Although Busino was evidently impressed with the spectacle there is no sign, for instance, that he realised that the Indian in the first pageant car was supposed to represent 'Industry', one of the chief symbols of the entire Show, let alone that he noticed the detail that she was holding 'a faire golden Ball in her hand, vpon which [stood] a golden Cupid' (sig. B1v).[186] Middleton's 'Castle of Fame or Honor', his venue for the traditional survey of the Company's great and good, becomes simply 'a fine castle' for Busino.[187] In the textual commentary, in contrast, Middleton invests this pageant with considerable importance as he here outlines the Grocers' history:

> the Noble Allen de la Zouch, Grocer, who was Maior of London the two and fiftieth yeare of the same Henry the third, which Allen de la Zouch, for his good Gouernement in the Time of his Maioralty, was by the sayd King Henry the third, made both a Baron of this Realme, and Lord Chiefe Iustice of England: Also that Famous Worthy, Sir Thomas Knoles, Grocer, twice Maior of this Honorable Citty. (sig. B3v)

This historical digression is unlikely to have featured in the day's entertainment; it pertains to the text, not the event. The placards about which Jonson was so scathing in his part of *The magnificent entertainment* may well have been of assistance to Busino. Jonson stated 'neither was it becomming, or could it stand with the dignity of these shewes . . . to require a Truch-man [interpreter], or (with the ignorant Painter), one to write. *This is a Dog*; or, *This is a Hare*' (*B. Ion: his part*, sig. B2v).[188] One can imagine that Dekker's disclaimer in *Londons tempe* might be aimed at Jonson or someone of a similarly pedantic outlook. Dekker anticipates criticism as follows:

> Some Hypercriticall Censurer perhaps will aske, why hauing Tytan, I should bring in Apollo, sithence they are both names proper to the Sunne. But the youngest Nouice in Poetry can answer for me, that the

Sunne when he shines in heauen is called Tytan, but being on earth
(as he is here) we call him Apollo. (sig. C1v).

Regardless of Jonson's views, these devices were used in pageantry
from time to time. One of the pageants for Queen Anne's entry into
London in 1533 had placards and scrolls bearing Latin phrases, and
Dekker's account of the 1604 royal entry makes it clear that some
of the figures were labelled.[189] In France in 1600 a royal entry supplied a considerable degree of explication: as was commonplace, the
printed text for the triumph was, in McGowan's words, 'crammed
with commentaries on the meaning of images, Latin inscriptions
and emblems'. However, in addition, the actual procession included
'summaries of the principal content . . . translations into French
of the inscriptions, and indications of the meaning of the entire
enterprise'.[190]

Some writers – Munday in particular – were keen to assist
their audiences *and* readers in comprehending the allegories and
emblems the Shows used. Indeed, Munday's approach could be
quite direct. The figure of Time addresses the Lord Mayor towards
the end of *Metropolis coronata* with the aim of summing up all
the preceding pageantry: 'Time hath nothing else to tel you', he
says to John Jolles, 'but the briefe meanings of these seuerall
inuentions' (sig. B3v). The 'meanings' are duly conscientiously,
if somewhat laboriously, worked through: 'a Spheare or Globe',
for example, stands for 'the world' (sig. B4r). The following year
Munday's text follows the same pattern: the whole array of devices
are lined up 'neere to the little Conduit' on the Lord Mayor's
return to St Paul's for the sermon, and once again their meanings are fully expounded, just in case Leman had missed anything
earlier in the day (*Chrysanaleia*, sig. C2v).[191] Zeal's speech in
The triumphs of truth works as a supplement to the visual symbolism the staged character of Truth possessed, explaining it for
those who had not picked up on every aspect of the significance
of Truth's attire and properties.[192] Both possible ways of glean-
ing the symbolic meaning are thereby covered. Zeal tells the
audience:

> That Crowne of Starres showes her descent from heauen;
> That Roabe of white fild with all Eagles eies,
> Her piercing sight through hidden mysteries;
> Those milke-white Doues her spotlesse Innocence;
> Those Serpents at her feete her victory showes
> Ouer deceite and guile, her rankest foes,

And by that Cristall Mirrour at her Brest,
The cleernesse of her Conscience is expresst.

(sig. B3v)

In his 1616 Show Munday helpfully 'impos'd' (his term) on the figure of William Walworth a requirement to explicate, at some length, the meaning of each individual device (*Chrysanaleia*, sig. C2v). In the same work he also comments that the characters of 'Iustice, Authority, Lawe, Vigilancy, Peace, Plentie and Discipline . . . as all the rest [of the Show's figures], are *best* obserued by their seuerall Emblems and properties' (sig. B4r; my emphasis).[193] In *Camp-bell* the figure of 'Religion' is clothed in 'a Virgin vesture of pure white, vayled round with a flame colour Tinsell shadowe. She holdes a rich Booke in one hand, and a siluer rod in the other, as her Ensignes of good reward and encouragement' (sig. B1r). 'Religion' is thus made recognisable both by colour (as we will see below) and by her traditional 'Ensignes'. Munday's use of the pelican in *Chrysanaleia* is a good example of the use in these works of the conventional qualities of an animal to serve as an emblem: in this case, the pelican's selfless care for her progeny epitomises the Lord Mayor's equivalent role in relation to the citizenry, just as she does in Whitney's *Choice of emblemes* (see Figure 14). *Sidero-Thriambos* makes the motivation for the use of such emblems clearer still. Here Munday explains their multiple functions, some very practical, and puts forward a defence of the idea that a picture speaks a thousand words. He writes that

> for better understanding the true morality of this deuice, the person-ages haue all Emblemes and Properties in their hands, & so neere them, that the weakest capacity may take knowledge of them, which course in such solemne Triumphes hath alwaies beene allowed of best obseruation: both for auoiding trouble to the Magistrate, by tedious and impertinent speeches, and deuouring the time, which craueth diligent expedition. (sig. C1v)

As Munday implies, emblems often had a didactic function. Indeed, Jonson himself differentiated pageant devices from simple 'hieroglyphickes' on the basis that the former bore a message peculiar to the occasion: 'the Garments, and Ensignes deliuer the nature of the person', he writes, 'and the Word the present office' (*B. Ion: his part*, sig. B2v).[194] As Munday's use of the phrase 'the true moral-ity of this deuice' indicates, this use of emblematic figures drew on conventions going back to the morality dramas of the preceding centuries. The figures of 'Iustice, Authority, Lawe' and the rest thus

Quod in te eſt, prome.

Ad eundem.

Tн е Pellican, for to reuiue her yóunge,
   Doth peirce her breſt, and geue them of her blood:
Then ſearche your breſte, and as yow haue with tonge,
With penne proceede to doe our countrie good:
    Your zeale is great, your learning is profounde,
    Then helpe our wantes, with that you doe abounde.

Parad. Poët.
Cor Pharius roſtro figit
pelecanus acuto, :
Et ſe pronatis ſo ne-
cat ipſe ſuis.

De par-

14 'Pelican' emblem from Geffrey Whitney, *A choice of emblemes* (sig. L4r)

have their roots in this allegorical tradition. As Bergeron notes,
Munday's use of the word 'emblem' both here and in other texts
such as *Chrysanaleia* demonstrates that 'he quite obviously understands the tradition'.[195] In addition, Munday's practice in these
two works exemplifies Kiefer's claim that pageant writers 'were
mindful that spectators might need help in understanding what they
saw'.[196] Munday is also concerned here to make use of the inherent
economy of the emblem: its ability to encapsulate meanings which
when expressed verbally might be 'tedious' to the onlooker. In
other works he is more expansive. In *Chruso-thriambos* Leofstane
describes 'the Orferie or Pageant' at length on behalf of the Lord
Mayor, making an exception only for those aspects 'that do sufficiently speake themselues in their distinguished places . . . [where]
your eye of heedefull obseruation may spare their further relating'
(sigs C1v–C2r).

   Not all these writers took the same approach, though. In contrast, Heywood was more of Jonson's mind, and his discussion of
how one should interpret his 1631 Show echoes his contemporary's
contemptuous phraseology in *The magnificent entertainment* quite

closely. It is noticeable, in addition, that Heywood writes as if his readers would have witnessed the Show and also would have had no difficulty 'deciphering' the symbolism he had used:

> I have forborne to spend much paper on neede lesse and Impertinent deciphering the worke, or explaining the habits of the persons, as being freely exposed to the publicke view of all the Spectators . . . I shall not need to point vnto them to say, this is a Lyon, and that an Vnicorne, etc. (*Londons ius honorarium*, sig. C4v)

He is not altogether consistent, though, for in the same text Heywood does imply that 'Labels' were supplied to 'shew what fruit [the trees] . . . beare', and Time and Truth have an 'inscription' showing their motto (as do Justice and Mercy later on) (sigs B2v–B3r). It is interesting to note that Munday's 'impertinent speeches' have been replaced by Heywood's 'Impertinent deciphering'. For Heywood, the printed text is not a comprehensive account of the visual spectacle of the Show, but rather a truncated supplement to it.[197] Dekker's approach in *Troia-Noua triumphans* is almost throwaway at times. There is a perfunctory feel to the list of figures in this work:

> Mercury hath his Caduceus, or Charming Rod, his fethered Hat, his Wings, and other properties fitting his condition, Desire carries a burning heart in her hand. Industry is in the shape of an old Country-man, bearing on his shoulder a spade, as the Embleme of Labour. (sig. B2v)

Webster, in contrast, goes to some lengths to ensure that the symbolism he employed was understood in its printed form. For instance, he writes of his description of a tableau which featured Sir Thomas White that 'this relation is somwhat of the largest, only to giue you better light of the figure' (*Monuments of Honor*, sig. B4v). His discomfort with having to take a middle way between the need for detailed exposition and the danger of insulting his heterogeneous audience and/or readership is clear. His text concludes with a brief epilogue which explains the problems he faced: 'I could, a more curious and Elaborate way haue expressd my selfe in these my endeauors, but to haue bin rather too teadious in my Speeches, or too weighty, might haue troubled my Noble Lord, and pusled the vnderstanding of the Common People' (sig. C2v).

'Neede lesse and Impertinent' such extrapolation may have been to Heywood, but Webster's anxiety is shown to be justified in one documented case. The German traveller von Wedel confesses that he remembered only part of the content of Peele's 1585 tableau: 'one of [the characters was] holding a book, another a pair of scales, the third a sceptre. What the others had I forget'.[198] He gives no indication that he understands the significance of the items cited. Although one has to factor in their nationality and hence probable lack of familiarity with some of the more arcane symbolism they witnessed, Busino's, Booth's and von Wedel's experiences of mayoral Shows, when taken alongside that of an Englishman, Gilbert Dugdale (of whom more below), do tend to bear out Wickham's assertion that 'the primary appeal of these occasional festivities . . . was visual'.[199] Furthermore, the difference in approach between Heywood and Webster echoes the debate within the theatre over the relative merits of seeing or hearing a play. Heywood touches on this issue in *Londini emporia* when he refers to onlookers 'who carry their eares in their eyes' (sig. B4r). As with Heywood, Kiefer writes that Jonson's 'condescension' towards those members of the audience who come to see, not hear, a play 'reflects distain for the multitudes who, missing a playwright's profundity, find more entertainment in what they see than in what they hear'.[200]

As an illustration of the potential difficulties, McGrath outlines the numerous contingencies upon which a complete understanding of the precise detail of pageantry (in this case, Rubens's 'Arch of the Mint') could be dependent: 'the keen-sighted spectator who knew something about the natural history of the New World – and . . . the subject would not have been unaccessible – would perhaps have recognised in the small, unprepossessing creature [otherwise designated a rabbit] . . . the chinchilla'.[201] All this, of course, is dependent on said well-informed spectator being sufficiently keen-sighted actually to spot this small animal and its 'somewhat weighty symbolism', let alone distinguish it from a rabbit. These difficulties aside, Watt is justified in her view that in this period 'a highly developed sense of visual allegory' existed, meaning that people were generally habituated to interpreting the more common and conventional forms of allegory and symbolism, which, after all, pervaded much early modern culture.[202] Thus a figure bearing a trumpet would doubtless have been readily identifiable as Fame, even to an onlooker who had not had the benefit of a classical education but who might have browsed a copy of Whitney's *Choice of emblems* or a similar work. At the same time, it is important to foreground the actualities of those occasions when the more 'writerly' dimensions of the Shows may have passed the audience by. Lublin emphasises that 'more than the productions of the professional [theatre] companies, the children's troupes, or even the court masques', the Shows 'deserve consideration primarily as a visual spectacle'.[203] For one thing, as Smuts comments, 'contemporaries had to content themselves with a . . . fragmentary view' of the pageantry, 'since painted emblems could not always be seen clearly from a distance and the noise of the crowd frequently drowned out recited speeches'.[204]

An important aspect of the material history of the Shows is thus the effect of practical constraints on the viewers' experience. The streets were thronged with people, disparate sources indicate that the speeches were at times inaudible and the onlookers must have sometimes struggled to make sense of the entertainment. As Lublin points out, 'the large crowds . . . no doubt created a level of ambient noise far greater than that which would have been found in the public playhouses'.[205] In addition, some of the onlookers would have failed to get much of a decent view of proceedings. The latter obstacle is certainly implied by Gilbert Dugdale's eyewitness account of James's 1604 royal entry, published as *The time triumphant declaring in briefe, the ariual of our soueraigne liedge Lord, King Iames into England*. Crucially, and unlike most of the other eyewitnesses discussed above, Dugdale was an *English* onlooker, and so linguistic difficulties cannot be blamed. Although his description is not of a mayoral Show, the same general issues would have applied. Dugdale attempted, not entirely successfully, to 'interpret' a figure on one of the ceremonial arches but he ended up mistaking the Genius of London for a hermit.[206] His account is reluctant to claim any particular authority and is full of provisos and apologies such as 'I was not very neare', 'I heard it not' and 'as I take it'.[207] When one considers how Busino and von Wedel retold their experiences of mayoral Shows it is plain that Dugdale's experience cannot have been unique. For instance, Dekker's 'Mermaids' are called 'Sirens' by one eyewitness of the 1612 Show, Abraham Scultetus.[208]

Smuts convincingly demonstrates that what might be regarded as irritating or inexplicable inconsistencies in fact 'help us grasp the variety [of] meanings that an occasion like this possessed and the complexity of the cultural issues it raised'. He concludes that 'the muddles and confusions in Dugdale's narrative are . . . revealing, for what they tell us about the difficulty of absorbing complicated pageantry while manoeuvring through tens of thousands of cheering and sometimes inebriated spectators'.[209] Munro too emphasises how 'the inaugural shows could be understood by contemporaries in terms of the violence, density, and impenetrability of the crowd'.[210] As Burden puts it, for many people the Shows were an opportunity 'to shout, wave, drink and in general live it up'.[211] Indeed, unauthorised use of 'squibs and crackers' could sometimes get one into trouble. In November 1629 Benjamin Norton, a Clothworker, appeared before the Court of Aldermen after having been 'arrested for throwing squibbs into the streete upon the Lord Maiors Day past'.[212] Busino relates how an outraged woman struck 'with a bunch of greens' a Spaniard thought to be part of the ambassador's party; the unfortunate man's fine garments were also 'embroidered' with 'soft, fetid mud'.[213] For Parry, even in the context of the aristocratic masque 'most of the actual audience of the time probably remembered it for an extraordinary series of capers cut by Prince Henry or Buckingham, or for the colourful costumes', rather than in its full metaphorical and symbolic complexity.[214] This is not to claim, however, that none of the audience outside of the Lord Mayor and his party were able to hear and understand any of the speeches, resulting in a 'purely visual' experience of the Show, as Bromham assumes: doubtless some of the speeches were audible and comprehensible to some people, and some not.[215] In any case, the Shows were sufficiently broad in their range to appeal to different tastes and interpretative abilities.

To be fair to the viewers, given the practical constraints of the day as outlined elsewhere, many of the pageants piled significance upon significance in a way unlikely to be readily or fully accessible to onlookers. In *Porta pietatis*, for instance, Heywood presents the figure of Piety, upon whose hand sits 'a beautifull Childe, representing Religion, upon whose Shield are figured Time, with his daughter Truth'. Piety is also accompanied in 'another co[m]partment' by representations of the blessed virgin, the 'three Theologicall Graces', and, in addition, the persons of Zeal, Humility and 'Constancies', all of whom bore the appropriate devices (sigs B4v–C1r). Such relatively tiny details would have been hard to ascertain from a distance, and might have been overcome by all the other distractions of the day. Visual impressions would inevitably have dominated the viewers' perceptions. Indeed, Watanabe-O'Kelly asserts that one should not assume that 'the learned aspect' of festivals was that which necessarily 'most interested the spectators'.[216] The speeches that 'explained' the tableau to its audience would have been helpful to them only if they were audible, and we do know that in some cases they were not. In *Metropolis coronata*, for instance, Munday warns that the first speech of the Show should be heard with 'such silence . . . as the season can best permit' (sig. A4v). Furthermore, despite what many modern commentators tend to assume, the descriptions in the printed pamphlets may not correspond precisely to what was experienced on the day. Smuts too argues that many 'have failed to recognise . . . that the elaborate allegorical schemes recorded in printed accounts of . . . processions often bear little relationship to what most spectators actually saw'.[217] Carnegie summarises the likely outcome thus: even if 'out of earshot of the speeches . . . [spectators] would see the mythological figures borne by baroque conveyances of scallop shells or sea-horses, catch the glint of sun on rich gilding . . . They would also see the array of silk flags and painted decoration . . . [and] would probably hear at least some of the music.'[218] There would have been plenty to enjoy even if the minutiae of the pageantry escaped many people.

'To humour the throng': 'popular' elements of the Shows

If the content of the mayoral Shows reflected popular London taste, at least to an extent, then they might be considered analogous to the popular taste in printed texts of 'the general [non-elite] reading public', where, as Watt argues, 'conservatism' and a 'persistence of old-fashioned beliefs' can be detected.[219] Accordingly, there were other elements to the entertainment that, perhaps because they were so taken for granted, or because the poets had little to do with them, were never mentioned in the printed texts. Long-standing traditional figures such as greenmen or 'wild men' should therefore not be overlooked, nor should ancillary roles like that of the man disguised as a giant who went on stilts 'to make roome' in the 1604 Show.[220] Machyn wrote of 'ij vodys [woods, i.e. wild men] and a dulle [devil] with squybes bornyng' in the 1554 Show.[221] Other eye-witness accounts demonstrate that such features of the Shows clearly made an impact on the audiences. They were sometimes employed in other forms of culture as metonyms for the overall entertainment. For instance, the giants in stilts are mentioned in Marston's *Dutch Courtezan*, where a character says 'Yet all will scarce make me so high as one of the Gyants stilts that stalkes before my Lord Maiors pageant' (sig. D4v).[222] Like *Eastward hoe*, which also refers to the Lord Mayor's Show, Marston's play was printed in 1605, suggesting that the semi-revival of the Shows in that year, after the plague hiatus, had increased their cultural currency.[223]

By foregrounding the 'special effects' employed in the Shows one can apprehend more clearly the reasons why the more spectacular aspects of the entertainments are so frequently cited in other works of the period, as well as why eyewitnesses remembered them so vividly. Considerable attention was paid to putting on the most impressive spectacle that ingenuity and funds permitted. I discuss the use of fireworks, one of the chief elements of this kind, further below, but the printed descriptions of the pageant devices themselves provide ample evidence of elaborate and complicated effects. In *The triumphs of honor and vertue*, for instance, Middleton gives an account of the two-part device called 'the Throne of Vertue, and the Globe of Honor'. The device would have taken considerable expertise to bring to life, for the text relates that this 'Globe suddenly opening and flying into eight Cants or distinct parts, discouers in a twinkling, eight bright Personages most gloriously deckt'. This 'Engine', as Middleton calls it, then 'conuert[s] it selfe into a Canopie of Starres: at the foure corners below are lac'd the foure Cardinal Vertues' (sigs C1v–C2r). As well as being quite a feat of early seventeenth-century engineering (no wonder Garret Christmas is called 'an Exquisite Master in his Art' in this text), the device must have been large enough to house eight performers; how the Globe was then transformed into a canopy of stars one can only imagine. Middleton rightly refers to the device as an 'Vnparalel'd Master-piece of Inuention and Art' (sig. C2v).[224] The 'Cristall Sanctuary' in the 1623 Show is equally ornate, with golden columns and silver battlements. Middleton states that it 'is made to open vp in many parts, at fit and conuenient Times', and it is also called 'an vnparaled Maister-peece of Art' (sigs B2v–B3r). Munday, in contrast, simply refers to the first device of *Sidero-Thriambos* as 'very ingeniously and artificially fitted [and] sutable to the dayes solemnity' (sig. A4v). Indeed, Munday's accounts of some of his Shows' more complex devices tend to be more self-deprecating than celebratory: in the latter text he concedes that 'fauourable conceit, must needs supply the defect of impossible performance' (*ibid.*). His disclaimer is borne out by the bathos later on conjured up by the British Bard, who 'smiteth [his] Staffe vpon his foot, & suddenly issueth forth the three seuerall letters of H' pertaining to the names of the Lord Mayor and both Sheriffs, all of which began with an 'H' in 1618.[225]

One cannot imagine Middleton admitting to an 'impossible performance'. Indeed, he and his collaborators had an especial interest in special effects, for their Shows tended to make greater use of them than some of their peers, and accordingly they pervade the printed descriptions. *The triumphs of truth* is particularly preoccupied with such tricks. As well as the 'fiue Islands' artfully

constructed on the river, the 'strange Ship' which conveys the King
and Queen of the Moors is expressly designed to 'astonish' the
onlookers by its ability to move with no visible means of control,
'it hauing neither Saylor nor Pilot' (sig. B4v). Elsewhere, the battle
between Zeal, Truth and Error, which forms the narrative spine of
this text, would have required much use of smoke, mists and the
like: the 'Mount Triumphant', for instance, is 'ouer-spred with a
thicke Sulphurous Darknesse . . . being a Fog or Mist raisde from
Error'. At Truth's command, this mist rises and is transformed into
'a bright spredding Canopy, stucke thicke with Starres, and [with]
beames of Golde shooting forth round about it' (sig. C2r–v). Zeal's
enemy Error has 'Mists hanging at his Eyes' (sig. B2r), the effect of
which was probably created by some kind of gauzy grey fabric. To
defeat these mists Truth bears 'a fan fild with all Starres . . . with
which she parts Darknesse' (sig. B3v). Some local butcher must
surely have supplied the supposedly 'human' heart that Envy eats
whilst seated on her rhinoceros.

As with these striking devices, other elements of the actual pageantry – such as Munday's inclusion of Robin Hood in *Metropolis
coronata* – may also have had a largely crowd-pleasing intent. Like
the giants and greenmen, 'popular' taste of this kind was indulged
but sometimes with ambivalence. Heywood, in particular, seems
regularly to express distain for populist entertainments. In *Londini
emporia* he dismisses the third show by land as 'a Modell deuised
for sport to humour the throng, who come rather to see then to
heare: And without some such intruded Anti-maske, many who
carry their eares in their eyes, will not sticke to say, I will not giue
a pinne for the Show' (sig. B4r). As there were no speeches within
this show – had there been any, he argues, they would 'be drown'd
in noyse and laughter' – he gives no further account of it. His use
of the term 'anti-maske' indicates an aspect of the pageantry that
might be considered antipathetic to the rest. It is hard to say if
Heywood is correct that crowd-pleasing spectacle was an essential
– if for him, perhaps unpalatable – part of the pageantry, or if his
words are more a reflection of personal bias. The frequency with
which he makes statements in his mayoral Shows along the same
lines, however, suggests it may be the latter. In *Londini artium*, for
instance, Heywood says little about the fifth show by land, on the
basis that 'the nature thereof being in the Poeme layd open euen
unto the meanest capacity' (sig. Cr), and in *Londini sinus salutis*
'the Third Plat-forme' is apparently 'contrived only for Pastime,
to please the vulgar, and therefore deserues no further Charractar,

then a plaine nomination, as devised onely to please the eye, but no way to feast the eare: and so I leave it' (sig. A8r).[226]

Despite this body of evidence, however, Heywood's treatment of an equivalent 'eye-pleasing' pageant in *Londini speculum* may, as Richard Rowland has argued, indicate a more teasing than wholly censorious approach.[227] Heywood here expounds in more detail, and with more empathy than in his other Shows, on the rationale for not including an account of a show which 'meerly consisteth of Anticke gesticulations, dances, and other Mimicke postures'. On the face of it, the rhetoric in this passage begins along the same lines as that quoted above, but Heywood does go on to say that these 'vulgar' devices are not 'altogether to be vilefied by the most supercilious, and censorious', for they take place in a heterogeneous environment – 'where all Degrees, Ages, and Sexes are assembled', as he puts it – and they should therefore be considered in a more generous light. All these constituencies, he argues, are 'looking to bee presented with some fancy or other, according to their expectations and humours'. Indeed – and for Heywood this acts as a kind of trump card – 'grave and wise men have been of opinion, that it is convenient, nay necessitous, upon the like occasions, to mixe seria iocis; for what better can set off matter, than when it is interlaced with mirth?' (sig. C2r).

One can look to the work of a contemporary of Heywood, James Shirley, for a less ambivalent treatment of popular entertainments. Like Jasper Mayne (whose work is quoted in Chapter 5), Shirley approached the Lord Mayor's Show from the vantage point of a court writer. He describes the Show in his 1633 play *A contention for honour and riches*, and here offers quite a lengthy and detailed satiric account of the persistence of 'popular' elements in the Shows of Heywood's period of dominance.[228] Two characters, Clod (a country gentleman) and Gettings (a London merchant), are at odds over the affections of a 'Lady' they are both courting. Their dispute ends in a duel, in the run-up to which Clod mocks Gettings's civic pretensions. The passage is worth quoting at length:

> the next day after Simon and Jude; when you goe a feasting to Westminster with your Gallyfoist and your pot-guns, to the very terror of the Paper-whales, when you land in sholes, and make the understanders in Cheapside, wonder to see ships swimme upon mens shoulders, when the Fencers flourish . . . when your whifflers are hangd in chaines, and Hercules Club spits fire about the Pageants, though the poore children catch cold that shew like painted cloth, and are onely kept alive with sugar plummes, with whom, when the

word is given, you march to Guild-hall, with every man his spoone in
his pocket, where you looke upon the Giants, and feed like Sarazens,
till you have no stomacke to Pauls in the afternoone: I have seene
your Processions, and heard your Lions and Camels make speeches,
in stead of Grace before and after dinner. (sigs B4v–C1r)

His satiric purpose to one side (lions and camels do not deliver
speeches in the Shows), Shirley provides some lovely detail in this
speech. He reveals the way in which 'whales' were constructed
from paper, the fact that the water-pageant featured ships and was
carried 'upon mens shoulders', that fireworks would have been used
to make 'Hercules Club' 'spit fire', and that Company dignitaries
carried their own spoons to the Guildhall banquet. Parodic or not,
the account appears to be accurate in a number of respects. For
instance, the Ironmongers' records for 1609 indicate that 'a whale'
was used in the water show: it was 'to row with Fins open for
Fireworkes at the mouth and water vented at the head' and it may
even have carried 'a Blackamore' in its mouth.[229] This beast must
have been quite a spectacle: if such devices were commonly used it
is no wonder that Shirley mentions it. In *Metropolis coronata* too
Munday describes a 'Sea Chariot . . . shaped like to a Whale, or the
huge Leuiathan of the Sea', which bears Fitz-Alwin and the 'eight
royall Vertues' (sig. A4r).

   Shirley and Heywood in their different ways reveal that traditions died hard. Despite Jordan's claim in the dedication to the
Grocers in *London's Joy* (1681) that 'in these Triumphs there is
nothing Designed, Written, Said or Sung, that was ever Presented
in any Show till this present Day' (sig. A2v), in fact where the
pageants reflected the traditional iconography and symbolism of
the Companies they were understandably reused, as the properties
were expensive. Indeed, on some occasions they were even borrowed between companies.[230] Not only were the properties reused
in subsequent Shows. In 1616 the Fishmongers' Company and the
Corporation liaised with the master of the King's barges to share
the use of barges for two events that happened to take place within
a few days of each other, the Lord Mayor's inaugural show and
Charles's investiture as Prince of Wales (the text of which Middleton
wrote and which was published as *Ciuitatis amor*).[231] Compared to
professional stage companies, MacIntyre and Epp assert, 'the same
few costumes and properties were generally used every year [for
the Shows], with only occasional updating'; the court masque, in
contrast, where money was not an issue, 'always used specially
designed garments'.[232] Munday, for instance, reworked a pageant

ship at least four times (five, if one includes *Londons loue*), signal-
ling the importance of ships to the trading companies to which many
Lord Mayors belonged. The ship was named the 'Barke-Hayes' for
the Drapers in 1614 (associated on this occasion with Sir Francis
Drake), was reinvented the following year as Jason's 'Argoe', and
then again as 'the Fishmongers Esperanza, or Hope of London' for
the latter company in 1616, where it also doubled up – 'by generall
sufferance', as Munday puts it – for 'the same fishing Busse, wherein
S. Peter sate mending his Nets' (*Chrysanaleia*, sig. B1r–v). If said
'general sufferance' is not forthcoming and the reader is not happy
to accept the analogy, Munday has another to hand: the ship can
alternatively be taken for 'one of those fishing Busses, which not
only enricheth our kingdome . . . but helpeth also . . . all other lands'
(sig. B1v).[233] In *The triumphs of the Golden Fleece*, a text which
uniquely focuses exclusively on the water show, Munday again
nominates the 'Barge of apt conueyance' as 'a beatifull and curious
Argoe . . . wherein Prince Jason, and his valiant Argonautes' went
to fetch the golden fleece (sig. A3v).

As this suggests, the Shows regularly reused pageant images, and
Munday is especially prone to take advantage of such economies.
In *Chruso-thriambos* Nicholas Faringdon, the four times Lord
Mayor from the Goldsmiths' Company, is wakened from his tomb
by the figure of Time; five years later William Walworth, an equally
famed Fishmonger, is similarly raised from death or slumber to
participate in that year's inauguration. Munday's liking for the
trope of resurrection is expounded in *Metropolis coronata* when
Robin Hood declares 'Since Graues may not their Dead containe,
/ Nor in their peacefull sleepes remaine, / But Triumphes and great
Showes must use them' (sig. C1v). Resurrection applies to the
devices themselves, too. *Chruso-thriambos* contains a number of
features of the pageantry that was to reoccur a few years later in
Chrysanaleia. As well as having tombs, an Indian king and queen
ride on a leopard in both productions. Munday goes beyond civic
pageantry to reuse some of the characters from his popular Rose
plays *The Downfall of Robert, Earl of Huntington* and *The Death
of Robert, Earl of Huntington* in *Metropolis coronata*, down to
the Skeltonic verse of Friar Tuck. Indeed, the text at this point
lapses into a dramatic dialogue that emphasises the extent to which
Munday is revisiting earlier works.[234] This practice of reuse was
not restricted to Munday's Shows, however. The 1637 Show has St
Katherine riding in a scallop drawn by a sea-chariot, a device with
many similarities to that used in other Shows, such as *Troia-Noua*

triumphans, although on the earlier occasion it was Neptune who rode in the scallop-shaped chariot. Heywood was then to revive the same chariot in *Londini status pacatus*, where this time the figure it bore was 'Nilus'.

As well as the devices, sideshows and so on, music was also an essential element of the Shows. Palmer writes that in civic pageantry music had from the very first been 'used to separate the various components of the procession and to emphasise the grandeur of both the occasion and the participants'. Even the instruments that were habitually employed – trumpets, drums and fifes – were those conventionally used for processions; they were chosen to produce the loudest and most robust sound possible.[235] On land, the City Waits usually stood on the leads above the porch of St Peter's church on Cheapside.[236] The trip back and forth to Westminster along the river also had a musical accompaniment, where again trumpets and drums were used.[237] In *The triumphs of the Golden Fleece* Munday testified to the employment of 'Drummes, Fifes, Trumpets, and other Iouiall Instruments' during the water show (sig. A3r–v). Trumpets were used particularly to punctuate proceedings and to draw the audience's attention to significant events, as in *Chrysanaleia*: 'so soone as the Lord Maior is come neere, and way made for his better attention: the Genius speaketh, the Trumpets sound their seuerall Surden flourishes [and] Walworth ariseth' (sig. B3r).[238]

The evidence indicates that accompanying music for the procession (especially on the water) was probably instrumental, but the pageantry did include songs as well as speeches, evidently sung by the characters in the various devices. These too are often overlooked. In *Tes Irenes Trophaea* 'The Song of the Muses' meets the Lord Mayor at Paul's Churchyard; the words and music are provided in the text. This 'song' looks to have been composed for the occasion: Euterpe and Terpsichore sing that they 'are come to meet thee [the Lord Mayor] on the way, / that vnto thy honours shrine, / We might dedicate this day' (sig. B2r). There is 'the Song of Robin Hood and his Huntes-men' in *Metropolis coronata*; in Dekker's *Londons tempe* the smiths sing 'in praise of Iron' (sig. B2v) and in *Troia-Noua triumphans* a song is heard from a hidden singer (sig. C3v). The Robin Hood song in *Metropolis coronata* has a ballad-style quality in keeping with the anachronistic tenor of the treatment in this work of Robin Hood and his crew. As in Squire's text, the song in *Troia-Noua triumphans* was also specific to the Show, for it picks up on the emblematic figures utilised in the pageantry such as Fame and Envy, and it also mentions Swinnerton, the new Lord Mayor, by name. The first device of *The triumphs of truth* features 'a sweet voyce married to [the] words' of a song, the music for which – or 'the Song with the Note', as the text has it – is also printed in this work. Going by the allusion to 'his Honors Confirmation', this song was also likely to have been composed for the day (sigs A3v and D3v–D4r).

To add to the din there was, according to Busino, 'an incessant shower of squibs and crackers' thrown from windows down on to the streets.[239] Once again, a focus on the printed text can give only a limited or perhaps even misleading sense of the full range of the day's festivities, some of which had little to do with the pageantry as such but which might have been there to offer what Williams calls 'light relief from allegory and history'.[240] Indeed, because there were no actual pageants in 1630 – and thus no printed text – this year is absent from most commentaries, although the Merchant Taylors' accounts make it clear that the full range of other entertainments did take place that year. Sideshows were surprisingly ubiquitous. As Shirley mentions 'fencers' in *A contention for honour and riches*, so the Merchant Taylors, for instance, employed 'viii men which did fyte with hand swordes' in 1602, as in other years, to provide the crowds with further entertainment.[241] In 1605 the Show included the traditional giant, carried about on stilts. Giants had since time immemorial been very common in all forms of civic drama, and they were sometimes included in the more formal pageant devices of the mayoral Shows in our period. For instance, Dekker has 'Ryot and Calumny, in the shapes of Gyants' accompanying Envy in the 'Forlorn Castle' device that concludes *Troia-Noua triumphans*; they then shoot off fireworks (sig. B4r).

As we saw above with Shirley's reference to 'Hercules Club [that] spits fire', fireworks were clearly extremely popular for these occasions, both on land and as part of the water show. Indeed, they stand as a metonym for the Show as a whole in Fennor's 1612 *Cornu-Copiae*, which refers to the spectators' experience of 'when . . . the fire-workes flye' (sig. H1r). Their use is quite extensive when one starts looking for it in the printed texts of the Shows themselves, and they demonstrate a range and originality that few other cultural forms from this period share. The whale used for the 1609 Show appears to have issued fireworks from its mouth, in much the same way, one can assume, as a hell mouth would have been used in earlier civic drama. Going by other references in livery company accounts, this effect was likely to have been created by the use of aquavitae, probably controlled by an operator inside the whale.[242] The use of fireworks in the water show is also signalled in *Londons ius honorarium*, where Heywood states that 'two craggy Rockes . . . are full of monsters, as Serpents, Snakes, Dragons, &c. some spitting Fier' (sig. A4r). *Londons tempe* has the figure of Jove with 'a Mace of Triple fire in his hand burning' (sig. B2r). In this instance we are fortunate to have a pictorial impression of the effect of his 'triple fire'. Booth's drawing of the 'London's tempe' pageant does show flames shooting out from Jove's hand; he calls the device 'the sceptre of triple fiery beams' (see Figure 6).[243] The three feathers used to indicate the arms of the Prince of Wales in *Monuments of Honor* somewhat riskily 'haue lights in them' to make 'a more goodly' show in the darkness (sig. C1v). Middleton too mentions the use of pyrotechnic devices throughout *The triumphs of truth*. On his arrival back at the City, the Lord Mayor is greeted by the figure of Zeal, dressed 'in a Garment of Flame-coloured Silke, with a bright haire on his head, from which shoot Fire-beames'; in his right hand he holds 'a flaming Scourge' (sig. B1v). At the end of the Show Zeal reappears with 'his head circled with strange Fires'. From his head – one assumes by dexterous use of a firework or by some combustible element being thrown – 'a Flame shootes out' and sets fire to Error's chariot 'and all the Beasts that are ioynde to it' (sig. D2v).[244] The wooden chariot and beasts would probably have had rosin thrown on them for even more spectacular incendiary effect when the flame reached them. This Show must have attained an extraordinary climax, especially if the chariot was left 'glowing in Imbers' in the dark October evening, as Middleton's text has it.

Pyrotechnic devices had practical as well as spectacular functions. Busino tells how in 1617 'there were . . . men masked as wild giants who by means of fireballs and wheels hurled sparks in the faces of the mob and over their persons'.[245] Zuizin saw the same device, which he recounted explicitly as part of a crowd control technique: 'people in masks', he wrote, 'carried palms with fireworks, and they threw from them sparkling fire on both sides because of the great press of people, that they might give way'.[246] Another contemporary source testifies to the regular appearance of such figures in mayoral pageantry, even in their early days. In Whetstone's *Promos and Cassandra* (1578) there are 'two men, apparrelled, lyke greene men at the Mayors feast, with clubbes of fyre worke' (sig. N1r). Going by eyewitness accounts and some contemporary images (see Figure 15), these 'fire clubs' look to have sprayed sparks around to produce what Butterworth calls 'a powerful pyrotechnic and

15 'Wild man' with fire club, from John Bate, *The mysteryes of nature, and art*, sig. N1r

dramatic effect'.[247] The greenmen were regularly accompanied by 'devils' spitting fire. No wonder they were remembered by onlookers for their effectiveness in clearing the way.

'All the bachelars in cremesun damaske hodes': colour and costume in the Shows

From the start of the day to its torch-lit end the spectacle was, of course, predominantly visual, and another way in which meanings were conveyed to the mayoral procession and to the onlookers was through the use of particular kinds of fabric and colour. The majority of the extant eyewitness accounts of mayoral Shows provide considerable detail of the clothing worn for the occasion, in terms of both colour and fabric, which echoes the attention paid to such matters in the livery company records.[248] The drawings of the Lord Mayor, sheriffs and aldermen in 1614 in van Meer's album, for instance, show them on fine horses wearing resplendent red robes (see Figure 16), echoing Machyn's repeated references in his diary to red, crimson and scarlet robes. Elements of costuming can also be gleaned from the illustrations relating to the 1616 Show. Smuts

16 The Lord Mayor in procession, from Michael van Meer's 'Album Amicorum'

has commented that 'the single most impressive expression of royal grandeur . . . was ornate clothing. In Tudor England the sight of rich silks, brocade and jewels was a compelling expression of prestige and power.'[249] His argument applies equally to civic 'grandeur'. Indeed, expenditure on fabric for the Company members and others in the procession encompassed a considerable share of the total cost of the Show, comparable in many cases to the costs of the pageants and greatly eclipsing the sums spent on costumes for the actual performers. The Merchant Taylors, for instance (who tended to spend lavishly on fabrics) paid over £170 for material for 'poore mens gownes' for the procession in 1602, a token of the importance the Companies attached to this aspect of the event.[250] Similarly, the Haberdashers' second largest outlay for the 1631 Show (after £200 to Christmas for 'pageantes and shewes') was over £140 for '17 blew clothes' alone.[251] Even the 'marryners that went in the Galley and Galley foyst' wore blue silk coats.[252] The Skinners were less extravagant, but even so they paid out almost £100 on the purchase of 'blew cloth' for '74 gownes & 44 coates' in 1629 (not including the additional expense of making the garments).[253]

Here is another divergence with the masque, incidentally. Although, as we have seen, they devoted considerable expense to furnishing their members and the usual roster of 'poor men' with clothing for the occasion, the Companies do not appear to be especially interested in the costumes used for the pageant performers. Their records tend to refer only rather tersely to 'apparelling personages', with no detail of what said personages were apparelled in. For earlier guild plays and for the Midsummer Watch, in contrast, it seems either that there was a store of properties and costumes held by the guilds or that these were purchased specially. For the Shows the responsibility for arranging costumes for the performers was invariably delegated to the writer and artificer team. As a result, only occasionally do the livery company records reveal much about how these costumes were acquired: they were hired in 1609, for instance – or 'old and borrowed', in the Company's view. Indeed, if, as seems likely in Munday's case at least, those who worked behind the scenes on mayoral pageantry had connections with the clothing trade, then costumes would have not needed any specific comment in Company records. It is equally possible that with the stage connections of almost all of the writers, and with the involvement of men like Thomas Kendall on occasion, the costumes may have been borrowed from theatre companies. In contrast, extensive records survive of the planning of masque costumes for their aristocratic performers, as well as quite a number of the actual designs. This also stands as a point of departure between the practices of the professional stage and those of the mayoral Shows: in the case of the latter the Companies appear to have had little interest in how the performers were costumed beyond requiring the creative team to organise 'apparel'.

There is one notable exception to this norm, however, in the Ironmongers' Court Book for 1629. As I have already signalled, these records are extraordinarily explicit about the content of the Show and as such have a great deal of as yet unexplored value for the history of pageant performance. They surely contain the text of Dekker and Christmas's original 'plot' for the various devices, which reveals the costuming of the characters in considerable detail, thus enabling even the modern reader to visualise their appearance. For instance, Oceanus, the King of the Sea, bore on his head 'a diadem' of gold, which was 'a Coronett of Siluer Scollops' topped with coral and pearl. The rest of his apparel is also described: 'his habitt is antique, the stuffe watchett [light blue] and siluer, a mantle crossing his body with siluer waues' and he also wore 'Bases and Buskins'. His wife Tethys, who rode on a sealion, had 'longe disheuelled' hair; she too wore a coronet, in this case of 'gold and [purple] pearl'. Her 'garments [were] rich' and her mantle made of 'Taffaty'. Of the other pageants, we are told that the Indian boy held 'a longe Tobacco pipe' and a dart, and that Lemnion's forge featured smiths dressed in 'waste Coats and Lether Aprons [with] their hair blacke and shaggy'.[254]

The royal couple's gold and silver attire exemplifies the richness of the colour and fabrics used on these occasions, evidence of which is available fairly often in the printed texts. Descriptions of costume also occur from time to time in eyewitness accounts (from the latter, for instance, it appears that the some of the performers wore masks).[255] One can readily visualise how the figure of Oceanus would have appeared in the 1620 Show, with his sceptre of green weeds, 'azure locks' and 'mantle of sea greene taffaty, lymed with waues and fishes' (*Tes Irenes Trophaea*, sig. A3r). In *Metropolis coronata* Munday describes how the argonauts wear 'faire guilt Armours' and carry 'Shields honoured with the Impresse of the Golden fleece'; even the rowers of the Argoe 'had all their garments . . . sprinkled ouer with golde, euen as if it had showred downe in droppes vpon them' (sig. A4r). Likewise, 'Londons Genius' in *Chrysanaleia* wears 'a golden Crowne on his head [with] golden Wings at his backe' and he bears 'a golden Wande in his hand' (sig. B3r). Gold and silver performed a dual purpose. They signalled the sheer ostentation of the event and the willingness of the Companies to spend lavishly, and they also added to the spectacle: one can imagine the light catching the gilded armour worn by Munday's argonauts.

It was not only the actual performers who were costumed. The Lord Mayor himself would have been resplendent in red, with his chain and cap of office, riding a horse with elaborate trappings (see Figure 16). To accompany him, the Bachelors of the Company were 'in foins' and 'budge' to mark their status within the Company.[256] Given the attention within the Companies' accounts to the cost of dressing their own members up for the inauguration, it is unsurprising that Busino devotes an entire section of his report to describing the attire of the civic dignitaries, especially the Grocers' liverymen:

> their gowns resemble those of a Doctor of Laws or the Doge, the sleeves being very wide in the shoulder and trimmed with various materials, such as plush, velvet, martens' fur, foynes and a very beautiful kind of astrachan, while some wear sables . . . Over the left shoulder they wore a sort of satchel, one half of red cloth and the other black, fastened to a narrow stole. There were other gownsmen in long cloth gowns with satchels of red damask . . . Others again wore another kind of appendage, also red, on the shoulder, and a fourth set had small stoles about the throat.[257]

Lupold von Wedel, over thirty years earlier, also began his description of a mayoral inauguration with his recollections of what the chief protagonists were wearing. His account demonstrates that the traditional attire had not substantially changed in the interim. On the day of the handover from one Lord Mayor to another in the Guildhall, 28 October, von Wedel reports that both the new Lord Mayor and his predecessor

> wear long coats of a brownish violet coloured cloth, lined with marten, and over these other coats of the same colour faced with calabar [squirrel] skins . . . On their heads they wear black caps . . . After them marched twenty-four councillors clad in the same manner, and in the town hall [Guildhall] stood forty-eight men . . . in long black coats also lined with marten, wearing on their backs large bags . . . of cloth half red half black, with a bandalier of the same colours over the shoulder and fastened before the chest.[258]

Vivid colour and the prevalence of luxurious furs and fabrics are among the strongest impressions one gains from the varied accounts of mayoral inaugurations. Indeed, the 'Tryumph' is cited alongside

'Maske, Tilt-yard [and] Play-house' by the anonymous author of
the anti-cross-dressing pamphlet *Hic mulier* as one of the specifically urban venues for the transgression of clothing norms.[259] The
use of fur and rich fabrics, naturally, was intended to reflect the
wealth and prestige of the Lord Mayor and his Company, whilst
colours would have helped the onlooker 'read' the Show as it passed
by. Anne Sutton concurs that 'the increasingly elaborate ceremonial
– of which liveries were such an important visual expression . . .
supported the authority of the civic officials'.[260] The display of the
symbolic regalia like the sword and the Lord Mayor's collar was
an important aspect of the procession. As Heywood puts it, 'you
this Day behold this Scarlet worne, / And Sword of Iustice thus in
publike borne; / The Cap of Maintenance, [and] Coller of Esses
[chain of S-shaped links]' (*Londini artium*, sig. B3r). Accordingly,
the image of the Lord Mayor in procession in van Meer's album
depicts the sword-bearer marching in front of the mayor, aldermen and sheriffs. Contemporary witnesses of the Shows would
have been habituated to 'reading' social status and other signs of
identity from clothing and regalia. Von Wedel comments that 'the
queen gives [a golden] chain to every newly elected [mayor], the
members of the town council who have been elected [mayor] once
before, wear likewise such chains, the other have only stripes of
black velvet on their coats'.[261] The significance of such accoutrements was well known: Dekker's Simon Eyre in *The Shoemaker's
Holiday*, for instance, cites the gold chain as a symbol of his newly
gained mayoral status.

Livery companies, of course, habitually used clothing as a
means of corporate identity, and this tendency was indulged to the
maximum during the Shows. Catherine Richardson notes that

> public displays of civic structures, designed to strengthen the percep-
> tion of hierarchies of government and the right ordering of society,
> necessarily employed visual spectacles of allegiance. The strength
> of identification with or exclusion from such groups was frequently
> negotiated and expressed through what people wore, especially on
> extraordinary communal occasions.[262]

To illustrate her point, one can see that certain colours had meanings
just as animals and other emblems did, such as red for the dignitaries
and blue for the 'poor men'.[263] The very distinction between those
Bachelors of the livery company dressed in 'foins' and those in the
lowlier 'budge' demonstrates how graduations in civic status were
reflected visually. Thus, as Richardson suggests, specific forms of

clothing can be seen as 'one of the boundaries between the personal and the communal'.[264] Children were also used as 'pages' within the procession, carrying nosegays of flowers on staffs.[265] One cannot, therefore, make hard and fast distinctions between costumed performers per se and those citizens who processed. The dignitaries in procession were an integral part of the spectacle, as were the 'poor men', dressed by the Company's munificence for the occasion and in themselves a public embodiment of that generosity.[266] Indeed, Archer notes that to manifest further the City's munificence 'the poor at the head of the procession carried shields with coats of arms of company benefactors'.[267] The temporary inclusion of representatives of 'the poor' into the corporate body of the livery is also another marker of the putative inclusiveness of the Show.

As well as clothing, to add to the overwhelming sense of colour and ostentation, banners, pavises, streamers, many made of silk and other expensive fabrics, as well as 'targettes' (decorated shields), featured heavily in the Companies' expenditure and were highly decorated for the occasion with coats of arms and so on.[268] Heraldic emblems were also an imporant part of the symbolic lexicon of Lord Mayor's Day. Munday notes in *Metropolis coronata* (a text particularly interested in heraldry) that a 'pelleted Lyon' and a 'sea-Horse' were chosen for heraldic reasons, the first being 'the supporter to the Drapers Armes' and the latter 'belonging to the Lord Maiors Armorie', as he puts it (sig. B2v). The Company records show that the banners and the like were usually painted and gilded and bore coloured silk fringes.[269] In addition, the barges were furnished with embroidered cloths. Typically, in 1610 the Merchant Taylors required 'fowre Banners, for the shipp, one with the kinges Armes, an other with the Princes Armes, one with the Citties Armes, and an other with the Companies Armes'.[270] One eyewitness, the Russian ambassador Zuizin, relates that the Lord Mayor travelled to Westminster in 'a decorated ship, painted in all sorts of various colors . . . and there were banners and great decorated flags'.[271]

Companies usually employed one or more ensigns to flourish their colours during the procession and feast. Here too the use of colour was predominant, for even the staves were painted ('whyte and blewe', in the case of the Merchant Taylors in 1602). The latter Company also paid £5 for 'fiftie pensilles [small pennants] a foote and a halff long a peece, wrought in fyne gould and silver in oyle'.[272] Large silk pavises were normally ordered, featuring the arms of the City, the monarch, the Lord Mayor himself, and his Company. For the banquet after the Show, the Guildhall was hung with tapestries for the Lord Mayor's feast, and often a painting of the monarch was brought in especially for the occasion.[273] The attention to detail is quite extraordinary: the Merchant Taylors stipulated, for instance, specific quantities of coloured and blue and white 'silke frindg' and twelve feathers for the standard bearers.[274] From starting the events with a procession accompanied by trumpeters to ending it with a feast served on gold and silver plate (even the 'ale potts' were gilded in 1622), no one could have been in any doubt that this was a special day indeed.

The high-profile splendour of Lord Mayor's day did not end at nightfall but was conferred a kind of immortality (or at least a greater longevity than that of a fleeting day) through the medium of print. There are, as I'll show further in the next chapter, many fascinating and complex relations between the event on the streets and the event perpetuated in textual form. Neither, I believe, should be regarded as having primacy: to understand the Show in its fullest dimensions, textual traces must be explored alongside and as a complement to the vestiges in the first-hand accounts and other contemporary witnesses discussed in this chapter.

Notes

1 *Rituals of Royalty*, pp. 1- 2.
2 'Occasional events', p. 180.
3 *The Early Stuart Masque*, p. 6.
4 Bad weather did not just threaten the inauguration: James Pemberton's election in September 1611, Munday notes, was characterised by such extraordinary weather (with 'Snow, Sleete, and rough winde') that it 'exceed[ed] the memory of man to speak the like'. Such was the auspiciousness of Pemberton's election, naturally, that at that instant the sun 'thrust foorth his Golden beames' to mark the moment (*Chruso-thriambos*, sigs C2v–C3r).
5 Paster, *The Idea of the City*, p. 139.
6 Booth's papers also contained the Utrecht panorama of the northern prospect of the City (he was a more than competent draughtsman). According to Edmund Howe, Christian, the Prince of Anhalt, adviser to the Elector Palatine, watched the festivities for William Craven's inauguration in 1610 and was then 'with all his Germayne trayne . . . entertained at the lord maiors feast' (cited in Sayle, *Lord Mayors' Pageants*, p. 86).
7 Van Meer's 'Album', fol. 90. These images were clearly made by an expert limner and would have been commissioned (see Schlueter, 'Michael van Meer's Album', p. 302). The album also contains illustrations of a St George's Day procession and of the King riding to Parliament, as well as the emblem of Virtue on a rock, which

may reflect the kind of symbolism repeatedly used in the Shows (*Brittannia's honor*, for instance, includes Amphitrite standing in the river on 'an Artificiall Rocke' (sig. A4r)), although there does not seem to be any direct link with any of the Shows that took place during van Meer's sojourn in London. Thomas Hayes, Lord Mayor in 1614, signed the album (this page has not survived).

8 See Astington, 'The ages of man', pp. 80 and 88 n. 3.

9 See the copy of STC 14756 held in the Houghton Library, Harvard University. This book has an extraordinary range of annotations in different hands.

10 'The ages of man', pp. 82 and 85.

11 There were other visitors, such as James's Danish brother-in-law Christian IV. In 1624 the *English* ambassador to the United Provinces, Sir Ralph Winwood, attended the Show. Such guests were often invited to the Lord Mayor's feast at the end of the day: Munday draws attention to 'the Lords of his Maiesties most honourable priuie Councell, and other great personages' who were at the feast in 1615 (*Metropolis coronata*, sig. B3r). The Earl of Leicester was a guest at the mayoral feast in 1560.

12 Jansson and Rogozhin, *England and the North*, pp. 160–2. On at least one occasion the Russian ambassadorial delegation refused to attend the mayoral inauguration because they could not accept being lower in precedence to the Lord Mayor (see Musvik, 'The King of Barbary's envoy', p. 231).

13 Munro, *The Figure of the Crowd*, p. 26.

14 Cowan and Steward, *The City and the Senses*, pp. 3–4.

15 Ravelhofer, *The Early Stuart Masque*, p. 5.

16 'The ages of man', p. 74.

17 Seaver, *Wallington's World*, p. 221 n. 33.

18 See Symonds, 'The diary of John Greene', p. 389. (Perhaps he had a hangover.)

19 Machyn's description is also reproduced in Sayle, *Lord Mayors' Pageants*, pp. 2–3. Smith's manuscript is now in the British Library; part of it is reproduced in Munday, ed. Nichols, *Chrysanaleia*, pp. 8–10. (I am very grateful to Andy Gordon for sharing his transcription of this text with me.) Smith wrote the 'citizens' play', *The Hector of Germanie*, in 1613.

20 Machyn was a parish clerk who had an interest in the history of London as well as contemporary events; he was also a Merchant Taylor. Nichols, who edited the diary in the 1840s, comments that Machyn 'takes a lively interest in the pageantry and holidaymaking of the City' and 'seldom fails to notice the Shows of Lord Mayor's day' ('Preface'). Thomas Heywood himself claimed in *Troia Britanica*: 'I haue beheld our Soueraign, Strangers feast, / . . . But chiefely when the royall Brittish Iames, / at Greenwitch feasted the great King of Danes' (sig. S6v).

21 Mortimer, 'Tudor chronicler or sixteenth-century diarist?', p. 983.
22 *Ibid.*, p. 995.
23 For instance, some eyewitness accounts of one of Elizabeth's progresses include the detail of how the Queen reacted to the deaths of three spectators caused by the collapse of a wall (see Archer and Knight, 'Elizabetha Triumphans', p. 17).
24 'Abram Booth's eyewitness account', p. 19.
25 *CSP Venetian*, vol. XV, p. 62. This incident is also discussed in a similar vein by Smuts: see 'Occasional events', pp. 180–1, and 'Public ceremony', p. 75. Heinemann makes the plausible suggestion that this incident may have prompted Middleton's portrayal of Gondomar, the Spanish ambassador, in *A Game at Chesse* (*Puritanism and Theatre*, p. 129). The behaviour Busino describes may not have been uncommon: John Chamberlain wrote to Dudley Carleton in October 1600 that 'your cousin Lytton brings his son William to see the Lord Mayor's pageant, and these uncouth ambassadors' (*CSPD*, vol. CCLXXV, p. 100). Busino also left eyewitness accounts of the masque (see Ravelhofer, *The Early Stuart Masque*, pp. 22–3). Interestingly, Hirschfeld notes that 'ambassadors saw themselves as 'being "on stage" when they attended masque performances'; from the case of the Spanish ambassador in 1617, one can see that this was not always voluntary (*Joint Enterprises*, p. 62).
26 Utrecht MS 1196, fol. 50r (translated in Lusardi and Gras, 'Abram Booth's eyewitness account', p. 22).
27 'Abram Booth's eyewitness account', p. 22.
28 *Collections* V, p. 8.
29 'Abram Booth's eyewitness account', p. 21.
30 See *Collections* V, p. 7, and Lusardi and Gras, 'Abram Booth's eyewitness account', p. 19. Back in 1568 the pageant for Thomas Rowe's inauguration may have borne 'Verses or p'ceptes [precepts]' such as 'Feare god' and 'be wyse' (Robertson and Gordon, *Collections* III, p. 49).
31 Utrecht MS 1196, fol. 48v, and Lusardi and Gras, 'Abram Booth's eyewitness account', p. 22.
32 Taylor describes a pageant which takes 'the forme of a Citie . . . with walls, Battlements, Gates, Churches, Towers, Steeples and lofty Buildings' in *The triumphs of fame and honour* (sig. A7r). Dekker's 'London' pageant in *Brittannia's honor* sounds similar. It thus seems unlikely that Middleton would have omitted to mention it had the Show included such a device, which in these other instances is likely to have resembled a mini-version of Stephen Harrison's 'arches of triumph' from 1604.
33 Jansson and Rogozhin, *England and the North*, p. 164.
34 Werner, 'A German eye-witness', p. 252. Scultetus must have had an

excellent memory, for he wrote his description of the Show twelve years after the event.

35 Von Wedel, 'Journey through England', p. 255.

36 Cited in Davidson, *Technology*, p. 28.

37 Booth's journal has been translated as stating that the Lord Mayor and entourage 'returned [to the City] by land' rather than by barge (Lusardi and Gras, 'Abram Booth's eyewitness account', p. 22). However, there is no indication anywhere else that the tradition of travelling by water was not followed on this occasion.

38 See Werner, 'A German eye-witness', p. 252. The Elector was given generous gifts by the City at the Lord Mayor's banquet.

39 See Goldsmiths MSS vol. 14a. Booth's journal suggests that in 1629 the King and Queen watched the mayoral party 'from a window in Whitehall as the barges in orderly procession landed at Westminster' (*Collections* V, p. 6; see also Lusardi and Gras, 'Abram Booth's eye-witness account', pp. 20 and 22).

40 Mulryne, 'Introduction', p. 10.

41 Watanabe-O'Kelly, 'Early modern European festivals', p. 23.

42 *The Figure of the Crowd*, p. 71.

43 Paster, *The Idea of the City*, pp. 127–8.

44 Mulryne, 'Introduction', p. 10.

45 *Ibid.*

46 *Puritanism and Theatre*, p. 121.

47 Jansson and Rogozhin, *England and the North*, p. 164.

48 Levin notes that the monarch's Master of Ceremonies usually organ-ised suitable places for visiting dignitaries to watch the Show; householders charged a fee of between £3 and £5 for access to their windows (*Middleton: The Collected Works*, p. 1266).

49 *CSP Venetian*, vol. XV, p. 60.

50 He was apparently aided by translators during his travels and probably did not speak English very well, if at all (Ford, *Oxford DNB*).

51 Von Wedel, 'Journey through England', pp. 254–5. Von Wedel's account also provides information about a part of the ceremony never mentioned in the printed texts or in the livery company records, which is the 'handover' from old to new Lord Mayor, when the new incumbent swears an oath to the City itself in the Guildhall on the day before the actual Show (von Wedel even wandered into the Guildhall kitchens to inspect the preparations for the feast on that occasion).

52 From *The Excellent and Renowned History of the famous Sir Richard Whittington* (sig. A1r).

53 Cowan and Steward note that 'from the fifteenth century onwards fire-works were used for celebrations and . . . appreciated more for sound than for visual effects' (*The City and the Senses*, p. 14).

54 Machyn's Diary (1553): www.british-history.ac.uk/report. aspx?compid=45512. One should, however, be aware of the short-comings of Nichols's edition (see Mortimer, 'Tudor chronicler or sixteenth-century diarist?', pp. 982 and 984).

55 Randall, *Winter Fruit*, p. 141.

56 Tessa Murdoch cites an illustration of Taubman's 1686 Show on a fan as a rare instance where the audience is also represented ('The Lord Mayor's procession of 1686', p. 211).

57 Jonson, Chapman and Marston, *Eastward hoe*, sig. I4v. The galley foist too had currency outside of the Shows: for instance, the 1618 cautionary tale *Certaine characters and essayes of prison and prisoners* warned prisoners that 'going abroad' with gaolers was 'more charge-able then the Lord Maiors gally foyst on Simon & Iudes Day' (sig. C3v). This reference also demonstrates the widespread knowledge of the expense of the Shows.

58 Palmer points out that since the Great Twelve companies often used more than one barge, and some of the smaller companies accompanied them, 'it would have been possible to see a full complement of around twenty splendidly decorated barges on the Thames' ('Music in the barges', p. 171).

59 As was common, the Merchant Taylors borrowed 110 javelins from the Tower armouries in 1605, as they did in 1556 (see Sayle, *Lord Mayors' Pageants*, pp. 22 and 78).

60 See GH MS 15,869, fols 1–2.

61 Nichols, *The Progresses and Public Processions of Queen Elizabeth*, p. 254.

62 *Ibid.*, p. 258.

63 BL Add. MS 18016, fol. 147r–v.

64 *The Diary of John Manningham*, p. 72.

65 *Ibid.*

66 *Ibid.*, p. 73. in 1622 Peter Proby was advised by the Lord Chief Baron to take care to control 'rogues in the streets about Paules . . . [and] any offering to raise sedition' (BL Add. MS 18016, fol. 167r). (For more on contemporary fears about vast numbers of rogues and vagrants, see Griffiths, *Lost Londons*, pp. 39–44.)

67 *The Diary of John Manningham*, p. 73. Manningham was probably a fairly objective recorder of these speeches. In contrast, although Finch does note the substance of the Lord Chief Baron and Treasurer's replies (the supply of corn is invariably mentioned), they appear by his account to be quite perfunctory and benign compared to those recounted by Manningham (the Lord Treasurer barely said anything beyond prais-ing 'the flourishinge of the Citty' in 1623, apparently (*ibid.*, fol. 182r). Perhaps Finch 'edited' the Crown's replies somewhat. That said, a note of potential controversy does creep in in 1623, when Finch records that the Lord Treasurer Cranfield 'came [in] as I was in the middest of

my speech' (*ibid.*). This apparent discourtesy (and the fact that Finch recorded it) may have had something to do with the fact that Finch, in his parliamentary role as a member of the committee for grievances, was simultaneously 'play[ing] an important role in harrying the beleaguered lord treasurer . . . who stood accused of taking bribes' (Finch, *Oxford DNB*). The King was apparently 'irritated' by Finch's 'fawning' speech when the Lord Mayor, Martin Lumley, was knighted (*ibid.*).

68 For instance, the Skinners paid £50 'towardes the trimming and paynting' of Stephen Slany's house in 1595; the same sum had been put aside for the same purpose for Wolstane Dixie in 1585 (GH MS 30,727/4 and 30,708/2, fol. 120v). When John Leman, mayor in 1616, was first elected Sheriff in 1606 the Fishmongers conferred on him £100 'towerdes the charge of prepayring & furnishing of his howse': this was, however, largely because as Sheriff he was expected to entertain other dignitaries at his own expense. Clerics were paid in the region of 20s for their sermons on Lord Mayor's Day (see, for example, GH MS 30,727/6, fol. 343 (Skinners' Company)).

69 The Skinners held a dinner for the Assistants and Livery, for example, in 1631 (see GH MS 30,708/3, fol. 133r). Their mayoral dinners in the 1620s cost over £20. When their turn at the mayoralty came, the Companies allocated other tasks to their Bachelors, such as welcoming guests at the Guildhall and borrowing plate.

70 GH MS 5570/1, fol. 81. The Fishmongers' Company obviously preferred meat to fish on these occasions. The full cost and menu of the 1617 Guildhall feast is still extant. Music has survived for the feasts for mayoral Shows in the 1670s, and it is likely that the pre-Restoration Guildhall banquets were also accompanied by music and songs (see Hulse, '"Musick & poetry"', pp. 14–16).

71 Harding, 'Citizen and mercer', p. 30.

72 Robertson and Gordon, *Collections* III p. xxii. The Merchant Taylors employed 'Goodman Williamson' in 1602 to 'mend' the ship and other pageant items after the Show and a carpenter to hang up the 'Shipp' on ropes over a beam constructed specially in their Hall (GH MS 34,048/8).

73 GH MS 11,588/2, fol. 733.

74 Goldsmiths MSS vol. 14a, fol. 18r.

75 See Homer, 'The Pewterers' Company', p. 109, and GH MS 34,048/10. The chair was obviously traditional, for the Clothworkers hired one too, in 1599 (Clothworkers' accounts 1599–1600, fol. 10v).

76 Machyn's Diary (1561): www.british-history.ac.uk/report.aspx?compid=45528, von Wedel, 'Journey through England', p. 255, and Jansson and Rogozhin, *England and the North*, p. 164. There is a cryptic reference to 'Gleyns daughter' in the Goldsmiths' records for the 1523 Midsummer show which has been taken to mean that she

acted in the entertainment; three other female names also occur in the context of Midsummer shows in 1534 (see Kathman, *Biographical Index of English Drama*, and Robertson and Gordon, *Collections* III, pp. 14 and 24).

77 Munday, ed. Nichols, *Chrysanaleia*. The five senses were a commonly used device: they also appeared, for instance, in the 1604 royal entry and in the *Gray's Inn Revels* of 1595.

78 GH MS 15,869, fol. 7v. Kendall also supplied clothing for Oxford University's entertainment for the King in 1605 (see MacIntyre and Epp, '"Cloathes worth all the rest"', p. 278). For more on Kendall, who at the time of the lost 1604 Show was also a shareholder and patentee of the Children of the Queen's Revels theatre company, see Munro, *Children of the Queen's Revels*, p. 182.

79 *The Child Actors*, p. 36. 'Error' in *The triumphs of truth* is called an 'elf', suggesting a child actor, and Heywood refers explicitly to 'beautifull Children' in *Londini speculum* (sig. C3v). Boy singers were also employed by the City Waits.

80 GH MS 16,969/2, fol. 225r.

81 See Rees, *The Worshipful Company of Grocers*, p. 129.

82 GH MS 11,590, fol. 6v. These commodities were bought in large quantities (114 lb of ginger, for instance).

83 *CSP Venetian*, vol. XV, p. 61. As Dutton points out, the spices must have been distributed in 'small packages' as 'to throw loose spices would seem merely wasteful' (*Jacobean Civic Pageants*, p. 124 n. 3).

84 *CSP Venetian*, vol. XV, pp. 61–2.

85 It is not always clear whether Native Americans or denizens of the East Indies are meant by those called 'Indians' in the Shows. I explore this issue in more detail in Chapter 5.

86 'Costuming the Shakespearean Stage', p. 156.

87 GH MS 16,967/2, fol. 66b.

88 Davies and Saunders, *History of the Merchant Taylors' Company*, p. 142. In 1628 the Skinners paid 'Mr Dun of Blackwell hall' 40s 'for the Children in the Pageants' (GH MS 30,708/6, fol. 361). 'Mr Leese' (Richard Lee), schoolmaster of St Anthony's, supplied children for the 1556 Show (Robertson and Gordon *Collections* III, p. 40). Children acted in Midsummer Watch pageants too (*ibid.*, p. 33).

89 Dekker, *The magnificent entertainment*, sig. B4v. The civic entry *Chesters triumph*, welcoming Prince Henry to Chester in 1610, featured 'boyes of rare Spirit, and exquisite performance', according to the preface of the printed text (sig. A2v).

90 Dekker mentions Bourne by name as 'one of the seruants to the young prince' (*The magnificent entertainment*, sig. H4r).

91 GH MS 11,590, fol. 6v.

92 See GH MS 30,048/9. For a summary of the little that is known about Thomas Rowley, see Kathman, *Biographical Index*. Another player,

John Johnson, about whom nothing seems to be known, accompanied Rowley.

93   Bentley, *The Profession of Player*, p. 60. A reference to 'Mumford', a 'tumbler' in these Drapers' accounts, has been taken to mean John Mountsett, an actor who also appeared in Norwich in 1638 (see Kathman, *Biographical Index*, and Robertson and Gordon, *Collections* III, p. 128).

94   Bentley, *The Profession of Player*, p. 60.

95   *Staying Power*, pp. 26–7. In later years the use of black performers is more conclusive: for instance, there are references to 'Negroes' in Tatham's 1663 Show and in many others thereafter (indeed, they seem to have been quite ubiquitous in the 1670s).

96   See Palmer, *Ceremonial Barges*, p. 5. Jane Palmer states that 'in fair weather the journey from Three Cranes Wharf to Westminster Stairs took about one hour' ('Music in the barges', pp. 172–3). Chamberlain testified to 'great winds on the water' for Lord Mayor's Day in 1612; some of the barges had to turn back and the Lord Mayor 'with much ado came almost alone to Westminster' (cited in Fairholt, *Lord Mayors' Pageants*, vol. II, p. 5).

97   *CSP Venetian*, vol. XV, p. 59.

98   Cited in Davidson, *Technology*, p. 28. Unfortunately no printed mayoral Show from this period has images of pageant wagons: the earliest such depiction was an engraving of the Chariot of Justice (on a folded sheet) in Settle's 1698 Show, *Glory's Resurrection*.

99   Wickham, *Early English Stages*, vol. I, p. 59.

100 Munday, ed. Pafford, *Chrysanaleia*, pp. 14–15; see also Manley, *Literature and Culture*, p. 272. The route of royal entries was rather different, beginning at the Tower and processing westwards back to Westminster.

101 *CSP Venetian*, vol. XV, p. 62. Booth's drawings of the 1629 pageants, in contrast, bear no sign of the means of transportation; indeed, if anything they look quite fixed; they also don't appear to be tiered.

102 GH MS 16,969/2, fol. 223v.

103 '"Rival traditions"', p. 210.

104 'English pageant wagons', p. 368 (incidentally, this is the same size given by Davidson for medieval wagons in York: see *Technology*, p. 23). Similar pageant wagons were used on the continent: in the Low Countries they were called 'praalwagens' and were sometimes wind-powered (see Cartwright, 'The Antwerp *Landjuweel*' and Schlueter, 'Michael van Meer's Album', p. 303). The pageant wagons were usually made and stored in Leadenhall. The Haberdashers' records suggest that Christchurch was used as a place to make or store their pageants, as the churchwardens received £1 in 1604 for the use of their 'rome' (GH MS 15,869, fol. 7v).

105 'English pageant wagons', p. 361. Davidson points out that pageant

wagons did have steering mechanisms: the narrow lanes of cities like York and London would have required such a means of negotiation (*Technology*, pp. 19–20).

106   Pre-Reformation pageants also had various levels, used to reflect the hierarchy between the human and divine, as shown in the 'Pentecost' pageant reproduced in Davidson, *Technology*, p. 22. The height of medieval pageant wagons has been estimated at 'about five foot above street level . . . [with] the roof . . . about eight feet above the stage' (*ibid.*, p. 29).

107   Jansson and Rogozhin, *England and the North*, p. 164.

108   See, for example, Goldsmiths MSS vol. 14a, fol. 19v. Porters were paid for carrying the pageants from Blackwell Hall, where they were often stored before the event. Blackwell Hall was on the west side of Basinghall Street, located conveniently close to the Guildhall, to which it was connected by a passage; it was evidently still being used for the same purpose in the 1660s. Company records often indicate the need for the pageants to be 'contynually watched' (as the Merchant Taylors put it) in the run-up to the event; in 1621 the pageant was watched for seven days by 'a poore man' (GH MS 34,048/10). As before, the pageant and shows in 1610 were made in 'Xpist [Christ] church'; the ground of the church was paved to accommodate this (GH MS 34.048/10). In later years a barn in Whitecross Street, in Cripplegate just north of the City, was used (see, for example, GH MS 34,048/13; see also my *Anthony Munday*, p. 136).

109   GH MSS 34,048/8 and 34,048/9. A hundred porters were paid in 1610 for carrying the 'Pageant, Chariott, Shipp, and all the rest of the other shewes' (GH MS 34,048/10). For more on porters and their roles within livery companies, see Ward, *Metropolitan Communities*, pp. 58–64. There is an illustration of a 'pageant litter' carried by men in Davidson, *Technology*, p. 18.

110   See Jansson and Rogozhin, *England and the North*, p. 163.

111   McGrath, 'Rubens's Arch of the Mint', p. 208.

112   See Fairholt, *Lord Mayors' Pageants*, vol. I, pp. xviii–xix. In sixteenth-century Antwerp the pageant of the Mount of Parnassus was moved around by means of a sledge (*ibid.*, p. xxvii). Illustrations of pageant wagons with clothed undercarriages (from Louvain in 1594) are reproduced in Davidson, *Technology*, pp. 21–2.

113   See Nichols, *The Fishmongers' Pageant*, pp. 12 and 16.

114   GH MS 15,869, fol. 7v. One of the pageant wagons for the 1686 Show was drawn by 'nine white Flanders horses' (Murdoch, 'The Lord Mayor's procession for 1686', p. 208).

115   GH MS 11,590, fol. 14.

116   For a French royal entry horses disguised as elephants were used to transport the triumphal cars (McGowan, 'The Renaissance triumph', p. 32). There is a somewhat fanciful image of such a 'disguised'

pageant in Fairholt's *Lord Mayors' Pageants* (vol. I, p. xvii). In *Cornu-Copiae*, contemporary with Dekker's 1612 Show, Fennor implies that porters are employed 'vpon that solemne day, / when as the Pageants through Chepe-side are *carried*' (sig. H1r; my emphasis).

117 Later on Webster remarks that only 'twelue of the foure and twentie Cities' endowed by Sir Thomas White had been placed on one of the pageants, 'for more would haue ouer-burthened it' (sig. C1r).

118 *Jacobean Civic Pageants*, p. 181 n. 4.

119 Goldsmiths MSS vol. 14a, fol. 20r. The porters were also required to act as 'bouncers' outside the Company Hall to keep out 'loose people'.

120 GH MS 34,048/8; GH MS 34,048/10. Fortunately, it does not appear that any of the musicians was injured by this surely rather dangerous practice.

121 GH MS 34,048/10.

122 GH MS 34,048/13.

123 Robertson and Gordon, *Collections* III, p. 54.

124 GH MS 30,708/3, fol. 38v. William Stokes, another gunner, was lucky to escape the carnage with only 'splinters in his hand' (fol. 38r). An eyewitness account of an Elizabethan progress records that a firework set fire to nearby houses (see Butterworth, *Theatre of Fire*, p. 168). The amount of engaging human detail in these records is very striking: in 1602 the Merchant Taylors, for instance, reimbursed 'a poore woeman . . . towardes the buying of a hatt, her husband having lost one' (GH MS 34,048/8).

125 GH MS 15,333/2, fol. 184.

126 'The ages of man', p. 81.

127 *CSP Venetian*, vol. XV, p. 61. The Drapers used thirty dozen whifflers' staves, seventy-six javelins, and two and a half dozen 'trunchions' to order the crowds in 1621, which totals around 450 men (Drapers' Bachelors Accounts, fol. 27). In 1613 the Grocers paid the City Marshall £4 for his assistance on the day (GH MS 11,590, fol. 6v).

128 GH MS 34,048/13 (one can imagine him standing there with his clipboard).

129 GH MS 11,588/2, fol. 512.

130 Economical to the last, Munday here adapts the images he used in *Himatia-Poleos*: 'Night folding up bright day in dimme mantles of darknesse . . . the Starres seeme to leaue their places in their fixed Spheares, and to become as many bright flaming Torches to grace our worthy Magistrate home . . . in the malice of black fac'd night' (sig. C2v).

131 'Music in the barges', p. 171. As an indication of the importance of the Company barge, in 1622 the Grocers dismissed their barge master from any further service to the Company for 'the greate wronge and abuse offred to this Company' and the 'disgrace' they received as a result of the 'slowe and heavy' barge he provided (GH MS 11,588/3,

fol. 225). The Companies supplied food and drink for those travelling on the barges.

132 Machyn's Diary (1555): www.british-history.ac.uk/report. aspx?compid=45516.

133 Jansson and Rogozhin, *England and the North*, p. 163.

134 In a fit of charitable nostalgia, in 1988 the City re-enacted the water show from Middleton's 1613 Show. The barges used in 1988 were, accurately, around 80 feet long.

135 *A History of the Worshipful Company of Drapers*, p. 80.

136 Jansson and Rogozhin, *England and the North*, p. 163.

137 Von Wedel, 'Journey through England', p. 253. The Merchant Taylors hired two barges to accommodate their liverymen in 1612 (see GH MS 34,048/10).

138 Drapers MS III, fol. 104. In a gesture that rather undermines the Salters' extravagance, Hartwell was made to promise that he would never request more than this annual sum ('John and Goodwife Hartwell had been supplying barges, drummers and trumpeters for the Company since the 1620s, mainly for Lord Mayor's Day' (Barty-King, *The Salters' Company*, p. 51)). James Ruffell was paid £40 'for the galley and the galley foist and all other things belonging to them' in 1604 (GH MS 15,869, fol. 8r); 'Samuell Erbury' some £27 by the Skinners for the 'Gallifoyst' in 1628 (GH MS 30,708/6, fol. 359). The Goldsmith' first barge was built in 1617, the Mercers' in 1632, the Fishmongers' in 1634 and the Grocers' in 1637; prior to these dates they would have hired barges (Palmer, *Ceremonial Barges*, pp. 24 and 33; Munday ed. Nichols, *Chrysanaleia*, p. 25).

139 GH MS 5770/2, fol. 196. The Drapers 'hired the great barge of the Archbishop of Canterbury' in 1533 and 'the Greyhound, the royal barge of Henry VIII' in 1540, and the Skinners had used Wolsey's barge back in 1518 (see Palmer, *Ceremonial Barges*, pp. 30 and 42).

140 Williams, 'A Lord Mayor's show', p. 503.

141 Drapers' Bachelors Accounts, fol. 88.

142 See *Collections* V, p. 6 n. 4.

143 Only one copy of this work has survived, and unfortunately the side-note is cropped.

144 Such an entrenched misconception is puzzling, for the difference is clear from the Companies' records and would no doubt have been clear to onlookers too: for instance, in 1620 the Haberdashers paid £29 to 'Mr Erberry for the galley foist' and £7 5s to 'Mr Sparrowhawke for the barge' (GH MS 15,869, fol. 16r). Jane Palmer is one of those scholars who confuses the foist and the barge, leading her to misinterpret evidence from the Ironmongers' records ('Music in the barges', p. 171). Even the *OED* gets it wrong, calling it 'a state barge'.

145 GH MS 16,969/2, fol. 222r.

146 Carnegie, 'Galley foists', p. 66.

147 *Ibid.*, p. 50. He explains that 'it had in theory to be able to give armed protection to the lord mayor' (p. 53). A 'galley fuste' appears on the river in Visscher's 1616 panorama.

148 *CSP Venetian*, vol. XV, p. 59.

149 *Ibid.*, p. 60.

150 Jansson and Rogozhin, *England and the North*, p. 163.

151 GH MS 16,967/4. In 1618, according to the Ironmongers, a cannon fired off 'almond comfetes [comfits]' rather than shot (Robertson and Gordon *Collections* III, p. 97).

152 Drapers' Bachelors Accounts, fol. 28. Exactly the same arrangement took place in 1623.

153 See GH MS 34,048/8. The Merchant Taylors tended to use 120 'brasse chambers', each firing twice (the noise must have been deafening): see, for instance, GH MS 30,048/9. The Goldsmiths' Company, for one, bought its own powder.

154 GH MS 34,105, fol. 2. Numerous trumpeters were also required for the Show.

155 In some royal progresses, in contrast, natural features were not available, such as the entertainments held for Elizabeth in 1591 at Elvetham where an artificial lake had to be dug for the occasion.

156 Robertson and Gordon, *Collections* III, p. 70.

157 *Ibid.*, p. 85.

158 GH MS 11,590, fol. 6r. In *Zelauto* Munday refers to 'a Pageant' as well as 'a number of strange deuices' (sig. Eiir).

159 Robertson and Gordon *Collections* III p. 87.

160 Robin Hood, Friar Tuck and 'his other braue Huntes-men', Munday comments, were 'at last' able to address the Lord Mayor at the very end of the day: their 'dutie . . . the busie turmoile of the whole day could not before affoord' (sig. C1r). (Note that Munday's remark is retrospective.)

161 The function of the lengthy and almost incomprehensible account of Pythagorean mathematics in his 1637 text remains obscure (*Londini speculum*, sigs B4v–C1r). Heywood's inveterate classicism can result in unintentional bathos: in *Porta pietatis* the historical archive has produced the snippet that in 'Arabia [sheep] have tayles three Cubits in length' (sig. B1v).

162 Stow himself participated in mayoral pageantry for his Company, the Merchant Taylors. He was in 1561 one of the eight Company members appointed to 'attend vpon the pageant to see that it be not borne against penthouses & to attend vpon the children and theire appell [*sic*] and to see it [the pageant] be safely sett vp within the hall accordingly'; in 1568 he acted as a whiffler (Robertson and Gordon, *Collections* III, p. 41).

163 The Merchant Taylors' accounts for 1601–3 show an annual pension being paid to 'John Stowe a brother of this company and a maker

of chronicles' (GH MS 34,048/8, fol. 35). Stow was paid 10s by the same Company in 1602 for the 'great paynes by him taken, in [searching] for such as hath byn Maiors, Shereffs, and Aldermen of this Companie' (*ibid.*). The results of Stow's labours may have been reused five years later, when James I was presented with 'a roll listing all those who had been chosen honorary members of the Company' (Davies and Saunders, *History of the Merchant Taylors' Company*, p. 162). As an example of how Stow's fame as a citizen historian outlived him, Mayne's *The citye match* (1639) has a satirical reference to a 'Merchant Taylor that writes chronicles' (sig. B2r). The historian and mapmaker John Speed was also a member of the Merchant Taylors, as was William Fleetwood, the Recorder of London. Sullivan has helpfully documented the library purchases of chronicles and related texts like Stow's *Survay* by some of the Companies (see 'London's early modern creative industrialists', pp. 316–19).

164 As discussed elsewhere, Stow would have been scornful towards Munday's error in *Chrysanaleia* where he claims that the City arms feature Walworth's, rather than St Paul's, dagger (sig. C3v; see also my *Anthony Munday*, pp. 159–60).

165 *Middleton: The Collected Works*, p. 1251.

166 Machyn's Diary (1554): www.british-history.ac.uk/report.aspx?com pid=45514.

167 Cited in Sayle, *Lord Mayors' Pageants*, p. 2. Smith implies that this pageant was carried along with the rest of the procession.

168 See Davies and Saunders, *History of the Merchant Taylors' Company*, p. 142, and Munday, ed. Nichols, *Chrysanaleia*, p. 9. See Kipling, 'The King's advent', p. 107, for a discussion of the same phenomenon in a royal entry in Antwerp.

169 Cockayne's coat of arms featured three cocks too.

170 The Ironmongers asked for 'two Estriches of Silver' from Grinkin in 1609 (perhaps the wooden animals were painted silver) (GH MS 16,969/2, fol. 223v).

171 See Utrecht MS 1196, fol. 48v.

172 Kiefer, *Shakespeare's Visual Theatre*, pp. 16 and 213.

173 Sayle, *Lord Mayors' Pageants*, p. 21. Sayle states that 'a camel [was] hired from one Southwall for £1' (*ibid.*).

174 GH MS 15,842/1, fol. 119r.

175 Carnegie remarks that 'the spectator lacking [Webster's] explanation might be hard-pressed to identify Liberality on the sole basis of this [dromedary] . . . Possibly Liberality has another property as well' ('Introduction to *Monuments of honour*', p. 291). As Dekker chose to celebrate 'fur' in the 1628 Show for Richard Deane, a Skinner, he had to mention a whole 'wildernesse' of furry beasts, from wolves and leopards to ferrets and squirrels (*Brittannia's honor*, sig. C2r).

176 *The Figure of the Crowd*, p. 57.

177 Gadd, 'Early modern printed histories', p. 33.

178 'The emblematic nature', p. 182. I find Bergeron's imagined 'inveterate pageant-goer' watching the Shows with 'his well-thumbed copy of Whitney's *Choice of Emblemes*' just a little far-fetched, however (*ibid.*, pp. 197–8).

179 Kipling, *Enter the King*, p. 14.

180 *CSP Venetian*, vol. XV, p. 59.

181 Sayle, *Lord Mayors' Pageants*, p. 60.

182 Lindenbaum states that 'smaller properties were kept in one of the companies' great chests' ('Ceremony and oligarchy', p. 176). In the earlier period these properties were accompanied by 'records of the event "entred into a booke" so that the pageants could be reproduced in "tymes hereafter"' (*ibid.*, p. 181). The Clothworkers had a 'pageant house' for storing the artefacts for their Shows (*Collections* V, pp. 4 and 15–16).

183 *The Magnificent, Princely, and most Royall Entertainments*, sig. C2r. This text also describes mermen and mermaids, Jason's ship with the golden fleece and the figure of Envy, amongst others, all of which appear in mayoral inaugurations too. Indeed, although it lacks civic imagery, in other respects this latter work is so reminiscent of a Lord Mayor's Show that one wonders if one of the pageant poets may have had a hand in it (the text, unfortunately, is anonymous).

184 Palmer, *Hospitable Performances*, p. 119. Munro too comments on how Busino's eyewitness account has received 'surprisingly little critical analysis' (*The Figure of the Crowd*, p. 60).

185 Smuts, 'Occasional events', p. 181.

186 Ravelhofer points out that Busino was very short-sighted and so may not have been able accurately to make out the detail of what he saw on these occasions (*The Early Stuart Masque*, p. 23).

187 Levin's account of the way in which the devices were designed 'with an eye toward their effect in performance' and 'need only be seen' rather understates the importance of the complex imagery to which the printed texts devote so much space (*Middleton: The Collected Works*, p. 1252).

188 Jonson, of course, is being unfair: such simple images would not have been identified in such a fashion, only the more obscure mythical figures: for an alternative view, see Dekker, *The magnificent entertainment*, sig. B1v.

189 See Osberg, 'Humanist allusions', p. 29.

190 McGowan, 'The Renaissance triumph', p. 33.

191 As Levin remarks, by summarising all the devices in this fashion, Munday's mayoral works 'segregate performance and explication' (*Middleton: The Collected Works*, p. 1251).

192 Bergeron comments that 'with slight variation Middleton's Truth could have walked off the pages of Peacham's [emblem book] *Minerva Britannia* and into the pageant' (*Middleton: The Collected Works*, p. 967).

193 Munday's interest in emblems was of long standing: he wrote a prefatory poem to, and may have co-edited, John Bodenham's *Bel-vedére, or, The Garden of the muses* (1600), a miscellany of commonplaces which took much of its material from emblem books.

194 Bradbrook comments that Truth in *The triumphs of truth* was 'copied in the greatest detail from that Truth whom Jonson had depicted in the Barriers for the marriage of the Earl of Essex [in 1606]' ('The politics of pageantry', p. 69).

195 'The emblematic nature', p. 171.

196 Kiefer, *Shakespeare's Visual Theatre*, p. 21.

197 Heywood appears to have had an especial interest in emblems: as Bath points out, two of his other 1630s works contain a large quantity of emblematic material (*Speaking Pictures*, p. 25).

198 Von Wedel, 'Journey through England', p. 255.

199 Wickham, *Early English Stages*, vol. I, p. 81. Ravelhofer discusses a similarly baffled foreign eyewitness of a court masque (*The Early Stuart Masque*, pp. 1–3).

200 *Shakespeare's Visual Theatre*, p. 8.

201 'Rubens's Arch of the Mint', p. 196. Ravelhofer argues, in relation to a late court masque, *Salmacida Spolia*, that 'spectators needed eagle eyes and advanced emblem reading skills to identify the small grasshopper squatting on the proscenium arch as "Affection to the Country"' (*The Early Stuart Masque*, p. 264).

202 Watt, *Cheap Print*, p. 138.

203 'Costuming the Shakespearean Stage', p. 157.

204 Smuts, 'Public ceremony', p. 67.

205 'Costuming the Shakespearean Stage', p. 156.

206 See Bergeron, *Practicing Renaissance Scholarship*, p. 156. Smuts comments that 'it is easy to understand how a Genius with loose hair and a long robe might have been mistaken for a hermit, especially when seen from a distance' ('Occasional events', p. 197).

207 *The time triumphant*, sig. B3r–v. Christine Stevenson comments on Dugdale's 'authentic spectatorship' ('Occasional architecture', p. 41).

208 See Werner, 'A German eye-witness', p. 252.

209 Smuts, 'Occasional events', p. 197.

210 *The Figure of the Crowd*, p. 72.

211 Burden, '"For the lustre of the subject"', p. 586.

212 Court of Aldermen Repertories, vol. 44, fol. 2r.

213 *Middleton: The Collected Works*, p. 1267.

214 Parry, *The Golden Age*, p. 45.

215 'Thomas Middleton's *The Triumphs of Truth*', p. 17.

216 Watanabe-O'Kelly, 'Early modern European festivals', p. 23.

217 Smuts, 'Public ceremony', p. 67. I will return to this issue at greater length in the next chapter.

218 'Introduction to *Monuments of Honour*', p. 231.

219 Watt, *Cheap Print*, p. 330. As an illustration of her point, Munday's medieval-style 'romances', some of which were first published in the 1580s, were still being reprinted well into the 1660s.

220 In 1604, the Haberdashers record a payment of £5 to those who 'served as greenemen with fireworks' (GH MS 15,869, fol. 8r). The terms 'woodsmen', 'greenmen' and 'wildmen' can be treated as synonyms in this context. These characters persisted into the later seventeenth century: greenmen were still used to clear the route in 1686 (see Murdoch, 'The Lord Mayor's procession of 1686', p. 210). I have seen no reference in the context of mayoral Shows to the 'morris dancers' who Munro claimed performed on the day, although they were definitely employed for the Midsummer Watch (*The Figure of the Crowd*, p. 52; see also Robertson and Gordon, *Collections* III, p. 17).

221 Machyn's Diary (1554): www.british-history.ac.uk/report.aspx?compid=45514. 'Wild men' also featured in royal pageantry and progresses.

222 Dekker is particularly likely to refer to aspects of the Shows in his other works: for instance, the galley foist features in *Westward hoe*, *The honest whore II* and *Match mee in London*.

223 Rick Bowers notes that Dick Whittington (and his cat) feature for the first time with the full famous and apocryphal story in two 1605 plays, one of which is *Eastward hoe* ('Dick Whittington', p. 34); Whittington was also the subject of a ballad produced in the same year.

224 In *Brittannia's honor* Dekker praises 'the workes, that for many yeares, none haue been able to Match them for curiosity'; they are, however, 'not Vast, but Neate, and Comprehend as much Arte for Architecture, as can be bestowed vpon such little Bodies', and on that basis he commends Garret and John Christmas (sig. C2v).

225 Perhaps he was aware of the deficiencies of this work, which is comprised in the main of unrelated and often rather banal emblems. For instance, it's not clear why he introduced the figure of the British Bard, and the Show as a whole does have a rather tired feel to it compared to some of his others. Given its date, it is possible that his edition of Stow's *Suruay* had taken up most of his time and energies.

226 The Ironmongers' minutes say of this third pageant that it is 'an Antique pageant for pleasure' (Robertson and Gordon, *Collections* III, p. 123).

227 *Heywood's Theatre*, pp. 262–3.

228 Shirley himself was to collaborate only the following year over the production of a masque with Rowland Bucket, a painter-stainer who

worked on a number of the Shows (*Middleton: The Collected Works*, p. 1262).

229 GH MS 16,969/2, fols 222r and 243v. The whale 'vented' water through 'squirtes', according to the Ironmongers' accounts.

230 It is likely that the Companies already owned some theatrical-style properties dating back to the pre-Lord Mayors' Shows period of pageantry (see MacIntyre and Epp, '"Cloathes worth all the rest"', pp. 279–81).

231 Bergeron, *Practicing Renaissance Scholarship*, p. 118. The Prince's drummers and fifers were employed by the Merchant Taylors in 1610 (see GH MS 34,048/10). In 1599 the Clothworkers hired a barge from 'Mr Dorrett', the master of the Queen's barge (Clothworkers' accounts 1599–1600, fol. 7v).

232 MacIntyre and Epp, '"Cloathes worth all the rest"', pp. 277 and 282.

233 In the same vein, as far as Munday is concerned the crowned dolphin in *Chrysanaleia* 'can serue indifferently' for two symbolic purposes (sig. B1v). For the King and Prince Henry's entertainment at Merchant Taylors' Hall in 1607 a ship was hung from the roof, bearing three men attired as sailors who sang accompanied by a lute (Nichols, *The Progresses*, vol. II, pp. 141–2) (I am grateful to Anne Saunders for drawing this to my attention).

234 Munday has Friar Tuck state that with Christmas approaching 'our seruice may appeare, / Of much more merit then as now', suggesting that they may be presented before the Lord Mayor at greater length. Perhaps, in the course of a fictional appeal for festive patronage Munday is covertly requesting that his own be considered 'when any occasion shall require' (sig. C2r–v).

235 Palmer, 'Music in the barges', pp. 171–2. The court masque, in contrast, employed 'noble wind instruments' and lutes (Ravelhofer, *The Early Stuart Masque*, pp. 199–200).

236 See GH MS 34,048/10 and GH MS 34,048/13, where the Merchant Taylors' Company states that this (surely rather dangerous) practice had been allowed 'in former yeares'.

237 See Wood, '"A flowing harmony"', p. 561.

238 'Surden', probably a variant of 'sordine' or muffled, appears to be a neologism.

239 *CSP Venetian*, vol. XV, p. 60. Somewhat hyperbolically, Munro concludes from Busino's account that this Show was more like a 'near-riot' than a 'dignified marriage of mayor and city' (*The Figure of the Crowd*, p. 61). Butterworth defines a squib as 'a firework that squirmed erratically to produce a fizzing shower of sparks that sometimes ended in a small report' (*Theatre of Fire*, p. 1).

240 Williams, 'A Lord Mayor's show', p. 515.

241 See GH MS 34,048/8. The Goldsmiths employed fencers in 1611 (see Goldsmiths MSS vol. 14a, fol. 8v) and in 1620 'Mr Bradshawe fencer

and his sonnes' were paid £8 5s 'for their service with others with two handed swordes' (GH MSS 15,869, fol. 16r). As late as 1671, a rope dancer called Jacob Hall (whose fame is testified to in a poem about Bow church) performed at the Lord Mayor's Show (see *Oxford DNB*, 'Hall, Jacob' and Fairholt, *The Civic Garland*, p. xiii).

242 See Butterworth, *Theatre of Fire*, pp. 15 and 81. In this same Show St George is accompanied by 'his conquered Dragon', but Munday does not say if the dragon issued fire (*Camp-bell*, sig. B2v).

243 Lusardi and Gras, 'Abram Booth's eyewitness account', p. 22.

244 The Russian ambassador Zuizin does not mention this undoubtedly impressive incident: perhaps his party had departed the City by then. As we have seen in Chapter 2, Middleton praises Humphrey Nichols's work in this aspect of the Show. Butterworth has shown that other dramatic performances in this period required 'the ability to target fire in some sort of controlled way'; he reproduces a sixteenth-century image of a man spouting fire through a tube (*Theatre of Fire*, pp. 5 and 40). Taylor's 1613 text *Heauens blessing, and earths ioy* demonstrates the elaborate effects that seventeenth-century pyrotechnics could aspire to.

245 *CSP Venetian*, vol. XV, p. 61. Scherb dates the use of giants in civic pageantry back to at least 1415 ('Assimilating giants', p. 71). They persisted despite a decline in 'belief in the existence of real, historical giants' 'among the educated classes' in the late sixteenth century (Woolf, *The Social Construction of the Past*, p. 326). Woolf comments that giants 'frequently featured in processions, entries, and certain other sorts of local ritual, as ludic figures of aberrant nature, as symbols of misrule, and, sometimes, as examples of men of humble origin achieving fame and prosperity' (p. 327).

246 Jansson and Rogozhin, *England and the North*, p. 164.

247 *Theatre of Fire*, p. 2. They appear to have been made with cane baskets or pasteboard and canvas clubs attached to a long pole (see *ibid.*, pp. 22–3): John Babington's *Pyrotechnia* gives instructions on how the effect could be attained (sigs D3v–D4v) (I am grateful to Elaine Tierney for this reference).

248 Bergeron notes 'the concern for costume' in Elizabeth's 1559 royal entry (*Practicing Renaissance Scholarship*, p. 39). Costumes and fabrics for the latter event were loaned to the City by the Revels Office, as they had been for previous royal entries (see Streitberger, *Court Revels*, pp. 220, 285 and 298). Again, costumes were a major aspect of the 1988 re-enactment, where 'metres of bright coloured silk and polyester chiffon' were used to create some seventy-eight individual costumes (see *The Lord Mayor of London's Jacobean Thames Pageant*, p. 9). For royal funerals and coronations even greater outlay on cloth took place (see Loach, 'The function of ceremonial', pp. 67–8).

249 Smuts, 'Public ceremony', p. 71.

250 See GH MS 34,048/8. By way of context, this is some £50 more than

a relatively expensive masquing suit provided for the King in 1634 (see Ravelhofer, *The Early Stuart Masque*, p. 150). As one might expect, given the nature of their trade, the Merchant Taylors' accounts provide more detail than is usually the case about how the coats and gowns were actually manufactured. Taffeta sarsnett ('a very fine and soft silk material made both plain and twilled, in various colours' (*OED*)) is one of the fabrics most commonly used. In 1610 and 1612 the cost of the 'azure' fabric for 'poore mens gownes and Coats' came first in the list of the Merchant Taylors' expenditure (GH MS 34,048/10).

251 GH MS 15,869, fol. 26r.

252 GH MS 34,048/10. The Goldsmiths made similar arrangements for the watermen (see Goldsmiths MSS vol. 14a, fol. 19r).

253 GH MS 30,708/6, fol. 361.

254 GH MS 16,967/4.

255 See Jansson and Rogozhin, *England and the North*, p. 164.

256 See Glover, *A History of the Ironmongers' Company*, p. 63. Tittler comments that 'observations of proper dress . . . seems [*sic*] to have been expected of officials in the guildhall at all times, and, indeed, often in the streets on daily business' (*Architecture and Power*, p. 107). Liveried Company members often attended funerals too; indeed, with Company arms being displayed in the procession, 'poor men' in attendance and dinners being held at Company halls after the events (as well as the short timescale for organisation), funerals bore many resemblances to civic pageantry (see Harding, *The Dead and the Living*, pp. 241–4 and 248, and for John Leman's funeral in 1632, pp. 251–2). Michael Neill writes that 'funeral "shewes" belonged to precisely the same order of pageantry as coronations, royal weddings, entries, and progresses – all were forms of "Triumph"' ('Exeunt with a dead march', p. 154).

257 *CSP Venetian*, vol. XV, p. 61. One of the texts produced to mark Christian IV's visit to London in 1606 devotes almost two pages to detailing the garments worn by both the performers and the procession of dignitaries (*The king of Denmarkes welcome*, pp. 4–5).

258 'Journey through England', p. 252.

259 *Hic mulier*, sig. C1r. Similarly, Prynne's *Histrio-mastix* mentions 'pageants' as one of many 'reliques of Paganisme' to be avoided by Christians (sig. D3r), and he repeatedly cites pageants alongside stage-plays, 'enterludes' and similar abominations: 'how many men are vainely occupied for sundry dayes (yea sometimes yeeres) together', he asks, 'in making theatricall Pageants, Apparitions, Attires, Visars, Garments, with such-like Stage-appurtenances, for the more commodious pompous acting and adorning of these vaine-glorious Enterludes?' (sig. Rr1r–v).

260 Sutton, 'Civic livery', p. 21. She focuses on the role of the Lord Mayor's sword-bearer, who marched at the front of the procession to

emphasise the power and authority of the City's leader. Her discussion of a mayoral inauguration in 1419, with its emphasis on 'the suits of [the participants'] respective mysteries', shows that this dimension of the Lord Mayor's inauguration was a long-standing tradition (p. 22).

261 Von Wedel, 'Journey through England', p. 253.

262 Richardson, 'Introduction', p. 14.

263 Ravelhofer notes that 'the early Stuart court . . . was obsessed with colour symbolism', and, as we see here, that 'colour determined a social dress code' (*The Early Stuart Masque*, p. 159). Lublin writes that, as red was 'the color of the court', the donning of red attire 'serves to identify [the city oligarchy] as servants of the monarch'; the act of swearing allegiance to the Crown at Westminster underscored the same function of the day ('Costuming the Shakespearean stage', p. 163).

264 'Introduction', p. 15.

265 Astington likens these pages to 'tiny maids of honor accompanying modern brides', and he notes that those selected to perform this role were probably the 'younger sons of prominent members of the company from which the Mayor had been chosen' ('The ages of man', pp. 80–1). The 'serjeants' also played a part in the procession: Sutton writes that 'they accompanied the leading civic officials about their business as required and particularly on ceremonial occasions, clearing the way for processions' ('Civic livery', p. 12).

266 The livery companies regularly provided poor men with clothing, not just on Lord Mayor's Day. Sheila Sweetinburgh has commented that 'the giving of clothing . . . offered donors the opportunity to act charitably towards their social inferiors, using the form of the gift to reflect the relative status of the benefactor and beneficiary'. She usefully refers to this exchange as a kind of 'symbolic capital' ('Clothing the naked', pp. 112–13). Harding writes that 'a hundred poor men attended the funeral of Sir Cuthbert Buckle in 1594 . . . [and] seventy-two were at Sir William Webbe's funeral in 1599' (*The Dead and the Living*, p. 243). Hardin, somewhat implausibly, likens the poor men on such occasions to 'captured slaves' (*Spectacular Constructions*, p. 154).

267 Archer, 'The arts and acts of memoralization', p. 122.

268 Barron discusses the use of heraldry in mayoral processions from the sixteenth century onwards ('Chivalry, pageantry and merchant culture', pp. 231–2).

269 The Merchant Taylors stipulated that the Lord Mayor's banner should be made from 'rich' silk (GH MS 34,048/10). Imported silk was extremely expensive.

270 GH MS 34,048/10. Woolf notes that 'in the course of the sixteenth century, arms increasingly figured as domestic, ecclesiastical, and civic decorations' (*The Social Construction of the Past*, p. 102).

271 Jansson and Rogozhin, *England and the North*, p. 163.

272 GH MS 34,048/8.

273 As was customary, the Grocers appointed twelve members of the Company 'to welcome the Guests' at the feast (GH MS 11,588/2, fol. 784). In 1617, the new Lord Mayor's butler, Francis Downes, was sent to the Company court to request the loan of plate and linen for the feast (see GH MS 11,588/3, fol. 57).

274 GH MS 34,048/8. It's no wonder that the Company also needed to purchase 'a paper booke to wryte the chardges of the busines in'.

4

'A briefe narration of each seuerall shew': the Show from street to print

From 1585 onwards the Lord Mayor's Show was with increasing frequency transmitted from event to text in the form of short pamphlets produced in print runs ranging from 200 to 800 copies. It is perhaps ironic that such ephemeral publications, relating to a fleeting day's celebrations, have gone on to have a life beyond their immediate context. Indeed, they have almost invariably been studied as literary 'works' quite separate from the event upon which they are based. As a consequence, most of the commentary on these texts is predicated on the assumption that the printed text mirrors the Show unproblematically – if indeed this question is raised at all.[1] The books of the Lord Mayors' Shows were, however, rarely, if ever, straightforward records of what took place on that day in late October. Smuts has commented that 'printed accounts of . . . London pageants . . . *appear to be* full accounts of historical occasions'. However, he continues, 'whenever we can check these narratives against other sources, we generally discover significant omissions and biases'.[2] Bergeron's assertion that 'the printed word . . . offers a kind of stability to the spoken word', and Taylor's similar observation that printed works 'memorialise the momentary' should therefore be tempered by an awareness that the printed word is not always identical to the spoken.[3] As we saw in the previous chapter, there will always be elements of the festivities that print cannot capture. My intention is to bring the printed narratives alongside their sources, not in order to prioritise one over the other but rather to combine these divergent but equally important aspects of the Shows. The fundamental question to be considered is, when we talk of the Lord Mayor's Show, what entity do we actually mean? The performance, the printed text or some ambiguous combination of the two?

Building on the large and growing body of knowledge about the London book trade, this chapter will explore who the printers and publishers of the texts were and what connections they may have had with the writers, artificers and/or the livery companies.[4] I will also address the questions of where and by whom the texts were distributed, and who owned and/or bought such books. Any proprietory authorising issues in relation to the Stationers' Company and other bodies are also discussed here. In addition, some of the printed texts had dedications and other prefatory material: this chapter will look into the significance of such paratexts. Other questions about the printed Shows will be addressed, such as whether the texts were programmes, souvenirs or prospectuses, or a combination of all three, whether they were printed before or after the Show and, as far as it is possible to ascertain, what the relationship of the printed text to the actual event tended to be.[5] These mostly unanswered – even largely unasked – questions reflect another important aspect of the Shows where scholarship has let us down. Even Peter Blayney excludes 'all masques, pageants and entertainments' from his account of printed playbooks, on the basis that the former were not really plays.[6] Blayney's view, which is not atypical, is part of the problem, for as hybrid cultural productions the Shows do not fit neatly into any of the categories habitually used within literary scholarship. As a consequence, no one has yet studied the full range of these texts, as a genre, in bibliographical terms.[7] Indeed, the question of genre remains vexed because the Shows straddle more than one of them – or perhaps should have a new one invented for them. As an instance, the copy of *Porta pietatis* held in the National Library of Scotland has been categorised both as a 'coronation' and as an 'English play', when it is in fact neither.

In some ways, of course, treating the printed Shows as straightforward literary texts is understandable. They were, after all, largely written by professional writers and they contain what can broadly be regarded as 'literary' content. Indeed, it is possible to argue that, with the presence of dramatists and the like from Peele's time onwards, there was a literary imperative for a title for these printed works, as with other 'authored' works such as plays.[8] At times, the desire to have an impressive, classical-style title could result in authorial error. Greg notes that Munday's secondary title for *Himatia-Poleos*, 'The Triumphs of Old Drapery', 'suggests that the words "Himatia Poleos" are intended to represent . . . a possible Greek equivalent of "old drapery", but the form "Poleos" points to confusion with . . . "of the city"'.[9] Nevertheless, in the printed text the writer perforce becomes dominant, despite the conventional acknowledgements of the crucial input of the artificer (of whom more elsewhere). Most of the title pages thus refer to the text as having been 'invented' or 'devised' by the poet. Indeed, an often overlooked and perhaps unexpected difference between the printed Shows and the equivalent accounts of monarchical or aristocratic ceremonial events is the way in which the author is foregrounded in the Shows but often uncertain in the latter type of text, in much the same way as authorship is similarly uncertain in a large number of play-texts. Conversely, for the period in question none of the printed Lord Mayors' Shows is anonymous.[10] Regardless of the claims of title pages, however, the collaborative reality that lies behind these texts illustrates Susan Anderson's argument that in ephemeral texts 'authorship must be seen as part of a set of conditions that shape the production of an occasional entertainment and its textual traces, despite the claims to authority that individual authors may make'.[11]

There are significant issues that pertain exclusively to the printed work rather than the Show on the streets. Even the titles of the printed texts – Middleton's *The triumphs of truth*, for instance – do not necessarily relate in a straightforward fashion to the day's entertainment.[12] Nowhere in the livery companies' records detailing the commissioning of and expenditure on the Shows (even where the Company in question deals explicitly with the nature of the 'devices', which is infrequently) have I found the *titles* of the books cited, as they appeared in print. This indicates that the titles were invented purely for the instance of the printed work, perhaps at the behest of the writers. It is certainly the case that from the relative obscurity of some early writers the role of 'the poet' had moved more to the centre-stage by the end of our period, at least as far as the printed works are concerned. Heywood's late 1630s Shows, *Porta pietatis* and *Londini status pacatus*, both declare on their title pages that the texts were 'Written by Thomas Heywood', the author's name being separated out by two rules to emphasise it.

The titles of these works tend to allude either to the central thematic concerns of the Show, such as 'honour and industry', or to the name of the Lord Mayor (*Camp-bell*, for instance), or to the name or trade of his livery company, as in *Chruso-thriambos. The triumphes of golde*. The livery company records, in contrast, almost always only refer to 'the book', or 'the book of the speeches', which may indicate that the Companies usually had only limited interest in, or perhaps only limited sway over, this aspect of the Shows. The latter term is used by the Merchant Taylors to refer to Dekker and Heminges's 1612 Show, for instance, the printed text of which was considerably more complex than the phrase 'the booke of the speeches' suggests.[13] What is noticeable is that, where the printed text (assuming there was one) has not survived, neither has any definitive title for that year's Show. Indeed, a couple of the very earliest texts have no 'literary' titles, as such, but are simply called, descriptively, *The device of the pageant* or similar.[14] Peele's 1591 production, printed with the title *Descensus astraeae*, is the first surviving printed work with a specific name of the kind that soon became ubiquitous. The titles thereafter became increasingly formulaic: a large number of the post-1655 printed Shows were simply called *London's Triumph*, or approximations thereof.[15]

Even the names of the individual pageants and devices within a particular Show are not always the same across the texts and the livery company records. For example, the Grocers' accounts call one of Middleton and Christmas's 1622 pageants 'the East Indian Paradise' whereas the text twice explicitly states that this pageant bears 'the title of the Continent of India'.[16] One cannot tell if the discrepancy reflects a change in the title from project to printed text (where perhaps the Company were unaware of any changes), or whether the former name is simply the one the Company preferred. Equally, the Grocers mention 'the Iland' in their accounts for 1617 but no device of that name appears in Middleton's text.[17] Unusually, the Drapers' accounts for both 1638 and 1639 state explicitly that the 'Pageants or showes' are 'particularly described' by 'the printed booke'.[18] It is rare indeed for Company records to comment on the relationship between the pageantry and the associated text, let alone to emphasise the authenticity of the latter in this fashion. Perhaps this instance indicates, as we will see further below, that in some cases the printed work was based closely on the 'plot' which the Company had commissioned; in both years a close correlation between the work of the artificers, the Christmas brothers, and Heywood is implied. At any rate, it certainly appears that the Drapers were especially pleased with the texts, as they ordered additional copies on both occasions, and in 1638 gave the poet £10 as a result 'of the Companies well liking it'.[19]

But there is still a question as to why the Shows were printed and published at all.[20] This ostensibly simple question is another that is rarely posed.[21] Ephemeral texts relating to court entertainments, royal entries, tournaments and so on had been printed for some time before the practice extended to the mayoral Shows. For instance, in Munday's 1580 work *Zelauto* the eponymous hero reads from a 'Book' of 'a gallant deuice presented in a Tournament' (sig. Eiiir).

The kind of immediate political contingencies cited by Smuts as reasons for the appearance in print of the more infrequent monarchical entries, progresses and other entertainments from the 1570s onwards cannot really apply to the Lord Mayor's Show, so we must seek other explanations as to why Peele's *Deuice of the pageant* was published in 1585 and why it was succeeded by others.[22] Manley suggests that the recourse to print came on the back of 'an apparent heightening of tensions between the City and both Crown and Parliament' in the 1580s, in the face of which it was considered necessary to encapsulate these moments of civic celebration in more permanent form. The ensuing texts can be seen as part of a wider 'ceremonial consciousness' and 'civic assertiveness', in Manley's useful phrases, also exemplified by works like the *Apologie of the Cittie of London*, produced the year before Peele's 1585 text.[23] It is certainly the case that the publication of Peele's 1585 Show was considered a significant enough moment for the text to be transcribed in its entirety – even down to the slightly amended authorial citation 'Done by George Peele, M. A. in Oxford' – in Strype's 1720 edition of Stow's *Survey*.[24] In the latter, Peele's text appears in a list of mayors and sheriffs under Lord Mayor Dixie's coat of arms; the only overt explanation for its inclusion is the marginal note 'A Speech at this Ld. Maior's Show' underneath Strype's initials, to show that this was an addition to the preceding editions of this work. Strype's inclusion of Peele's text clearly indicated an interest in these works on the former's part which has received surprisingly little commentary, for the transcription of the 1585 text does not stand alone but is followed by regular, although not comprehensive references to later Shows, beginning at 1611. Strype must have had Munday's 1611 text to hand – as he must have had Peele's – for he paraphrases its title page quite closely:

> Chruso-Thriambos. The Triumphs of Gold. Being a Description of the Shows at the Inauguration of this Maior, James Pemberton, Knt. at the Charge of the Goldsmiths. Devised and written by Anthony Munday, Citizen and Draper of London. Imprinted at London by William Jaggard, Printer to the Honourable City of London, 1611.[25]

Strype goes on to cite Munday's *Chrysanaleia* and Heywood's texts for 1631, 1632 and 1633 in the same manner.[26]

As far as the *purpose* of these works is concerned, unlike with plays and their repeated performances, printed texts of occasional events like a Lord Mayor's Show had no further practical function once the day was past. Indeed, a large number of the Show texts bear the date of the entertainment, as if to underscore the point. They were, after all, only ever printed at around the same time as the event. Here they differ from masque texts, which in some cases (Jonson's masques are of course the most notable of these) were republished, sometimes amended, a while after the performance took place. In this respect the printed texts generated by the mayoral Shows are more reminiscent in content, form and purpose of the works produced to commemorate royal progresses and the like. As with these works, printing the Shows may have been intended as largely a commemorative act.[27] In addition, the level of symbolic and emblematic sophistication on display on these occasions might have made it helpful to have a written description to refer to. Writing of Jonson and Dekker's accounts of James's royal entry, Parry observes that the triumphal arches 'were so dense with meaning [and] . . . their detail so extravagantly superfluous to the occasion . . . that it is not surprising that . . . detailed report[s] . . . [were published] so that they could be studied and deciphered at leisure'.[28] Jonson, for one, however, appears to have taken no prisoners with the navigability of his printed text.

Regardless of any possible difficulties on that score, this kind of retrospective scrutiny by readers may well have been essential, for the printed texts, as well as the Shows on which they were based, certainly became more complex as the seventeenth century progressed. Peele's early printed Shows were minimalist (the 1585 text contains only the speeches despite also promising 'the Deuice'), and even in 1605 the Merchant Taylors reimbursed Munday solely 'for printing the bookes of the speeches in the Pageant and other shewes'.[29] It should be noted, however, that the eventual text for the latter year was rather more extensive than this record implies, as Munday included a substantial historical discussion before the speeches, as was his wont. Bergeron raises the possibility that mayoral Shows began to be printed as a way of 'expanding and tapping into a larger audience not bound to the occasion', although such a theory presumes a wider readership for the texts than would be the case if they were simply distributed to members of the Company, who would almost invariably have seen the Show anyway.[30] The relationship between event and text did not always operate in the same way in all occasional works. Lauren Shohet argues that the court masque was initially 'an elite, private . . . performance form . . . but one that was conveyed regularly into a nascent print public sphere'.[31] For the Shows, the opposite was true: the performances were open to all but the texts were produced in relatively limited numbers and probably to a more exclusive readership. Indeed, putting print runs and company records side by side, there does seem to be a degree of congruence between the number of copies of Shows printed in this period and the number of livery members of the Companies that commissioned them. It is therefore *possible* that the bulk of the copies were designed for these recipients.

The Companies certainly had a stake in the books of the Shows. Once the tradition had got fully under way in the early seventeenth century, the habitual publication of at least 200 copies of these works in this period is a phenomenon that tempers somewhat Gadd's conclusion that the livery companies 'were generally uninterested in how contemporary printed works were being employed to disseminate those same [corporate] attributes that they valued so highly'.[32] In some ways these works can be seen to aid the dissemination of the livery companies' public image. The indebtedness of the writers to the generosity of the livery companies is emphasised from the title pages of these texts onwards, and as one might expect, all the writers are at pains to celebrate traditional civic values. Although the printing of the texts was secondary in importance to the enactment and celebration of the mayoral inauguration itself, the companies' expenditure on the texts, even if as a kind of 'vanity publishing', must have been for a reason. On those infrequent occasions when the printed text of a mayoral Show was entered in the Stationers' Register to demonstrate its ownership and thus the right to publish, there must have been a concern about possible piracy of the text, or perhaps of the publication of a competing account of the Show (unlikely though this may seem).

It is a slightly different case for those ephemeral texts that describe royal events, the publication of which was most likely to have been trading on the celebrity of the protagonists as well as the immediacy of the event(s) and where a wider readership is therefore to be expected. Kipling notes that the political significance of some royal entries in the sixteenth century led to their texts being 'published in several languages and distributed all over Europe'.[33] This level of interest would no doubt have been the motivation for the dual publication in 1613 in both London and Edinburgh of *The Magnificent, Princely, and most Royall Entertainments giuen to the High and Mightie Prince, and Princesse*, an account of the entertainments held in Heidelberg to welcome the Elector Palatine and his new English spouse, Princess Elizabeth.[34] In addition, as with other works of this kind, there would have been a 'reportage' aspect, where the readership might have expected to learn more about the activities of the great and the good. These texts would have acted more as a kind of news pamphlet rather than a souvenir or programme.[35] Such a work would most likely have been printed and offered for sale in the usual fashion, which is not often, if at all, the case for the mayoral Shows. This 1613 text itself (which is anonymous – another difference from the Shows) is silent about the rationale for its publication: perhaps this would have been too obvious to need comment. John Taylor's account of the 'Sea-fights & Fire-workes' that accompanied these marriage celebrations, fortunately, takes the reverse approach. Indeed, Taylor is extremely candid about the purpose of this text, beginning it with the explanation that

> I do not write nor publish (this description of fire and water triumphs) to the entent that they should onely reade the relation that were spectators of them to such (perhaps) it will relish somewhat tedious like a tale that is too often told: but I did write these things, that those who are farremoted, not onely in his Maiesties Dominions, but also in foraine territories, may haue an understanding of the glorious pomp. (*Heauens blessing, and earths ioy*, sig. A3r)

Taylor's estimation of the likely reach of his readership is perhaps over-ambitious (although the text does seem to have gone to at least two editions) but he does helpfully flag up the 'reportage' element of such works. Later in the seventeenth century a number of ephemeral works were produced to accompany – or to cash in on – the infamous Pope-burning processions in London in 1679–81, which also had a propagandist function. Again, these works were published anonymously, although, suggestively, it looks as though Elkanah Settle, a writer of mayoral Shows in the 1690s, may have been involved in the Pope-burning processions too. Events of the latter kind and any ensuing texts were, of course, much more a product of topical political contexts than the mayoral Shows – and in the case of the Pope-burning processions they were only temporarily accommodated by the authorities – but all the same they appealed to the same appetite for street pageantry, in the widest sense of the term, as did the Shows.

'A Booke of the Presentatiens': printing the Shows

Although they were in some ways anomalous and we should keep these differences in mind, it is at the same time instructive to examine the printed texts of mayoral Shows in the context of the usual printing and publishing practices of the period. They were, after all, printed in the same shops by the same printers as numerous other works. However, as we have seen with so many aspects of the Shows, the history of their appearance in print is not clear-cut. The earliest instance where at least part of a Show seems to have made it into print is 1566, when 5s was paid by the Ironmongers for printing the 'poses speches and songs, that were spoken and songe by the children in the pagent' (the resulting text has not survived).[36] Robertson and Gordon speculate that this early printed text 'may have been for use by the performers rather than for the convenience of the spectators'.[37] They do not cite any evidence to support this claim, though, nor is there any indication in the Ironmongers' records of how many copies were printed, nor by whom. Peele's 1585 *Deuice of the pageant* thus appears to have been the first printed for wider circulation in a relatively straightforward fashion.

The identity of the printer is one of the few aspects of the printed Shows that we can almost always be sure about.[38] The printers used for the Shows often had extant connections with the writers. This is the case for Robert Raworth and Heywood in the 1630s, a time when Raworth was simultaneously printing some of Heywood's plays.[39] Indeed, from the evidence of the company accounts, where the name of the printer is often left blank, the Companies do not appear to have expressed any especial interest in who printed these works, which suggests that they were content to leave these arrangements to the writers and artificers. Professional writers were, after all, often well placed to liaise with printers. Munday, for instance, had a long-standing connection with Edward Allde, having been apprenticed to his father, John, at the same time as Edward in the late 1570s.[40] Allde junior printed *Himatia-Poleos* (and, it seems, *Camp-bell*, another Munday work, too, for which the imprint is lost) as well as *Londons loue* and other works of this type such as the second edition of Dekker's *Magnificent entertainment*.[41] William Jaggard printed two of Munday's extant Shows (1605 and 1611). Jaggard's connection with Munday may well have derived from the lineage of the former's print shop in Cripplegate, home consecutively to Charlewood, Roberts and then Jaggard, all of whom printed Munday's works.[42] The Stationer Henry Gosson, one of the few *publishers* involved with printed mayoral Shows, had a close relationship with John Taylor over some twenty years and probably published his Show in 1634.[43] Similarly, Nicholas Okes, who printed *Troia-Noua triumphans* in 1612, also printed *The famous history of Sir Thomas Wyatt* (a Dekker and Webster collaboration) in the same year and Dekker's *Guls horne-book* in 1609.[44] Okes had been printing Heywood's works since at least *An apology for actors* in 1612 and their relationship was to persist until Okes's death. In his *Apology* Heywood testified to Okes's care and industriousness as a printer, even if he did so in passing in the course of a savage attack on the 'negligence' of the printer of a previous work.[45] Interestingly, in 1623, when Middleton and Munday were wholly responsible for separate sections of the Show (the water show and the land show), the resulting two texts were produced by different printers: Nicholas Okes printed Middleton's share and Thomas Snodham, Munday's. Munday, in fact, is the least likely of these writers to have developed a consistent relationship with one particular printing house. Of the nine mayoral works by Munday printed between 1605 and 1623, five different printers were involved, including Okes, Purslowe and Allde.

Nicholas Okes was also the printer of some of Webster's plays and his solitary mayoral Show. Indeed, John and Nicholas Okes were by some measure the most commonly used printers for the Shows, being responsible for seventeen of the thirty-one extant works from this period. Okes senior dominated the printing of mayoral Shows from 1612 until 1633; only a handful were produced by other printers in that period.[46] There was a break in the Okes family's hegemony in 1634, when John Taylor wrote the Show text and probably brought his own publishing and printing team along with him. Taylor's Show does not cite a printer, but he was likely to have been Augustine Mathewes, who printed all Taylor's books published by Gosson in 1634–35 (the text is neatly but very sparingly printed, with the use of only rather primitive devices). The standings of the printers varied. The majority, like Raworth and Okes senior and junior, were associated with what Watt calls 'cheap print' – pamphlets, play quartos, popular histories, and so on – whereas others, like the Printer to the City, William Jaggard, had more stature in civic circles. Nicholas Okes was primarily a printer and typesetter of drama and as such would have had the right kind of experience to print mayoral pageants, for, as well as being set out in similar ways to play-texts as far as the verse elements were concerned, the printed Shows were almost all quartos, the form many plays first appeared in (*Londini sinus salutis* and *The triumphs of fame and honour* are, unlike most, in octavo format). Since the texts were published unbound and in quarto or octavo form, their tendency to survive in only very small quantities (if at all) is perhaps only to be expected.[47] Given the extent of Okes's experience by the time he was involved in printing mayoral Shows, one can only assume that the poor quality of the print job evident in some texts was as much the result of a lack of time as of a lack of expertise, and possibly that by the mid-1630s John Okes – who obviously had less experience than his father – may have increasingly been taking over the business.[48] That said, Blayney argues that 'less reputable establishments' 'would have offered the publishers low rates and speedy delivery', both of which would have been relevant factors for the printing of mayoral Shows. Of Nicholas Okes in particular he concludes that 'it is unlikely that workmanship was as high on [his] list of priorities as was profit', and he characterises Okes's output as 'small and cheap'.[49]

In at least two cases – *Chruso-thriambos* (1611) and *The triumphs of truth* (1613) – two substantially different *editions* of the work were printed, which does show that it was thought worthwhile to issue a revised edition, as a printer or publisher's decision to reprint would indicate that further demand for the work was expected. In the case of Middleton's text, the most egregious mistakes were corrected for the second edition, when, Greg argues, the work was 'completely reset'.[50] The opportunity was then taken to combine with *The triumphs of truth* another Middleton text, *The manner of his Lordships entertainment on Michaelmas day last.*[51] This is an account of the entertainment held when Sir Thomas Middleton was elected to office in September at 'that most Famous and Admired Worke of the Running Streame', the Lord Mayor elect's brother, Hugh Middleton's 'New River'. Greg comments of the latter, combined text that

> this publication is unusual. It is possible that the printer intended two simultaneous issues, one containing the oath-day entertainment only, the other the election entertainment as well. It seems more likely, however, that when the copy for the latter was received the type of the four sheets of the earlier [mayoral Show only] issue was still standing, and that advantage was taken of the fact to print a further impression (with . . . alterations) and append new matter to it.[52]

Unfortunately Greg does not address the question of *why* a second edition of Middleton's text was printed. What motivation could there have been to reissue a work that was printed for a particular occasion in limited numbers and not offered for general sale? Perhaps, contrary to the usual assumptions, the second edition, with its additional text, *was* to be sold commercially. Indeed, this yoking together of two or more distinct works is much more commonly seen in relation to royal entertainments, masques and the like than with mayoral Shows. If, as speculated below, Shows were sometimes sold in the conventional way, then this might increase the likelihood that this was the fate of the second edition of Middleton's 1613 Show.

In fact, Middleton's text has a more complex bibliographical history still: it is not simply a matter of the second edition being produced to make corrections to the first. There are a large number of corrections to various copies of Middleton's 1613 text, the extent of which suggests to me that there may, in fact, have been (at least) *three* discrete issues, not two. Three copies of the 'first edition' (STC 17903) survive. The two copies held at the Guildhall Library and Longleat differ from the British Library copy in quite a few respects. Although all three have been categorised as the first edition, each varies from the others, sometimes including corrections that otherwise appear only in the *second* edition. Conversely, the Bodleian copy of this second edition (STC 17904) bears a different set of corrections to the first edition from the British Library copy of the 'same' edition, resulting in another mixture. All in all, in October 1613 Okes's workshop seems to have been busy making press corrections and other amendments in a seemingly arbitrary way, resulting in a confusingly large number of variant states of Middleton's text.

As far as *Chruso-thriambos* is concerned, Pafford, its editor, has stated that the two editions of Munday's Show 'were not of the same impression' (although he believes that both versions of this work were included in the total of 500 copies which were ordered), and he concurs with Greg that STC 18267.5 'was probably in part a corrected reprint' of STC 18267. Although the final pages appear to be unaltered, there are numerous small differences between the two editions of this work, especially on sheets A–B, which appear to have been completely reset. In the process, a couple of unequivocal errors have been amended, but STC 18267.5's 'corrections' are sometimes less accurate than its probable predecessor, and quite a few seem solely to be what Greg calls 'indifferent variants' which may reflect either the compositor's preferred spelling or that of the author, if the printer was working from an authorial manuscript.[53] It is possible that special care may have been taken over the second attempt at this text because the Goldsmiths were expecting members of the royal family to be present at the Show. In addition, on those regular occasions where the authors were responsible for co-organising the printing of the Shows, then it would have been more likely that they would have had a role in correcting proofs. Indeed, Munday's characteristic preference for double vowels has persisted in many of his printed Shows, which, taken with his background as a printer as well as his extensive experience as a jobbing writer by this date, perhaps indicates a close relationship with the printing process.[54]

As well as the two works already discussed, some copies of other mayoral Shows also contain considerable differences from each other. A key example is Middleton's 1622 *Triumphs of honor and vertue*. The corrections to the copy of this work held in the Folger constitute a case that this work exists in variant states, with the BL copy perhaps reflecting an earlier state.[55] Although Greg notes only one variant (on the title page) the Folger copy actually shows numerous minor and not so minor press corrections to typographical errors present in the BL copy, as well as other changes in the second half of the work. Amongst other things, the later compositor – or perhaps Middleton himself – seems to have preferred to use capital letters for nouns and adjectives.[56] The most significant difference is the insertion of two lines of verse on sig. B3v missing in the BL copy. Heywood's *Londini artium* is another text where individual copies bear both minor and more substantial corrections. As well as showing quite a few press corrections to typographical errors, one of the two surviving copies has a passage missing from the second dedication (to the Sheriffs) that does appear in the other copy. Part of this passage, it seems, was originally erroneously placed in the first dedication to the Lord Mayor, and, when the mistake was realised, moved to its correct location in the text and printed with amendments. As with other Okes print jobs, however, the (possibly) earlier imprint has fewer typographical errors than the (later?) one with the dedications accurately printed. Perhaps, again, what we have here is two editions of the same work.

There is an important distinction to be drawn between those fairly numerous opportunistic texts produced to cash in on an event of national significance – such as the marriage of the Count Palatine and Princess Elizabeth – and the commissioned Lord Mayors' Shows texts. For one thing, some of the former texts were printed with noticeably more care and expense than the majority of the Shows, perhaps in the anticipation of financial recompense. Munday's *Londons loue*, for example, which was printed by Allde, features a great deal of (expensive) white space, devices and a large woodcut of a ship as a frontispiece.[57] As the cases discussed above indicate, the Shows were often hastily and clumsily printed, although it is, of course, possible that some of the errors may have originated from the manuscript from which the compositors were working. Nicholas Okes appended an address to the reader in Book Four of Munday's *Amadis de Gaule* (1618), where he (Okes) apologises for 'such slips and errors' he had missed in the printing (sig. A2v). This is the same year as Munday's *Sidero-Thriambos*, also printed by Okes, so it is therefore likely, at that juncture at least, that Okes did not have a dedicated person in place to correct proofs. One can also suppose that a text like a mayoral Show, printed in a short timescale and not, it seems, in any way treated like an elite publication, would have been given only a cursory check-over. Although press corrections were clearly made to mayoral Shows, mistakes did slip through the net. It is certainly the case that some copies of both Nicholas and John Okes's Shows have numerous uncorrected errors, some quite substantial.[58] At the same time, one has only to compare *The triumphs of truth* and all its variants with, say, those works printed by Purslowe, *Metropolis coronata* and *Chrysanaleia*, to see how well mayoral Shows *could* be printed.[59] Indeed, some Shows made greater demands on the printers by including musical notation and foreign languages. Heywood makes repeated recourse to Greek and Latin, for instance, in his Shows, and there are speeches in French and Spanish in *The tryumphs of honor and industry* and in French in *Brittannia's honor*. Musical notation was printed in two Shows, *The triumphs of truth* and *Tes Irenes Trophaea*.

Although they raise many vexing questions, thanks to the diligent bureaucracy of the livery companies the printed texts of the Lord Mayors' Shows can be used to throw light in aspects of printing in this period that cannot readily be gleaned in other contexts. As with the commissioning of the Shows, the Companies' accounts offer information about the cost and size of the print runs. The usual print run appears to be 500 copies (although it was sometimes as few as 200 or 300) and the cost to the Company was between £2 and £4.[60] Owing to some unspecified demand, the Drapers' records for 1638 indicate an additional print run and subsequent cost; in this instance it appears that the (unnamed) printer, John Okes, was paid direct by the Company, rather than via Heywood or the Christmas brothers as intermediaries as was the usual practice.[61] In the following year, Okes – this time named in the Company records – was again paid a further sum for printing 'three hundred bookes for the Companie over and above the number they were to have, by agreement of Mr Christmas'.[62] A total print run of 800 copies, as on this occasion, is large for a mayoral Show, but not an unusual quantity in the general context of early modern printing practices (Blayney cites 800 as the normal print run for a play-text).[63] Taken together with the unusual degree of interest in the printed text evidenced by the Drapers' accounts (as discussed above), perhaps the Companies were belatedly taking the publication of these works more seriously as the 1630s – and the heyday of the Shows themselves – drew to a close.

The cost of printing was generally paid to the writer and/or the artificer, who would have liaised with the printer, although in some cases (such as 1613 and 1617), there was no such intermediary.[64] Munday was paid an unusually generous £6 by the Merchant Taylors in 1605 for the cost of printing the books, perhaps because Jaggard was more expensive than the likes of Okes.[65] The Drapers appear to have had established some kind of relationship with John Okes, whose name (as we have already seen) is mentioned specifically in their accounts in 1639; as with his father in 1613, he appears to have been paid personally – albeit with the 'agreement' of Christmas – rather than via an intermediary. This, however, is an unusual state of affairs: in the majority of cases, the livery company records do not show the name of the printer (nor, frequently, the number of copies ordered). Mayoral shows do not sit comfortably within the category of 'commercial' or 'speculative' print, for sure. In the case of the Shows the printers were simply responding to a payment to print on command a specific number of copies rather than making any kind of independent decision about their commercial viability.

Indeed, by taking payment for arranging to have the texts of the Shows printed, as was commonly the case with these works, the writer and artificer team (or the artificer alone, in some cases) were effectively acting as the *publisher* of the work in question, and may have earned money from commercial sales of the works – assuming this took place – in those cases where they were also responsible for *distributing* the texts. Bald, Bergeron and Munro all assume that the texts were distributed privately and gratis by the Company, which might be the obvious conclusion to come to were it not for the citation of a publisher in three separate mayoral works. There is a reference in the imprint of *Troia-Noua triumphans* to John Wright, a bookseller who was also a publisher of many best-selling books: 'Printed by Nicholas Okes, and are to be sold by Iohn Wright dwelling at Christ Church-gate' (sig. A1r).[66] Middleton's

1621 work *The sunne in Aries* was printed by Edward Allde for 'H. G.' (probably Henry Gosson).[67] *Descensus astraeae*, an early Show, also cites a bookseller and publisher, William Wright, on its title page (the actual printer is not known).[68] That three of these texts refer to booksellers makes it less likely that the printer simply used the wrong imprint on either occasion. Perhaps practice differed: from a payment by the Drapers to 'Mr Mondayes man for bringing the bookes' in 1623 it is probable on this occasion that they were delivered to the body which had paid for them, suggesting that the Company distributed them as well.[69] The texts printed to celebrate royal entries and other such non-civic entertainments appear more regularly, although not invariably, to have publishers (masques, in particular, almost always have both a printer and a publisher).[70]

Only rarely were the printed Shows entered in the Stationers' Register. Indeed, only six were entered in this period: of the surviving works, these were *The triumphs of truth*, *Troia-Noua triumphans*, *Chrysanaleia* and *The triumphs of fame and honour*, along with two works which are no longer extant (Peele's 1588 text and the text for 1604).[71] Royal entries and other entertainments, in contrast, such as Elizabeth's entry into Norwich in 1578 and Christian of Denmark's London entertainment in 1606, appear to have been entered in the Register more consistently. This indicates that such works were treated as more regular kinds of publication (perhaps with sales to the general public) than mayoral Shows.[72] Some Shows, such as Middleton's *Triumphs of truth*, were not entered until after the Show had taken place, suggesting, as Greg notes, that 'unless entrance [to the Register] was delayed the print cannot have been ready on the Lord Mayor's oath-day'.[73] Others, however, were entered beforehand. For instance, Peele's 1588 text was entered in the Stationers' Register by Richard Jones, the printer, on 28 October, i.e. the day before the Show, and 'uppon Condicon that it maye be lycensed', which means it had not yet been authorised for publication.[74] The Stationers' proviso is interesting, for it also indicates that the Company thought it not worth the risk of licensing this text *without* the authority of the censors, as, according to Blayney, they were sometimes prepared to do for texts which were unlikely to offend or which were not considered sufficiently important to need licensing.[75] Without an extant text, however, it is impossible to ascertain why such a tentative decision was made. Another Stationers' Register entry for a lost text relates to 1604 (the year in which Jonson was involved in the mayoral inauguration in some capacity), where the printer Felix Kingston entered 'a

thing touchinge the pagent' on 29 October, the day of the Show.[76]
The word 'thing', as opposed to 'booke' as with all other entries in
the Register, perhaps indicates a very slight publication, more like
a broadsheet than a pamphlet. Two works were entered before or
at the same time as the Show: *Chrysanaleia* on the day of the Show,
to Purslowe, its printer, and Taylor's 1634 text on 14 October to
Henry Gosson.[77] Allde may have got into trouble for *not* entering *The sunne in Aries*. William Jackson speculates that this title
may have been one of the four works which been printed 'without
lycense or entrance', for which offence Allde was reprimanded by
the Stationers in early October 1621.[78] We do know that *Troia-
Noua triumphans* was entered in the Stationers' Register on 21
October, a week before the Show, when, as before, Nicholas Okes
was allowed to print the work 'When yt is further Aucthorised'.[79]
Werner argues on this basis that a manuscript of the text was submitted to Okes for printing by this date, a week or so before the
Show.[80] In contrast, *The triumphs of truth* was not entered until 3
November and there is no stipulation that this text be authorised
in the Stationers' records.[81] Werner's supposition about the 1612
Show is made more plausible because, as he points out, the printed
work shows no awareness that its intended guest, Henry, Prince of
Wales, was not able to attend the Show. 'It is evident therefore', he
writes, 'that Dekker did not revise the text after 29 October, that
it is not a description of the actual event [in this respect], and that
it was either already in print, or in the process of being printed,
just before or simultaneously with the pageant'.[82] Conversely, since
The triumphs of truth was not entered until a week *after* the Show,
this is likely to indicate that the work had not been printed by 29
October and hence may not have been available for distribution on
the day.

This raises two questions: who did the distributing of these hundreds of books, and at what point did this take place? It is rather
difficult to tell, for we do not know whether the printed texts of
Shows were actually sold or simply given away. Only after the
Restoration do the texts have prices or other signs of sale on them.[83]
The assumptions underpinning scholarship in this area are ripe for
full re-examination. A tantalising reference in a work published
in a timely fashion in October 1617 suggests that mayoral Shows
were to be found on booksellers' stalls alongside plays, ballads
and the like. Henry Fitzgeffrey's *Satyres: and satyricall epigrams*
cites 'Sightes, to be read: of my Lo. Maior's day's [*sic*]' in its list
of the 'rout / Of carelesse fearlesse Pamphlets' that populated 'our

Time-stalles' (sig. A4r).[84] The situation becomes clearer after 1660. Settle's 1698 Show, *Glory's Resurrection*, appears to have the word 'price' printed on the title page underneath the imprint (the 'e' of 'price', if 'price' it was, has been cut away).[85] One copy of Settle's *The Triumphs of London* (1695) appears to have a price of 3d written in a contemporary hand on its title page, along with the date of the Show, '29 Octob.'. Had the earlier texts been sold, their retail price would probably have been analogous to quarto play-texts, which Blayney has calculated to range from around 4d to 10d per copy, partly depending on the number of pages.[86] The automatic assumption on the evidence available would be that these texts were simply commemorative and distributed to a select readership, at least in the first instance. If this is an accurate view of the mayoral Shows, then they were, naturally, most likely to have been given away gratis, although such liberality must be put alongside the fact that the Company members, who may have been those who received the books, had to pay to be part of the procession anyway. In any case, whether the texts were sold or not, as we have seen, the printers would have been under pressure to finish printing the texts as quickly as possible, while the event still had the maximum currency for *any* potential reader.

Levin argues that 'a somewhat specialised audience for [the printed Shows] . . . is implied by their tendency to assume a reader's familiarity with the overall shape and geography of the shows'.[87] Heywood does refer back to a previous Show in *Londini artium* in such a way as to suggest that he is expecting a degree of continuity in his readership. Since the 1632 Show was presented on behalf of the Haberdashers' Company for the second year running, Heywood once again brings in St Katherine, the company's patron saint. In the second text he states that there is no need to rehearse 'the Etymologie of her Name, her Royal Birth, her Breeding, the Life and Death [because] in the last yeeres Discourse I gaue a large Charactar' (sig. B2v). He also signals an expectation of a fairly erudite readership, refraining from explaining the 'Hystory' of Perseus and Andromeda, 'but rather referr[ing] the Reader to Ouid, who hath most elegantly expressed it': the side-note 'Meta-' is obviously a reference to the relevant Ovid work to which the reader is encouraged to refer (*ibid.*, sig. B3v).

Some clues about how these events were translated into print can be gleaned from another one-off text, printed in 1639, *Mars, his triumph*. This was written by William Barriffe to commemorate military exercises by men of the Artillery Garden at Merchant

Taylors' Hall in October of the previous year and it bears similarities in terms of its context to mayoral Shows, especially in its address to a metropolitan audience. In the dedication Barriffe explains his recourse to print with helpful candour:

> the well contriving and exact performance [of the exercises] . . . induced many of the judicious Spectators to desire copies: which through severall transcriptions became so imperfect, that I was requested by many to bring it to the Presse . . . This I was the more willing to suffer, by reason no more were to pass the print, then barely might serve such Gentlemen who were desirous of them, being members of our own Company. As not being willing that so rough and unpolishd a draught should be exposed to the publick view.[88] (sig. *4r)

Although his stance of authorial modesty is a commonplace in this period, Barriffe does reveal aspects of the way in which his work made it into print from its initial manuscript circulation. Clearly, although it bore the name of both a printer ('I. L') and publisher (Ralph Mab), this text was expressly not intended for a wide audience. Barriffe's dedication tells us that it was effectively an 'on demand' publication, produced after the event, and intended to supplement successive manuscript transcriptions with their inherent instability. Only 'Spectators' of 'our own Company' are cited as a potential readership. An account of a Jonsonian masque performed at the house of Lord Haye on 22 February 1617 is claimed by Greg to have been 'apparently printed for private distribution on the occasion of the performance', although there is nothing specific in the text itself to give this impression apart from the absence of an imprint; unlike Barriffe's work, there is no explanatory preamble.[89]

The writers of the Shows, unfortunately, tend not to be so expansive. Those texts that do not scrupulously describe all the pageantry (Heywood's are a case in point) *may* have been produced as programmes, issued on the day to onlookers with no particular requirement to be comprehensive. In its initial pages John Squire's *Tes Irenes Trophaea* quite clearly positions itself as a programme through its use of the present tense and in the way in which it represents the relationship between the book and the event. In the dedication the author expresses the wish that the text will add to the 'pleasure' he hopes the Lord Mayor 'will conceiue at view of those reall Tryumphs' (sig. A2r). It is as if Francis Jones had been handed a copy before the day's festivities began, although the main body of this text, oddly, is written in the *past* tense. The Ironmongers'

Court minutes certainly imply that this Company was responsible for distributing the printed texts to its members and other worthies, for in 1629 Garret Christmas and Dekker were instructed to 'give' the Company 500 copies once they were printed, as were Heywood and the Christmas brothers six years later.[90] As we have seen, the onlookers at large were given souvenirs, of a kind, in the form of various items scattered from the pageant cars and tableaux stations, such as coins, spices and in 1610, 'Tynn Compters [counters] which were throwen out of the Shipp, into the Streetes amongst the people'.[91]

As the uncertainty about their circulation indicates, the printed texts of Lord Mayors' Shows did not fit altogether neatly into normal commercial publishing practices. In 1611, the books were given to the Goldsmiths' Company to disseminate, although Robertson and Gordon claim that 'there is no evidence that [the books] were ever distributed as programmes'.[92] Their theory is that the books were only commemorative and issued after the event, although if this was the case then the 'explanations' of the more arcane symbolism that some of the texts contain would have been of no help to the onlookers if they were not available on the day itself; putative readers would have had to rely on their memory. As we will see below, the commonplace use of the present tense also indicates that the texts could, in principle, have been used as guides to the proceedings.[93] Cressy writes that 'printed programmes' were sold to spectators of the Gunpowder Plot firework display held in 1647 'which explained . . . each tableau', so it is at least possible that the same arrangement could have taken place for some of the Shows in the years previously.[94] Although very brief, this latter text, *A Modell of the Fire-works to be presented at Lincolnes-Inne Fields on the 5th of November 1647*, certainly follows the 'description of tableau followed by explanation of its meaning' format that had become usual practice with printed mayoral Shows by then. This is certainly the approach Middleton takes in *The triumphs of integrity*. Towards the end of the text he pauses to offer his readership some elucidation: 'I thought fit in this place to giue this [pageant] it's [*sic*] full Illustration', he writes (sig. B4r). It seems, then, most likely that practice simply varied: in some years the books were distributed on the day and in others not.

Unlike mayoral Shows, continental 'festival books' were usually composed of both text and image. As Ravelhofer writes, these 'aimed at a comprehensive account of a courtly spectacle, which at best included full illustrations of the event'.[95] The printed texts of London mayoral Shows, however, were themselves exclusively textual. As a result, pictorial images relating to the Shows are even rarer than the printed texts, and raise similar questions about form and function. Who created them? What was their purpose? To whom were they given? Are they accurate representations of the pageants produced on the day? Alongside Booth's sketches (discussed in Chapter 3), the best known, most extensive and as a result the most reproduced illustrations are those associated with the 1616 Show, the originals of which are still in Fishmongers' Hall, though in poor condition. These images, known as the Fishmongers' Pageant Roll, mostly bear handwritten captions, written in the past tense. For instance, the picture of the 'fishing busse' is captioned 'This bursse [*sic*] served on land and so did all the rest of the shewes following'.[96] The use of the past tense might indicate a commemorative function for these images. More evidence for this supposition can be gleaned by the comment 'This remaineth for an Ornament in Fishmongers Hall' written above the picture of the King of the Moors; similar notes are appended to a number of the other devices. The writer helpfully adds that one of the pageants was 'unfit' to be kept as an 'ornament' owing to the large number of children used to 'beautify' it, and recommends for future reference that 'if the house will have a pageant to beautify their hall they must appoint fewer children therein'.[97] The repeated references to the images being displayed at the Company Hall show that, whatever their *original* purpose, they ended up being used commemoratively, and the latter quotation implies that this may have not been uncommon practice. It is thus possible that similar illustrations were produced for other Shows as part of a team's 'project' but not kept. The survival of these images to this day shows that, unlike the Show books, they were and remain prized by the Fishmongers' Company.

However, as with the printed works, one should not assume that the pictures necessarily truthfully represent the pageants displayed on the day. On the King of the Moors image the reader is told to 'note' that the other Moors, although there depicted on foot, actually 'ridd on horsebacke' (as Munday's text also states). Such discrepancies may have been inevitable, of course, given the different media concerned. The drawing of Walworth in his bower, for instance, is perforce static, whereas the staging of the pageant has Walworth waking from sleep or death, sitting up and speaking (see Figure 17). Indeed, the caption on this particular image states as much, echoing Munday's text: 'this was a tombe or monum[en]t placed in Powles Church Yeard whereon ley Sr Wm Walworth who

17 The pageant of Walworth's bower/tomb from *Chrysanaleia*

risse from the same & made a speech to the Lord Maior & so ridd on horsebacke for that day'.[98] The 'conceit' of this pageant was indeed probably impossible to realise in a drawing, for Walworth is described first as 'a Marble Statue' who then rises and takes horse (sig. B3r). Furthermore, a degree of artistic licence is in evidence. The pageant chariot of Richard II in the printed text, for example, is described as having wheels by means of which it was moved around, but in the drawing the pageant in its entirety (including the wheels) is shown fixed to a block, with chains suggesting the edifice was drawn along in some unspecified fashion, making the wheels redundant (see Figure 9). As depicted, it is hard to see how the pageant could have been transported, and the presence of a similar block structure on some of the other images suggests that these were drawn for display rather than practical purposes.

It is equally unclear who produced these images and wrote the notes on them. The captions do not seem to be in Munday's hand, nor are they in the hand of the Fishmongers' clerk who wrote the Court minutes for 1616. It is possible that they were drawn by 'Mr Colle a Carver or graver', whose name appears (albeit in a different hand) on the Walworth bower image, as it seems logical that the artisan who made the pageants would have been best placed to draw them. If this was the case, they could conceivably have been based on working drawings for the pageants, to accompany the writer's and artificer's 'plot', perhaps with written annotations added with a view to posterity. This is not conclusive, however, for the images also include members of the procession on horseback dressed in the usual attire and it would seem unnecessary for those bidding for the commission to illustrate an aspect of the event which would have been the same as always. As with the use of the past tense, the whole purpose of the illustrations may have been commemorative and their origin retrospective. Perhaps it is understandable that Nichols does not speculate about the timing and function of the images.

'Fauourable conceit, must needs supply the defect of impossible performance': text and event

A fundamental question I will now address is the nature of the relationship between the printed text and the event it sought to represent. Palmer reminds us that such a relationship was not necessarily straightforward: 'the pageant experience is typically converted into an authorised text that *claims* to simply report the entertainment. In making such a claim, these texts mystify their own part in a secondary shaping of everyone and everything included in the original performance'. As he notes, 'scholarship has yet to recognise these kinds of secondary shapings'.[99] Furthermore, as well as being distinct from the performance, as time progressed the printed texts became much more than simply a reproduction of the speeches given on the day. These texts are therefore in the main a complex hybrid of description *and* interpretation. They are, Hentschell writes, 'self-consciously *textual*', bearing elements such as dedications, prefatory matter, printer's details and so on, all of which she usefully describes as 'extra-theatrical, giving the reader more and new information than would have been allowed the spectator'.[100] Middleton's *Tryumphs of honor and industry* is a case in point: unless the printed text *did* function as a programme, the translations provided in the printed text of the speeches given on the day in French and Spanish are unlikely to have been available to the audience on the day; hence, perhaps, Middleton's statement that only 'a small number' of those present would have understood them (sig. B2r).

The discrepancies between text and performance were not always as well disguised as one might assume. The authors of a number of the printed Shows are surprisingly frank about the logistical and other problems that may have affected their ability to present the entertainment as it had originally been planned. Bergeron offers a neat conceptualisation of the dialectic between text and event, arguing that

> as the book seeks to 'fix' the event . . . it apparently liberates the dramatist to create materials not represented in the street entertain-ment . . . [T]hrough this gap he moves with digressions, descriptions and discourses on sometimes arcane topics. That gap may also consist of ellipses – omitted details of the dramatic event. We therefore come to experience the pageant . . . texts as events themselves, resembling but differing from the show.[101]

Even Stephen Harrison's printed illustrations of the arches he created for James's coronation entry, which one might assume would be accurate representations, do not provide identical details to the written descriptions given by Jonson, Dekker and Middleton.[102] Gasper has noted that Dekker, in particular, chooses to record 'not what the King saw and heard, but what Thomas Dekker thought the King ought to have seen and heard'.[103] These texts had their own agendas, and faithful representation of what happened on the day was not necessarily chief among them. After all, it was not until the seventeenth century that the printed texts attempted to do more than simply publish the speeches. Watanabe-O'Kelly asserts that 'the official account [of a festivity] sets down and explicates the political programme of the festival as depicted in the official iconography of that festival'.[104] As a result, we should be cautious about how much we credit their representations, for, as she states, such texts tend to 'narrate what the organisers hoped would happen rather than what did happen'.[105] These texts are, crucially, fashioned and authored, and some, as we will see, are noticeably self-conscious about their literariness: as Bergeron has argued, 'textual performance here fantasises theatrical performance'.[106] Johnson has pointed out that the texts sometimes 'read much more like the script of a contemporary play than the account of public experience'.[107] The regular commissioning of playwrights to produce these texts was only ever going to enhance this aspect of them.

Probably the most extreme example of a disparity between the printed text and Show itself occurred in 1605, where the Show was brought to an untimely end by very inclement weather and then repeated a few days later on All Saints' Day. Indeed, given the timing of the Shows in late October it is quite remarkable that this seems to be the only year when the weather was so bad that the event had to be completely called off, although there are other occasions – 1612, for example, where high winds nearly ruined the water show – when the festivities were to some extent curtailed.[108] The expense and, of course, the underlying importance of the event was such that in most cases those concerned tried to soldier on. The 1605 Show, however, was restaged in its entirety: even the sword-players were re-employed. Munday's text, however, gives no sign of this eventuality (perhaps it was printed before 29 October), and if it were not for the Merchant Taylors' accounts recording the loss of the 'great coste . . . bestowed upon their Pageant and other shewes' and the additional expenses of 'repairing' the 'shewes' so that they could be replayed, one would not know that this had taken place.[109] The case of the 1605 Show, together with other more trivial instances, demonstrates that more uncertainties are introduced if one accepts that the relationship between the event and the printed text is contingent rather than straightforward.

As we have seen in relation to so many facets of the Shows, practice varied. Some, although not many, printed texts made explicit claims to represent the day's events both fully and faithfully. *Troia-Noua triumphans* states on its title page that '*All* the Showes, Pageants, Chariots of Triumph, with other Deuices, (*both* on the Water and Land) [are] here *fully* expressed' (sig. A1r; my emphases). Similarly, in *Londons tempe*, Dekker's title page claims that 'All the particular Inuentions, for the Pageants, Showes of Triumph, both by Water and land [are] here fully set downe' (sig. A1r). These instances resemble the way in which in this period play-texts were almost invariably printed with some variant of 'as performed by X company at Y playhouse' on their title pages: in both cases, a kind of authority is being claimed. However, of the other pageant writers only Taylor takes the same line. He is quite emphatic about the authority of this work, stating on his title page that 'The particularities of every Invention in all the Pageants, Shewes and Triumphs both by Water and Land, are following fully set downe' (sig. A2r). More typical is the relationship between the text and the event as outlined in *Tes Irenes Trophaea*, which merely offers on its title page an 'explication of the seuerall shewes and deuices', with no definite guarantees that the 'explication' did reflect how the 'shewes and deuices' materialised. Indeed, this phraseology does not even guarantee that Squire was responsible for *originating*, as well as 'explicating', said shows and devices, although at the same time it is unlikely that he would have been asked simply to write them up. The title page of Middleton's 1613 Show simply says that it contains 'all the Showes, Pageants, Chariots, Morning, Noone, and Night Triumphes' (sig. A1r). Munday is more ambiguous in *Sidero-Thriambos*, stating in his dedication to the Ironmongers that 'the whole scope of the deuices aymed at, and were ordered according to [the Company's] direction: are briefly set downe in this Booke' (sig. A3r). Here the ability to present the 'whole scope' might be seen as potentially in conflict with Munday's stated aim to 'briefly set downe' the content of the Show.

These texts were indeed composed of different elements, and the writers did not all approach the task in the same way. It is important to keep a distinction in mind between those aspects of the texts which pertain exclusively to print and thus to the reader's understanding of the work, such as preambles, dedicatory material and comments on the Show in action, and those parts of the texts, such as the speeches, which reflect the viewers' experience. As Manley comments, the printed Shows were 'no mere script'.[110] Munday's general practice was to embark on a historical overview of the City, the livery company and/or the Lord Mayor in question, then supply descriptions of the various pageants and devices, and then append the speeches almost as a supplement. Heywood took fewer pains to be comprehensive; indeed, he is often quite frank about the gaps in his text. Dekker and Middleton, in contrast, habitually switch from prose description to speeches and back again, in an attempt, one imagines, to give a full and authentic account of the day. The joins do sometimes show. The list of royal, ecclesiastical and ducal past members of the Merchant Taylors with which Dekker concludes the book entitled *Troia-Noua triumphans* clearly belongs only to the printed text rather than to the actual event. The list has no apparent function within the pageantry, and Dekker also explains to Swinnerton that 'if I should lengthen this number [of names], it were but to trouble you with a large Index of names only, knowing your expectation is to bee otherwise feasted' (sig. C3r). Dekker's expectation, it appears (borne out by the way he dedicates the work, discussed below), is that the Lord Mayor is following the text as the day unfolds.

Other texts indicate a more commemorative, or at least a retrospective function by being written or partly written in the past tense, although we must remember that it was quite possible that the past tense may have been used to confer an *air* of authenticity upon that which was *supposed* to have happened. *Tes Irenes Trophaea*, for instance, begins by stating that 'the first shew, or presentment, on the water, *was* a Chariot'; thereafter all such descriptions are in the past tense (sig. A3r). In contrast, Heywood refers to 'the Showes, *now in present* Agitation' in *Londini sinus salutis* (sig. A4v; my emphasis). *Chruso-thriambos* commences with an account of how 'First, concerning the seruices performed on the Water, when [the Lord Mayor] tooke Bardge, with all the other Companes towards Westminster; supposition must needes giue some gracefull help to inuention' (sig. A3r–v). The text then rapidly reverts to the present tense, however, suggesting that Munday may have adapted the scenario for publication by 'topping and tailing' its various sections to render it suitably retrospective. Even so, the text is so dense with historical and mythical explication that the capaciousness of a printed text must always have been in mind. The first pageant, the 'Orferie', is described not simply in terms of the appropriate figures it bears and their significance to goldsmithing, but with, in addition, a lengthy account of the 'back story' of Chthoon and her daughters Chrusos and Argurion, and of 'that greedy and neuer-satisfied Lydian King' Midas (sig. B1r). Even the 'Touch-Stone' that Chrusos bears on the pageant has its own history, as Munday's text reveals. Although Leofstane summarises some of this information in his address to the Lord Mayor at St Lawrence Lane, none of this earlier and wider contextualisation would have been readily available to the onlookers on the day of the inauguration in the absence of a book.

Munday's *Metropolis coronata* obligingly indicates how events actually unfolded on the day by mentioning measures taken to change the 'script' in order to deal with a delay. He writes that 'because after my Lords landing, protraction necessarily required to be auoyded . . . such speeches as should haue been spoken to him by the way, were referred till his Honours returne to Saint Paules in the afternoone' (sig. B3r–v).[111] Perhaps it had taken longer to get back down-river than anticipated. Heywood makes the same kind of gesture towards authenticity in *Londini speculum*, where he comments that 'these few following Lines may . . . be added unto Jupiters message, delivered by Mercury, which though too long for the Bardge, may perhaps not shew lame in the booke, as being lesse troublesome to the Reader than the Rower' (sig. B4r). In both cases, the writers' words make it pretty certain that these particular works were not finalised or circulated until after the Shows had taken place. Dekker's *Brittannia's honor* is an example of what seems to be the opposite case, for he is typically frank about a possible revision to the day's schedule in such a way as to make it clear that the text was printed before the event took place. As with Queen Anna in 1611 and Prince Henry in 1612, a royal visitor was expected in 1628 – Queen Henrietta Maria. Dekker writes that '*if* her Maiestie be pleased on the Water, or Land, to Honor These Tryumphes with her Presence, This following Speech in French *is then* deliuered to her' (sigs A4v–B1r; my emphases). Dekker also discloses that, had the Queen been present, she would have received a copy of 'a Booke of the Presentatiens' specifically decorated for its royal recipient, 'All the Couer, being set thicke with Flowers de Luces in Gold' (sig. B1r). A speech of welcome is also reproduced in the text, in both French and English. It is not clear whether the 'Booke' planned for the Queen was the present one with a fancy cover, or a special copy tailored for its recipient.

The texts' bearing on the events is therefore often uncertain. The 1590 text states in its final page, as a kind of afterthought following an account of Walworth's famous deeds, that 'it is to be understood that Sir William Walworth pointeth wherewith the king did endue [*sic*] him, which were placed neere about him in the Pageant' (*The deuice*, sig. A4r). It is unclear if those who are supposed to do the 'understanding' are subsequent readers, although this does seem the likeliest interpretation. The text concludes with a brief epilogue:

Time.
 Time serues for all things,
  Time runneth fast,
 We craue your patience,
  For the time is past.

(sig. A4r)

The pronoun 'we' perhaps indicates that these final words were spoken on the day and addressed to an audience rather than a readership. Nelson's text therefore seems to be gesturing towards both.

Perhaps because he was new to the genre in 1612, Dekker, despite the claims of accuracy on his title page as cited above, goes further still towards preserving contingency in his text. He writes in *Troia-Noua triumphans* at one point that '*either* during this speech [of Envy], *or else* when it is done, certaine Rockets flye up into the aire' (sig. C1r; my emphasis). In contrast, Middleton's *The tryumphs of honor and industry* is not only written in the present tense but by a complex use of personal pronouns invokes the reader's – or the viewer's – attention towards the spectacle before them, thereby exemplifying Palmer's assertion that 'commentary frames performance'.[112] Thus Middleton writes that 'about this Castle of Fame are plast many honorable figures . . . If you looke vpon Truth first, you shall finde her properly exprest' (sig. B4v). Here, as Levin comments, Middleton 'does not merely describe the emblematic participants, he takes us by the hand and points'.[113] Two years later Middleton expressed himself again in a similar fashion: 'let mee draw your attentions to his Honours entertainment vpon the water', he tells his readers (*The triumphs of loue and antiquity*, sig. A4v). In *Londini emporia* Heywood similarly remarks that 'the Fabricke it selfe [of the first water pageant] being visible to all needeth not any expression from me' (sig. A4v). *Sidero-Thriambos*, in contrast, comes across as having been presented to the Ironmongers' Company after the event, as Munday's dedication states that 'what the whole scope of the deuises aymed at, and were ordered according to your direction: are briefly set downe in this Booke' (sig. A3r). The descriptions of the devices themselves, one should note, are expressed in the dominant present tense. Indeed, Munday switches from past to present in the space of two consecutive sentences: 'Certain gallant Knights in Armour', he writes, '*haue* the charge or guiding of [a] Cannon . . . This *was* first imployed on the water, in the mornings seruice, and afterwards helpeth the dayes further Triumph' (sig. B2v; my emphases). I interpret this passage as having been partly derived from the original explanation of the devices, as presented to the Company and/or used to construct the pageantry, with a coda to explain what took place on the day added for the occasion of print. In the haste to bring these works to print by, or soon after, the day of the Show it is hardly surprising that one ends up with a composite of various sources, sometimes with the raw edges showing.

Accordingly, like *Sidero-Thriambos*, Munday's *Metropolis coronata* shows vestiges of the original plot offered to the Drapers in the very same sentence as evidence of how the actual Show turned out. He begins, somewhat incongruously, in a provisional manner ('as occasion best presenteth it selfe') and then turns to the actuality of the day:

> afterward, as occasion best presenteth it selfe, when the heate of all other employments are calmly overpast: Earle Robin Hood, with Fryer Tuck, and his other braue Huntes-men, attending (now at last) to discharge their duty to my Lord, which the busie turmoile of the whole day could not before affoord. (sig. C1v)

In *Londini sinus salutis* Heywood too sometimes describes the pageants in both the past and present tense, such as when he writes that 'the next Modell by Land, which was onely showne upon the Water, is one of the twelue Celestiall signes' (sig. A5v). For instance, he writes in the present tense of the firing of ordnance after a speech, but in the same sentence tells his reader 'now I come to the fift and last'. The writers occasionally add interventions in their own voices, so to speak. Towards the very end of *The triumphs of truth* the present tense used to describe the pageantry is mixed with an interpellation of authorial voice, when Middleton, in the middle of his account of the day's spectacle, thanks Nichols, Grinkin and Munday and then returns to his account as if the interruption had never happened (sigs D2v–D3r). Heywood also at times inserted himself into his text quite overtly, with an oddly defamiliarising effect. In *Londini sinus salutis* he cites only briefly those aspects of the Ironmongers' history and classical antecedents which he might have discussed at length: 'Heere I might enter into large discourse, concerning the commodiousnesse of Iron and Steele . . . with other fixions to the like purpose'. However, he tells how he deliberately chose not to serve up pre-used material, for 'these hauing been exposed to the publick view vpon occasion of the like solemnity, & knowing withall that Cibus bis coctus [twice cooked food], relisheth not the quesie stomackes of these times. I therefore purposly omit them' (sig. B1r). There is no question that this part of the text is retrospective.

Heywood similarly negotiates – not without awkwardness – the correct path through his material. There is an intervention in *Londini status pacatus* which again is located uncomfortably between the last two speeches of the day, although it might have been better placed in the prefatory section where he introduces the mayor and his Company in the traditional fashion, or alternatively tagged on at the end as an appendix. As it stands, it serves as another example of the fragmented nature of these texts.[114] Heywood writes, rather defensively:

> one thing I cannot omit, concerning the Wardens and Committies of this Worshipful Society of the Drapers; that howsoever in all my writing I labour to avoyd what is Abstruse or obsolete: so withall I study not to meddle with what is too frequent and common: yet in all my expressions either of Poeticall fancie, or (more grave History,) their apprehensions went equally along with my reading. (sig. C3v)

Heywood's practice in this respect differs quite markedly from some of his predecessors, especially Munday, who habitually made a point of giving the reader, if not the viewer, extensive historical contextualisation of the Shows in general, and often of the livery company in question, without any self-consciousness about its appropriateness. The use of personal pronouns is often indicative of the intended audience and/or readership, of course. In the speeches 'you' more often than not is directed at the Lord Mayor; in the expository material in prose, however, a readership is implied. 'I' and 'you', as Bergeron has remarked, 'imply a dialogue with a reader', and accordingly Taylor is even more preoccupied with the reader's experience than Munday tended to be. He concludes *The triumphs of fame and honour* with the explanation that 'these few expressions I thought fit to set downe here for the illustration of such words and places as may seeme hard and obscure to some meane Readers' (sig. B6v).[115] Middleton makes a similar point slightly more tactfully in *The triumphs of honor and vertue*, where 'to adde a little more help to the fainter Apprehensions' amongst his readership, he explains that 'the three Merchants . . . haue reference to the Lord Maior and Sheriffes' (sig. B2v). It seems unlikely that Taylor would address the dignitaries of the Clothworkers' Company, those whom he elsewhere terms 'the Noble Fellowship and Brother-hood of Clothworkers', in such terms, so a wider readership is signalled here. Indeed, Taylor goes to some lengths with his 'explanations', which form a series of appendices to the main body of the text. In case they were unaware of European geography, the reader is informed, for instance, that 'Po [is] a famous river in Italy [and] Seine a river in France which runs through Paris'; further afield, it is revealed that 'Ierusalem [is] the chiefe Citie of Iudea' (sigs B4v and B6v).

In *Troia-Noua triumphans* Dekker appends a note to explain that the water show does not feature in his text, despite the fact that the title page includes it:

> the title page of this Booke makes promise of all the Shewes by water, as of these On the Land; but Apollo hauing no hand in them, I suffer them to dye by that which fed them; that is to say, Powder & Smoke. I had deuiz'd One, altogether Musicall, but Times glasse could spare no Sand, nor lend conuenient Howres for the performance of it. (sig. D1v)

There are two points at issue here. On the one hand, Dekker had 'deviz'd' a suitably 'musicall' water show for which there was insufficient time, and, on the other hand, those aspects of the water show which were performed on the day – exclusively composed of cannon, it would seem – do not appear to have gained his approbation (perhaps he, as 'Apollo', had no hand in them). One gets the impression that Dekker was a bit displeased at how things turned out. This text generally retains so much that is tentative that it seems likely to have been based more on what was *intended* to happen than on the reality. Indeed, throughout Dekker's mayoral works we find sections that read more like a prospectus or a brief than a retrospective record. Envy's speech towards the end of this Show was intended either to be accompanied by or followed by gunfire, as Dekker's text rather awkwardly states: 'This done, *or as it is in doing*, those twelue that ride armed discharge their Pistols' (sig. C4v). Indeed, I would speculate that a large part of Dekker's printed text for 1612 was imported directly from his original 'plot' – with all the provisionality that this implies – with either no cognisance or no concern that the logistical tone throughout might strike the reader oddly.[116] Munday's account of the making of the 1616 Show also foregrounds the processes that lay behind the production. His use of the word 'our' alludes to the teamwork he and Grinkin engaged in, an impression underscored by the text's seeming use of the original brief in phrases like 'our first deuice' and 'we next present' (sigs B1r and B2r).

These instances serves as an instructive reminder that the printed work should not readily be assumed to be identical to the day's performance. The texts related to royal entries and other civic entertainments celebrating the monarch and his or her family are, however, more consistently commemorative. Even so, as with his later Show, Dekker's account of James's 1604 royal entry includes some speeches that were not heard on the day; the first edition admits that this was the case owing to the possibility of the King being wearied by overlong festivities.[117] Indeed, Dekker is especially likely to preserve contingency in his texts, perhaps because of his abiding interest in theatrical effect. Another of Middleton's civic texts may offer us some clues as to one of the relationship between printed book and event. In his second year as City Chronologer, 1621, he published *Honorable entertainments compos'de for the seruice of this noble cittie*, quite a long work comprising ten ad hoc entertainments in the form of verse, prose and speeches which took place before civic and Privy Council dignitaries during Easter week 1620.[118] The entertainments were centred on the marriage of Charles Howard, Baron of Effingham, and Mary Cockayne, the eldest daughter of the Lord Mayor for whom Middleton had also written the inaugural Show in 1619, the year before the entertainments in question.[119] The publication date confirms that Middleton's text is retrospective, and the dedication to Francis Jones, the current Lord Mayor, also establishes the printing of the text as between October 1620 and October 1621, the dates of Jones's mayoralty. Furthermore, the dedication implies that the dedicatees (the Lord Mayor, aldermen and other civic dignitaries) were present at the entertainments:

> Those things that tooke Ioy (at seuerall Feasts)
> To giue you Entertainment, as the Guests
> They held most truly Worthy, become now
> Poore Suiters to be entertaynde by you,
> So were they from the first; their Suite is then,
> Once seruing you, to be receiude agen,
> And You, to equall Iustice are so true,
> You alwaies cherish that, which honors You.
>
> (sig. A2r–v)

However, for this text to be printed at all indicates that there would have been a wider readership than simply those present at what was, in one case (and despite the presence of important public figures), essentially a private, family event. There must also have been a reason why the accounts of these disparate events were put together into a single work and issued a year or so later, when quite some time had elapsed.

Further ways of conceptualising the relationship between the printed text and the event emanate from the 1629 Show by Dekker and Christmas, which was printed as *Londons tempe*. *Londons tempe* is a unique instance where we have a printed work and an eyewitness account that includes sketches (Abram Booth's), as well as exceptionally full livery company records. For in this instance, fortuitously, the Ironmongers' Court minutes for 27 October (two days before the actual Show) contain an entry called 'The explanacion of the Shewe on the Lord Maiors day', which details each of the six individual pageants performed during the Show. That it exists at all is notable, for it is very unusual for Company records to preserve this level of detail about the *content* of the actual pageantry. The only equivalent instances where other Company records provide more than minimal information about the content of the Show were decades earlier, in 1561 and 1568, where the speeches given on the day of the mayoral inauguration were transcribed in the Merchant Taylors' records. If, as it seems, the Ironmongers' Company took an especial interest in the content of their Shows it is perhaps not a coincidence that Munday draws attention to his 1618 Show having been 'ordered according to [the Ironmongers'] direction' (*Sidero-Thriambos*, sig. A3r). However, there is no explanation for the Ironmongers' 'explanacion' of 1629: it appears at the end of the day's minutes accompanied by two marginal notes that simply state 'Pageantes' (see Figure 18). The descriptions are written in a different hand from the rest of the Company clerk's minutes, which does not appear to be either Dekker's or Christmas's, going by their signatures in these minutes.

The Ironmongers' descriptions of the pageants, although briefer than those in the printed text, do follow the latter very closely. Their account of the first 'Scene' of the Show begins as follows:

> The first Scene is a Watterworke presented by Oceanus Kinge of the Sea sitting in the vast shell of a Siluer Scollupp, reyning in the heads of two wild Seahorses their maines falling aboute their neckes shining with curles of gold. On his head is placed a Diadem whose bottome is a conceited corronett of gold.[120]

Londons tempe reads:

> The first scene is a Water-worke, presented by Oceanus, King of the Sea . . . He . . . sits Triumphantly in the Vast (but Queint) shell of a siluer Scollop, Reyning in the heads of two wild Seahorses, proportioned to the life, their maynes falling about their neckes, shining with curles of gold. On his head . . . is placed, a Diadem, whose Bottome, is a conceited Coronet of gold. (sig. A4r)

18 Extract from the Ironmongers' Company records (1629):
'the explanacion of the Shewe'

The identical use of adjectives ('vast', 'wild' and 'conceited'), in particular, is significant and suggests a common source, which might have been authorial and based on Dekker and Christmas's original brief, backing up the contention I made previously about Dekker's practice. In 1613 the Grocers recorded that Munday had presented to them a 'Devise or proiect in wryting sett downe', which he offered to read to the Company Court.[121] Assuming that this was common practice, it is therefore entirely feasible that the Ironmongers had access to Dekker and Christmas's plot in written form, making it easier to copy that plot into their minutes. Strangely, two of the passages in these minutes describe the pageants in the past tense ('The fourth presentation was Lemnions fforge', states one), although the

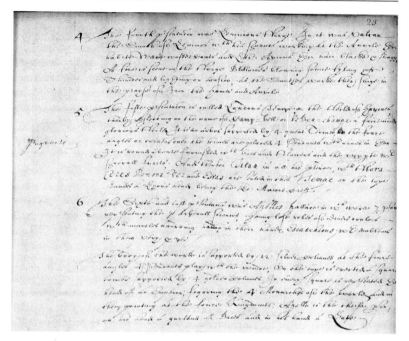

19 Extract from the Ironmongers' Company records (1629):
'the explanacion of the Shewe'

Show had not yet taken place (see Figure 19). In the printed text
they are all referred to in the present tense.

The exceptionality of this instance is demonstrated by juxtapo-
sition with another Dekker production, *Troia-Noua triumphans*,
and the livery company documentation associated with it. In their
accounts the Merchant Taylors do list the names of the pageants for
their 1612 Show, such as 'Neptunes Throne', but there is nothing
like the congruence between the disparate texts that we saw in the
case of the Ironmongers' Show for 1629. Indeed, the pageant that
the Merchant Taylors call 'Envies Castle', Dekker calls 'the Forlorn
Castle', and his fourth device, 'Fames high Temple', is not mentioned by the Company at all.[122] Similarly, the Company accounts
refer to 'the seaven liberall sciences' as being part of 'Neptunes
Throne' when in the printed work they appear within the second
device, 'the Throne of Vertue'.[123] Here it is clear that the Merchant
Taylors' list of individual pageants is cited purely and pragmatically
in terms of what they are paying for.

In sum, it seems to me most likely that in the majority of cases – particularly with Dekker's Shows – the main body of the printed works was based, sometimes with very little amendment, on the writer and artificer's scenario for the Show as commissioned by the livery company in question. Upon printing, the writers sometimes added (often jarring) comments about the vicissitudes of the day. The present-tense descriptions of the pageants, then, may have been a relic of their original address to the Company, and not necessarily directed to the witnesses of the Show on the day, although this may have been the eventual effect. Many of the texts – increasingly so through this period – then had dedications, historical preambles and the like appended to them when the work was prepared for publication, none of which would have had any particular function when the Show was commissioned. Heywood's recourse to historical and mythical record, in particular, often reads like rehashed classics lessons from his days as a student.[124] Middleton simply reproduced the first page of the preamble to *The triumphs of loue and antiquity* in *The triumphs of honor and vertue* three years later; although the texts were commissioned by different Companies, apart from a few words in parentheses, the two works are identical at this point.[125] Perhaps he thought no one would notice, or care.

'Tendred into your hands': patrons, readers and owners

These texts were produced, at least in principle, for a multiple audience and readership: the Lord Mayor, some of the onlookers and any subsequent readers. Bromham sensibly comments that 'the deviser of the pageant could assume a third audience, whose experience would have been exclusively verbal . . . [and who] might be capable of picking up verbal details that might or might not have registered in performance'.[126] Heywood evinces just such awareness in *Londini artium*, where he dismisses the third land pageant with considerable lack of tact (rather undermining this part of the Show in the process). Indeed, he labours the point to such an extent he is clearly assuming an educated readership, one which would not be offended by what he says:

> This [pageant] is more Mimicall than Materiail [*sic*], and inserted for the Vulgar, who rather loue to feast their eyes, then to banquet their eares: and therefore though it bee allowed place amongst the rest: (as in all Professions wee see Dunces amongst Doctors, simple amongst subtle, and Fooles intermixt with Wisemen to fill vp number) as

doubting whether it can wel appology for it selfe or no, at this time I afFoord it no tongue. (sig. B4r)

True to his word, the pageant is not described and no speeches are reproduced, unlike the other parts of the Show. Apart from the ambivalence towards 'the vulgar' manifested here, Heywood's text makes an explicit division between the taciturnity of the printed text and the actual performance of the Show, where the third land pageant would have taken place.

Some of the Shows and other printed texts of entertainments such as royal entries are more 'writerly' than others. In these works one can see many instances of where the writer hoped to supplement performance and to allow the meanings exemplified by the pageantry to come across more fully. Prefatory material in the printed text discussing historical matters pertaining to the Lord Mayor's Company, as presented by Munday and Taylor in particular, is one thing, and more or less relevant to the matter in hand, but, typically, Jonson's work is at the far end of this spectrum. To Dekker's disdain in his parallel text (Jonson's was published first), his colleague's part of *The magnificent entertainment* is stuffed with copious marginal notes, footnotes, Greek and Latin tags and other textual aspects which have little to do with the entertainment witnessed on the streets, and indeed would probably have been extremely distracting for any reader attempting to gain an impression of the day. Genius's speech of 'Gratulation', for instance, is wellnigh drowned out in the printed text by Jonson's exhaustive (and exhausting) scholarly notes, references and authorial amplifications.[127] Smuts has rightly commented that Jonson's work 'demands to be treated as a literary text rather than a record of a public occasion', and Kiefer argues along the same lines that 'it was not in [Jonson's] nature to make things easy for spectators . . . [P]erhaps only the readers of Jonson's masques find sufficient explanation . . . to comprehend fully what spectators beheld in performance'.[128]

Other 'writerly' features of such occasional texts include dedications, and it is chiefly in the dedications, for obvious reasons, that one tends to find explicit references to the actual day of triumph itself. Dekker's *Troia-Noua triumphans* is typical in this respect. He addresses Swinnerton as follows: 'Honor (this day) takes you by the Hand and giues you welcomes [*sic*] into your New-Office of Pretorship . . . I present (Sir) vnto you, these labours of my Pen, as the first and newest Congratulatory Offrings tendred into your hands' (sig. A2r). As time wore on, it had become more common

for printed Lord Mayors' Shows to bear dedications to the new
Lord Mayor or, occasionally, to his livery company.[129] However,
Bergeron is incorrect when he states that mayoral texts 'cite only
one patron: the current Lord Mayor (or occasionally also the
sheriff)'.[130] Munday's dedications never mention the new Lord
Mayor, and, where sheriffs are cited by other writers, such as
Heywood, it is always the two of them.[131] The convention was to
write a dedication to the Lord Mayor – Middleton's were generally
in verse – although Munday, where he dedicated his mayoral texts
at all, and he was less likely to do so than most of his contemporaries, chose to address the Master, Wardens and Assistants of
the Company in question.[132] Perhaps, knowing the way Munday
tended to operate, he did so in the awareness that future commissions of this type were more likely to emanate from those who
ran the livery companies than from an individual. He does write
in *Sidero-Thriambos* that he chose to dedicate the book to the
Ironmongers' governing body because theirs 'was the charge' for
the Show (sig. A3r). *The triumphs of the Golden Fleece* is addressed
to 'the Maisters, Wardens Batchelers, and their Assistant Brethren'
of the Drapers, with whom Munday had, as he puts it, 'runne
through the troublesome trauaile of so serious an employment'
(sig. A2r). That said, although many of the writers were otherwise
employed as dramatists – indeed, Bergeron has recently argued that
'playwrights helped shape these [pageant] texts to resemble many
other kinds of text' – such dedications did not really operate in
the ways one can identify in other printed works like plays.[133] In
the context of a mayoral Show the 'patronage' of the writer by the
livery company can be taken as read. It did not have to be sought,
nor, it seems, did writers require the protection of a patron, as was
sometimes the case with other kinds of publication. This points up
once again how the printed mayoral Show does not sit unproblematically alongside other works of this period.[134]

However, although the writers may not have *needed* to seek
patronage for their texts, some still used the same terminology as
elsewhere in their other works, and indeed in the majority of early
modern dedications. Livery company patronage thus underscores
the existence of these events, first on the street and then in print.
Middleton presents *The triumphs of loue and antiquity* to the Lord
Mayor: on 'this day', his dedication reads, 'my Seruice, and the
Booke' are offered to Cockayne (sig. A3r). Dekker is once again
gratifyingly open about the processes that lay behind his work.
As we have seen, addressing the new mayor in the dedication of

Troia-Noua triumphans directly, he writes 'I present (Sir) vnto you, these labours of my Pen, as the first and newest Congratulatory Offrings tendred into your hands'. The dedication thus presents the text as being offered to Swinnerton, almost as a physical gift, on the very day of his inauguration: 'Yesterday [you] were a Brother', Dekker states, 'and This Day a Father' (sig. A2r–v). Altogether, Dekker's text, written entirely in the present tense, does read as if the work had been handed ceremonially to the new Lord Mayor on the day itself.[135]

'These entertainments', Bergeron comments, 'by their nature serve and please patrons', and he notes that no mayoral text has a preface to the *reader* as such.[136] In these dedications, as he has argued, we can see the writers 'struggling to understand and characterise their cultural position . . . [and] what it means to be an author of such texts'.[137] Munday's lengthy dedication to the Fishmongers' Company in *Chrysanaleia* is a case in point. He here delineates his relationship with the Company (and, by implication, with the City as a whole), claiming that his authorship of the pamphlet derives from a deep-seated and lifelong allegiance. For Munday, as I have established elsewhere, his 'cultural position' (in Bergeron's terms) is inseparable from his personal one. Interestingly, Munday transfers the agency of patronage from the patron (the Company) to himself – it is almost as if he offers *them* the patronage. His dedication uses the metaphor of a river feeding into, and nourished by, the sea, to express his indebtedness to the Fishmongers. His dedication of the text to them is therefore a 'iust retribution and dutie', and their 'Patronage and protection' of the writer 'in right and equity belongs unto you'. The Company is exhorted to 'welcome' *their* patronage of Munday 'in loue and acceptance' (sig. A3r–v).[138]

The printed books of the Shows may, as speculated, have been handed around to various important people on the day. Subsequently, though, many have ended up far and wide from the City. I now move on to explore what can be learned about the ownership and use of these works. As a starting point, the physical form of the texts can tell us something about their genre and possible readership in their own time. Of the printed mayoral works that have survived, after Nelson's 1590 text, and with the sole exception thereafter of Munday's 1618 *Sidero-Thriambos*, part of which is in black letter to demonstrate the 'archaic' nature of that section of the text where a venerable Bard speaks, the Shows were uniformly printed in roman type.[139] This might suggest a certain status in the eyes of the printers and stationers for those books which might otherwise be seen simply as 'pamphlets', for although black letter was still used ubiquitously for proclamations and editions of the Bible, according to Blayney, 'the book trade [associated] roman type with a higher level of literacy and education than blackletter . . . [and it] did *not* perceive [books printed in roman type] as belonging to the same market as jestbooks and ballads'.[140]

Some printed Shows (as with university drama and masques) bore Latin on their title pages. Farmer and Lesser's interpretation of this phenomenon is that Latin 'attached itself most commonly to forms of drama that were . . . part of the elaborately classicized and allegorical displays of the court and city'.[141] The use of Latin also seems to be related to the frequency of an authorial attribution: where Latin exists on a title page so, most usually, does an author's name. *Tes Irenes Trophaea* bears a motto from Virgil, 'Parua sub ingentimatris se subijcit umbra', along with the initials 'I. S'. As noted above, with the minor proviso that the title page of *Campbell* has not survived, none of the mayoral Shows is anonymous. Farmer and Lesser note the 'remarkably high frequency [of author attribution] on the title pages of Lord Mayor's shows', 'surpass[ing] all other forms of drama'.[142] They also comment that 'we should probably assume that authors provided these [Latin] tags as part of the copy they gave to their stationers'.[143] This is possible, I suppose, but in the absence of much information about by whose agency the mayoral texts got into print, it remains speculation. Farmer and Lesser also state that 'the dramatists who most frequently employed Latin were, not coincidentally, the same authors who were attempting to establish their own literary authority', and they mention Jonson and (with some puzzlement on their part) Heywood in this regard.[144] They do not comment on the fact that two of Dekker's three Shows, *Londons tempe* and *Brittannia's honor*, also bear Latin mottoes on their title pages: their omission is perhaps because Dekker does not sit at all easily within their category of authors 'attempting to establish literary authority'. Only nine Shows have Latin on their title pages in any case, and most of these are simply the conventional motto 'Redeunt spectacula', although Farmer and Lesser are correct that this trend appears to have accelerated in the 1630s as far as the Shows are concerned. The phrase, which can be translated as 'the games will return', is extracted from 'Nocte pluit tota, redeunt spectacula mane, / Divisum imperium cum Jove Caesar habet', lines written by Virgil in praise of Emperor Augustus. All bar one of Heywood's Shows use this motto. Dekker's *London's tempe* has a line from Martial, 'Quando magis dignos licuit spectare triumphos?'. Dekker clearly favoured Martial, as *Brittannia's honor* bears another of his epigrams (plus its source reference); Webster too used Martial on *Monuments of Honor* (an epigram that also appears in the reader's preface to *The White Devil*).[145]

Although this evidence demonstrates that in various ways they appear not to have been categorised as what is often called 'cheap print', the Show texts, unlike a number of works commemorating royal entries and the like, were (as we have seen) published without illustrations. Robertson and Gordon suggest that the reason why the mayoral Shows were not illustrated (as they tended to be in continental Europe) was 'the limited resources of English book production'.[146] Astington, in contrast, argues that the difference between English and continental practice has been 'overstated': 'illustration was popular and more widespread than is commonly recognised'.[147] The English book trade was actually quite capable of producing illustrated 'festival' texts, even if these tend to relate to royal entertainments: one only has to look at the detailed engraving of 'the great Pond at Eluetham, and . . . the properties which it containeth' in *The honorable entertainement gieuen to the Queenes Maiestie in progresse, at Eluetham in Hampshire*, published in 1591, not to mention Harrison's *Arch's of triumph*.[148] It is more likely that Lord Mayors' Show texts were not illustrated by lavish plates, as on the continent, partly because this was not generally the custom in England, and also because of a lack of time in the printshop. Indeed, Blayney observes that texts composed of both verse and prose, as is the case for the Shows post-Peele, presented more difficulties for a compositor and printer than a text entirely in verse; to add to the complexity, as we have seen, some Show texts also included musical notation.[149]

As I discuss in more detail elsewhere in this book, unlike royal triumphs, the mayoral Shows were usually planned in detail only some three weeks before the event, which would not have made it possible for a printer to produce elaborate plates. Other forms of pageantry that took place with a longer run-up could produce illustrations, such as Thomas Lant's thirty plates for the printed commemoration of Philip Sidney's 1588 funeral procession, published as *Sequitur celebritas*.[150] As Orgel states, 'the market for printed masques [and other works of this type] in England . . . was not dependent on the elegance of the book'.[151] In general terms significant differences do exist between the printed texts of Lord Mayor's Shows and those produced on the continent to commemorate royal

or ducal triumphs. However, it is important to remember that one
is not necessarily comparing like with like: as Watanabe-O'Kelly
says, 'which form a festival book takes is largely determined by the
traditions of the court or civic or religious body which commissions
it'.[152] One major disparity is that instead of being produced in relatively large numbers by professional printers, as in London, those
works produced on the continent, in Watanabe-O'Kelly's words,
'were often customised for particular patrons by being printed
on vellum, hand-coloured or illuminated, so that the line between
mass-produced publication and one-off art object can become
blurred'.[153]

Evidence of who owned the printed Shows once they had been
distributed is, unfortunately, scant, partly because the rate of attri-
tion of the printed texts was considerable (for instance, of the 500
copies of *The sunne in Aries* only two have survived, which is not
atypical). Book collectors within whose collections mayoral Shows
reside include Robert Burton, Brian Twyne, Anthony Wood and
Humphrey Dyson.[154] For the most part, these were scholarly men
with no apparent London links and their copies were probably
gained some time after the actual Show took place. Only Dyson
was an immediate contemporary, and he was also the only one with
significant civic connections.[155] He signed the title page of a copy
of *Brittannia's honor* which is now bound into a larger volume of
related works. Dyson was a citizen of London (a member of the
Wax Chandlers' Company), which might in itself be sufficient cause
for ownership of at least one of these texts. His co-editorship of
the 1633 edition of Stow's *Suruey* (along with Munday and others)
also demonstrates his orientation towards the civic domain, not
least because Munday, Dyson's main collaborator and the preceding continuer of Stow's work, had himself been one of the most
successful pageant-writers of the past three decades. Indeed, it is
quite likely that Dyson and Munday were already working on their
massive expansion of the *Suruey* when Dekker's 1628 Show took
place; Dyson *may* even have somehow got hold of a copy of the
printed text as part of his researches.

Moreover, what is common to all the surviving copies of mayoral
Shows is that, where they exist at all, contemporary marginalia only
very rarely extend past the title page of the text; even there handwritten annotation tends to be solely owners' or readers' names.
One is drawn to the conclusion that it was generally considered
more important to own a copy of one of these works than to read
it, or at least to read it more than once, quite probably because the

majority of the owners had already seen the Show and so had little cause to want to revisit its content.[156] There are a few exceptions, however. One of the most heavily annotated books – the Bodleian's copy of *The triumphes of re-united Britania* – bears on its title page the names of various individuals in apparently contemporary or near-contemporary hands, as well as the strikingly appropriate comment 'Champion for the Citty or the Citty's Champion' next to Munday's name (although the comment may, of course, refer to the Lord Mayor). The rest of the text, however, is unmarked and indeed very clean. Similarly, one copy of *The triumphs of loue and antiquity* bears the handwritten note 'Free of the Skynners' on its title page, alluding to the Lord Mayor's Company. Generally speaking, although one is likely to find copies with dirty or stained covers, since the works were not originally produced with bindings, the majority of extant Show texts are both in excellent condition and lacking in signs of active use, which suggests they were prized, unread or perhaps both. Indeed, a copy of Heywood's *Londini status pacatus* was left uncut for a considerable time and thus cannot have been read by its immediate contemporary owner(s). Hardin's description of the printed Shows as 'a lasting account of how [the City oligarchy] wished to perceive themselves and the metropolis' therefore seems accurate only in principle: what is the value of 'a lasting account' that no one reads?[157] The likely ownership of certain copies of the Shows seems to have extended outside of the limited realm of the City companies, in any case. The Thynne family of Longleat, who had strong civic connections, may have owned their copies of *The triumphs of truth*, *Metropolis coronata* and *The triumphs of loue and antiquity* since they were first printed, especially since only a few years separate these works.[158]

A rare exception to the norm of non-annotation, as far as mayoral Shows go, is the Gough copy of *Londini status pacatus*, where someone has carefully counted the lines of the verses of every substantive speech and written the number at the end of the relevant passage. The title page of this book also bears, in what looks like the same hand, the comment 'G [i.e. good?] Speeches', which *may* – exceptionally – indicate a reader's aesthetic appreciation of the contents: perhaps the reader's liking for the speeches manifested itself in a desire to count their lines.[159] The same reader probably marked the number of lines of one speech (and numbered the pages) in a copy of Middleton's *Triumphs of loue and antiquity* which also forms part of the Gough bequest in the Bodleian. Interestingly, both of these copies bear more signs of use than is the norm.

Given that the usual assumption is that civic dignitaries were the initial recipients of these works, another, rather surprising aspect of the ownership history of these texts is their extreme scarcity in Company Halls. There seems to have been little or no incentive for the livery companies to keep copies of the printed Shows. Even the single copy of *Metropolis coronata* owned by the Drapers – the only contemporary printed Show I have been able to locate in a Company Hall – was probably bought by the Company a considerable time after 1615.[160] The Fishmongers' Company does have a copy of the lavish 1844 edition of *Chrysanaleia*, which was produced on its behalf, but this is an exception. The general view amongst livery company archivists is that such ephemeral texts were not at all prized by the Companies; most of the Companies had very little interest in 'literature' generally, even when they had paid for the printing of the works themselves. If this is the case, it, in this context, disproves Heywood's claim in 1631 that the Companies 'neglect not the studdy of arts, and practice of literature' (*Londons ius honorarium*, sig. C3v).

In contrast, as one would expect, the texts themselves foreground the livery companies in various ways. *Monuments of Honor* is the first printed Show to use the Company's arms. After 1624 it became common practice to display the arms of the livery company to which the Lord Mayor belonged on the title page of the printed work. This practice, it seems to me, may be connected to the defiant claims one finds *within* these texts too about the importance of the livery companies in the later Jacobean period and onwards, a topic which will explored in the next chapter.[161]

Notes

I am particularly indebted to Ian Gadd and Richard Rowland for their comments and advice on this chapter.

1 Michael Burden's discussion of the post-Restoration Shows is an exception in this respect (see '"For the lustre of the subject"').
2 'Occasional events', p. 180; my emphasis. As Watanabe-O'Kelly has cogently argued in relation to continental triumphs, 'festival books are . . . not simple records of a festival, but another element in it' ('Early modern European festivals', p. 23).
3 'King James's civic pageant', p. 230; 'Making meaning', p. 63.
4 There were between twenty-one and twenty-four printing houses in London in this period, and not all of them were prepared to print any text at all, although the Lord Mayor's Show is unlikely to have been

regarded as controversial (Blayney, 'The publication of playbooks', p. 405).

5 See Watanabe-O'Kelly, 'Early modern European festivals', p. 23, for a useful summary of the ways in which continental festival books might have been produced and consumed.

6 'The publication of playbooks', p. 384. Fortunately Greg did include the Shows in his bibliographies, although Watanabe-O'Kelly and Simon's *Festivals and Ceremonies: A Bibliography of Works Relating to Court, Civic and Religious Festivals* is not complete: it omits all pre-1605 printed Lord Mayors' Shows and all those written by Heywood, and includes only some of the texts held in the British Library, even those which are bound together in the same volume.

7 Bergeron has written a bibliographical study of one of Heywood's Shows. Farmer and Lesser do include some of the Shows in their account of the marketing of play-texts: as they state, 'some of the more interesting results may be found by comparing commercial drama to its university and closet counterparts, to masques, entertainments, and Lord Mayor's shows' ('Vile arts', p. 111). However, given that they consulted Greg's *Bibliography* when compiling their database of 'all qualifying title pages' the omission of some ten Shows is puzzling.

8 I am grateful to Ian Gadd for the development of this point.

9 Greg, *Bibliography*, vol. IV, p. 1682. Munday's classical scholarship was never all that secure; one cannot imagine Jonson or Heywood making such an error.

10 Farmer and Lesser note that masque texts only infrequently cite an author 'due to the courtly fiction that the patron of the masque is its true author and due to their coterie audience, assuring that anyone important would know the author of a masque without being told' ('Vile arts', p. 108 n.39).

11 'A true Copie', para. 39.

12 This point can be related to the one made by Peter Berek that generic terms (tragedy, comedy and so on) are more of a preoccupation for the producers of printed works, as marketing devices, than they are for performance ('Genres, early modern theatrical title pages', p. 161).

13 See GH MS 34,048/10. This backs up Northway's argument that the Companies 'thought about the shows as speeches' ('To kindle an industrious desire', p. 169).

14 From the Stationers' Register it would appear that Peele's lost 1588 text was entitled 'The device of the Pageant borne before the Righte Honorable Martyn Calthrop, Lorde Maiour of the Cytie of London' (Greg, *Bibliography*, vol. I, p. 965).

15 The title pages of these later works contained the same information as the earlier texts, largely set out in the same way, using the same kind of terminology: see, for example, the title page of Jordan's *London in*

Luster of 1679, with its conventional 'All set forth at the proper Cost and Charges of the Worshipful Company of Drapers', and so on.

16 GH MS 11,590, fol. 21; Middleton, *The triumphs of honor and vertue*, sig. B1v.

17 GH MS 11,590, fol. 14.

18 Drapers' Bachelors Accounts, fols 86 and 99.

19 *Ibid.*, fol. 86. For some reason the name of the printer and the number of extra copies is left blank in the 1638 accounts (perhaps such details were uncertain until a very late stage); Okes is named the following year, when an additional 300 copies were ordered.

20 The earliest surviving printed and illustrated text of a European royal entertainment – in this case, an entry into Bruges – was published in Paris in 1515 (see Kipling, 'The King's Advent Transformed', pp. 92 and 121 n. 4). Prior to that, manuscript accounts of fifteenth-century London pageantry were sometimes compiled (see Barron, 'Pageantry on London Bridge', p. 93). Comparative analysis of 'festival books' as a genre has been hugely aided by the British Library's online collection (which does not include mayoral Shows, however): www.bl.uk/treasures/festivalbooks/homepage.html.

21 Smuts is unusual in the way he foregrounds the issue, asking 'why did certain ephemeral events – but not others – acquire a second life through the relatively durable medium of print?' ('Occasional events', p. 183). His focus, however, is exclusively on the royal entry and progress rather than the Lord Mayor's Show.

22 See *ibid.*, pp. 188–94.

23 *Literature and Culture*, pp. 268–9.

24 Stow ed. Strype, *A Survey of the Cities of London and Westminster*, vol. II, pp. 136–7.

25 *Ibid.*, p. 140. There isn't a single volume which includes copies of all five of these Shows (the Huntington Library holds them all but the provenance varies), so Strype may have referred simply to those individual copies then available to him, or to a volume that has been broken up.

26 He also, more briefly, mentions the titles and authors of the Shows for 1672, 1673, 1677, 1680, 1681 and 1685.

27 One should not understate the commercial imperatives for some of these works: as Hunt points out, Mulcaster's account of Elizabeth's coronation was explicitly published to be sold (*The Drama of Coronation*, pp. 159–60).

28 *The Golden Age*, p. 3.

29 GH MS 34,048/9.

30 *Textual Patronage*, p. 49.

31 'The masque in/as print', p. 177.

32 *Guilds, Society*, p. 45. Blayney asserts that to make a profit on a play-text a publisher would have to sell 'about half the edition' ('The publication of playbooks', p. 389).

33 'The King's Advent Transformed', p. 92.

34 Norbrook comments of this moment that 'so great was the interest in the wedding that descriptions of the festivities sold very quickly, and one unscrupulous printer issued an account of the couple's arrival in Heidelberg eight days before they had left England' ('The Masque of Truth', p. 82).

35 Greg states that a copy of Jonson's *Masque of Blackness* bears 'an autograph dedication to Queen Anna signed "Ben: Jonsonius"' (*Bibliography*, vol. I, p. 403), suggesting that the text was given to her personally, although it is not clear when this happened; one copy of *The Masque of Queenes* has an autograph epistle to the Queen (*ibid.*, p. 416).

36 Robertson and Gordon, *Collections* III, p. 46. Somewhat anachronistically, the Ironmongers use the same phrase in relation to the printing of the 1609 work that became *Camp-bell* (GH MS 16,969/2, fol. 216v).

37 Robertson and Gordon, *Collections* III, p. xxxii.

38 The sole extant copy of *Camp-bell* is missing its first few pages and all remaining copies of Dekker's Shows for 1628 and 1629 lack an imprint.

39 Amongst other works by Heywood, Raworth printed two plays at around the same time as Heywood's 1635 Show, *The English traueller* (1633) and *A challenge for beautie* (1636), and a court masque, *Loues maistresse: or, The Queens masque* (1636). The connections may have been generated by the Shows, too, as Okes printed one of Squire's sermons in 1621, the year after Squire's sole mayoral Show (going by the ESTC, Okes does not seem to have printed Squire's works before).

40 Allde, a rather controversial figure, produced over 700 items during his career; however, he mostly acted as a 'trade printer', printing material for others.

41 Allde also printed Henry Roberts's *The King of Denmarkes welcome* (1606), one of a number of texts commemorating the royal visit, a copy of which is in Dyson's collection. Roberts himself, who had been producing these kinds of occasional texts since the 1580s, was a Stationer.

42 Munday was a neighbour during this period, too (see Hill, *Anthony Munday*, p. 32). (I am grateful to Peter Blayney for his advice on the Okes family.)

43 Watt states that Gosson 'specialised in the works of [this] one author'. He also appears to have published pamphlets at the more 'sober' end of the market (*Cheap Print*, pp. 291 and 359).

44 Okes was a fellow parishioner of John Webster senior in St Sepulchre without Newgate.

45 Heywood, *An apology for actors*, sig. G4r–v. This earlier work, *Troia Britanica*, had been printed by Jaggard in 1609, so Heywood's

contrasting experiences were the reverse of what one might expect, given Okes's reputation.

46 Nicholas Okes began his printing business in 1607. *Brittannia's honor* was printed by Okes and Thomas Norton in the first year of their (unauthorised) partnership. Okes had been printing works by both Dekker and Middleton for some years beforehand.

47 There are around ninety extant individual copies of the various Shows, of which I have personally examined eighty-seven.

48 See Bawcutt, 'A crisis', p. 412.

49 Blayney, *The Texts of* King Lear, pp. 27–9. Okes, it seems, also had a rather cavalier attitude to the various regulations governing printers' activities.

50 Greg, *Bibliography*, vol. I, p. 454.

51 Sullivan is therefore incorrect when she states that this combined text was 'reprinted two years after' the Show, in 1615 ('Summer 1613', p. 162 n.1; she repeats the claim on p. 164).

52 Greg, *Bibliography*, vol. I, p. 455. This work in its various incarnations illustrates Greg's comment that 'the distinction between editions, issues, and variants' can be 'occasionally worrying' (vol. IV, p. xxxii).

53 *Ibid.*, vol. I, p. 432.

54 Bergeron concurs: 'I think it reasonable to assume that the manuscripts which served as printer's copy for the pamphlets were probably Munday's foul papers or fair copies' (*Pageants and Entertainments*, p. xviii). Jackson argues that 'the presence of a dedication printed over Webster's name [in *The Monuments of Honor*] strongly suggests that the printer's manuscript copy must have derived from the author' ('Textual introduction', p. 251).

55 The Huntington Library copy is identical to the copy in the BL in every respect. Shows which demonstrate fewer and more minor press corrections between different copies include *The triumphs of health and prosperity* and *Londons ius honorarium*.

56 See Greg, *Bibliography*, vol. II, p. 531.

57 This woodcut appears to have been reused for Taylor's *Heauens blessing, and earths ioy* of 1613.

58 Bergeron has identified 'a number of manifest errors' in Okes's printing of *Londons ius honorarium* ('Heywood's "Londons Ius Honorarium"', pp. 225–6). There is a reference to 'faults' missed by the printer in *'Tis Pity She's a Whore* (sig. K4r), which was printed by Okes in the same year as *Londini emporia*. *Londons tempe* is also notably badly printed (probably by Okes), often using worn and damaged type.

59 See Middleton, *The triumphs of truth* (STC 17903), sig. C2v, for instance. Not all the ephemeral texts issued from Okes's workshop were of poor quality, however: Webster's *Monuments of Honor* is

neatly done and at least one impression of *The triumphs of honor and vertue* has been carefully corrected.

60 £2 appears to be the going rate that a publisher would pay an author for 'a small pamphlet' (Blayney, 'The publication of playbooks', p. 396).

61 Drapers' Company Court of Assistants Minutes. September 1603 to July 1640. MB 13. There were extensive links, if not always amicable ones, between the Drapers and the Stationers in this period (see Johnson, 'The Stationers versus the Drapers', *passim*).

62 Drapers' Company Court of Assistants Minutes. September 1603 to July 1640. MB 13.

63 'The publication of playbooks', p. 405.

64 'Nicholas Okes Stacioner' was paid £4 direct by the Grocers in 1613 (GH MS 11,590, fol. 6); in 1617 they again paid Okes £4 for printing 500 books (GH MS 11,588/3).

65 Jaggard printed mayoral Shows both before and after he became the Printer to the City of London in 1610.

66 Hardin asserts that the texts were printed 'for officials of the City and the livery companies' ('Conceiving cities', p. 24); Hentschell, in contrast, assumes that all the texts were sold to the general public (see *The Culture of Cloth*, p. 177).

67 Gosson (who may have been the nephew of the anti-theatrical polemicist and ex-actor Stephen Gosson) is described by Watt as 'the largest single producer of ballads' in this period, publishing 'over eighty separate ballad titles' (*Cheap Print*, pp. 275 and 291). Gosson was responsible for entering Taylor's 1634 Show in the Stationers' Register, having had a long association with the writer.

68 For William Wright, see Watt, *Cheap Print*, p. 277.

69 Drapers' Bachelors Accounts, fol. 36.

70 One of the editions of Dekker's *Magnificent entertainment*, for instance, was printed by Edward Allde for Thomas Man the younger; an account of James's progress from Scotland to England, published the previous year, was printed by Thomas Creede for Thomas Millington; Munday's *Londons loue* was printed by Allde for Nathaniell Fosbrooke; Middleton's *Ciuitatis amor* was printed by Okes for Thomas Archer; and the majority of the accounts of Christian IV's 1606 visit to England had both a printer and publisher.

71 Hentschell is therefore mistaken to claim that the Shows were 'often' entered into the Stationers' Register (*The Culture of Cloth*, p. 164).

72 The text of the Norwich entry, and Thomas Churchyard's accounts of the Queen's entertainments in Norfolk and Suffolk, were licensed to Henry Bynneman; Jonson's version of the 1604 royal entry was entered to Edward Blount on 19 March of that year (only four days later), and Dekker's to Thomas Man on 2 April: clearly some controversy resulted (see Greg, *Bibliography*, vol. I, pp. 19 and 316–18).

Allde entered 'a booke called the Kinge of Denmarkes welcome into England' on 8 August 1606 (the actual event took place on 18 July); an anonymous text celebrating the Palsgrave marriage on 14 February 1613, *The marriage of the two great princes*, was entered on 18 February of that year (*ibid.*, p. 22).

73 *Ibid.*, p. 453. Okes entered Middleton's text on 3 November.

74 Arber, *Transcript*, vol. II, p. 235. The Stationers' Register ascribes the 1588 Show to 'George Peele the Authour'. The Skinners' Company archives show that Peele won the commission for the 1595 Show too, but again in the absence of any printed text we know little about it; the text may have been printed but has not survived.

75 Blayney, 'The publication of playbooks', p, 398. 'Authority', he asserts, 'was officially compulsory, but in practice the [Stationers'] Company officers could decide when it was or was not required' (p. 404).

76 Arber, *Transcript*, vol. III, p. 115. Felix Kingston printed hundreds of (chiefly religious) works between c.1578 and c.1652; in particular, he printed a number of texts for Thomas Man (the publisher of Dekker's 1604 *Magnificent entertainment*) in the 1600–5 period, and he also printed another text produced to commemorate the new king's arrival into London, Michael Drayton's *A paean triumphall* (1604).

77 Arber, *Transcript*, vol. III, p. 276, and vol. IV, p. 302. On the latter occasion 'Master Taylor' is cited as the author; Munday's name does not appear in 1616.

78 Jackson, *Records of the Court of the Stationers' Company*, p. 138.

79 Arber, *Transcript*, vol. III, p. 228.

80 Werner, 'A German eye-witness', p. 253.

81 Greg, *Bibliography*, vol. I, p. 28. Unfortunately the Grocers' records do not say how many copies were printed.

82 Werner, 'A German eye-witness', p. 253.

83 Watt cites an instance where a printer got into trouble for trying to sell a text relating to a royal progress for 2d (*Cheap Print*, p. 263). Taylor claims that these works were 'either given away or sold at a heavily discounted price', although he does not, unfortunately, provide any evidence for the latter assertion (*Buying Whiteness*, pp. 125 and 410 n. 11).

84 Fitzgeffrey's text was entered in the Stationers' Register on 9 October 1617 (Arber, *Transcript*, vol. III, p. 284).

85 This work was printed for R. Barnham in Little Britain, and also features quite lavish engravings (which the title page calls 'Sculptures') of the individual pageants. That this work was produced for the open market is also underscored by the advertisement it bears on its last page for another text.

86 'The publication of playbooks', p. 421 n. 61. A handwritten note on one of Munday's translations, *The true knowledge of a mans owne*

selfe, records that its (possibly original) purchaser paid 7d for the book and bought it in London (this copy is in the Folger Shakespeare Library).

87 *Middleton: The Collected Works*, p. 1257. An alternative explanation, that the printed works were often based in large part on the 'plot' presented to the Companies, is further explored elsewhere in this book.

88 Barriffe appears to have specialised in texts about military exercises. See *Collections* III, p. 182, for a record from the Merchant Taylors relating to this entertainment; see also Ravelhofer, *The Early Stuart Masque*, for a discussion of Barriffe's text.

89 Greg, *Bibliography*, vol. II, p. 493. The text is *Louers made Men. A masque presented in the house of the right honourable the Lord Haye* (1617).

90 See GH MS 16,967/4. The same form of words was used for Munday's 1609 Show, where again he was required to give the Company 500 copies of the books. Of those 500, only one – incomplete – copy survives.

91 See GH MS 34,048/10. The Company bought 15 lb of these counters, which must have been a considerable number.

92 Robertson and Gordon, *Collections* III, p. xxxii. Pafford, who edited this Show in 1962, states (unfortunately without giving any concrete evidence) that copies 'were received by members of the Goldsmiths' Company in 1611', to whom the texts were given as free 'souvenirs' (*Chruso-Thriambos*, pp. 7 and 9).

93 A book of speeches was printed to accompany Elizabeth's civic entertainment at Bristol in 1574, and a copy was apparently given to the Queen to help her follow the proceedings (see McGee, 'Mysteries, musters and masque', p. 120 n. 61). Anne Boleyn may also have received a manuscript presentation copy of her 1533 entry into London (see Osberg, 'Humanist allusions', p. 31).

94 Cressy, *Bonfires and Bells*, p. 163. The text is a one-page broadsheet, ascribed to George Browne, gunner.

95 *The Early Stuart Masque*, p. 84.

96 The images were reproduced, with hand-colouring, by Henry Shaw and published in 1844; it is these versions I have used here although one has to treat them with some caution as the images have been slightly altered to make them fit the Victorian notion of 'Tudorness'. I am grateful to Stephen Freeth and John Fisher of the Guildhall Library for their advice on these illustrations.

97 Munday ed. Nichols, *Chrysanaleia*, p. 16.

98 See also Munday, *Chrysanaleia*, sig. B3r.

99 Palmer, *Hospitable Performances*, pp. 119–20.

100 Hentschell, *The Culture of Cloth*, pp. 164–5.

101 Bergeron, *Textual Patronage*, p. 50.

102 McGowan asserts similarly of continental triumphs that 'the texts which were published to commemorate the celebrations usually

recorded the details of all the edifices in full, and described projected structures as if they had been erected' ('The Renaissance triumph', p. 28).

103 Gasper, *The Dragon and the Dove*, p. 41. Bergeron comments 'maddeningly, Dekker does not tell us which speeches the performance omitted or cut' (*Textual Patronage*, p. 56).

104 Watanabe-O'Kelly, 'Early modern European festivals', p. 19.

105 *Ibid.*, p. 22.

106 Bergeron, *Textual Patronage*, p. 56.

107 Johnson, 'Jacobean ephemera', pp. 162–3.

108 For the 1612 Show, see Sayle, *Lord Mayors' Pageants*, p. 98. Thomas Churchyard's printed account of Elizabeth's entertainment at Norwich, in contrast, deals unashamedly with the consequences of inclement weather.

109 See GH MS 30,048/9.

110 *Literature and Culture*, p. 276.

111 Palmer points out that it would have taken a while for all the boatloads of people to disembark ('Music in the barges', p. 172).

112 Palmer, *Hospitable Performances*, p. 123.

113 *Middleton: The Collected Works*, p. 1252. This is a useful discussion, although it takes a somewhat text-centric approach: she does not consider that, if it functioned as a programme, the text may be guiding the attention of a viewer as well as, or even rather than, a reader.

114 Middleton interrupts *The triumphs of truth* in a similar fashion: Bergeron comments that this moment 'suggests Middleton's having a conversation with himself' (*Middleton: The Collected Works*, p. 964).

115 *Ibid.* For more on Taylor's readers, see Capp, *The World of John Taylor*, pp. 67–75.

116 Hardin's sensible suggestion in this regard – 'it seems reasonable to conjecture that [original plots] contained much of the same material found in the printed accounts' – has not been pursued by any other commentators ('Spectacular Constructions', p. 17).

117 Dekker, *The magnificent entertainment*, sig. I4r. Indeed, the very first substantive page of this work commences with 'a device (projected downe) . . . that should haue serued at his Majesties first accesse to the Citie' (sig. A2r).

118 Commemorative texts were sometimes printed or reprinted as parts of larger composite works: as well as *The triumphs of truth*, issued with *The Manner of his Lordships Entertainment*, Jonson's *A particular Entertainment of the Queene and Prince their Highnesse to Althrope*, was issued with *B. Ion: his part*.

119 Middleton and Rowley dedicated their 1620 masque *The world tost at tennis* to Lord Howard, his wife and her father, William Cockayne.

120 GH MS 16,967/4.

121 Robertson and Gordon *Collections* III, p. 86.

122 See GH MS 34,048/10 and *Troia-Noua triumphans*, sigs B4r and C1v. In 1624 the Company reverted to the usual form by merely referring to 'all the land and water shewes Pageants, [and] Chariott' (GH MS 34,048/13).

123 GH MS 34,048/10 and Dekker, *Troia-Noua triumphans*, sig. B2r.

124 Fairholt comments, with some justice, that many of the speeches Heywood produced for the Shows 'are rather turgid and bombastic, and . . . remarkably full of pedantic allusions' (*Lord Mayors' Pageants*, vol. II, p. 58).

125 Middleton also reuses here, again with little emendation, his account of previous Grocer mayors which had previously been printed in *The tryumphs of honor and industry*. The title pages of his Shows from 1619 onwards are almost identical, bar (naturally) the name of the Lord Mayor and livery company.

126 'Thomas Middleton's The *Triumphs of Truth*', p. 4.

127 See Jonson, B. *Ion: his part*, sigs B3r and D1v–D2r, for example. Jonson's text must have presented Valentine Simmes and George Eld, its printers, with considerable challenges. As Dutton comments, 'Dekker's account is altogether more relaxed' (*Jacobean Civic Pageants*, p. 21). Dekker praised Middleton's contribution without equivocation.

128 Smuts, 'Occasional events', p. 197; Kiefer, *Shakespeare's Visual Theatre*, pp. 20 and 23.

129 Dekker's 1612 Show is the earliest extant printed Show to have a dedication: Bergeron regards 1613 as 'a fault line' in the history of dedicatory prefaces (*Textual Patronage*, p. 51).

130 *Ibid.*

131 In contrast, as well as being dedicated to the Lord Mayor, Harrison's *Arch's of triumph* does have an address to the reader, at the very end of the text. Tatham's text of the 1660 Show is less equivocal about its status than its predecessors, as it has a preface to the reader.

132 Given his usual practice in the dedications of his other prose works, which are often very effusive, as Bergeron comments, Munday shows an unusual 'reticence' here (*Textual Patronage*, p. 67).

133 *Ibid.*, p. 19.

134 Heywood has been singled out by Cyndia Clegg as a notable writer of prefaces to the reader: this may be the case for his plays, but not for his Shows, which only bear prefatory addresses to civic dignitaries rather than to readers as such ('Renaissance play-readers', p. 27).

135 This may be an authorial device, as the text was entered in the Stationers' Register a week before the Show.

136 *Textual Patronage*, p. 49.

137 *Ibid.*, p. 51.

138 See also Hill, *Anthony Munday*, pp. 23–4.

139 1590 is the date cited by Lesser for the establishment of roman type, and he notes that black letter often signalled 'past-ness' in early

printed books ('Topographic nostalgia', pp. 101 and 107). The use of
black letter in playbooks after 1609 was extremely low at less than 7
per cent (*ibid.*, p. 114), which points up the exceptionality of *Sidero-Thriambos* in this regard.

140 'The publication of playbooks', pp. 414–15.

141 'Vile arts', p. 99.

142 *Ibid.*, p. 109 n. 45. The list of Shows in this article is incomplete,
however (a third of them are missing), and so their figure of 91 per
cent for authorial attribution – and indeed their other statistics about
the Shows – should be treated with caution.

143 *Ibid.*, p. 99.

144 *Ibid.* Heywood's use of Latin is ascribed by Farmer and Lesser to his
attempts in the 1630s 'to put together a collection of his dramatic
works', Latin being part of a strategy 'to develop literary authority'
(p. 101).

145 Such mottoes were traditionally used in royal and continental triumphs too. Interestingly, Munday, who had two authorial tags for
many of his other works, did not use Latin on his Shows (see my
Anthony Munday, pp. 49 and 52).

146 Robertson and Gordon, *Collections* III, p. xxxiii n. 3. See Kipling,
'The King's advent transformed', p. 111, for an example of such a
complex engraved printed illustration, in this case from a royal entry
that took place in Antwerp in 1582. In some cases, he adds, texts of
royal entries circulated in 'de luxe, hand-coloured versions' (*ibid.*,
p. 122 n. 9).

147 'The ages of man', p. 87.

148 Reproduced in Greg, *Bibliography*, vol. I, plate XXXI. Harrison's text
is also in folio, unlike the usual quarto format of mayoral Shows.

149 'The publication of playbooks', p. 406. Settle's 1698 Show, *Glory's
Resurrection*, has four lavish plates to accompany the text. To demonstrate the continental mode, a Venetian text printed in 1591, *Funerali
antichi di diversi Popoli et Nationi*, has twenty-three plates and a
frontispiece (see Society of Antiquaries, *A Catalogue*, p. 6).

150 This text Goldring calls 'unprecedented . . . [as] nothing like it had
been published in England' ('The funeral of Sir Philip Sidney', p. 210).

151 'The book of the play', p. 28.

152 'Early modern European festivals', p. 22.

153 *Ibid.*

154 Anthony Wood had a collection of programmes for Encaenia and
determination ceremonies at Oxford University, where he often wrote
his impressions of the music and speeches that took place at these
events (see Kiessling, *The Library of Anthony Wood*, p. xxx).

155 The sole surviving copy of Munday's *Chruso-thriambos* (STC 18265-5)
is part of the Puckering bequest in Trinity College, Cambridge. It is
just possible that this copy's provenance can be traced back through

the Puckering family to its date of publication. There is a strong likelihood that members of the royal family attended the Lord Mayor's Show in 1611, and, given the connection between the royal household and Thomas Puckering, it seems to me at least possible that this copy was actually given to a member of the royal party (perhaps Puckering himself) on the day of the Show. Unfortunately, despite the expert assistance of David McKitterick, I have not been able to authenticate this possibility.

156 I am grateful to Maureen Bell for her elucidation of this point.

157 Hardin, 'Spectacular Constructions', p. 17.

158 Christiana, a daughter of Richard Gresham (Lord Mayor in 1537) and sister of Thomas Gresham (the founder of the Royal Exchange) married Sir John Thynne in the sixteenth century (see Blanchard, *Oxford DNB*, 'Gresham, Sir Richard').

159 There are also some marginalia inside the Bodleian's unique copy of Peele's 1585 Show; unfortunately, most of them have been covered over by the binding with the result that they are barely legible.

160 The ESTC omits this copy. I am grateful to Penny Fussell for her advice on this work.

161 The first post-Civil War printed mayoral Show, *Londons triumph* (usually ascribed to John Bulteel) bears the coat of arms of the City Corporation on its title page, rather than the arms of the relevant livery company.

5

'To prune and dresse the Tree of Gouernment': political and contemporary contexts of the Shows

Bergeron helpfully reminds us that 'by definition civic pageants are *political* events. They involve the presence of the ruler . . . they utilise public monies of city or guilds, they take place in the public arena, and they celebrate national and civic virtues.'[1] The latter are not inconsiderable concerns, although the political dimensions of the Shows have been widely overlooked. In general terms, the Shows repeatedly personified traits of good government as well as threats to the City's peace and stability such as Envy or Ambition. In so doing, they inevitably engaged with political questions in the broadest sense. In this respect, as in others, they contrast to the royal masque, where, as Norbrook has argued, 'overt religious imagery and overt political comment are kept under strict control'.[2] The Shows also displayed the City's sense of itself, often in implicit or, more rarely, explicit contrast to the values of the court. Mayoral pageantry was therefore a reflection of a civic culture grounded in the values of a local government which was, in Withington's words, 'elitist, elective, pragmatic, patriarchal, and more often than not committed to civil and godly reformation'.[3]

My account of the Shows will demonstrate the ways in which they engaged with the changing socio-economic scene of the City and with court and city politics, in the widest sense, in the pre-Civil War period. Indeed, the chasm between the courtly and civic domains widened as the seventeenth century wore on. By the middle of the century, Withington has argued, the monarchy and its closest supporters were 'actively suspicious of citizens and the powers they wielded'.[4] This is not, however, to posit some fundamental opposition between these two centres of power through the whole period. The Crown needed the City's money – increasingly so as the seventeenth century progressed – as much as the City needed the Crown's distribution of monopolies and its continued, if contingent, acceptance of its much-prized autonomy.[5] As Brenner points out, those at the top of the civic hierarchy, in particular, were 'drawn, unavoidably, into perpetual contact, and collaboration, with the royal government'.[6] Equally, out-and-out criticism of state policy or of the shortcomings of individuals, royal and otherwise, did not feature in the Shows. Such sentiments in civic circles at large were sometimes inchoate in any case; where they were expressed, this tended to occur subtly and tentatively, in coded language and through the careful use of selected figures and emblems.[7] I therefore follow Curtis Perry's judicious approach: one should see the Shows not as 'points on a graph leading to increased opposition between the city and the court', he writes, 'but as successive reformulations of civic pride occasioned by James's withdrawal from the center of London's political consciousness'. The situation, he stresses, was 'more complicated than simple rivalry' between Crown and City.[8]

Alongside larger historical changes, this chapter will also explore those more immediately contemporary aspects of the Shows which Leah Marcus calls their 'present occasions'.[9] Numerous opportunities for what Manley terms 'fine-tuned topical analysis' are offered by the Shows.[10] Alongside the regular mayoral inaugurations, civic entertainments of other kinds were sometimes put together as a direct response to, or intervention in, a local issue or event. For instance, the ceremony to mark the opening of the New River in 1613 was scheduled specifically to take place at the same time as the election of the Lord Mayor in September, and, as we'll see further below, it was no coincidence that Ralegh was executed on 29 October 1618. Thus, although the overt politicisation of the Shows was to accelerate from the 1650s onwards, my account of the Shows will dispute that of A. M. Clark, who wrote of the Shows that 'their "history" [was] lore from the past, rather than the events of a sixteenth or seventeenth century present', and that their politics were 'purely conventional'. I will demonstrate that the Shows were not uniformly 'studiously couched in the language of generalities and compliment', as Clark asserts.[11] Civic pageantry was undeniably drawn towards historical tradition and the *assertion* of unbroken continuities, but at the same time it was capable of responding to more immediate concerns and its attempt to establish a harmonious civic community (at least textually) was not always entirely successful. Manley expresses the precarious balance between long-standing tradition and politically aware response to contingency well. Civic pageantry, he writes, was 'endowed with an aura of timelessness . . . but it was never simply the case that performance straightforwardly re-enacted tradition . . . An element of improvisation proceeded against a background of customary events and practices.'[12] Such 'improvisation', as we will see, could manifest itself as the Shows' engagement with political events and tensions.

At the most fundamental level, an essential aspect of all these entertainments was *instructive* support: 'the performance of good counsel', in Hunt's useful phrase.[13] Praise, the ostensible purpose of the mayoral Show, was a double-edged sword, for it is composed of both compliment and, potentially, criticism, inhabiting a precarious place between the two. The figures invoked by mayoral pageantry perform the function of gentle – and, as we'll see, sometimes not so gentle – moral exhortation. Munday, true to form, summarises this rationale when he baldly states to the new Lord Mayor that the tale of Jason and the golden fleece has been used for a purpose. 'By way of Morall application', he has Fitz-Alwin declare, 'Your Honour may make some relation / Vnto your selfe out of this storie' (*Metropolis coronata*, sig. B1v). For Munday, 'no Monsters dare confront [Jolles's] way' (*ibid.*), but other Shows did sound a note of warning about the challenges that lay ahead for the new incumbent. For Middleton, who, as we will see below, generally stresses the rigours of the mayoralty, Edward Barkham will confront risks in his 'Yeares voyage'. 'There is no Voyage set forth to renowne', the figure of Jason states, 'That do's not sometimes meete with Skies that frowne, / With Gusts of Enuie, Billowes of despight, / Which makes the Purchase once achieu'd, more bright' (*The sunne in Aries*, sigs A4v–B1r).[14] Using a similar metaphor, Dekker has Neptune caution John Swinnerton that 'thou must saile / in rough Seas (now) of Rule: and euery Gale/ will not perhaps befriend thee' (*Troia-Noua triumphans*, sig. B1v). The point is reiterated later on, when Fame informs Swinnerton that he faces a 'dangerous yeare' in which 'Each Eye will look through thee, and Each Ear / Way-lay thy Words and Workes' (sig. C1v).

Richard Deane, Lord Mayor in 1628, is issued with a series of quite stringent instructions: to remember the poor, to watch out for 'Dangers farre off', and to 'Kisse Peace [and] let Order euer steere the Helme' (*Brittannia's honor*, sig. B3r). At the end of the Show Deane is advised to trust no one as he takes his year's voyage through the mayoralty (here the ship of state appears again), 'for Officers Sell / Their Captaines Trust'. Dekker's approach here, as he admits, is admonitory: 'You May: you *Must*', he writes, for 'I counsell not, but *Reade / A Lesson* of my loue' (sig. C1v; my emphases).[15] Heywood could be even more demanding: there is something almost threatening in his use of the mirror as a metaphor in *Londini speculum*, whereby, he writes, 'I have purposed so true and exact a Mirrour, that in it may be discovered as well that which beautifies the governour, as deformes the government' (sig. B2v). The message to Richard Fenn thus seems to be that there is no hiding place from the intense scrutiny he is about to experience. Nautical imagery features too in Heywood's first Show, where he uses Scylla and Charybdis as tokens of the hazards the Lord Mayor must try to escape. Ulysses informs Whitmore that he must 'Keepe the even Channell, and be neither swayde, / To the right hand nor left'. The range of challenges that he must evade include 'Malicious envie . . . Smooth visadged flattery, and blacke mouthd detraction, / Sedition, whisprings, murmuring, [and] private hate' (*Londons ius honorarium*, sig. B1v). One would hardly be surprised if Whitmore had wished his election had never taken place upon hearing such a series of ghastly threats in store.

Being included in Fame's record – or not – was often used as a motivating force for the new incumbent: 'for the Encouragement of after ages', as Middleton put it in *The sunne in Aries* (sig. B1v). Indeed, the recitation of what Middleton calls 'the Glory of illustrious Acts' (*ibid.*, sig. B2r) that we see in so many Shows may have worked as much as a marker of how far short the new Lord Mayor may come to his predecessors than as an inspiration to emulate their achievements. In *The sunne in Aries* Edward Barkham, only very recently a member of the lowly Leathersellers' Company, is presented with exemplars whose worthy deeds range from being 'Colledge Founders [and] Temple-Beautifiers' to 'Erecters . . . of Granaries for the Poore'. Indeed, by stating that 'no Society, or Time can match' the achievement of that most famed and primary of Lord Mayors, Fitz-Alwin, who served 'for twenty-foure Yeares compleate' (*ibid.*), Middleton more or less rules out Barkham making an equivalent impression. In *Troia-Noua triumphans* it is possible that the difficulties Dekker antici- pates Swinnerton confronting may have something to do with the 'spite that murmur[ed] at the Choice' of the new Lord Mayor that Dekker rather impolitically mentions (sig. B3v). Conditional rather than unconditional approval of the new Lord Mayor is therefore a consistent feature of the Shows' rhetoric. Indeed, 'Expectation' features as a discrete character in *Sidero-Thriambos* expressly to 'intimate' to the Lord Mayor that 'there will be more then ordinary matter expecte[d] from him' (sig. B4v). More bathetically, Munday's extended simile of the Lord Mayor as the nursing pelican in *Chrysanaleia* leads him to warn John Leman, as the City's parent, to expect 'broken sleeps [and] daily and nightly cares'; indeed, he almost implies that, if he is to 'iustly answere to our Emblem', then, like the legendary pelican, Leman will expire at the end of his term of office (sig. B2r). There is then a recap at the end of this Show, where Leman is warned in even more drastic terms of what lies ahead for him:

> Continuall cares, and many broken sleepes,
> Heart-killing feares, which waite on Eminence
> Hard at the heeles, and (torturingly) still keeps
> Within the soule imperious residence,
> As whippes t'afflict both hope and patience . . .
> These you hardly will auoide this yeere.
>
> (sig. C3r)

All is not doom and gloom, however, for Munday offers the reassurance that with the assistance of 'Discretion, Policie, and Prouidence, / Courage [and] Correction', even the 'busiest troubles' will be 'sweetly qualified' (*ibid.*).

All these references to threats and troubles demonstrate that the London represented in mayoral pageantry was a more complex, fractured entity than Paster assumes when she writes of 'the clear atmosphere of the communities of praise' and of an absence in the Shows of any 'ambivalence about urban life'.[16] In themselves, as a starting point, the mayoral Shows' nostalgia and reification of the past were ideological strategies, attempts to fend off what was perceived by the City's great livery companies as an undesirable decline in their power and influence. As Hentschell has written in relation to the cloth trade, there was 'in the late sixteenth and early seventeenth centuries, a recurrent strain of loss and nostalgia in the writings about [this] industry'.[17] Furthermore, the sometimes aggressive economic actions and motivations that underscored the City's wealth could here be represented in a more benevolent light. In mayoral pageantry, Palmer has argued, 'malevolent ambition [is translated into] a felicitous vision of mercantile endeavor and aspiration'.[18] The invocation of past and present civic glories stands as a contrast to the eventful, crisis-ridden reigns of the Stuart kings before the civil wars.

'London's secure, with peace and plenty blest': responses to crisis in the Shows

Whether or not a full-scale Lord Mayor's Show took place was in itself dependent on immediate contingencies. In times of plague, as we have already seen, only minimal entertainments were put on and the route was usually changed to abbreviate the procession. There was thus no Lord Mayor's Show in 1625 owing to James's death and a severe outbreak of plague in London. In the following year's Show Middleton belatedly praises Allan Cotton, the Lord Mayor of 1625, and comments that at his 'Inauguration . . . Tryumph was not then in season, (Deaths Pageants being onely aduanc'st vppon the shoulders of men)' (*The triumphs of health and prosperity*, sig. B2r).[19] Thereafter, during the Caroline period, civic entertainments suffered generally, not exclusively because of unfortunate circumstances such as plague but also owing to a lack of interest on the part of the monarch. There is a precedent here in the early years of James's reign, when the Shows seem to have elapsed for a while and were in 1609 'reviued againe by order from the King', as Munday puts it in the 1633 edition of Stow's *Survey* (sig. Eee3v). Heywood's near-contemporary mayoral Show of 1635, *Londini sinus salutis*, perhaps to underscore the difference between James and Charles in this respect, also comments that on the inauguration of Thomas Campbell in 1609 'all the like Showes and Triumphs belonging unto the solemnitie of this day, which for some yeeres, had been omitted and neglected, were by a speciall commandement from his Majestie, King Iames, again retained' (sig. A4v).[20] In this instance, as both Munday and Heywood emphasise, even though his concern for pageantry was shortlived, the King did take action to renew mayoral entertainments. His son's approach was rather different. An insight into the attitude of the Caroline court to civic pageantry can be gleaned from Jasper Mayne's *The citye match*, a sub-Jonsonian play commissioned by the King and first performed at court. The 'Epilogue at Whitehall' praises the critical acumen of its aristocratic audience, stating that the author

> . . . hopes none doth valew [the play] so low
> As to compare it with my Lord Maiors show.
> Tis so unlike, that some, he feares, did sit,
> Who missing Pageants did or'esee the wit.

(sig. S2r)

Interestingly, the 'Epilogue at Black-friers' which follows in the printed text reins in the hostility towards civic entertainments manifested in the Whitehall epilogue. In its Whitehall incarnation, however, the play epitomises the Lord Mayor's Show as the kind of contemptible entertainment which stands in opposition to courtly pleasures.[21]

Charles's own indifference towards civic pageantry began to manifest itself very early on. At the very start of his reign, in 1626, the new monarch called a halt to the already quite advanced preparations for the traditional civic celebration of a sovereign's accession, which had already been postponed from 1625 owing to the plague (Middleton had been employed to design some of the pageantry). 'Almost worse than the last-minute cancellation', Randall writes, Charles I 'ordered the pageants torn down immediately, despite the fact that his subjects had gone to great expense to build them'.[22] The Venetian ambassador reported that 'five most superb arches . . . will prove useless and they have already begun to dismantle them amid the murmurs of the people and the disgust of those who spent the money'.[23] Indeed, a contemporary witness, George Wither, relates in *Britain's remembrancer* that walking through the desolate post-plague city

> . . . my eye did meet,
> Those halfe built Pageants which, athwart the street,
> Did those triumphant Arches counterfeit,
> Which heretofore in ancient Rome were set . . .
> The loyall Citizens (although they lost
> The glory of their well-intended cost)
> Erected those great Structures to renowne
> The new receiving of the Sov'raigne Crowne.
>
> (sig. K2v)

Bergeron comments that it is 'more accurate' to call Charles's royal entries '"non-Entries", because it seems to have been this king's particular penchant to build up anticipation for a state entry and then for some reason to fail to follow through on the plans'.[24] As far as civic visibility is concerned, Charles's royal entry into London from Scotland in 1641 was therefore too little, too late.

The first Show of Charles's reign might be seen to comment on the King's cessation of the royal entry. After the 1625 hiatus the Shows returned in 1626 with Middleton's last one, *The triumphs of health and prosperity*, a work which is quite a bit shorter than many of its predecessors, perhaps a reflection of uncertain times. Middleton strikes a dark note in the first speech, doubtless alluding to the dual misfortunes of 1625, plague and the death of a monarch, writing that 'a cloude of griefe hath showrde upon the face / Of this sad City, and vsurpt the place/ Of Ioy and Cheerfulnesse' (sig. A4r). Middleton uses the image of a rainbow to suggest a silver lining to these recent clouds in the person of the new Lord Mayor and the chance to celebrate his inauguration. Although Charles himself was not present at the Show, Middleton took the opportunity to outline the relative roles of City and Crown. Indeed, one could see *The triumphs of health and prosperity* as a criticism of the King's recently abandoned royal entry. Middleton's text begins with what looks like the usual historical survey of civic record, but he singles out the importance of inaugural ceremonial with notable hyperbole:

> if you should search all Chronicles, Histories, Records, in what Language or Letter soeuer; if the Inquisitiue Man should waste the deere Treasure of his Time and Ey-sight, He shall conclude his life onely with this certainety, that there is no Subiect vpon earth receiued into the place of his Gouernement with the like State and Magnificence, as is his Maiesties great Substitute into his Honorable charge the City of London. (sig. A3r)

The King, the subtext of Middleton's prologue seems to imply, and as all readers of this work would have known, refused to be 'receiued into the place of his Gouernment' in the time-honoured fashion. The Show's celebration of Charles's 'great Substitute' (a phrase reiterated in the first speech) with all the appropriate 'State and Magnificence' therefore could be seen to act as a kind of reproach to the King's neglect, and to appropriate the glamour that should have belonged to the royal entry further to magnify itself.

The effect is subtly conveyed, for Middleton is ostensibly simply reusing prefatory material he had written for *The triumphs of truth* and then recast slightly for *The triumphs of integrity* in 1623. He had made some small but significant changes from the original wording from 1613, however, which may have had a particular valency in the context of 1626. Here, for instance, the phrase 'great Substitute' is preferred to 'the Lord Maior of the Citty of London' as used in the 1613 work, a tactic which points up the status of the Lord Mayor *vis-à-vis* that of the King whose absence from that same City had recently been so glaringly apparent. It also suggests that the mayoral Show is itself a kind of substitute for the royal entry. Indeed, as if to emphasise the point, Middleton comments that London bears 'the Inscription of the Chamber Royall'. This title is one traditionally used for London during the royal entry rather than the Lord Mayor's Show, so its citation in this context is rather odd (London bore the name as an 'inscription' for James's 1604 entry, for instance). By stressing that the current occasion is 'no lesse illustrated with brotherly Affection then former Tryumphall times haue beene partakers of' (*ibid.*), in its 1626 moment the text could also be drawing attention to a period within those 'former times' when 'affection' towards the City was lacking. It is in the preface that the majority of these encoded comments occur, interestingly: perhaps with a more select civic readership any criticism of the monarch could be safely made more tangible than in the public speeches.[25] In the latter, Middleton contents himself with the more vague statement that in recent times 'Delight, / Triumph and Pompe had almost lost their right' (sig. A4v). The blame for this state of affairs is left unspecified. Indeed, although dutiful acknowledgement is made in the Show's speeches of the loyalty due to the monarch from both mayor and people, ultimately the burden of the text is that the king may be the head of the body politic but the City is the heart. Middleton calls it 'the Fountayne of the bodies heate: / The first thing [that] receiues life [and] the last that dyes' (sig. B2v).

Middleton's emphasis on the importance of the City to the health of the country as a whole is a common, if carefully negotiated, theme in mayoral inaugurations. Recorder Finch claimed in his Exchequer speech in 1623 that the City is 'the center in which all the lines of the kingdome meete'.[26] Dekker uses another kind of metaphor in *Brittannia's honor* to encompass the idea: for him, London is 'the Master-Wheele of the whole Kingdome: [and] as that moues, so the maine Engine works'. As if the notion is not clear enough, he supplements yet another representation of it, whereby 'London is Admirall ouer the Nauy royall of Cities: And as she sayles, the whole Fleete of them keepe their course' (sig. A3v). In *Himatia-Poleos* Munday takes London's primacy further still, and has Fitz-Alwin, the first mayor, explain that his role came into existence to make up for shortcomings in the system of sole sovereign power that preceded it. In earlier times, Fitz-Alwin says, 'men thought fit / In the Kings iudgement Courts to sit'. Contention over this arrangement (about which Munday is unhelpfully if perhaps understandably vague) resulted in chaos: 'wrongs vnredrest, offences flowing, / Garboyles & grudges each where growing'. To ensure consistent and peaceful government, therefore, monarchical authority had to be supplemented: 'so would he [the King] plant a deputie, / To figure his authority, / In the true forme of Monarchie' (sig. C1v). The message is clear: the security of the state requires both sovereign *and* Lord Mayor. In *Metropolis coronata* (as I have discussed at greater length elsewhere), the Lord Mayor's stature almost displaces that of the monarch. Jolles is likened to 'an immortall Deitie' who is 'this day solemnly married to Londons supreame Dignitie'; the Show itself is akin to 'a Royall Maske' (sig. B4v).

The Shows can therefore be seen to represent the monarchy and its relationship with the City in a way that was receptive to changing times. Peele, with his court connections, and writing at a time before the printed mayoral Show had become an established genre with its own specifically metropolitan values, made much of 'our faire Eliza', the 'peerless Queene', in *Descensus astraeae*, the very title of which aligns the Show with one of Elizabeth's favoured personae (sigs A2v–A3r). When compared to the work of his successors, Peele's integration of the Queen into his mayoral Show illustrates Perry's argument that 'King James's departure from Elizabeth's civic persona released London from the affective bond of . . . mutual obligations . . . [resulting in] alterations in the civic self-fashioning of the first decade of his reign'.[27] Thus for the later pageant writers the figure of 'Fame', although repeatedly associated with Queen Elizabeth throughout her reign, was not an exclusively monarchical image but one which could readily be borrowed to praise the City and its mayors. Some years later, Munday may have made a rather compromised attempt to genuflect to the new sovereign in *The triumphes of re-united Britania* but this was not the mayoral Shows' usual mode.[28] In their treatment of the Crown, the Shows can be seen to express a potentially critical response to James's much-cited lack of interest in public display in civic forums. As we have seen, Middleton was particularly likely to accentuate the Lord Mayor's status as the royal 'substitute'. For Middleton, the glory tends to reflect back on the monarch from the Lord Mayor, not vice versa. Thus, he cannot resist commenting in *The triumphs of loue and antiquity* that for a member of the monarchy to pay their debts to 'Merchants' – in this case, 'Philip [*sic*]', Edward III's queen – is an act 'rare *in these dayes*' (sig. C2r; my emphasis). Middleton foregrounds royalty only in his final Show, *The triumphs of health and prosperity*, and even there, as I have argued above, he does so to critique rather than praise. As Manley comments, Taylor presents a 'wonderfully ambiguous' take on the king's power *vis-à-vis* that of his 'substitute':

> For no Kings Deputy, or Magistrate
> Is with such pompous state inaugurate,
> As Londons Mayor is, which most plainly showes
> The Kings illustrious greatnesse whence it flowes.[29]
> *(The triumphs of fame and honour*, sig. A3v)

The circularity of Taylor's argument in these lines is reminiscent of that put forward in the Recorder of London's speech at the

Exchequer in 1624. On this occasion Finch stated that "tis for the honor of the kinge that he be honoured whome the kinge honored': although he hastily explained that he was not saying that the king was not supreme, whose the real 'honor' was remains highly ambiguous.[30] Heywood too could sometimes be quite bold in his defence of the City's primacy versus that of other cities, notably Westminster. In *Porta pietatis* he writes that although London and Westminster are 'Twin-sister-Cities', 'London may be presum'd to be the elder, and more excellent in Birth, Meanes, and Issue; in the first for her Antiquity, in the second for her Ability, in the third, for her numerous Progeny' (sig. A3r–v).[31]

Such a defence of London's supremacy took place within the context of a debate about its boundaries and its freedoms which accelerated through the seventeenth century. As is often noted, concerns about civic governmental and livery company jurisdiction in the face of the expansion of the city into the suburbs increased into the seventeenth century to become, in Harding's words, 'one of the important and enduring characteristics of early modern London'.[32] Whether or not these concerns were entirely justified or were shaped partly for rhetorical purposes, as Griffiths has recently proposed, it is still the case that there was undeniably a *perception* that the City was under threat from various quarters.[33] Following the model established in the early years of King James's reign, when in 1607 he issued new charters to some livery companies as part of his move to bring them more under his purview, the London suburbs were incorporated by the Crown in 1636, an act that implicitly endangered the City's monopoly over legitimate trade within its boundaries.[34] With this 'New Incorporation', Hardin writes, 'the line separating sanctioned from unsanctioned commercial activity disappeared, rendering the original corporation no longer unique'.[35] The effective result was that the City now had a rival. In response to challenges of this kind, and to the growth of unregulated trade in the suburbs, the City made efforts in the 1630s to reinforce its boundaries by, for instance, rebuilding the Gate at Temple Bar and, later, in 1640, setting up an iron chain between the City limits and Middlesex.[36] Concurrently, City oligarchs were ordering more scrutiny of the City wall and its gates and ditches. Despite all this – or perhaps due to all this – as Harding states, 'the sense of the boundary was weakening'.[37]

The Shows' response to these infringements and challenges varied. For one thing, the suburbs were invariably edited out of the 'London' represented in the pageantry: as Griffiths argues, 'there was no wish to celebrate larger metropolitan identities incorporating the ribbon-developments that sapped specific senses of civic identity'.[38] Relatedly, one sees a defiant stress on the full, extended limits of mayoral authority, especially in the Shows of the 1620s and 1630s. Here the river Thames is often used as a metonym for the extent of the civic realm. Thamesis's statement in *Londini emporia* that Ralph Freeman is the 'great Lord in cheife' 'up [river] to Stanes and downe as farre as Lee' (sigs A4v–B1r) echoes Dekker's more explicit treatment of the same theme a few years earlier.[39] The latter writes that 'the extention of a Lord Maiors power, is euery yeare to bee seene both by Land and Water: Downe as low as Lee in Essex: [and] vp as high as Stanes in Middlesex' (*Brittannia's honor*, sig. A3v). Heywood's *Londini speculum*, which took place the year after Charles I's 'New Incorporation', also addresses the changing political and economic landscape of London and, in particular, the Crown's recent innovation, which he mentions towards the very end of the Show. Unavoidably perhaps, Heywood engages with the New Incorporation directly, using a maternal image to explain its genesis and to present the newcomer as the progeny of the original City. His imagery, however, is not without implied tension. London, he writes, 'in her age grew pregnant [and was] brought a bed / Of a New Towne'. Although this infant allegedly adds 'to her more grace', it is still described as a 'burthen' (sig. C4r). Hardin asserts that the arrival of the 'New Towne' is 'recast as a natural process', thus dispelling any sense of danger or threat to the City, but I would argue that the force of the word 'burthen' is not so easily discounted; in addition, the phrase 'to her more grace' is held in abeyance by parentheses.[40]

Towards the end of this period, as the political temperature in London rose still higher, the mayoral Shows were constrained in their entirety. In 1640 the Royalist Sir William Acton, a Merchant Taylor, was initially elected as Lord Mayor. He was, however, subsequently discharged from the offices of Lord Mayor and Alderman by the Commons (he was later imprisoned by Parliament in 1642), and was succeeded as Lord Mayor by Edmund Wright, a Grocer. The Merchant Taylors made no entries in their minute books or accounts of anything associated with Acton's putative mayoralty.[41] Acton is also omitted by John Tatham from the list of previous Merchant Taylor mayors that he provided in his 1660 Show.[42] The Grocers did treat Wright's nomination more conventionally, although it was certainly not accompanied by anything like the usual fanfare (the total expenditure was some £200 less than the

Grocers paid out in 1622).[43] They also, perhaps understandably, made no reference to Wright being a replacement for Acton when they set up their usual arrangements in early October. Members of the livery were thereafter assessed for their contributions, barges were rowed up and down river, the procession evidently took place with torches, whifflers, trumpeters, banners and so on, and the event was concluded with a dinner – what was missing was the pageantry. The Company decided in May to forgo its usual anniversary dinner owing to 'the inconveniences and unfitnes of the times for publike feasting', so it may be that the same rationale came into play in respect of Lord Mayor's Day, although it still held the feast on that occasion, albeit a 'moderate' one.[44] As far as the pageantry is concerned, the Grocers baldly stated that 'their [*sic*] is noe publike show eyther with Pageats [*sic*] or upon the water' (the livery paid a reduced subscription as a result of the lesser expenditure) but refrained from saying why.[45]

Nevertheless, although they seem to have been relatively understated when compared to previous years, in the same way as the theatre managed to continue in a much reduced form after 1642, civic festivities did not come to a total halt in the 1640s. Indeed, turning the usual convention of entertaining the monarch on its head, there was a 'great and generous welcome' given to members of Parliament at Grocers' Hall in January 1641.[46] As far as civic posts were concerned, the Grocers in the usual fashion conferred a benevolence upon a Sheriff elect for the beautifying of his house and the ordering of plate for a feast in October 1642, when one might have expected them to have other things on their minds – or maybe that was the point of continuing in the traditional manner. In October 1645 the livery members of the Painter-Stainers 'still met at the Hall in their gowns, the Assistants wearing their distinctive badges, and past Masters their foynes'.[47] Equally, Lord Mayor's Day still took place throughout the Commonwealth period, though there is little evidence from Company records that it was accompanied by much in the way of entertainment. In 1654 the Grocers ordered that their barge be repaired and trimmed 'as also trumpetes and others to bee agreed with by Mr Wardens as formerly', indicating that the procession still went down river to Westminster as it had done since time immemorial.[48]

In the context of a very charged political atmosphere Heywood's 1639 Show, the last Show with any pageantry before the first civil war broke out, is entitled (quite deliberately ironically, it seems, or in Rowland's terms, 'wistfully') *Londini status pacatus; or, Londons*

peaceable estate. The Show was written to celebrate the inauguration of the royalist mayor Henry Garway, a Draper, and Heywood
takes care to negotiate the pressing issues of the moment.[49]
Rowland rightly calls Heywood's treatment of civil war 'visceral
and intense'.[50] From the outset this text demonstrates an awareness
of its dangerous times: for one thing, Heywood specifically and
perhaps optimistically praises the new Lord Mayor's qualities as a
peace-maker. As with Munday's 1618 Show, although on a much
larger scale, Heywood's text deals explicitly with the calamity of
'sedition, tumult, uproares and faction'. The fifth pageant is the
central one, sharing its name with the text itself. Here are displayed
'a Company of Artillery men compleatly armed, to express Warre'.
In the preamble to the description of the show Heywood states
specifically that 'Domesticke War is the over-throw and ruine of all
Estates and Monarchies . . . most execrable, begetting contempt of
God, corruption of manners, and disobedience to Magistrates'. He
goes on to argue that civil war is worse than foreign warfare, the
latter of which is, in comparison a 'more gentle and generous contention' (sig. C2r–v). In any other moment we might expect to see
foreign warfare treated with anxiety – indeed, we see this in some
Shows from the previous decade – but for Heywood it is very much
the lesser of two evils. With some prescience he warns that

> any War may be begun with great facility, but is ended with much
> difficulty; neither is it in his power to end it, who begins it . . . &
> therefore much safer and better is certaine peace, than hoped for
> Victory: the first is in our Will, the latter in the Will of the Gods. (sig.
> C2v)

'Our neighbour Nations' (one of which was Scotland), he states
later in the text, are already in the 'throwes' of war, and he issues a
plea that both gratitude and 'Pious cares' should strive to preserve
peace at home.

Indeed, Peace, the antithesis of war, comes in for considerably
more sustained attention than in any other Show of this period: it
becomes a central focus of the latter stages of Heywood's text. The
embodiment of the City itself, the Genius of London, is given the
keynote speech in which these concerns are articulated. From the
vantage point of a moment where peace must have seemed more
and more endangered, Heywood produces what sounds with hindsight like a plaintive call for what he describes as 'the Tranquillity,
and calme quiet of kingdomes, free from Section, tumult, uproares
and faction'. Peace, he continues, as if aware that it is a precarious

quality in 1639, asks 'no lesse wisedome to preserve it, then valour to obtain it' (sig. C2r). It is naivety, he argues, to consider War but a 'pleasant showe' like the mayoral inauguration, for it is rather a dreadful prospect to be avoided at all costs. Indeed, Heywood illustrates its horrors very vividly: 'when slaughter strowes the crimson plaine with Courses' and 'Massacre, (all quarter quite denying) / Revells amidst the flying, crying, dying', the reality of civil war will strike home, but by then it might be too late. The lines invoking a situation in which 'The Harmlesse, armelesse; murder one another: / When in the husbands and sad Parents fight' (sig. C3r) show strikingly accurate foresight of how the widespread conflict to come was to manifest itself.

The impassioned treatment of warfare here goes far beyond the usual, brief invocation of such figures as Error and so on, who were traditionally conjured up in order to be defeated by the new Lord Mayor. For Heywood in 1639, writing during the Scottish war, warfare – and specifically *domestic* warfare – merits more prolonged attention, and he thus alludes to prior manifestations of the conflict that was to result so soon in civil war across the whole of Britain. He does so quite overtly, too. In the same work he has the figure of Janus give the Lord Mayor a 'golden key' with which to release certain political prisoners, 'those Gaild / For Capitall crimes' (sig. B3r). Rowland argues that this recalls 'the MPs who were imprisoned after the king prorogued Parliament in 1629 [one of whom] Sir John Eliot, had already died in the Tower'.[51]

Heywood's intervention apart, one cannot posit wholesale antagonism from the Companies towards Charles and his policies, however: for one thing, the political and religious affiliations of the City oligarchs varied from hardline Calvinist to loyal royalist. In addition, as Elizabeth Glover comments, during the troubled 1640s the Companies generally sought to stay on the safe side: 'the official line will always have been cautious and conciliatory to whichever side was in power'.[52] Nevertheless, Clark understates the significance of Heywood's portrayal of civic strife, arguing that his location of such upheaval in Germany rather than England – which takes place via a marginal note 'As lately in Germany' – displaces the contemporary urgency of the message of Heywood's Show.[53] Rowland's reading, in contrast, regards the citation of Germany as a reminder of 'the Caroline regime's failure to relieve the torments of protestants abroad'.[54] Indeed, only a few years previously John Taylor's Show stated quite explicitly that 'fire and sword doth Germany molest' (sig. A7v). Heywood's is, after all, only a marginal note, and, even if it can be seen to act as a slight disclaimer, the numerous witnesses of this Show, unlike its readers, would not have known about it. In any case, and by any standards, the page after page of overt concern about potential upheaval is too apparent to be so dismissed. 'Long may [peace] last' is Heywood's final word, although he has conferred little confidence that his hopes would be borne out (sig. C4r).

A military note is also struck in earlier mayoral Shows. The figure of War speaks to Francis Jones in the 1620 Show, eventually yielding to Peace, the subject of the title of the printed work. The advice 'Warre' gives to the new Lord Mayor suggests that peace is not guaranteed. Jones is told that he should 'resolue of future hazards; and prepare / Me such prouisions that if times should cease, / To be vnto this land as now they are, / Warre might restore againe the Palme to Peace' (sig. C1v) 'Warre' ends the day by defending Jones's gates with 'fire and sword' (sig. C2r). 'Future hazards' are made to sound inevitable. Although I am not arguing for a direct connection (the text is not that specific), the background to the 1620 Show and its preoccupation with peace was a conflict between the Protestant Palatinate and Spain which made all-out war amongst the European powers, including England, look more likely than it had done for years.[55] There was, after all, a real interest and religico-political investment in England in the fortunes of Frederick of Bohemia, the Elector Palatine, who had since 1613 been the King's son-in-law, and who was to become, along with his wife Elizabeth, James's daughter, the bearer of (ultimately thwarted) Protestant hopes against Spanish hegemony on the continent.

The strains were perhaps already in the air, for in characteristic style Middleton strikes a topical note in *The triumphs of loue and antiquity*, staged the year before Jones's inauguration. At this juncture William Cockayne, that year's Lord Mayor, was, as Middleton notes, 'Lord Generall of the Military Forces'. 'Expectation' implies a dual celebration of both aspects of Cockayne's importance, for

> two Tryumphs must on this day dwell,
> For Magistrate, one, and one for Coronell [Colonel],
> Returne Lord Generall, that's the Name of State
> The Souldier giues thee; Peace, the Magistrate.
>
> (sigs A3r and B1v)

The text highlights Cockayne's military role throughout, stressing that alongside the conventional procession of aldermen and sheriffs one should not overlook

> the Noble paines and loues of the Heroyick Captaines of the Citty, &
> Gentlemen of the Artillery Garden, making with two glorious Rankes
> a manly and Maiestick passage for their Lord Generall, his Lordship,
> through Guild-hall yard; and afterward their Loues to his Lordship
> resounding in a second Noble Volley. (sig. C1v)

Manley too cites this text's 'topicality', arguing that 'the unusu-
ally heavy use [in this Show] . . . of the City Trained Bands, whose
Lord-General Cockayne became with his inauguration, may reflect
the City's eagerness . . . to contribute to war with Spain'.[56] In the
Honorable entertainments of 1621, also written for Cockayne,
Middleton once more refers to the Lord Mayor as the 'L.[ord]
Generall of the Military forces' (sig. B1r), a title which, Parr com-
ments, 'inflates [Cockayne's] authority over the city militia'.[57]

By the mid-1630s, as we have already seen, warlike imagery
was both more widespread and had taken on a more urgent note.
As well as the negotiation of civil versus foreign war in *Londini
status pacatus*, there is 'an Imperiall Fort . . . defenc'd with men
and officers' in *Londini speculum* (sig. C2r). Perhaps with a recent
outbreak of unrest in Scotland in mind, Heywood is notably defensive about why he has used such an image for his fourth show.
'Nor is it compulsive', he writes, 'that here I should argue what a
Fort is, a Skonce, or a Citadell, nor what a Counterskarfe, or halfe
Moone, &c. is; nor what opposures or defences are: my purpose is
onely to expresse my selfe thus farre'. The 'onely purpose' of this
'project', he stresses, is to signify London's status as 'his Majesties
royall chamber' (sig. C2r). Nevertheless, a certain nervousness
persists. He stipulates that what he writes about 'Warre' has in it
no 'impropriety' nor anything 'that is dissonant from authority',
and he then cuts short an explanation of the history of the goddess
of war, Bellona, with the interjection that 'this Discourse may to
some appeare impertinent to the project in hand, and therefore
I thus proceed to her speech' (sig. C2v). A similar image is given
more sustained treatment in *Londini sinus salutis* (1635), where
'Bellipotent' Mars is placed in 'a Castle munified with sundry Peeces
of Ordnance; and Accomodated with all such Persons as are needfull for the defence of such a Citadell' (sig. A8v). Heywood is still
somewhat vague about Mars's function here, though. Moreover,
the statement that Mars has witnessed 'so many Sonnes of Mars . . .
In compleat Arms, Plum'd Casks [casques], and Ensigns spred' does
not specify *where* such military figures have been seen. Heywood
does add that although London itself is currently 'peacefull', it
'could to a Campe, it selfe change in an houre', indicating that a

military threat may not be all that remote (sig. A9r–v). It is possible, therefore, that Dekker's praise for England in *Brittannia's honor* as a beacon of peace in the context of a Europe that he describes as 'Frighted with Vproares, Battailes, Massacres, / Famines, and all that Hellish brood of warres' is at that juncture more hopeful than realistic. In the late 1620s it was becoming more difficult to sustain the image of a 'blessed Land . . . that seest fires kindling round, and yet canst stand / Vnburnt for all their flames . . . When all thy Neighbours shrike, none wound thy brest' (sig. C2r). Warfare is undeniably a present – and geographically close – reality for Dekker here.[58] The following year he cites more directly the foreign powers with which England was intermittently in conflict in this period: 'Horrid Sea-fights, Nauies ouerthrowne, /. . . The Dunkerks Hell, / The Dutchmans Thunder, and the Spaniards Lightning' (*Londons tempe*, sig. A4v). His references to 'Pyrates' and 'Dunkerk' would probably have been understood by the informed onlooker as alluding to the problems English merchant ships had had on that score for some years and which reached a height in 1628, the year of this Show.[59]

These later instances mark a substantial change from the well-nigh bucolic city invoked by Peele back in 1585, where the most common adjective used for London is 'lovely', where the Thames is a 'sweet and daintye Nymph' within whose waters 'leaping fishes play', and where 'the Husbandman, / layes downe his sackes of Corne at Londons feet' (*The deuice*, sigs A2r–A3r). Peele's text does include a soldier, but his role is vaguely defined and quite passive when compared to those invoked by Middleton and Heywood in the Jacobean and Caroline periods. Later texts differ quite markedly too from those produced by Munday in quieter times. In *Camp-bell* Munday has St George rebut concerns about 'inuading Enuie, or homebred trecherie' with a simple 'So much for this' (sig. B3v). In the 1611 Show, *Chruso-thriambos*, Leofstane tells the new Lord Mayor that he will be ruling in 'sweeter singing times' than 'those dayes of disturbance and rough combustion' that he himself knew (sig. B2r). In *Chrysanaleia* Munday's account of the long-distant Peasants' Revolt is positively dismissive of it: 'leauing the matter, a case of desperate Rebellion [and] the manner, a most base and barbarous kinde of proceeding', Munday focuses instead on 'that triumphant victorie' within which Walworth played such a notable role. Victory over the enemies of 'King and State' is the keynote here, even though the depiction of Richard II has the 'triumphing Angell' 'hold[ing] his Crowne on fast, that neither forraine

Hostilitie, nor home-bred Trecherie should euer more shake it'
(sig. B3v). In any case, 'Treason and Mutinie' are conspicuously
outnumbered by the combined forces of 'Truth, Vertue, Honor,
Temperance, Fortitude, Zeale, Equity [and] Conscience', backed
up by 'Iustice, Authority, Lawe, Vigilancy, Peace, Plentie and
Discipline' (sigs B3v–B4r).

'Of Trafficke and Commerce': representing merchants and merchandise in the Shows

As cultural forms very close to the changing realities for civic bodies
such as the livery companies, the Shows did engage with the economic pressures on those who commissioned and paid for them.
For the companies, a major concern as the seventeenth century
wore on was their increasing failure to control economic activity
by 'foreigners', and their decreasing powers even over those who
had gained the freedom.[60] In their transition from guild to livery
company these bodies had become more focused on merchandising
than on the production of commodities, and the members of the
oligarchy from which the Lord Mayors emanated were increasingly
turning to trade to maximise their income, by controlling where the
commodities were bought and sold as well as the manner in which
they were produced. For instance, about one-sixth of the livery of
the Drapers in this period were also members of trading companies
such as the Merchant Adventurers.[61] These trends resulted in what
Hirschfeld calls a 'bifurcation during the Elizabethan and Stuart
years between craft and mercantile interests'.[62] The Merchant
Adventurers themselves in turn became more and more displaced by
newer bodies like the East India and Levant Companies. As we will
see further below, in their efforts accurately to represent and hence
celebrate the mercantile activities of the Lord Mayors, the pageant
poets perforce engaged with the shifts and tensions inherent in this
important transition.

As early as 1605 Munday emphasised the trading dimensions
of the companies. In *The triumphs of re-united Britania* Epimeleia
states that at the point at which the Merchant Taylors gained their
present name, in the reign of Henry VII, 'they traded, as no men
did more, / With forren Realmes, by clothes and Merchandize, /
Returning hither other Countries store' (sig. C3r). As this demonstrates, despite the underlying tensions, mercantile values are
ostensibly represented in a positive light by the Shows wherever
feasible, creating what Manley calls 'new rationales for the city

and its bourgeois pursuits'.[63] Heywood provides an epitome of the approach in *Londini emporia*, which, as its title suggests, foregrounds 'Merchants and Merchandise'. The benefits of these two, he writes, are numerous. As well as making commodities 'conducible and frequent', by merchants' 'glorious' 'Aduenture and Industry vnknowne Countries haue beene discouered, Friendship with forreigne Princes contracted, [and] barbarous Nations to humane gentleness and courtesie reduced' (sig. A3r). Middleton's take on the latter aspect of 'merchandise' in *The triumphs of truth* is typical. Here the Moorish king relates how he was converted from heathen belief by 'commerce' with 'English Merchants, Factors [and] Trauailers' (sig. C1r): even a religious discussion is coded in the language of trade as 'commerce'. Later in his civic career Middleton strikes the same note. In *The triumphs of honor and vertue* the 'blacke Queene' states that she was drawn to knowledge of 'Christian holinesse' through her encounter with 'English Merchants'; the colonies of Virginia and Bermuda are called 'those Christianly Reformed Islands' (the accuracy of Middleton's account of foreign trade is somewhat imperilled, though, by the citation of Virginia as an island) (sigs B2r and C2r). In this respect Middleton and his peers were in touch with changing realities. Oligarchs from the Great Twelve livery companies were deeply imbricated with the Merchant Adventurers, the Virginia Company, East India Company and the like, as well as with colonial endeavours in Ireland.[64] The City plutocrats made considerable financial investment into these new venturing bodies as the seventeenth century progressed, and unsurprisingly this increasingly significant aspect of the City made its way into pageantry.

In some cases, this was a result of pageant writers' tendency to provide an overview of the new Lord Mayor's career and notable roles. This trend within the Shows began quite early in the period and accelerated from then on. Via his usage of the ship 'The Royall Exchange' in *The triumphes of re-united Britania* Munday references the new Lord Mayor's involvement in foreign trade (Holliday was a founder of and was to become the Treasurer of the East India Company). We can see an amplification of this aspect of the City's activities from Munday's rather brief treatment of Holliday's trading links to their prominence later into the seventeenth century. In 1629 Dekker accurately cites the powerful merchant James Campbell's freedom of the East India Company as well as the fact that he was the 'Maior of the Staple, Gouernor of the French Company, and free of the East-land Company' (*Londons tempe*, sig. B1v).[65] In the same way, in 1637 Heywood discusses Richard Fenn's membership of the Merchant Adventurers, 'as also of the Levant, or Turkey, and of the East India Company'; indeed, the Haberdashers are rather eclipsed in the text by Fenn's trading links (*Londini speculum*, sig. B3r). Heywood also lists all the trading companies to which Morris Abbot belonged in 1638, emphasising his significance to overseas trade: 'the present Lord Major . . . [is] free of the Turkey, Italian, French, Spanish, Muscovy, and was late Governour of the East Indy Company' (*Porta pietatis*, sig. A4r).[66] In *Londini status pacatus* he flags up his awareness that Garway's 'breeding hath beene chiefly in Mercature' as well as of his 'personal Travell in [his] youth' (sig. A2r). Such knowledge of the new Lord Mayor's past and present was expected of pageant poets. Middleton refers similarly to the manner in which his namesake had escaped 'great and many incident dangers, especially in forraigne Countries in the time of [his] Youth and trauels' (*The triumphs of truth*, sig. A2r–v), and Peter Proby's recovery from 'so long a Sicknesse' is mentioned in *The triumphs of honor and vertue* (sig. B3r).

By the 1630s, the time of Heywood's dominance of the writing of the Shows, bodies like the East India Company had considerable importance for the City, and as a result their significance emerges clearly in Heywood's works. In the dedications of his 1632 Show Heywood highlights the new Lord Mayor's Lincolnshire breeding (like his own), and the membership of the Merchant Adventurers held by both of the City Sheriffs, but does not mention the Haberdashers until well into the text. Heywood's emphasis forms an instructive contrast with, say, Munday's Shows of some twenty years earlier, where the livery companies and their domestic enterprises are his primary concern. Heywood's Shows can therefore be seen – willingly or unwillingly – to represent the decline of the livery companies and the new hegemony of the merchants. Indeed, there is a defensive, as well as hyberbolic, note to the way in which Heywood describes the Merchant Adventurers' Company in *Londini speculum*. Before discussing the actual shows (in an echo of Munday's strategy with regard to 'old drapery' back in 1614 and 1615, discussed below), he hastens to tell his readers that the Company

> were first trusted with the sole venting of the manufacture of Cloth out of this kingdome, & have for above this 4 hundred years traded in a priviledged, & wel governed course, in Germany, the Low Countries, &c. and have beene the chiefe meanes to raise the manufacture of all wollen commodities to that height in which it

now existeth . . . whereby the poore in all Countries are plentifully maintained. (sigs B2v–B3r)

Merchants generally are heroic figures for Heywood, making 'discovery of all Nations' by bravely 'plow[ing] the bosome of each unknowne deepe' whilst 'others here at home securely sleepe', as he puts it in *Porta pietatis* (sig. B3r). Even figures from classical legend are reworked to fit this notion. Jason's Argo becomes anachronistically 'the first choise peece [i.e. ship]' to trade across the sea and it is stressed that this voyage had no other pretext than to stand as the first mercantile endeavour (sig. B4r). In *Londons ius honorarium* he states that as kings arrive at their status 'eyther by succession or Election', so the Lord Mayor is elevated to that role 'by Commerce and Trafficke, both by Sea and Land, by the Inriching of the Kingdome, and Honour of our Nation' (sig. C1r). There is nothing here about good deeds – in this instance trade is paramount. Whitmore's involvement in the East India and Virginia Companies is surely the referent of the dangers encountered by 'Commerce' in this text, where his ships travel 'through a Wildernesse of Seas, / Dangers of wrack, Surprise, [and] Desease' (*ibid.*, sig. C3r). In *Porta pietatis*, too, Heywood expresses the aspiration that 'that Fleete / Which makes th'East Indies with our England meete, / Prosper' (sig. B1r–v). *Londini status pacatus* is even more expansive, listing the numerous places where overseas trade was taking place, from Ireland to Newfoundland. Henry Garway, the Lord Mayor on that occasion, was a mainstay of the East India Company in the 1630s (as had been his father in the Levant Company); as Rowland has pointed out, Heywood's information about Garway's various roles is both correct and 'absolutely current'.[67] In *The triumphs of honor and vertue* too Middleton mentions the banners displayed on the 'Globe of Honor' as 'the Armes of this Honorable City, the Lord Maiors, the Grocers, and the Noble East-India Companies' (sig. C2r). Heywood notes that Hugh Perry and Henry Andrews, the Sheriffs in 1632, were both members of the Merchant Adventurers; their 'Trafficke and Commerce', as he puts it, 'testifie to the world your Noble Profession' (*Londoni artium*, sig. A3r).

The following year, Heywood's pseudo-historical preamble in *Londini emporia* is primarily concerned with celebrating the antiquity of 'Merchants and Merchandise'; as with *Londini speculum* his account of the Clothworkers' Company is secondary (sig. A3r). Although by judicious use of a shepherd the Clothworkers form the topic of the first Show on land, the second is dedicated to 'the

Trade of Merchant-Aduenturers'. This second show features the rather more lofty figure of Mercury in the somewhat unusual if timely guise of 'the God of Barter, buying, selling, and commerce in all Merchandise whatsouer' (he is also, fortuitously, associated with 'Showes, Ouations, [and] Triumphs') (sigs B2v–B3r). Mercury boasts about the Merchant Adventurers' commerce across the world, from exotic locations such as 'Musco', Persia, Turkey, China and Greece to the more familiar 'Genoua, Luca Florence, Naples . . . Norway, Danske, France, Spaine, [and] the Netherlands' (sig. B3v).[68] Picking up on the note of merchant heroism struck elsewhere, Heywood also stresses the potential dangers inherent in the Merchant Adventurers' overseas forays and includes a reference to the military force that such foreign adventures sometimes necessitated. Freeman's ship, he writes, 'though a woodden Fabricke', is

> . . . so well knit,
> That should inuasiue force once menace it
> With loud-voic't Thunder, mixt with Sulpherous flame,
> 'T would sinke, or send them backe with feare and shame.
>
> (sig. B3v)

As with Holliday's ship above, Heywood here alludes to the importance of ship-owning for these leading merchants, a link he makes even more apparent in *Londini emporia*, where the second show on land 'is a Ship most proper to the Trade of Merchant-Aduenturers' (sig. B2v). Taylor's citation of a range of rivers from the Danube to the Indus in *The triumphs of fame and honour* makes their importance to trade very apparent. Thames states that 'for [the City's] commodities I'le ever flow' bearing 'silks and velvets, oyle, and wine, / Gold, silver, Jewels, fish, salt, sundry spices, / Fine and course linnen, [and] drugges of divers prices' (sig. A5v).[69]

As cultural forms grounded in the shifting reality of the sources of the City's wealth – chiefly the East India Company and the Merchant Adventurers – the Shows undeniably do negotiate the 'otherness' of non-Europeans encountered on trading voyages. As Ania Loomba asserts, the mayoral Shows create 'a fantasy that enacts the possibilities of contemporary colonial trading practices, and thereby [they mobilise] the national pride and commercial optimism necessary for such ventures'.[70] Loomba contextualises the ways in which the Shows increasingly focused on traffic with foreign and sometimes colonised nations. In particular, she argues that through the widespread use of racial 'others' in these works (especially, although not exclusively, those produced for the

Grocers' Company), 'emperors, queens, or other representatives of riches, plenitude and exotic grandeur' are staged for the watching masses. Her judicious discussion emphasises, however, that in the Shows we do not habitually find 'savage or wild peoples' as in some other early modern cultural forms. Through their overseas adventures, as she comments, City merchants came into contact with 'sophisticated courts' with 'long standing commercial and trading histories', and these accordingly found their way into mayoral pageantry, even if they were so invoked only to be depicted as largely passive.[71] To bear her out, Middleton's 'Indians' in *The triumphs of honor and vertue* are 'Commerce, Aduenture and Traffique, three [of them] habited like Merchants' (sig. B1v). The group is headed by the 'Queene of Merchandize' (there is no king in this instance), who makes the speech to the Lord Mayor. The majority of 'Indians' or 'Moors' represented in these works are indeed kings and queens.

In a contrasting approach, although Rebecca Bach too gives the Shows valuably extensive discussion, and her account is well-informed about the socio-economic background of these works, her reading is too ready simply to castigate their treatment of black characters. She asserts categorically that 'pageants and masques depend on and instantiate coordinated oppressions', and she imposes an assumption that all non-European figures in the Shows are 'colonial' or 'imperial' subjects.[72] Although the treatment of non-European subjects in the Shows is not enlightened by modern standards (surely one can hardly expect it to be), as Taylor has argued, the Shows do at least give them some exposure and, crucially, in some cases, a voice.[73] Middleton's Indian Queen takes the 'most eminent Seate' in the Continent of India pageant, and she states that 'I'me beauteous *in* my blacknesse', not in spite of it (*The triumphs of honor and vertue*, sigs B1v–B2r; my emphasis). For Bach, in contrast, this queen is 'an inarticulate displayed anti-self'.[74] Taylor, who also criticises Bach's neglect of the wider cultural context, instances her reading of the Shows as an example of 'New Historicist and Foucauldian scholarship, [which is] dedicated . . . to the assertion of synchronic epistemic totality, without individual agency and difference'.[75] Bach's approach to the audience of the Shows also bears out Taylor's concerns. I am troubled by the pronouns she uses in her unevidenced assertion that the audiences of the Shows 'could celebrate their own desired transformations into vastly wealthy white English subjects at the same time as they celebrated the whitening of *their* imperial subjects'.[76] For one thing, the trading nations in the far and near East Indies, the focus of *The*

triumphs of honor and vertue's depiction of the spice trade and a
number of other Shows produced for the Grocers' Company, were
in no way the 'imperial subjects' of England in this period (even the
colonised parts of the Americas were not referred to in these terms
in the early seventeenth century).[77] When writers like Middleton
refer to 'Indians', sometimes 'Indians', i.e. the inhabitants of India
or the East Indies, is exactly what they mean. Moreover, as Bach
concedes, 'pageant audiences . . . were at least as diverse as the
denizens of Jonson's city comedies'.[78] Not all those who witnessed
the Shows would have shared the city oligarchy's ideological stance
(inasmuch as it is possible to generalise about this), let alone its
wealth. Such was the heterogeneity of the population of London in
this period that some of the onlookers may even have been black, or
Irish, themselves, and thus hardly likely to 'celebrate' their 'whiteness' or their supposed status as colonial oppressors.[79] Relatedly,
as discussed above, if Fryer is correct that some of the performers
may actually have been black, this would complicate the scenario
still more.

'The Court and City two most Noble Friends': the Shows and Stuart state policy

At the same time as city merchants and their associates were venturing across the globe, there were problems at home to deal with. It
is possible to trace the impact of contemporary domestic exigencies
– for instance, the Cockayne Project and its catastrophic effect on
the cloth trade – upon mayoral pageantry.[80] Even the selection of
the Lord Mayors in 1614 and 1615 may have been informed by the
ongoing crisis in the cloth trade, for, according to Hentschell, 'the
widespread concern for the state of the cloth among London merchants' may have encouraged them to nominate two Draper Lord
Mayors consecutively.[81] Hardin writes that Munday's 1614 and
1615 Shows provide 'a consistent ideological spectacle of social and
commercial stability and historical continuity'. In the context of a
rising crisis in the cloth trade at this juncture, however, such continuity and stability can be regarded as a critique, or at least a defence
of the status quo. Hardin argues that in the course of an 'attempt
to assimilate changes in the cloth industry' these entertainments
'expose [the Drapers'] anxieties about the changing market'.[82]
Hentschell credits Munday's works with still more edge, writing
that 'recalling the past becomes, for Munday, a radical act where
current policies can be challenged'.[83] The critique, she argues,

operates by means of an invocation of the 'venerable past' of the Company in Munday's two Shows, an invocation that highlights the shortcomings of a monarch 'who would not respect that past'.[84]

The fortunes of the cloth trade had an impact that went well beyond the specific interests of the Merchant Adventurers and the livery companies involved in the trade, such as the Drapers and Clothworkers. Supple argues that during the period of the Cockayne Project 'in a very real sense England's prosperity had become the object of a gigantic gamble'.[85] Munday's Shows for 1614 and 1615 participate in a debate about the relative merits of the traditional mode of 'old drapery' versus the risky innovations inherent in the Cockayne Project. The thoroughgoing emphasis on 'oldness' in *Himatia-Poleos* works to remind the audience of the privileges of 'Old Drapery' – herself impersonated in the Show – which were at this point being undermined by the attempted monopoly of 'new' drapery in the putative Cockayne Project. It is, paradoxically, in its evocation of antiquity and tradition that Munday's Show engages most acutely with very contemporary issues, for October 1614 was a moment right in the middle of the imposed transition from 'old' to 'new' drapery; by the end of the year, Supple writes, Cockayne and his fellow projectors 'were left in control of the [cloth] trade to Germany and the Low Countries'.[86] In *Himatia-Poleos* – which celebrates the inauguration of Thomas Hayes, who was both a Draper *and* a member of the Merchant Adventurers, the company most affected by Cockayne's plan – there is therefore an insistent hearkening back to 'those blest daies of olde' 'when yea and nay was greatest Oath'. Even the language Munday uses is old-fashioned, such as 'good woollen Cloath ycleped Englands Draperie' (sig. C1r). Old drapery exports had reached an all-time high of 127,000 cloths in 1614: by early in 1615, however, they had fallen by some 50 per cent.[87] Nevertheless, in the following year, the subtitle of *Metropolis coronata* continues to invoke 'ancient' drapery. In a probable spirit of nostalgia for the years of successful trade with the continent that peaked in 1614, in this Show Munday foregrounds the way in which the Lord Mayor's ship is represented as being 'lately returned, from trafficking Wool and Cloth with other remote Countryes' (sig. B2v). (It is perhaps ironic, given the turmoil of 1614–15, that Cockayne himself was to become Lord Mayor only a few years later, in 1619.)

In *Himatia-Poleos* Munday also anachronistically elides the functions of manufacture and retail which for the Drapers, as for most Companies in this period, had long since become separated.

Indeed, if anything this Show foregrounds the former aspect of the Drapers' craft at the expense of the latter. There is a Cotswold shepherd, but no London merchant, and the fact that Drapers were at this point chiefly responsible for selling rather than producing cloth barely registers. 'The best aduantage' of the Company, Munday declares, 'euer ensued by *making* of woollen Cloathes' (sig. B2r; my emphasis). Furthermore, Hentschell argues that Munday's Shows for the Drapers can be seen as 'nationalistic', celebrating as they do 'the product [wool] most closely tied to England's understanding of itself'.[88] By the manner in which they chose to put on mayoral Shows the Companies themselves, of course, somewhat ironically, were great consumers of the expensive, imported textiles – the kind of 'fantastick habites' that Munday criticises in *Himatia-Poleos* – that were damaging the English cloth trade (sig. B1r). As Hentschell argues, the figure of the shepherd in *Himatia-Poleos*, probably dressed in 'plain, homespun wool', would have stood out as 'an oddity in [the] sea of sumptuousness' represented by the assembled dignitaries of the City in their red garments and furs.[89] Indeed, Middleton (in unusually pacific mood) finesses the potential for conflict between the manufacture and importation of fabrics in another Drapers' Show, *The triumphs of integrity*, where he reconciles old and new by focusing on what he calls 'the Moderne vse of this Antient and Honorable Mistery [of the Drapers]'. He also draws attention to the importance of drapery by writing that 'it clothes the Honorable Senators in their highest and richest Wearings, all Courts of Iustice, Magistrates, and Iudges of the Land' (sig. B1r).

Even earlier still there may be signs of strain in the Shows' representation of their contemporary moment. There are traces of a response to dearth in Nelson's 1590 Show, which includes references in the first speech to food being expensive and people begging for 'releefe'. Specifically, Nelson's text implies a decline in the fish trade, claiming that if people kept 'fish dais as wel as flesh' the cost of the latter would decline, the position of those involved in fishing would improve, and stores of 'butter, cheese and beefe' would be increased (*The deuice*, sig. A2r). Later on, however, 'Plentie' makes more complacent comments about England being a land of milk and honey, chief of the 'Christian nations' (sig. A3r). Northway posits a rather mechanistic relationship between attitudes to work and consumerism in the Shows and the supposedly consequent behaviour of the populace. She argues, for instance, that the encouragement in Nelson's Show to eat more fish 'worked', as consumption of fish rose during the 1590s.[90] Of course, people would have been perfectly capable of making a rational decision to purchase cheaper food, especially in a time of scarcity, without having been 'urged' to do so by a character in a Lord Mayor's Show, assuming they had seen the Show in the first place. And it was, after all, a Fishmongers' Company Show: one would expect fish to be mentioned.

Economic circumstances also seem to feature in Munday's *Chruso-thriambos*, where a rather odd marginal note gives an account of the price of some basic commodities at the time of the famed medieval Lord Mayor Nicholas Faringdon, supplied to back up Munday's point about the 'plenty' of those days. Bergeron simply calls this moment 'puzzling', whereas Palmer invests it with more significance, arguing that the note 'makes clear [Munday's] quotidian desire . . . [to make Faringdon's] resurrection an accounting problem'.[91] Furthermore, Palmer posits a 'provocative' aspect to Munday's ostensibly banal observations, claiming that Munday is indirectly calling attention to 'the royal debt [of] approaching £720,000'.[92] Money certainly was in short supply in this period. The King had recently suspended Parliament as a reaction to its criticism of his profligacy, and there was considerable concern from the crown that currency was being debased. There are, then, grounds to support Palmer's sense of the contemporary edge of *Chruso-thriambos*. Earlier in 1611, by attending the event, James had placed an unusually strong emphasis on 'the trial of the pyx', an annual ceremony held to gauge the purity of the gold and silver used by the King's Mint. This unprecedented action was backed up nine days later by 'A proclamation against melting or conueying out of the Kings Dominion of Gold or Siluer'. Marcus argues that the way in which James handled this traditional ceremony acted as 'a reminder of his power, a strong hint that [the Goldsmiths] would do well to abandon certain aspects of their search for "priuate lucre" and heed his proclamation for the preservation of money'.[93]

Munday's Show for the Goldsmiths therefore came at a politically sensitive moment for this Company in particular, and the decision to stage a version of the pyx ceremony in the Show can be seen to act as an implicit commentary on James's actions only a few months previously.[94] For Munday, the testing of gold is wholly the Goldsmiths' responsibility, and that the Mint belonged to the Crown and that the Master of the Mint was a royal post are facts largely excluded from the representation of the 'ingenious Say-Maister' in the Show. One can read Munday's little scene as an indirect engagement with James's attempts to control the purity of coinage. Like James at the Mint only five months earlier, the Goldsmiths' 'Essay-Maister' is an 'absolute Tryer of [gold and silver]'s vertue'; he 'makes proofe of them in his Furnaces, and of their true worth or value' (sig. C1v). His task is to

> distinguish those precious Mettals of Gold and Siluer, from base adulterating or corruption . . . euen to the smallest quantities of true valuation, in Ingots, Iewelles, Plate or Monies, for the more honour of the Prince and Countrey, when his Coynes are kept from imbasing and abusing. (sig. A4v)

Although a variety of commodities are mentioned, only 'Coynes' have a specific bearing on the 'honour of the Prince and Countrey', a phrase which also acts to foreground the connection with the ceremony at the Royal Mint. Although Marcus's identification of Munday's avaricious 'Lydian king' (Midas) with James is a tempting one to make, it is, as she concedes, 'blurry'.[95] Munday is nowhere *overtly* critical of the King's policy. As we have seen, he does add that the practice of assaying is intended to enhance the 'honour of the Prince and Countrey'. Exactly whose 'Coynes' are 'his', however – the (unnamed) Prince's or the Goldsmiths' Say-Maister's – is left ambiguous.

Other forms of engagement with Jacobean policy can be identified in mayoral Shows written by those more outspoken than Munday tended to be. Dekker's 1620s Shows make their point by stressing at length, but only in general terms, how powerful the City and its oligarchs are, such as when in *Brittannia's honor* he has the figure of London tell the Lord Mayor that 'the Christian World, in Me, reads Times best stories, / And Reading, fals blind at my dazling Glories' (sig. B2v). Middleton, as one might expect, offers a compelling example of how more explicitly topical political interventions can be identified in mayoral Shows. *The triumphs of integrity* of 1623 can be seen to offer a reaction to the prospect of the failure of the proposed 'Spanish marriage' between the Prince of Wales and the Spanish infanta of the same year.[96] Indeed, Prince Charles and the Duke of Buckingham had arrived back in England in the same month as the Show took place, and doubtless the issue had too much currency and popular appeal to be overlooked. Thus *The triumphs of integrity* seemingly cannot avoid an implicit reference to the recent failure of the marriage negotiations.[97] Indeed, given the fame (or notoriety) of *A Game at Chesse* in the following year it would have been more surprising if Middleton had refrained from commenting on one of the key political issues of the day in any of the high-profile works he produced in this period.

In *The triumphs of integrity*, then, under the pretext of invoking the usual joy at the inauguration of the new Lord Mayor with the use of the conventional image of the sun breaking through cloud, Middleton at the same time gestures towards another, more pressing and controversial, source of popular celebration. In a speech located at the 'Imperiall Canopy', a device topped with the King's motto, 'Beati Pacifici' and his coat of arms, Middleton presents one of the most direct commentaries on current events within the whole canon of mayoral pageantry. He prefaces this with an announcement that he is just about to go beyond purely civic matters to 'bring Honor to a larger Field' and engage in 'Royall Businesse'. He certainly delivers on his promise. A fairly neutral account of the three graces and the three crowns of James's triple kingdom is then followed by the explanation that the cloud represents:

> Some Enuious Mist cast forth by Heresie,
> Which through [James's] happy Raigne, and Heauens blest will,
> The sun-beames of the Gospell strikes through still;
> More to assure it to Succeeding Men,
> We haue the Crowne of Brittaines Hope agen,
> (Illustrious Charles our Prince,) which all will say
> Addes the chiefe Ioy and Honor to this Day.
>
> (sig. C1r)

The term 'heresie', standing for Catholic Spain and clearly opposed to the 'sun-beames' of the (Protestant) 'Gospell', can readily be regarded as a commentary on contemporary events when put together in the same speech as a reference to Prince Charles, as well as to the succession. The nation has been saved from the prospect of future Catholic monarchs, Middleton implies. The sense of relief generated by the failure of the planned marriage is also surely the referent of 'we haue the Crowne of Brittaines hope agen'. As Bergeron points out, the use of the word 'agen' raises the question of where Prince Charles had been before he came home – the answer, of course, was Spain.[98] Middleton's intervention was expressed in a speech, not confined to a textual preamble, and would thus have been heard by at least some of the onlookers on the day as well as being transmitted into print. The 1623 Show can therefore be seen to partake in the same high level of public interest in the failure of the Spanish match exploited within texts such as *The ioyfull returne, of the most illustrious prince, Charles,*

also printed in October of that year.[99] In *The triumphs of integrity*
Middleton provides another example of how a traditional pageant
device – in this case, 'a Golden and Glorious Canopy' with the three
crowns and sunbeams taken from the Drapers' arms – could be
reworked to suit the present occasion.[100] Only two years previously,
in *The sunne in Aries*, Middleton had referred to James, albeit in
parentheses, as 'that ioy of honest hearts' and as the king 'that
Vnites Kingdomes [and] who encloses / All in the Armes of Loue'
(sigs B2v–B3r). A rather more contingent form of goodwill towards
the royal family and state policy is in evidence in 1623.

As we have seen in relation to *Himatia-Poleos*, *Chruso-thriambos*
and *Metropolis coronata*, Munday's texts can also be seen to have
contemporary political dimensions. However, if he did comment on
the underlying moment of the 1618 Show – the execution of Ralegh
taking place simultaneously along the river at Westminster – he did
so quite obliquely.[101] *Sidero-Thriambos* does foreground threats,
not solely to the Lord Mayor's administration as we see repeatedly
in these works, but perhaps on a wider scale. The negative elements
which Munday invokes as challenges to the new Lord Mayor have
a slightly different flavour to the norm. 'Those vile Incendiaries',
as Munday puts it, are on this occasion 'Ambition, Treason, and
Hostility', rather less abstract entities than Error and the like; the
former relate more directly to matters of state than to civic policy.
Treason (with an underlying element of ambition) was, of course,
the offence for which Ralegh had been charged and executed. As I
have argued elsewhere, Munday does stress that 'this yeare' needs
to be 'better secured, against all their violences and treacherous
attempts' (sig. C1v). No other Lord Mayor's Show cites 'treason'
twice in this fashion, and the sense that Munday's text has a bearing
on contemporary state politics is amplified further on where, in
an interesting moment of slippage, Munday states that 'Feare and
Modesty' are on hand to assist, 'through the darkest obscurities,
when any disorder threatneth danger to *Maiesty*, or to his carefull
deputie' (sig. C1r–v; my emphasis).

The figure of Francis Drake, another Elizabethan hero who
is repeatedly invoked in Shows (especially those written for the
Drapers' Company) by a range of writers, takes on a special significance in the 1620s, in a period when his enterprises against
the Spanish would have had a particular valency, and when
there was a political point to be made from celebrating notable
aspects of Elizabeth's reign.[102] Drake appears as one of 'Seuen
worthy Nauigators' in Webster's *Monuments of Honor*, where

he is celebrated for having 'brought home gold, and honor from sea-fights' (sig. A4v). Naturally, for Webster Drake is a worthy navigator rather than a privateer, as the Spanish would have seen him. His antagonists in these 'sea-fights' (and those of his peers such as Hawkins and Frobisher), including, implicitly, the 1588 Armada, are not named, but it would probably have been obvious. (Although Webster does not cite this aspect of their fame, navigators like Frobisher had also had an important part to play in the opening up of trade routes for the enrichment of the City.) In *The triumphs of health and prosperity*, produced during a time of open conflict between England and Spain, Middleton makes a point of linking Drake with another traditional Drapers' icon, Jason. Drake is therefore for Middleton 'Englands true Iason', almost mystical in the greatness of his deeds. Drake, he claims,

> did boldly make
> So many rare Adventures, which were held
> For worth, unmatcht, danger, vnparaleld,
> Neuer returning to his Countries Eye,
> Without the Golden Fleece of Victory.

(sig. B1r)

The unspecified 'dangers' which confronted Drake and over which he was, allegedly, always victorious, were, of course, the Spanish. Middleton has elided Drake and Jason to such an extent that it is difficult to see where one ends and the other begins. The work that Middleton makes such conventions do exemplifies the imaginative ways in which pageant writers used traditional forms of representation to speak to their immediate moment. The critical edge that can be detected in the Shows – especially those by Middleton – goes some way towards refuting the notion put forward by Easterling that they 'showcase, seemingly without irony, the values and foundational principles [Middleton's] comedies so vividly call into doubt'.[103]

Middleton certainly established a habit of commenting on foreign relations during the later Jacobean period. Levin has recently posited that Spain and France, the 'twin objects of England's secret admiration and obsessive fears, come in for special treatment' in *The tryumphs of honor and industry*. By staging a member of each of these nations in the Show, and having them specifically 'utter their gladness' at Bolles's inauguration, Middleton, she argues, was playing to the crowd's likely antipathy towards Frenchmen and Spaniards. Indeed, she argues for a specific connection between

this Show and 'the latest conspiracy theory at court', which was
about a supposed French and Spanish plot to kidnap the King and
Prince Charles, invade England and establish a Catholic regime.[104]
'Court circles', however, are not the same as civic circles: there
would probably have been enough general anti-Spanish and anti-
Catholic feeling in the City at large to prompt the audience reaction described by Busino, as discussed previously. Middleton also
updates Munday's approach in *The triumphs of re-united Britania*
to King James as the embodiment of union when in *The Triumphs
of loue and antiquity* he has 'seuerall Countries . . . all owing Fealty
to one Soueraigne'. By 1619 James's realm, as depicted in the
Show, has expanded across the seas to include the colonial subjects
not mentioned by Munday, who concentrated on 'Britain'.[105] For
Middleton, however,

the Noble English, the faire thriuing Scot,
Plaine hearted Welch, the French man bold and hot,
The ciuilly instructed Irish man,
And that kind Sauage, the Virginian,
[Are] all loungly assembled.

(sig. B3v)

'These twelve Noble Branches': intra-Company politics

Commentary on current events and controversial figures within
the confines of the City itself can also be traced in the Shows.
Everyone knew that the Lord Mayors were members – even if in a
few cases only very recent members – of what Dekker called 'the
twelue superior Companyes' (*Troia-Noua triumphans*, sig. B3r).
It was not usually 'done' to draw attention to the disputed hierarchy within that twelve, but in *Londini emporia* Heywood tact-
lessly reminds the Clothworkers that they are 'in count the last of
Twelue'. Indeed, he rather labours the point, explaining over the
course of an entire page, and with reference to the debate about
precedence in the two English universities, his argument that 'in all
numbers there is a compulsiue necessity of order, onely for method
sake'.[106] The hierarchy of the Great Twelve had more than simply
a methodological rationale, of course, and the Companies were
more concerned with precedence and status than Heywood makes
out, despite his protestations that 'I hold them all equall without
difference' (sig. A4r). There is an irony, too, in his citation of
the supremely unpopular John Spencer as one of the City's 'best
Magistrates' (he also mentions the unfortunate Thomas Skinner,

'who dyed before hee was Knighted') (*ibid.*). Perhaps because he himself was not free of the City Heywood was less aware of or less deferential to civic sensibilities than some of his contemporaries. Despite the convention of ignoring those instances when a civic dignitary did not practise the trade of the Company to which he belonged, Heywood also states in *Londini artium* that Rainton, the new Lord Mayor, 'though free of this Worshipfull Company of the Haberdashers . . . yet was by Profession a Mercer'. This is not simply a passing reference, for the reader is given more detail of Rainton's involvement in mercery than is strictly necessary, being told that Rainton's 'chiefe Trading was in Florence for Sattins, Tafatties, and Sarsnets, in Luca for Taffaties, in Gene [Genoa] for Gene Veluets, Damasks, &c. In Bolognia for Satins, Cypresse, and Sarsnets' (sig. B4r).

One of the most controversial cases of 'the custom of London' coming into play related to Edward Barkham, the Lord Mayor in 1621 for whom Middleton wrote *The sunne in Aries*. Barkham was a member of the Leathersellers' Company, very much a minor concern in the hierarchy of the City, and he did not begin the process of translation to the Drapers until only four months before his mayoralty commenced. He was not welcomed, either: the prolonged negotiations over accepting Barkham are clearly visible in the Drapers' Company minutes for that year, and the matter was resolved only on the intervention of the Privy Council.[107] Although *The sunne in Aries* does not exactly exude enthusiasm for the new Lord Mayor, at least, fortuitously, Middleton was able to cite a precedent to legitimate Barkham's troubled move to the Drapers, because the Lord Mayor in 1578, Richard Pipe, had translated via the same route.

Closely associated with the question of primacy, and often as controversially, was the issue of antiquity. Being able to claim first place in the historical chronology of the livery companies was a prized honour, and one which pageant writers naturally engaged with. Munday, whose Shows are closely identified with the Companies compared to those of some of his contemporaries, begins *Himatia-Poleos* by stating that time-honoured tradition, dating back to the Romans, has distinguished between the 'most memorable Societies' and those he dismissively calls 'other[s] of lesse note and merite' (sig. A3r). This process of selection, he continues, has in the context of the City itself resulted in 'twelve graduations of honour and dignitie'. Naturally, given the sponsors of the occasion his text is celebrating, Munday then claims the status of 'the first Companie of all other in this Citie' to belong to 'the ancient fellowship or Societie of Drapers' (sig. A4v). Corroboration of this claim is produced by reference to historical authorities – 'William Fitzstephen, Iohn Bale, Roger Houedin, and others' – in a way that brings to mind Munday's marshalling of 'Antiquaries' like Camden to defend himself elsewhere in this text. Munday's confidence in said authorities, however, must have been tempered by the need to add a marginal note to explain that Fitzstephen (in case the reader was unaware) 'liued and wrote in the time of King Stephen' (*ibid.*).[108] From the Drapers, the preface goes on, the trades of 'the diuers other Companies' were derived, like the subsidiary branches of a tree.

As I have discussed at length elsewhere, Munday then becomes embroiled in a convoluted attempt to extricate himself from the embarrassment of having in 1611 ascribed Fitz-Alwin, the first mayor of London, to the Goldsmiths rather than to the Drapers.[109] He proffers a (kind of) apology, but pretty much cancels this out by stating that the end justifies the means: 'I might well *iustly* be condemned', he protests, 'if I should seeke after any other argument . . . then [the Drapers'] own due deseruing, so long time sleeping in obliuion, yet now reuiued, to their endlesse honour' (sig. B1r; my emphasis). After this prolonged period of 'obliuion' the Drapers were in the civic limelight quite regularly from 1614 onwards, and the following year Munday was again writing a Show for his Company. *Metropolis coronata* accordingly begins with a reference back to *Himatia-Poleos*, where, Munday writes, he himself had 'sufficiently approued the true antiquitie, and primary Honour of Englands Draperie' (sig. A3r). Once again, antiquity and primacy go hand-in-hand, and once again Fitz-Alwin is asserted in this text to have been a member of the Drapers, 'a Draper Brother', as he puts it (sig. B1r). Although he was always drawn to the historical – or pseudo-historical – record, Munday was not alone in making such claims for the Drapers. Later writers reiterated the appropriation of Fitz-Alwin to that Company in Shows written on their behalf: Heywood in *Porta pietatis* (sig. A3v), and Middleton in both *The sunne in Aries* (sig. B1v) and *The triumphs of health and prosperity* (sig. B1v).[110] In the latter text Middleton also stresses the fact that Cuthbert Hacket had been the sixth Draper Lord Mayor in the last twelve years (sig. B3v). In *Metropolis coronata*, however, Munday visibly stages the Drapers' primacy rather than restricting his claims to a preface available only to the text's readers. Towards the end of the day a

> goodly Monument or Pageant, with the glorious Sunne in continuall
> motion ouer it, appertaining to the Drapers Armory; presents yee
> London in the supreme place of eminence, and the twelue Companies
> (her twelue Daughters) all seated about her in their due degrees,
> onely Drapery is neerest to her, as being *the first and chiefest honored*
> *Society before all other.* (sig. B4r; my emphasis)

One can only imagine what the Mercers and Grocers, the two
Companies that had for exactly one hundred years before this Show
traditionally preceded the Drapers in the hierarchy of the Great
Twelve, would have made of this public act of lèse majesté. As this
suggests, Munday's approach towards the Drapers' Shows, due
no doubt to his membership of that Company, could sometimes
be openly partisan. At the very end of *Himatia-Poleos*, seemingly
carried away with enthusiasm for the task in hand, he takes the
opportunity to remind his readership that the Drapers' 'loue to the
Citie [had] very manifestly prooued their worth' when in 1591 there
were no volunteers for the vacant role of sheriff. 'As many refus-
alls still hapning day by day', he relates, 'to the great disquiet of
the Companies, and mighty delay of time, yet when no one would
vndergoe the Office and charge, a Draper hath done it, worthily
and willingly'. 'Maister Benedict Barneham, a learned and iudicious
Gentleman' duly stepped into the breach and 'chearefully vnder-
took the Shrieualty' (sig. C3v). 'Three cheers for the Drapers, and
let that be a lesson to the rest of them', Munday seems to be saying.

As this discussion demonstrates, despite their ostensible purpose
of celebrating civic harmony and shared values, there are moments
when dissensions within the livery companies made their way into
civic pageantry. One of the most celebrated civic links was that
between the Fishmongers and the Goldsmiths, but the treatment
of that relationship in mayoral Shows reveals that even friendship could be contingent. In an early Show, one of the characters,
addressing a Fishmonger Lord Mayor, John Allot, says of the
Goldsmiths that they 'haue long in loue to [the Fishmongers] been
vnited' (*The deuice*, sig. A2v). In *Chrysanaleia* Munday makes
even more of the long-standing bond between the two Companies.
Their 'league of loue and fellowship' he dates back to the time of
the Crusades through a frankly rather unpersuasive account of how
the merchants then 'trading in fish, oyle, flaxe, silkes and other
commodities' were 'most frequently then termed Fishmongers'; the
Goldsmiths in turn offered 'many friendly helpes and furtherances'
(sig. A4r). The friendship, once established, continued back home
in the City and was exemplified by the joint work of rebuilding

London's wall and establishing Moorgate and Cripplegate. To enforce the importance of the bond, later in the same Show the King of the Moors is accompanied by

> tributarie Kings on horse-backe [who] carry Ingots of golde and siluer . . . and in this order they attend on him: shewing thereby, that the Fishmongers are not vnmindfull of their combined brethren, the worthy Company of Golde-smithes, in this solemne day of triumph. (sig. B1v)

When five years previously he had produced a Show on behalf of the Fishmongers' ostensible great allies, the Goldsmiths, however, Munday then stressed that 'the ancient loue and cordiall amity' between the two Companies did not extend to sharing the costs:

> Yet let no censure stray so far at large,
> To think the reason of that vnity
> Makes Fish-mongers support the Goldsmithes charge,
> And their expenses shared equally:
> No, t'is [*sic*] the Gold-Smiths sole Society. [*sic*]
> That in this Triumph beares the Pursse for all . . .
> Their loues (herein) may not be thought the lesse,
> But rather virtuall, and much stronger knit.
> (Chruso-thriambos, sig. C2r–v)

His intention was probably to underscore the great wealth of the Goldsmiths' Company. However, in typical Munday style he labours the point to such an extent that the end result, despite his probable intention, is to make it sound as if the much-vaunted amity is based on rhetoric alone with no material manifestation.

The general approach within the Shows to the inauguration of the new Lord Mayor was to focus on the new post holder with little explicit reference to his predecessors beyond the standard invocation of continuity and tradition, often via the impersonation of some suitably historically remote incumbent such as Fitz-Alwin, Walworth, Eyre or Faringdon. Heywood's rather guarded approach in *Londini sinus salutis* takes the middle ground. He writes in relation to previous Ironmonger Lord Mayors that

> I shall not neede to borrow my Introduction from the Antiquitie of this Famous Metropolis . . . [these] being Arguments already granted . . . and yet I hold it not altogether Impertinent to remember some few things of remarke. (sig. A4r)

He then proceeds to highlight notable incumbents and moments in civic history in the usual fashion. Munday's somewhat peculiar approach to asserting the continuity of the mayoralty in *Chrysanaleia*, pursuing the image of the selfless pelican to which he likens the role, states that 'though the maine Authoritie of Gouernment (in him) may be sayd to dye: yet it suruiueth in other Pellicans of the same brood' (sig. B2v).[111] On the eve of the 1620 Show, however, Middleton produced an entertainment to mark not Francis Jones's inauguration but rather the *termination* of William Cockayne's mayoralty. The entertainment was held in the private confines of Cockayne's house but published within the composite work *Honorable entertainments* in 1621. Here Middleton offers quite a different perspective on the transition from one Lord Mayor to another. This slight piece, comprising only a couple of speeches, represents the end of Cockayne's term of office as a kind of funeral – 'a sad Pageant', as Middleton calls it. The entertainment begins with 'one attir'd like a Mourner' accompanied by instruments 'expressing a mournfull Seruice'. Middleton then supplies a pseudo 'Last Will and Testament', which has Cockayne bequeathing to his unnamed 'Successor' 'all my good wishes, paines, labours and reformations'. The piece concludes with an 'epitaph' bemoaning the end of 'a Yeare of goodness, and a Yeare of right' (sigs C1v–C3r). Rhetorically, the speeches present only very limited hope and expectation that such virtue would continue into the next mayoralty.[112]

I have yet to come across another such an 'anti-pageant' in printed form. Middleton had written not only Cockayne's mayoral Show but also the entertainments for his daughter's wedding, and he was then in his first year as City Chronologer, having taken on the post in September 1620, mid-way through the various entertainments included into this composite work and during Cockayne's term of mayoral office. Despite Cockayne's leading role in the disastrous 'new drapery' cloth monopoly of only a few years earlier, Middleton appears to have had an especially close relationship with Cockayne as a patron in this period.[113] Hence, perhaps, this anomalous take on the transition to another incumbent. Parr points out that a reader of this work would be quite able to differentiate Middleton's enthusiastic representation of Cockayne from the way in which he celebrates the Haberdashers rather than Jones himself in the entertainment that follows this one.[114] As we'll see, Middleton was not averse to letting his personal feelings about members of the City oligarchy become evident in his writing. It is perhaps not a coincidence that although he would, for various reasons, have been the obvious candidate, Middleton did not write the Show for Cockayne's successor, Francis Jones (this was John Squire's sole foray into the genre). Middleton was, however, to pick up the reins again in 1622; indeed, he wrote four of the following five extant Shows, running right up to the year of his death, 1627.[115]

As this instance demonstrates, Bald's assertion that in his civic works Middleton 'attempted no more than to flatter his hearers with what they most wanted to hear' underestimates the extent to which, as in his plays, Middleton was his own man.[116] As Hutchings and Bromham have argued, it is not the case that once he embarked on his civic works 'Middleton abandon[ed] his probing vision of the problems of life in the expanding city for . . . a craven attempt to please his new employers'.[117] There are, they write, 'expressions of concern for the poor and the powerless throughout Middleton's work'.[118] As we have already seen, careful scrutiny of Middleton's Shows can therefore reveal much implicit – and sometimes quite explicit – critique. In *The triumphs of truth*, written for his name-sake Sir Thomas Middleton, a man of decidedly Calvinist views, Middleton takes the moral high ground from the outset. He has Error claim, for instance, that there are 'a thousand of our Parish, besides Queanes, / That nere knew what Truth meant' (sig. B3r).[119] In this text Middleton's tendency towards criticism of the City's inhabitants can also be seen to extend to its oligarchy. It is therefore impolitic, to say the least, to have the personification of maternal 'London' say to the new Lord Mayor that

> . . . some Sonnes I haue
> Thanklesse, vnkind and disobedient,
> Rewarding all my Bounties with Neglect,
> And will of purpose wilfully retire
> Themselues, from doing grace and seruice to me,
> When they have got all they can, or hope for, from me . . .
> And now they show themselues, yet they haue all
> My blessing with them, so the world shall see
> 'Tis their vnkindness, no defect in me.
>
> (sigs A4v–B1r)

As Hutchings and Bromham observe, this work 'does not present the city family as harmonious and united'.[120] Indeed, the phrase 'And now they show themselues' suggests that 'London' is allud-ing to those dignitaries actually present at the Show, as does the use of the present tense in 'some Sonnes I haue'. There is a similar aspect to Error's speech as quoted above, where some of those who allegedly do not know what truth is are said to be 'e'en in this Throng'.[121] As far as the figure of 'London' is concerned, the evils she mentions appear to emanate from some others who have previously held the mayoralty. In the course of an extended period of what Lobanov-Rostovsky calls 'dramatic irony', Middleton has Error give a very authentic-sounding account of how a corrupt mayoralty would work:

> Heres Gluttony and Sloth, two pretious Slaues,
> Wil tell thee . . . the worth of euery Office to a Haire,
> And who bids most, and how the Markets are, . . .
> They'l bring thee in Bribes for Measures and light Bread,
> Keepe thy eye winking, and thy hand wide ope,
> Then thou shalt know what Wealth is, and the scope
> Of rich Authority.[122]

(sig. B2r)

As Heinemann asserts, here Middleton presents an 'explicit treatment of bribery and corruption' that with its critical edge goes beyond the traditional praise of civic good works one might expect to find in mayoral Shows.[123] Although Error's speech works as a rhetorical temptation to the Lord Mayor with the expectation that she will be eventually defeated by Zeal, at the same time if you put these two passages from the same work together Middleton might be implying that some of Sir Thomas Middleton's predecessors, rather than acting as exemplars for their successor in the usual manner of mayoral pageantry, had actually abused their office. Nepotism is an issue here, perhaps: Sullivan has speculated that Middleton may be expressing 'some unease about a Welsh hegemony, given the number and importance of Myddeltons in London in 1613', although significant family groups were not that uncommon in the City and Middleton himself was, of course, the new Lord Mayor's namesake.[124] Certainly, Error's accusation that 'wealth' and 'authority' (or 'Power and Profite', as she has it elsewhere) result from the mayoralty could be seen as being a bit close to the bone when addressed to men motivated and advantaged by both attributes, especially when presented in front of a large audience who, as Stock notes, might have 'half expected' 'all the abuses of office' the Lord Mayor is tempted to engage in. Stock argues, rightly, I think, that in this work Middleton 'takes Dekker's insistence on the conditional nature of civic honour even further by demanding evidence of the mayor's probity and honour . . . on the spot'.[125] As Lobanov-Rostovsky argues, 'the morality structure of this show reinforces the public awareness of such abuses . . . [and] the contingency of praise in Middleton's pageant threatens the political value of the spectacle'.[126]

'All such pious and religious Magistrates': politics and religion in the Shows

The triumphs of truth is perhaps the most outspoken of Middleton's Shows, but a cautionary note occurs in other works. Issues of religion and trade were at the heart of early seventeenth-century English politics. Reflecting these preoccupations, one can detect a seriousness about many Lord Mayor's Shows which goes beyond the double edge of instructive praise as discussed above. Middleton's *Triumphs of loue and antiquity*, for instance, warns the Lord Mayor that his year of office will require 'Labour' to avoid the perils inherent in the role, with a particular emphasis on the temptations of office:

> The Rude and thorny wayes thy care must cleare,
> Such are the vices in a City sprung,
> As are yon Thickets that grow close and strong:
> Such is oppression, Cosnage, Bribes, false Hires,
> As are yon catching and entangling Briers.
>
> (sigs B2v–B3r)

There is also an aside in the same vein in the later work *The sunne in Aries*, where Fame comments that the notable deeds of civic worthies have not always been upheld by their successors. Past Lord Mayors, Middleton writes, were 'Erecters some, of Granaries for the Poore, / Though now conuerted to some Rich mens Store / (The more the Ages misery)' (sig. B2r). Again, it is almost as if Middleton has someone specific in mind who has so degraded their predecessors' benevolence. He emphasises in *The triumphs of honor and vertue* that Proby's wealth was attained 'with an unusuring hand'. This feat implicitly differs from the way in which others enriched themselves, for Middleton adds that this 'is not the least wonder worthy note' on Proby's inauguration (sig. B3v). The point is made clearer still later in the same work, when 'Honor' claims that Proby is due honour because he 'stands free' from the unworthy conduct indulged in by others, such as 'making Frends / Of Mammons Heapes, got by unrighteous Ends' (sig. C3r).[127] Without this kind of personal reference to the new Lord Mayor Middleton covers much the same ground in *The triumphs of integrity*, where the virtues of the past are compared to the failings of the present. Men like Fitz-Alwin, it is asserted, 'heapt up Vertues, long before they were old [whereas] This Age sits laughing vpon Heapes of Gold' (sig. B2r). One wonders how this speech would have been received by a civic oligarchy which was so notably founded on 'Heapes of Gold'.

Such tactics were not confined to Middleton's work. Less stringently, Munday too has Fitz-Alwin mourn the decline of the representatives of civic paternalism, 'right worthy men' as he calls them, in *Metropolis coronata* (sig. B1r). Heywood could be as outspoken as Middleton on occasion. Rowland has argued that in his final Show Heywood puts forward 'a provocative interrogation of [the new Lord Mayor] Garway's reputation' which amounts to 'an act of considerable effrontery'.[128] In this text Heywood takes the opportunity to run through some instances in Roman history where civic rulers engaged in conduct damaging to their citizens. These ostensibly historically remote examples of how not to run a city can, however, be regarded as admonitory when directed towards a Lord Mayor whose loyalties tended to lie more in the direction of Whitehall than the Guildhall. Indeed, Janus 'admonisheth all Magistrates . . . to be constant in all their courses', especially when it comes to matters spiritual. Heywood enjoins Garway both to establish and maintain 'true Religion' in such a way as to suggest that such sustenance is required (sig. B2r). Moreover, he stresses how important 'free and frequent Preaching of the Word and Gospell' is for the 'Prosperity, Plenty, Health [and] Wealth' of the country (sig. C2r). The emphasis on 'free and frequent Preaching' of the gospel aligns Heywood – if not Garway – with a particularly stringent Protestant stance. Four years earlier Heywood seemed to have been expecting Clitheroe to be a veritable paragon of virtue, for *Londini sinus salutis* recommends that he fosters traits of 'constancy of mind', 'gentlenesse', 'sincerity', philosophical patience, 'placabilitie', and 'humanitie', as well as the kind of exacting and ardent religious zeal one finds in Middleton's works (sigs B1v–B2v). There is an equally Middletonesque note to the figure of Piety, the eponymous pageant in *Porta pietatis*, who is accompanied by Zeal with her ever-burning heart, although in *Londini sinus salutis* Heywood seems considerably more positive about the new Lord Mayor's stance on matters religious than on the later occasion.

As this suggests, Middleton was not alone in attempting to put ethical and spiritual constraints on the Lord Mayor's behaviour. The preamble to *Londini emporia*, for instance, lists the eight 'Offices of Piety [which] are in a Merchant required'. Amongst these, Heywood touches on those activities which have the strongest bearing on how men like Ralph Freeman gained their wealth and prestige. Like many of his peers, Freeman was active in trading companies such as the Levant Company. All the same, he is told to abjure 'all fraud and deceite in bargaining', to avoid the practice of 'Extortion and

Oppression', 'out of his abundance to bee open-handed vnto all, but especially the poore and indigent', and 'to bridle the insatiate desire of getting' (sig. A3r–v). Heywood also attempts to mystify the reality of overseas commerce. Mercury states that trade with numerous European countries is almost altruistic: 'What's best in them, comes frequent to our hands. / And for transportage of some surplus ware, / (Our owne wants furnisht) what we best can spare' (sig. B3v). There is no mention here of how fraught these trading connections often were in this period. Moreover, realistically, of course, a desire for great wealth was integral to these men's practices, and Heywood's moral exhortations to Freeman do sit somewhat uncomfortably with the unmitigated praise for merchants and merchandising elsewhere in this text. In this respect Heywood's tricky position may have been the result of the ideological conflicts that lay behind it. Rowland argues that 'the symbiotic relationship Heywood posits between the upholding of religious principle and the conduct of trade was a profoundly and increasingly contentious issue at precisely the moments at which Heywood introduced it into his writing, and the Merchant Adventurers [of which Freeman was a member] were at the heart of the controversy'.[129]

A similarly serious note pervades Middleton's mayoral Shows, in particular. One cannot imagine such a high-minded writer including knockabout verses by Robin Hood and his comrades, as Munday does in *Metropolis coronata*.[130] As Heinemann argues, in *The triumphs of truth* Middleton attempted 'much more in the way of sustained moral allegory than was usual' in mayoral Shows.[131] O'Callaghan concurs, writing that this work 'is notable for its promotion of godly Protestantism' and that Middleton 'sees public office in distinctly Calvinist terms'.[132] Although all Shows highlight to various degrees the labours and personal sacrifice inherent in the Lord Mayor's term of office, Middleton does so in a particularly emphatic fashion. Indeed, Middleton's characteristic tenor can be used to dispute Bach's assertion that the Shows were 'first and foremost mercantile spectacles'.[133] For Middleton, almost invariably, *moral* questions are first and foremost. To demonstrate the point, on his return to his house at the end of the Show in 1621, Middleton has Edward Barkham greeted by a positive army of moral qualities. 'Iustice, Sincerity, Meeknes, Wisedome, Prouidence, Equality, Industry, Truth, Peace, Patience, Hope, [and] Harmony' are all present, along with Fame, to remind the new Lord Mayor of his responsibilities, 'illustrated by proper Emblems and expressions' to emphasise the point (*The sunne in Aries*, sig. B3v). Middleton, could, however, produce work on behalf of those whose political position was not wholly civic. He highlights Peter Proby's court connections in *The triumphs of honor and vertue*, emphasising in the dedication that Proby was a man who 'hath seru'd / Two Royall Princes' and was a 'Scholler, Souldier, Courtier [and] Citizen' (sigs A4r and B3v). That this was an unusual combination is revealed by the manner in which Middleton foregrounds Proby's transition to civic authority: the figure of Antiquity informs the City that 'you haue a Courtier now your Magistrate' (sig. B3v).[134] O'Callaghan argues plausibly that this demonstrates that 'it is difficult to sustain the argument that Middleton's civic entertainments are motivated by an ideological opposition between the city and the court', or at least not a wholesale one.[135]

All the same, Middleton's first Show, *The triumphs of truth*, can be characterised as stern, seeking to instruct much more than to entertain. As well as being the longest Show from the period, it makes its moralistic point again and again and again, and dramatises the threats to the Lord Mayor perhaps rather too aggressively for popular taste. O'Callaghan rightly characterises the key figures of Zeal and Truth as 'militaristic' and 'God's soldiers', as with Heywood's 'Church militant' in one of his Shows some years later.[136] In *Metropolis coronata* Munday's equivalent character is named 'Discreet Zeale' (sig. B2r): there is nothing discreet about Middleton's version in *The triumphs of truth*. Munday's treatment of the threats to the new Lord Mayor in the former work consists simply of a rather throwaway reference to 'all occasions which may seeme sinister or hurtfull' (sig. B2r–v). In this respect *The triumphs of truth* also differs a great deal from some of the early, pre-1600 Shows, where various virtuous figures greet and bless the Lord Mayor with little sign of any danger to any of them. Nelson's 1590 text, for instance, presents a bevy of civic virtues, including 'Plentie', 'Wisedome', 'Gods Truth', 'Pollicie', 'the peace of England', 'Loialtie and Concord' and others; 'Ambition', the sole negative figure, is allowed only one brief speech (*The deuice*, sigs A2v–A3v). It is notable Middleton's next Show – after a three-year hiatus – was more purely celebratory than *The triumphs of truth* (as well as being a great deal shorter – perhaps he had received some feedback), with only a passing moment of potential conflict between 'Reward' and 'Justice', speedily resolved.[137]

There is also something rather ascetic about Middleton's Shows. Even in the lavish *Triumphs of truth* 'Perfect Love' emphasises that 'from this Feast of Ioy' 'all Excesse [and] Epicurisme' are prohibited (sig. D1r). There may be a feast, but it is a 'Reuerend' one. In *The triumphs of integrity* Middleton produces such a sustained defence of true virtue that the form of the event itself comes into question: "tis not showes, Pompe, nor a House of State / Curiously deckt, that makes a Magistrate', he claims (sig. B2v). Perhaps inevitably, given its conceptual focus on unshowy integrity, the Show (on the evidence of Middleton's text) seems to have used less exciting pageantry than many others from this period. Even the 'Cristall Sanctuary', the device that culminates the day, although undoubtedly beautifully designed, does not have the spectacular features of the pageants and devices employed in *The triumphs of truth*, for instance. There is little here of the crowd-pleasing nature of the pitched battle between Zeal and Envy, or fireworks setting fire to a chariot, which the audience would have seen in 1613. The later work does have a rather static and preachy quality, being concerned with that which is 'manifest, perspicuous, plaine, and cleere' (sig. B3v). A 'Temple of Integrity' featuring 'Santimonious Concomitants' is probably not what the audience would have expected or appreciated, despite Middleton's claim that it is aimed at 'the content of the Spectators' (sig. B2v). To a lesser extent, *The sunne in Aries* too implicitly undercuts its own status as a lavish triumph. Here Middleton has Fame argue that the most virtuous are the least likely to boast about their merits:

> Diamonds will shine though set in Lead, Trueworth
> Stands alwaies in least neede of setting forth:
> What makes Lesse Noyse then Merit? Or Lesse Showe
> Then Vertue?
>
> > (sig. B4r)

Only 'the Vulgar Will' is impressed by 'Vaine-glory', it is stated, somewhat paradoxically given the context. Likewise, the new Lord Mayor is invited to the feast at the end of *The tryumphs of honor and industry* in the usual form, but the promised feast is but a 'solemne pleasure', where 'all Epicurisme is banisht'. At this event, the writer stresses, 'Moderation and Grauity are alwayes attendants' (sig. C1r). In this later instance it is possible that Middleton deliberately tempered this aspect of the day's celebrations to fit the predilections of the Lord Mayor, George Bolles. Heinemann calls Bolles a 'Sabbatarian', and there is an anecdote that, immediately after the publication of James's *Book of Sports*, he allegedly intervened to stop the royal retinue in its progress through the City on a Sunday, during church services.[138] She also argues that the 1613 Show too was 'evidently tailor-made to suit [Sir Thomas Middleton's] personality and interests'.[139] The phrase 'tailor-made' is an over-simplification, however, and her potentially reductive approach to the relationships between mayoral politics and Middleton's own agenda has recently been critiqued by O'Callaghan.[140] Another problem with Heinemann's approach (important though it is for Middleton criticism) is that it implies that Middleton chose the men for whom he wrote mayoral Shows, depending on the congruity of his views and theirs, rather than the Lord Mayor's Company choosing him.

Nevertheless, there is undeniably a 'godly' aspect to Middleton's Shows. In *The triumphs of loue and antiquity* he emphasises 'the noble and reuerend Ceremonies which Diuine Antiquity religiously ordained' (sig. C4r). A Websterian note is struck in *The triumphs of honor and verue*, where the Globe of Honor contains 'eight bright Personages . . . representing the *Inward Man*, the Intentions of a Vertuous and Worthy Brest' (sig. C1v). This device serves to depict an almost doctrinal struggle between virtue and human frailty (a theme which, on the face of it, does not appear altogether suitable for spectacular pageantry). The mist that descends over the globe is intended to demonstrate that 'the best men haue their Imperfections, and worldly Mists oftentimes interpose the cleer-est Cogitations' (sig. C2r). Another statement in the same work reinforces Middleton's views on the importance of real virtue: 'It may be said you did but late passe by / Some part of Triumph that spake Vertuously, /And one such Speech suffices; 'tis not so' (sig. C1r). *The triumphs of truth* certainly does not content itself with only one 'vertuous' speech. The rarefied religious politics of Middleton's Shows compares interestingly to Heywood's rather more targeted approach. As Rowland has demonstrated, in *Porta pietatis* Heywood specifically celebrates the brothers of the new Lord Mayor, both of whom were clerics of a distinctly nonconform-ist persuasion. As Rowland argues, Heywood is 'enthusiastic' about the anti-Laudian Archbishop of Canterbury, George Abbot, a man who had come into conflict with both the present monarch and his father.[141] The pageant of Piety with which this Show concludes seems full of confidence in the religious rectitude of the new incum-bent, invoking a time when Piety, 'shining in her pure truth', stands firm in the face of both 'Atheists' and 'Schismaticks' (sig. C1v). She has no need to fear what Heywood calls 'the Faggot and the stake', the instruments of *Catholic* religious persecution.

Although he does not always spurn them altogether (the

Companies were unlikely to have sanctioned this), in his earlier
works in this genre Middleton is less likely than his peers to spend
time on the history of the Company in question, such as anecdotes
about previous Lord Mayors. His preference wherever feasible
is for lengthy moralising exhortations to the new incumbent.
Middleton's practice is in notable contrast to that of at least one of
his contemporaries, Munday, who often placed figures from civic
history and mythology at the forefront of his Shows. Middleton's
first Show contains nothing of the Company's history whatsoever;
perhaps he was required to include such detail, albeit briefly in
some cases, in his later Shows. Where he does place the new Lord
Mayor in a historical lineage, as in *The triumphs of integrity* with
its procession of rulers who rose exclusively from 'humble beginnings', this often serves, as Heinemann writes, to emphasise his
'central theme', which is 'that greatness derived from merit is far
superior to greatness derived from high birth'.[142] Rather than celebrating monarchical greatness, the text puts civic meritocracy in
the foreground. 'All this is instanc't onely to commend', Middleton
writes in this work, 'the low condition whence these Kings deesend';
even King David is cited in this regard, as not scorning 'to be a
Shepheard' (sig. A4v). 'Low-obscure beginnings' are no impedi-
ment to 'Fame' as far as Middleton is concerned (sig. A4r). The
main body of this work thus belies its dedication, where Middleton
praises Martin Lumley's 'Descent Worthy . . . [being] Sprung of an
Antient, and most Generous Race' (sig. A2r). As its title suggests,
in this work Middleton defends quite boldly the superiority of 'vertuous strife' over 'high Place', emphasising that 'meane wombs /
No more eclipse braue Merit, then rich Toombes / Make the Soule
happy' (sig. A4r–v). His rhetoric here brings to mind the dedication
in Webster's *Dutchesse of Malfy*, where the latter writes that 'the
ancient'st Nobility [is] but a rellique of time past, and the truest
Honor indeede [is] for a man to conferre Honor on himself' (sig.
A3r). There is a degree of irony, given its setting, in the final line
of the argument Middleton presents in the speech in the 'Mount
Royall'. The repetition of the harsh consonants 't' and 'd' conveys
the scorn in the sentiment quite strongly:

> 'Tis the Noblest Splendor upon Earth,
> For man to adde a Glory to his Birth . . .
> Then to be Nobly-borne and there stand fixt;
> As if 'twere Competent Vertue for whole Life
> To be Begot a Lord.
>
> (sig. A4r–v)

Similarly, in *The triumphs of truth* the Lord Mayor is asked the rhetorical question, 'For what is Greatnesse if not ioyn'd with Grace?' (sig. D2r). Naturally, Webster's own mayoral Show takes the same line, pursuing a theme of 'honour' derived from noble deeds, not noble birth. Sir John Hawkwood relates that 'My birth was meane, yet my deservings grew / To eminence . . . From a poore common Souldier I attained, / The stile of Captaine, and then Knight-hood gaind' (sig. B2r). Taylor focuses on the specifically civic means by which one could attain the heights, in the process giving a more direct account of the route to 'fame' and 'honour' taken by the Lord Mayor himself. As 'Great Rivers have their heads in little Rills', he explains, so

> from th'apprentice seven yeares servitude
> Proceeds the grave gowne, and the Livery Hood,
> Till (in the end) by merit, paines and care,
> They win the Grace to sit in Honours chaire.
> (*The triumphs of fame and honour*, sig. B1r)

Dekker writes more broadly in *Troia-Noua triumphans* that 'Arts, Trades, Sciences, and Knowledge' are 'the onely staires and ascensions to the Throne of Virtue' (sig. B2v). Once again social status associated with high birth does not get a look-in. Indeed, Dekker reminds the reader that 'Time hath his wings, Glasse, and Scythe, which cuts downe All' (*ibid.*). In a proto-existentialist moment Dekker expresses the idea that it is all about proving yourself. Swinnerton is sombrely told by Fame at the culmination of the day's festivities that his previous successes are irrelevant and must now be laid aside,

> . . . for the wayes which thou hath past
> Will be forgot and worne out, and no Tract
> Of steps obseru'd, but what thou now shalt Act.
> The booke is shut of thy precedent deedes.
>
> (sig. C1v)

Dekker emphasises to Swinnerton that 'in this Court of Fame / None else but Vertue can enrol your Name' (*ibid.*). Middleton concurs, arguing in *The triumphs of integrity* that ''tis the Life, and Dying / Crownes both with Honors Sacred Satisfying' (sig. A4r). In *Londons ius honorarium* Heywood addresses the Lord Mayor thus, echoing Middleton, Dekker and Webster before him: 'more faire and famous is it to be made, then to be borne Noble, For that Honour is to be most Honored, which is purchased by merit, not

crept into by descent' (sig. A2r).[143] Furthermore, 'Vertue' reminds
the courtier Peter Proby in *The triumphs of honor and vertue* that it
is a mistake to place wealth and power above moral sanctity: 'Selfe-
Opinions Eye', she announces, may pass her by 'As if the Essence
of my Deitie / Were rais'd by Power, and not Power rais'd by me'.
Those rulers who make this mistake, it is warned, 'build the Empire
of their Hopes on Sand' (sig. C1r). Given that Proby's rise to civic
power was generated in part by his connections with *royal* power,
this is a potentially cutting observation. All these works bear out
Paster's argument that 'the pageants ministered to the city's self-
esteem by challenging aristocratic assumptions that birth, courtly
grace, and royal favor matter most of all'.[144] An entirely different
perspective on merit and advancement is offered by Mayne's 1639
court play *The citye match*, where, amidst a number of what *The
Knight of the Burning Pestle* calls 'girds at citizens', the merchant
Warehouse bemoans his *lack* of high-born nobility with reference
to Lord Mayor's Day. Warehouse is, he admits, 'a man that hath
/ No scutcheons but them of his Company, / Which once a yeare
doe serve to trim a Lighter / to Westminster and back againe' (sig.
M2v). Livery company 'scutcheons' are much more highly rated in
the Shows, naturally.

The concerns in terms of large-scale political changes which this
chapter has dealt with so far can now be brought together. As I
have argued elsewhere, the Shows tend to cite historical monarchs
only in terms of what they have contributed to the livery company
in question and/or to the City as a whole. That these charters, rights
and monopolies had at times been 'wrestled from English kings',
in Manley's phrase, is an aspect of them which the Shows usually
leave unspoken, although there is such an implication in the way
in which in *Monuments of Honor* Edward III is made to state that
these eight kings 'held it a special honor, and renowne . . . to unite
themselues into the [Merchant Taylors'] Brotherhood' (sig. B3r).[145]
Nevertheless, selectivity was the inevitable consequence. The effect
of such a perspective on *Monuments of Honor* is to produce a roll of
honour with unexpected results. 'Henry the sixt' is both 'religious'
and 'unfortunate'; Edward IV is 'Amarous and Personable', and
Richard III manages to be both a 'bad man' and a 'good King . . . for
the Lawes he made in his short Gouernment' (Munday deals with
King John in much the same way: his evil deeds are outweighed by
his generosity towards the City). For Webster, the highest place in
the Merchant Taylors' pantheon is reserved for Henry VII, the 'wise

and politique' king during whose reign the Company received its charter (sig. B2v). Dekker's pageant 'Brittannia's Watch-tower' represents solely 'those Kinges . . . whose loues and Royall fauors' were bestowed upon the City: accordingly, only Edward the Confessor, Richard I, King John and Henry III are mentioned (*Brittannia's honor*, sigs B4v–C1r).

Famous Lord Mayors of antiquity, in contrast to monarchs, were regularly represented in the Shows to act as exemplars, and they were often introduced alongside Fame, to emphasise the point. Companies such as the Fishmongers (whose chief hero was William Walworth) and the Mercers (who could boast Dick Whittington) would no doubt have expected the pageant writers to exploit previous glories associated with the company in question.[146] As Woolf has stated, Walworth 'turns up again and again in mayoral processions, up to the end of the eighteenth century', although he points out that 'the reputation of such a character could be inflated and embellished over time'.[147] Middleton foregrounds the rather more obscure Henry Barton, a Skinner whose mayoralty was notable not for saving the nation from rebellion but for the more prosaic feat of being the one in which 'for the safety of Trauellers, & strangers by night through the Citie, caused lights to be hung out fro[m] Alhollontid [All Hallows] to Candlemas' (*The triumphs of loue and antiquity*, sig. B4v). Indeed, figures like Walworth, Faringdon, Fitz-Alwin and the rest had taken on a pseudo-mythical character over the years, as the dispute between 1611 and 1614 about Fitz-Alwin's corporate affiliation shows.

For this reason pageant writers like Munday felt able to play fast and loose with the historical record by placing real historical figures alongside those of dubious provenance such as Robin Hood, and by juxtaposing classical, legendary and medieval contexts even if this practice was criticised by chroniclers, Stow included. Indeed, Bradbrook argues that combining disparate contexts in this fashion – as Munday did in *Metropolis coronata* where he has Robin Hood as Fitz-Alwin's son-in-law – 'is something better than mere ignorance': in this Show, she writes, Munday 'joined the ancient figure of woodland freedom . . . with an ancient emblem of civic power'.[148] As with Robin Hood, the Shows also included references to figures with limited civic significance, but who could be used to reflect the thematic concerns of the production, such as Sir Francis Drake, who as we have seen features in a number of Drapers' Shows as a famous 'brother' of the Company.[149] That Drake was repeatedly juxtaposed to Jason and his argonauts as part of the treatment

of the golden fleece trope points up the hybrid nature of the Shows'
sources. The bulk of the spectators of the Shows would have been
very likely to be familiar with these characters from the City's past
and elsewhere, even if their sense of the historicity may not have
been all that secure.[150] Other contemporary sources such as Stow's
Suruay and various chronicle histories, as well as the profileration
of London-focused plays during this period (some written by the
same men as the mayoral Shows) repeatedly rehearsed the notable
and charitable deeds of deceased dignitaries.[151] They did so, too,
with the same kind of nostalgic valorisation of these men that one
finds in the Shows. As Hardin notes, the invocation of, and, in some
cases, actual impersonation of previous Lord Mayors accentuates
'the sense of historical immutability by bridging the gap between
the thirteenth century . . . and the early seventeenth century'.[152]

Past mayors also acted as models for the current incumbent and
his administration, although not always positive ones. Northway
presents a complex, if at times convoluted, account of what lies
behind an apparently harmless song contained within Dekker's
1629 Show for the Ironmongers, *Londons tempe*. Dekker's use
here of a vernacular verse form indebted to Richard Stanyhurst's
derided translation of *The Aeniad*, she argues, works as an implicit
message to the new mayor, James Campbell, *not* to follow the path
of his unpopular father Thomas, Lord Mayor in 1609. 'A copy of
something bad', she states, can take the form of 'an egregious translation, [or] an unpopular mayor'.[153] In the same Show, however,
Dekker does not in any way criticise the City itself. Indeed, he
presents a characteristically patriotic defence of the Thames against
all comers, claiming that all other supposedly great rivers of the
world – the Ganges, Nile, Euphrates and so on – 'would weepe
out there eyes, / Madde that new Troys high towers on tiptoe rize
/ To hit Heauens Roofe'. Heywood is just as nationalistic at times:
compared to the Thames, he boasts in *Londini artium*, the Seine is
but 'a Brooke' and Rome's famous Tiber is merely 'a Ditch' (sig.
B1v). (That Rome is the capital of Catholicism may have had an
impact on Heywood's approach here, as with his claim in *Londini
status pacatus* that Rome 'Tyranniz'd over the whole World' (sig.
A3v).) Dekker begins *Brittannia's honor* in the same style, praising
London as a city 'able to match with the Fairest in the World . . .
renowned Abroad [and] admired at Home'. Indeed, in 'Forraine
Countries' London, he claims, 'is called the Queene of Citties'.
Westminster, one should note, is but London's 'Royall Daughter'
(sig. A3r). 'Fully to write downe all the Titles, Stiles, and Honors of

this our Metropolis', he concludes, 'would weary a 1000. pennes' (sig. A3v). Indeed, the three full pages of civic hagiography which he supplies are for Dekker only a taster. In his preamble, he writes, he has merely 'shewne you the Toppes onely of our City-Buildings; and in a little Picture drawne the Face of her Authority, giuing but a glimpse of her Prator as hee passes by' (sig. A4r). Heywood is equally prone to this kind of exaggeration, writing in *Londini status pacatus* that 'Rome it selfe the Metropolis of the Roman Empire' could not, even 'in her most flourishing estate and Potency . . . in the least compare with London' (sig. A3v).

The treatment of London's primacy in these works, as I have indicated above, at times engages with the central political battles of the age, such as the intermittent conflict between England and the Catholic nations on the continent, and with the growing domestic tensions between the Crown, City and Parliament at home. Echoing his chauvinistic treatment of London versus its foreign competitors above, in *Londons tempe* the famed 'Sposalizio del Mare', the marriage of the sea ceremony at Venice, is for Dekker merely 'a poore Lantscip' when compared to the 'full Brauereis of Thamesis' (sig. B1r).[154] To some extent Dekker is being typically bombastic, but his representation of the Thames in *Londons tempe* is only a wider-scale version of the way in which Munday had claimed the status of 'Queene of all Britanniaes streames' for the river in *The triumphs of re-united Britania* (sig. B4v). Webster too has Oceanus correct Thetis's misapprehension that they are witnessing 'the marriage of the sea'. 'That beateous seate is London', he states, which with its 'Eminent Marchants . . . [is] as rich, and venturous as euer grac't, / Venice or Europe' (*Monuments of Honor*, sig. A4r). 'Th' rest ath World', Webster claims, 'cannot shew the like' worthies as Drake and the other famous English sailors, a fact which, he asserts, generates envy in foreign nations (sig. A4v). In the 'Temple of Honor' pageant Webster locates 'Troynouant or the City' seated above other 'eminent' but 'admiring' cities: 'Antwerp, Paris, Rome, Venice and Constantinople'. Heywood takes the idea further still, arguing in *Londini speculum* that London's virtues are such that 'all forraigne Cities' are taught by it 'how to correct their vices' (sig. B1r). To further demonstrate the superiority of the English capital Webster marshals 'fiue famous Schollers and Poets of this our Kingdome' from Chaucer to Sidney; the latter, as Carnegie comments, is 'not only a poet but also a soldier', and a soldier 'who fought and died in the Low Countries for the Protestant cause', to boot (sig. B1r).[155]

Such nationalistic pride does not constitute wholesale xenophobia,

though. As with *Monuments of Honor*, many of these texts only
care to diminish the achievements of *Catholic* countries. In the same
vein, Taylor has the figure of London announce that for 'Rome, and
all Cities that hold Rome supreme, / Their glorie's [*sic*] are eclips'd
or but a dreame' (*The triumphs of fame and honour*, sig. A7v).
Indeed, in his mayoral Shows as well as in the speeches he wrote
for James's 1604 royal entry, Dekker emphasises the amity between
the City and certain kinds of 'foreigner': those from Protestant
nations or denominations. In *Troia-Noua triumphans*, Gasper has
argued, Dekker demonstrates the triumph – in more senses than
one – of 'militant Protestantism' by celebrating both the marital
alliance between the Stuart monarchy and the Elector of Palatine
and 'the emergence of a new religious-political figurehead' in Prince
Henry.[156] In his text Dekker welcomes

> our best-to-be beloued friends, the Noblest strangers, vpon whom,
> though none but our Soueraigne King can bestow Royall welcomes;
> yet shall it be a Memoriall of an Exemplary Loue and Duty (in
> those who are at the Cost of these Triumphs) to haue added some
> Heightening more to them then was intended at first, of purpose to
> do honor to their Prince and Countrey. (sig. A3v)

The 'well-beloved' overseas visitors on this occasion were Frederick,
the Elector Palatine and his entourage.[157] Dekker was clearly aware
of the implications of the presence of the new ruler of Bohemia
and leader of the Protestant Union – soon to be James's son-in-
law – when he states that the Company in question, the Merchant
Taylors, took it upon itself to 'heighten' the welcome he received
(his comment also reveals that their attendance was confirmed late
in the day). Frederick's coronation as Elector had already been
marked with celebratory bonfires in London. The year 1612 (or
at least part of it) was an encouraging one for English Protestants.
Prince Henry looked set to be their ideal monarch in due course,
and during the year his father had established strong links with
overseas Protestant states and communities, leading to the Palatine
marriage of 1613. Henry's untimely death, however – his attendance at Dekker's Show was expected but thwarted by terminal
illness and he died about a week later – only increased the sense in
some quarters that James took too conciliatory an approach to the
Catholic nations (we have already seen one response in mayoral
pageantry to the proposed Spanish match of 1623). For Dekker in
October 1612, however, Henry was still the great Protestant hope.
To that end, his description of the pageant of the House of Fame

stipulates that 'a particular roome [is] reserued for one that repre-sents the person of Henry the now Prince of Wales' (sig. C1v).[158]

Even after his early death (perhaps in a way heightened by it) Henry remained a totem for many Protestants, and a decade later Webster revived the prince in *Monuments of Honor*. Webster had written *A monumental columne*, an elegy for Henry (Heywood also wrote one), published in 1613, and the former took the opportu-nity to resurrect the figure of one of the few Stuarts with whom the Protestant City was then able to feel comfortable.[159] The topicality of this Show is relatively pronounced, in fact. Carnegie suggests quite plausibly that since the figure of Queen Anna in Webster's Show 'seems to have been identifiable only by an escutcheon bearing the arms of Bohemia, spectators may well have imagined her to be James's daughter, Elizabeth of Bohemia, the current exile from the Palatinate'. Furthermore, the use of 'the impresa of Amadeus V of Savoy' might, for a well-informed spectator, have brought to mind 'the intended marriage of Elizabeth's dead brother Henry' as well as the continued significance of Savoy to continental Protestantism.[160]

Within the Show's emphasis on the 'monuments' of dead wor-thies the dead Prince is given considerable prominence, partly as a famed previous member of the Merchant Taylors, the Company behind the Show, but also as a model of virtuous princedom. After a passing reference to the year in which Henry was conferred the freedom of the Company (1607), Webster's last and most sig-nificant pageant then centres on Henry, who is impersonated like a statue or funeral monument upon 'an Artificiall Rocke, set with mother of Pearle, and other such precious stones'. This rock, as Webster puts it, 'expresses the riches of the Kingdome Prince Henry was borne Heire to'. The figure of Henry himself stands 'vpon a pedestall of gold' 'with his Coronet, George and Garter; in his left hand he holdes a Circklet of Crimson Veluet' (sig. C1v). At the very end of the Show 'Amade le Graunde' delivers a speech to the Lord Mayor which emphasises Henry's importance through an extended tribute to the latter's virtues:

> This [pageant] chiefly should your eye, and eare Imploy
> That was of al your Brother-hood the Ioy,
> Prince Henry fames best president,
> Cald to a higher Court of Parliament,
> In his full strength of Youth and height of blood,
> And which Crownd all, when he was truly good . . .
> Such was this Prince.
>
> (sig. C2r-v)

Celebrating the qualities of English Protestantism's lost cause in such a pronounced fashion only a year after the furore over the proposed marriage between Henry's brother and a Spanish Catholic princess might, at least in principle, have thrown a less than flattering light on to Charles, only a year away from his own accession. Webster's Show demonstrates how powerful the myth of Henry was in the 1620s. Twelve years after his demise, Henry, Webster asserts, is still a 'Iewell [that has] not quite lost his Ray'; the Merchant Taylors, standing in for a wider constituency, 'Haue not forgot him who ought ner'e to dye'. Charles himself is alluded to in far less enthusiastic terms only as Henry's (nameless) successor, who 'seconds' his brother in 'grace' and '*may* second him in Brother-hood, and place' (sig. C2v; my emphasis). Indeed, Charles featured by name in only one civic pageant (either as prince or as king), and this sole citation took place, as we have seen, in the course of Middleton's trenchant take on the failed Spanish match in *The triumphs of integrity*. Henceforth, Charles's lack of sympathy with civic pageantry was to work both ways.

The gulf between the mayoral Shows and a gradually more beleaguered monarchy can, in retrospect, be glimpsed in those Shows produced in the mid-1620s. Although the Shows were to continue in increasingly strident terms to articulate civic values for another fifteen years, the positive involvement of the Stuarts in mayoral pageantry, pre-Restoration, seems to have ended with Webster's belated panegyric to Henry. When the Shows were restored along with the king in the 1660s, although attempts were made to conjure up the glory days I have been exploring, they could never retain their confidence nor their unique ability to comment in such complex ways on their own moment. It is therefore perhaps inevitable that once the eighteenth century arrived they soon experienced what can be described as a dying fall. All the same, their vigour and their relevance belonged to, participated in, and, I would argue, helped to shape the early modern moment in the many ways which I have attempted to encapsulate in this book.

Notes

1 *English Civic Pageantry* (revised ed.), p. 5. Northway has demonstrated that the adherence to the ideal of 'industriousness' in the Shows extends to their poetic form, too (see 'To kindle an industrious desire', pp. 173–4).

2 'The masque of truth', p. 86.

3 'Urban political culture', p. 260.

4 *Ibid.*, pp. 240–1. Withington quotes Hobbes to demonstrate the important role played by the City of London in the 'ousting' of Charles I (p. 266).

5 Brenner has argued that 'the company merchants of London [shared] a profound dependence on the Crown-sanctioned commercial operations that provided the foundations for their protected trades'; conversely, 'the merchants offered loans and taxes, as well as political support, to the Crown' (*Merchants and Revolution*, pp. 83 and 200).

6 *Ibid.*, p. 201.

7 Such a strategy, Bradbrook argues, 'did not involve the difficulty of putting new political statements into direct words' ('The politics of pageantry', p. 73).

8 *The Making of Jacobean Culture*, p. 209.

9 'City metal', pp. 44–5. However, the connections between these kinds of productions were probably not as direct as she assumes when she claims that *Sidero-Thriambos* was 'Munday's response to [Jonson's masques] *The Golden Age Restored* and *The Vision of Delight*' (*ibid.*, p. 44).

10 *Literature and Culture*, p. 221.

11 *Two Pageants*, p. 3. Richard Rowland, as we will see, has ably shown how Heywood's Shows responded to the heightened politics of the 1630s.

12 'Civic drama', pp. 294–5.

13 *The Drama of Coronation*, p. 9.

14 Recorder Finch's speech given when Barkham took his oath at Westminster also strikes a sterner note than usual, although that might be largely a reflection of the extent to which Barkham's predecessor, Francis Jones, had failed to live up to the demands of the mayoralty. 'Magistrates are not sett in Authority for their owne sakes', Finch proclaimed, 'but for the people'. The office of Lord Mayor, he emphasised, involved 'a number of cares' which 'cannot [be] putt off with [the Lord Mayor's] clothes now layed under his pillow', and those who take on high office ought to 'consider well the weight of government' (BL Add. MS 18016, fl. 149r).

15 In this context, the way Heywood addresses Richard Fenn in the 1637 Show is unusually apologetic: he asks the Lord Mayor to 'excuse' his 'boldnesse . . . in presuming to prompt your Memory in some things tending to the greatnes of your high place and Calling' (sig. A2r).

16 *The Idea of the City*, p. 125.

17 *The Culture of Cloth*, p. 5.

18 'Metropolitan resurrection', p. 382.

19 There was no Guildhall feast that year either. The records of the Court of Aldermen for 1625 contain many references to pesthouses, the appointment of surgeons and the like, and also to numerous reversions

of civic roles which must have come about because of the death or
desertion of the incumbents.

20 In 1609 the King apparently returned from hunt specifically 'to demonstrate his respect for the Lord Mayor's Show' (Wright, 'Rival traditions', p. 199).

21 Conversely, as Robertson and Gordon point out, in *The triumphs
of truth* 'Middleton takes over a figure from the masque [Jonson's
Hymenaei] and applies it to the uses of the citizens' (*Collections* III,
p. xl). Court writers targeted civic pageantry on other occasions too,
such as William Hopkins (a friend of Davenant and Jonson), who
made sarcastic reference to 'the learned layes / That make a din about
the streets' (cited in Rowland, *Heywood's Theatre*, p. 335).

22 *Winter Fruit*, p. 142.

23 Cited in Bergeron, 'Venetian state papers', p. 42. There's a full account
of the delays to and subsequent cancellation of Charles's abortive
royal entry in *Middleton: The Collected Works*, pp. 1898–1900. Ian
Gentles argues that Charles's lack of interest in civic ceremony was
'fatally to weaken royal charisma in such a way that the king was
unable to control London on the eve of, and during, the Civil War'
('Political funerals', p. 206).

24 'Charles I's royal entries', p. 91. Brenner dates 'the profound aliena-
tion of the [City] merchants from the Crown' from the beginning of
Charles's reign onwards (*Merchants and Revolution*, p. 218).

25 Since only the schematic 'plot' was generally agreed to by the livery
company, it seems likely that the printed work gave the writer the
chance to add 'unauthorised' material, especially when the writer
often liaised with the printer directly.

26 BL Add. MS 18016, fol. 178v. In 1624 he pronounced that the
'dignity' of London was 'above my power of expression', and that
the City was not only the highest in the land but also above 'most of
the cittyes of the world' (fol. 184r).

27 *The Making of Jacobean Culture*, p. 190.

28 As Woolf notes, in early modern London, memories of monarchs
'invariably revolve around something done by a king *to* or *for* London
and its citizens' (*The Social Circulation of the Past*, p. 321; see also my
'Monarchs and mayors', pp. 22–4).

29 *Literature and Culture*, p. 284.

30 BL Add. MS 18016, fol. 186r.

31 See also Rowland, *Heywood's Theatre*, pp. 343–4.

32 'City, capital, and metropolis', p. 137.

33 See *Lost Londons*, pp. 8–11.

34 The building of the new Exchange outside of the City on the Strand in
1609 was also perceived as a rival to the Royal Exchange in the City.
For more on the varying responses to urban growth within the City
and the Crown, see Griffiths, *Lost Londons*, pp. 50–2.

35 'Conceiving cities', p. 20. As he comments, the new system of gaining 'freedom' of this New Incorporation on payment of 20 or 40 shillings to the Crown 'is reminiscent of King James's sale of baronetcies' (p. 24).

36 See Robertson, 'Persuading the citizens?', p. 530.

37 'City, capital, and metropolis', p. 137.

38 *Lost Londons*, p. 5.

39 The City Corporation had had since the twelfth century the responsibility for managing the river from Staines to Yantlett Creek, Kent. (Civic control of this stretch of the river was kept until 1857.) A reminder of this responsibility often featured in the speeches given at the Lord Mayor's oath-taking by the representatives of the Crown (see, for instance, BL MS 18016, fol. 167r).

40 'Conceiving cities', p. 34.

41 Sayle, *Lord Mayors' Pageants*, pp. 124–5.

42 Tatham had to change his tune quite radically in the space of two years. Whereas in 1658 Honour's speech begins 'Though some dark clouds do interpose our joy', with a marginal note to explain that this relates 'to the death of the Protector' (*Londons Tryumph*, sig. C1v), in 1660 Tatham's mayoral text was loyally entitled *The royal oake*, and by 1664 his Show included speeches addressed to the King and Queen.

43 See GH MS 11,590, fol. 30. Fewer than half the number of non-members of livery Companies were assessed for contributions in 1640 compared to 1613. It was a different story when the incumbent was a parliamentarian: a letter from Isaac Pennington, the radical Lord Mayor and eventual regicide, in the Grocers' Court minutes for August 1643 refers to 'great . . . danger this cittie is in . . . [from] the kings forces' (GH MS 11,588/4, fol. 83).

44 GH MS 11,588/4, fols 3 and 15. The Wardens' election day feast did go ahead, however. Another 'moderate' dinner ('without any second course') was ordered on Lord Mayor's Day the following year, when two members of the Grocers also pleaded to be released from their duties as Stewards (their request was granted on payment of a fine of £25 apiece) (GH MS 11,588/4, fol. 34).

45 GH MS 11,588/4, fol. 15. The Grocers do refer to 'deepe' debts in the same minutes, and it is clear from contemporary Corporation records that the Crown owed considerable sums to the City of which the latter saw little prospect of repayment.

46 Fairholt, *London Pageants*, p. 70 (as he notes, the City entertained Fairfax and Cromwell in 1649).

47 Englefield, *The History of the Painter-Stainers Company*, p. 120.

48 GH MS 11,588/4, fol. 330. A 'moderate dinner' was the order of the day for the Grocers in October 1650 and 1652 (GH MS 11,588/4, fols 254 and 296). The Companies' records of expenditure on Shows retain exactly the same format in the Restoration period; apart from

some price rises it is almost as if nothing had changed between the 1630s and 1660s. Randall argues that this 'marked a calculated effort [on the part of the City] to pull things together [and] to construct an image of normalcy' (*Winter Fruit*, p. 142). Englefield writes of the Painter-Stainers that 'the ordinary [Company] records . . . succeed each other with astounding sang-froid at periods when the train bands were marching out to meet the victorious Royalist Army, [or] when the plague cart was making its ghastly round of the city streets' (*The History of the Painter-Stainers Company*, p. 91).

49 *Heywood's Theatre*, p. 360. As Rowland points out, Garway had in fact already been involved in impressing men to serve in the campaign in Scotland. George Whitmore, for whom Heywood wrote the 1631 Show, was also a supporter of Charles I: when the first Civil War broke out he was imprisoned by Parliament. Nicholas Rainton, in contrast, Whitmore's successor, was allied to the more radical elements in the City, such as Isaac Pennington, and has been described as having 'undoubted puritan sympathies' (see Brenner, *Merchants and Revolution*, p. 310). Heywood tells Freeman, Rainton's successor, that there is no 'better President to imitate then your Predecessor' (*Londini emporia*, sig. A2v).

50 *Heywood's Theatre*, p. 358.

51 *Ibid*, p. 351.

52 Glover, *A History of the Ironmongers' Company*, p. 64.

53 *Two Pageants*, p. 10.

54 *Heywood's Theatre*, p. 358.

55 'In August 1620 Spain's Army of Flanders had invaded the Palatinate' (Brenner, *Merchants and Revolution*, p. 248). Morris Abbot (to become Lord Mayor in 1638) had apparently investigated the possibility of support for an Anglo-Dutch war against Spain in 1620–21, and in 1621 Parliament openly if unsuccessfully asked the King to declare war (*ibid.*, pp. 249 and 252).

56 *Middleton: The Collected Works*, p. 1399.

57 *Ibid.*, p. 1432.

58 Fairholt claims that Dekker's use of the phrase 'the wilde boar has tusked up his vine' in *Londons tempe* is 'an allusion to the famous thirty years war . . . Dekker's simile is obtained from Psalm lxxx, verses 8 and 13; the vine is the church, or the true faith; the wild boar its enemies' (*Lord Mayors' Pageants*, vol. II, p. 185).

59 Earlier that year Christopher Clitheroe (the Lord Mayor in 1635) made a speech to Parliament about the dangers of Dunkirk privateers (see Thrush, *Oxford DNB*, 'Clitherow, Sir Christopher').

60 See Kellett, 'The breakdown of gild and corporation control', pp. 382–4. 'Foreigners' were non-free inhabitants of the City; 'aliens' or 'strangers' were the terms used for those from overseas in this period.

61 See Hardin, 'Spectacular Constructions', p. 76. Brenner writes that the Merchant Adventurers 'at the turn of the seventeenth century

. . . held unquestioned leadership in London's merchant community'
(*Merchants and Revolution*, p. 3). The fact that Brenner's 700-page
overview of the rise of overseas trade within the City barely mentions the *livery* companies speaks volumes, and backs up Manley's
argument that the merchant companies were 'bypassing and rendering obsolete the traditional government and companies of the City'
(*Literature and Culture*, p. 291).

62 *Joint Enterprises*, p. 10.

63 *Literature and Culture*, p. 292.

64 The East India Company was founded in 1599; thereafter, a number
of livery companies 'underwrote' its activities and as we can see from
the Shows their oligarchs were frequently members of it. Brenner has
calculated that 'of the 140 aldermen elected in the period 1600–1625,
about half . . . were overseas traders' (*Merchants and Revolution*,
p. 82).

65 In the preceding year's Show, however, although Dekker refers in
passing to the 'Armes of the foure Companies' of which Richard
Deane is free (along with the Skinners, these were the Levant, Virginia
and North West Passage companies), the latter three are not named
and as a result are not given anything like the profile we see elsewhere,
although the Russians he depicts and the 'goodly Russian prize' he
cites may refer to the Russia Company (*Brittannia's honor*, sigs B4v
and C2v).

66 Rowland calls Abbot's governorship of the East India Company
'aggressive' (*Heywood's Theatre*, p. 342).

67 *Ibid*, p. 346. Brenner comments that 'what is truly impressive is
the degree to which the leading merchants who originally established the [Levant] trade in the later sixteenth century were able to
make their influence felt through their descendants' (*Merchants and
Revolution*, p. 72). The 'great wealth' this trade generated 'routinely
provided [City merchants] with the opportunity for magistracy', and,
ultimately, the mayoralty in the case of Richard Saltonstall (1597),
Thomas Middleton (1613) and Ralph Freeman (1633) (*ibid.*, p. 74).
Although Brenner does not mention the fact, of the five men who held
senior positions in the East India Company in the 1630s, all but one
had been Lord Mayor: indeed, they dominated the mayoralty in this
period (see *ibid.*, p. 78).

68 Rowland has demonstrated the interconnections between trade and
nonconformist religion for the Merchant Adventurers' Company,
especially in the 1630s (*Heywood's Theatre*, pp. 340–2). Heywood's
list makes it clear that the Merchant Adventurers did *not* trade with
the Americas or West Indies. This is not to say, of course, that colonies and plantations were insignificant in this period, but rather to
stress that those who engaged with these more risky and unpredict-
able colonial areas were 'an entirely new group of traders, originating

almost totally outside the company merchant community' (Brenner, *Merchants and Revolution*, p. xii; see also pp. 108–12). Only infrequently did City merchants become involved in the Virginia Company (Thomas Hayes, Lord Mayor in 1614, was one).

69 Taylor makes the point that the rowers were two 'Saylours [and] two watermen', a distinction that the other writers were less likely to be aware of. His empathy with boatmen comes across when he writes that 'being ouer-joyed . . . every one of them drinks his Kan as a health . . . and presently fall[s] into a Rugged friskin daunce' (sig. A6r).

70 *Middleton: The Collected Works*, p. 1718. I would dispute her blanket use of the term 'colonial', however.

71 *Ibid.*, p. 1716.

72 *Colonial Transformations*, p. 161.

73 See, for example, *Buying Whiteness*, where Taylor calls Middleton's King of the Moors 'an 'unequivocally positive representation of a black speaker' (p. 126). Bach also does not appear to realise that the 'exotic animals' employed in the Shows, such as the ostrich or camel, were traditional emblems of the Companies and employed for that reason rather than to foster a sense of 'wildness' (*Colonial Transformations*, p. 161).

74 *Ibid.*

75 Taylor, *Buying Whiteness*, p. 411 n. 17.

76 *Colonial Transformations*, p. 162; my emphasis. (I am grateful to Stephen Gregg for his advice on this section.)

77 Middleton here distinguishes between those countries where the East India Company was actively trading, in which England had no imperial or colonial interests at this juncture, and 'plantations' like Virginia. Trade with the *East* Indies (particularly the spice trade) was, as Brenner writes, 'of great significance to the overall structure and character of London's merchant establishment'; conversely, 'by the end of the 1620s, all of the great City merchants had entirely forsaken the American trades' (*Merchants and Revolution*, pp. 77 and 92).

78 *Colonial Transformations*, p. 162.

79 There is evidence of 'blackamores' living in London from at least the 1590s onwards; parish records also show that the urban population was quite mixed in terms of its nationality and ethnicity, which included Irish people (see Griffiths, *Lost Londons*, pp. 72–6).

80 I don't propose to rehearse at much length the series of events that has become known as the Cockayne Project: for a full account of the series of events and their consequences, see Supple, *Commercial Crisis and Change*, pp. 33–51. Hardin notes that Jonson was commissioned by William Cockayne to write an entertainment in support of his attempt to secure a monopoly over the cloth trade ('Spectacular Constructions', pp. 72–3).

81 *The Culture of Cloth*, p. 162.

82 'Spectacular Constructions', pp. 75–6.

83 *The Culture of Cloth*, pp. 154 and 163. She goes so far as to call Munday's approach 'subversive', which may be overstating the case (p. 171).

84 *Ibid.*, pp. 162–3. Brenner calls James's support for the Cockayne Project 'an unspeakable betrayal' of the Merchant Adventurers (*Merchants and Revolution*, p. 210).

85 Supple, *Commercial Crisis and Change*, p. 34. 'Old drapery' refers to the long-standing trade in high-quality undressed and undyed English broadcloth.

86 *Ibid.*

87 See *ibid.*, pp. 34 and 39.

88 *The Culture of Cloth*, p. 168. It is certainly noteworthy after all the discomfort inherent in Munday's construction of 'Britishness' in *The triumphes of re-united Britania* that by 1614 he has defaulted to calling the nation 'England' once again.

89 *The Culture of Cloth*, pp. 168–9; see also Northway, 'To kindle an industrious desire', p. 178.

90 'To kindle an industrious desire', p. 176.

91 *Pageants and Entertainments*, p. 70 n. 225.

92 'Metropolitan resurrection', p. 379 (see also my *Anthony Munday*, p. 146).

93 'City metal and country mettle', p. 29. 'Priuate lucre' refers to the fraudulent practices associated with the manufacture and circulation of coinage. Edmund Howe's account of the 1611 ceremony is reproduced in Wortham, 'Sovereign counterfeits', pp. 334–5. The King's goldsmith in 1611 was Hugh Middleton, sponsor of the New River.

94 James's policy may have had an impact on the election of Pemberton in 1611, for it was rare for a Goldsmith to become Lord Mayor.

95 'City metal', p. 33. Once again Munday's weak classical knowledge lets him down: as Marcus points out, Midas was from Phrygia – King Croesus was from Lydia.

96 O'Callaghan offers a similar account of this text (*Thomas Middleton*, p. 97).

97 The failure of this match led to widespread celebrations in the City; the parishioners of St Mary Whitechapel even put up a plaque to record their 'thankfulness' that Charles had returned unscathed and unengaged from 'the Dangers of his Spanish Journey' (see Merritt, 'Puritans, Laudians', pp. 952–3). Cressy also discusses the 'spontaneous' and 'improvised' celebrations in London in 1623 of Prince Charles's return from Spain, writing that the Prince's 'participation in the celebration was minimal' (*Bonfires and Bells*, p. 101).

98 *Middleton: The Collected Works*, pp. 1767–8.

99 This latter text was entered in the Stationers' Register on 13 October
1623, a few days after Taylor's similar work *Brittaines Joy* (Arber,
Transcript, vol. IV, pp. 67–8).

100 Philip Collington suggests that the staged figure of Antonio's dead
wife in *The Revenger's Tragedy* is an early example of Middleton's
habitual use of the 'animated emblems' which so regularly feature in
his mayoral Shows ('A puppet-play', pp. 114–15). His characterisation
of Middleton as a writer who 'creates scenes that are visually dazzling,
morally edifying, and thematically controversial all at once' can be
applied as much to the Shows as to Middleton's plays (*ibid.*, p. 123).

101 John Aubrey wrote that 'the time of Sir Walter Raleigh's execution
was contrived to be on my Lord Mayor's day, that the pageants and
fine shows might avocate and draw away the people from beholding
the tragedie of the gallantest worthie that England ever bred' (cited in
Fairholt, *Lord Mayors' Pageants*, vol. II, p. 261). One can compare
this moment with the timing of Sidney's funeral *vis-à-vis* the execution
of Mary, Queen of Scots, in 1588 (see Goldring, 'The funeral of Sir
Philip Sidney', pp. 209–10). I have discussed the contemporaneity of
Sidero-Thriambos elsewhere (see *Anthony Munday*, p. 159).

102 Merritt argues that the figure of Elizabeth was invoked in the 1610s–
20s as a means of expressing 'anti-Spanish' Protestant feeling and
accompanying reservations about James's 'pacific' attitude towards
the erstwhile Catholic enemy ('Puritans, Laudians', p. 953). Cressy
writes that 'London and rural churches tended to celebrate Elizabeth's
accession day more enthusiastically than her successor' (*Bonfires and
Bells*, pp. 59–62).

103 Indeed, Middleton's first foray into mayoral pageantry, *The triumphs
of truth*, has a title notably similar to *The Masque of Truth*, a political masque which takes up a strongly pro-Protestant position towards
the imminent marriage between Frederick, the Elector Palatine, and
Princess Elizabeth. Norbrook has speculated that Middleton may have
written the masque, which was unperformed for disputed reasons. As
he points out, Middleton did write another court masque celebrating a
Jacobean union, the scandalous marriage of the Earl of Somerset and
Frances Carr in December 1613 ('The masque of truth', p. 94).

104 *Middleton: The Collected Works*, pp. 1252–3. Although she does
acknowledge his 'obvious and ardent anti-Spanish sentiments', I
would treat Busino's eyewitness account of the Spaniards in the Show
and in the crowd with more caution than Levin does, as this would
surely have been mediated by his role as chaplain to the *Venetian*
ambassador (*ibid.*, p. 1264).

105 Squire too refers to 'our foure Kingdoms, England, Scotland, France
and Ireland' in *Tes Irenes Trophaea* (sig. B2v).

106 Rowland argues that Heywood stresses procedure at this juncture
'because he was aware that this was one company amongst several in

which artisans were agitating, with increasing intensity as the 1630s wore on, for more extensive participation in the choice of their governors' (*Heywood's Theatre*, p. 305).

107 See Drapers MS MB13, fols 163–4. Bergeron helpfully summarises the debate over Barkham's translation in *Middleton: The Collected Works*, pp. 1586–7.

108 Bergeron notes that 'Fitzstephen's history of London is included in Stow's *Survay*': perhaps Munday's research was not so extensive as he makes out (*Pageants and Entertainments*, p. 83).

109 See my *Anthony Munday*, pp. 166–71.

110 According to Hentschell, Taylor may have been following Munday's example (or, given its date, possibly Middleton's) in respect of Fitz-Alwin in *Taylors pastorall*, an 'historicall and satyricall' work about sheep and shepherds (sig. D2r–v) (*The Culture of Cloth*, p. 170 n. 38).

111 This text is unusual too in listing all previous Lord Mayors from the Fishmongers' Company, not just the famous ones (see sig. C1v).

112 See Patterson, 'Married to the town', p. 160, for a discussion of the recorder of King's Lynn's 'reservations' about the abilities and religious views of the new mayoral incumbent.

113 Manley argues that Middleton's use of the figure of Orpheus in his Show is a compliment to Cockayne's famous eloquence, and he comments on Cockayne's 'complex place' within the 'current political scene' in the early 1620s (*Middleton: The Collected Works*, pp. 1398–9).

114 *Ibid.*, p. 1434.

115 Middleton may have been foresighted: as we have already seen, Jones fled the City and his creditors before the end of his term of office (see Chapter 2, above).

116 Middleton, ed. Bald, *Honourable Entertainments*, p. vi.

117 *Middleton and His Collaborators*, p. 12.

118 *Ibid.*, p. 13.

119 Taylor's loose description of Thomas Middleton, the new Lord Mayor, as a 'Puritan' is rather unhelpful (*Buying Whiteness*, p. 131): for a more nuanced account of Middleton's religio-political preferences, see Welch (rev. Dickie), *Oxford DNB*, 'Myddleton, Sir Thomas'.

120 *Middleton and His Collaborators*, p. 13.

121 Bromham claims that in this text Middleton is attacking Robert Carr and the Howard faction at court. Dutton writes that this might explain why 'George Chapman, who was identified with court patronage, and especially Robert Carr . . . sneered at Middleton's [1613] pageant' (*Jacobean Civic Pageants*, pp. 138–9). Heywood comes close to the same position in *Londini status pacatus* when 'Nilus' speculates about the likelihood of 'crocodiles' breeding 'here . . . in place and office' (sig. B1v).

122 Lobanov-Rostovsky, 'The Triumphs of Golde', p. 887.

123 Heinemann, *Puritanism and Theatre*, p. 128. Bribery is also cited as something to abjure in *The sunne in Aries* (sig. B3r).

124 'Summer 1613', p. 169. She notes the prevalence of Welsh references in Middleton's *A Chaste Maid in Cheapside*, produced in the same year (pp. 171–2).

125 'Something done in honour of the city', p. 143.

126 'The Triumphes of Golde', p. 890. This is a valid reading of Middleton's text but it is somewhat undercut by Lobanov-Rostovsky's two problematic assumptions: that City oligarchs were all uniformly hostile to theatricality (a point I have addressed elsewhere), and that the livery companies took subtle dramatic ironies into account when conferring the commissions for Shows. I have seen no evidence of the latter kind of deliberation.

127 To contextualise Middleton's 'Mammon's heapes', Brenner states that 'a fortune of £10,000 was a minimum requirement for eligibility' to become a member of the Court of Aldermen (*Merchants and Revolution*, p. 81). William Cockayne left around £72,000 at his death in 1626.

128 Rowland, *Heywood's Theatre*, p. 348.

129 *Ibid*, pp. 340–1.

130 Woolf discusses the ubiquity of Robin Hood in forms of popular culture; he points out that 'Robin featured prominently in May games and morris-dancing' (*The Social Construction of the Past*, p. 336). Owing to an unduly narrow definition of 'drama', however, he does not challenge Malcolm Nelson's assertion that Robin Hood features only in one work from the early Stuart period, Jonson's incomplete *The Sad Shepherd*; Munday's *Metropolis coronata* makes this claim erroneous ('Of Danes and giants', pp. 191 and 206 n. 80).

131 *Puritanism and Theatre*, p. 127.

132 *Thomas Middleton*, p. 92. In *Londini sinus salutis* Heywood pronounces that 'every Magistrate is a minister vnder God', an unusual take on the role (sig. B1v).

133 *Colonial Transformations*, p. 155.

134 Middleton's treatment of Proby is echoed in the Recorder's speech at the Exchequer. Finch commented that Proby attained the freedom of the City 'by guift', and on the basis that he already had the patronage of the recently deceased Queen Anna. Despite his court connections, though, Finch's speech makes it clear that Proby's suitability for the mayoralty derives wholly from his election by his civic peers; royal favour, it is implied, is in itself inadequate (BL Add. MS 18016, fol. 166v).

135 *Thomas Middleton*, p. 94.

136 *Ibid.*, p. 92. Middleton's opinionated manner manifests itself elsewhere, too. Rather digressively, he praises Queen Anne, the wife of Richard II, for being the first to introduce riding side-saddle for

women: 'Who it was that taught 'em [women] to ride stradling', he rages, 'there is no Records so immodest that can shew me, onely the impudent Time, and the open profession' (*The triumphs of loue and antiquity*, sig. C2v).

137 Northway has usefully charted the length of the speeches in the Shows in this period, with a noticeable peak in 1613 for *The triumphs of truth* and an equivalent dip for Middleton's next Show in 1617, the shortest in the whole period (see 'To kindle an industrious desire', p. 170).

138 *Puritanism and Theatre*, p. 128 n.14; see also *Middleton: The Collected Works*, p. 1254.

139 *Puritanism and Theatre*, p. 128.

140 *Thomas Middleton*, pp. 93–4.

141 Rowland, *Heywood's Theatre*, p. 343. The Lord Mayor himself, Morris Abbot, had been 'a prominent member of the vestry of St Stephen's, Coleman Street', one of the most fervently nonconformist parishes in London (and incidentally, Munday's parish for his last decade or so) (*ibid*, p. 344). For more on the Abbot family in the 1620s, see Brenner, *Merchants and Revolution*, pp. 224–5.

142 *Puritanism and Theatre*, p. 129.

143 In some cases the dignitaries celebrated by the Shows did not have unproblematic pasts: Sir Thomas Middleton, for instance, had been committed to Newgate for 'contempt and refusall of his oathe [of Alderman]' ten years before his mayoralty (Corporation of London Reps, vol. 26, fol. 159v).

144 *The Idea of the City*, p. 149.

145 *Literature and Culture in Early Modern London*, p. 221.

146 For more on Whittington's role in the Mercers' 'corporate memory', see Robertson, 'The adventures of Dick Whittington', p. 61.

147 *The Social Circulation of the Past*, p. 314. Henry Machyn, as Woolf notes, misremembered Walworth's notable deed at Smithfield.

148 'The politics of pageantry', p. 66.

149 Drake and his fellow mariners Hawkins and Frobisher feature in Heywood's 1637 text, *A true description of His Majesties royall ship* (sig. D4r), as they do in Webster's *Monuments of Honor* (sig. A2v).

150 Woolf discusses how in this period 'the division of sacred from secular, with respect to the past . . . did not prevent the intermingling of episodes from the Bible with those of classical, medieval or recent history' ('Of Danes and giants', p. 176).

151 Howard argues that London-focused plays 'educate[d] playgoers about the lives and deeds of the city elite' (Howard, 'Competing ideologies of commerce', p. 170; see also Wheatley, 'The pocket books of early modern history', pp. 190–2).

152 'Spectacular Constructions', p. 86.

153 'To kindle an industrious desire', p. 183.

154 The gold ship used on this occasion (the Buchintoro) was described by a slightly less partisan witness, Thomas Coryate, as 'a thing of marvellous worth [and] the richest galley of all the world' (cited in *Middleton: The Collected Works*, p. 1265).

155 'Introduction to *Monuments of Honour*', pp. 233 and 246.

156 *The Dragon and the Dove*, p. 131. Behind this denigration of Venice may have lain the reality of 'the perceptibly declining power' of Venetian trade in the Mediterranean (Brenner, *Merchants and Revolution*, p. 45).

157 An eyewitness account of this Show by one of the party is discussed in Chapter 3. Visitors attending the 1624 Show included members of the Dutch government, in town for negotiations with King James over a truce with Spain.

158 Bradbrook comments that the 'Merlin in the rock' device for the lost 1610 Show 'reproduced the [Arthurian] theme of Prince Henry's Barriers of that same year' ('The politics of pageantry', p. 67).

159 Interestingly, Recorder Finch's speech at the Lord Mayor's oath-taking in 1624 also emphasises continuity and perpetuity in a way that resembles Webster's text. After a reference to the raising of 'Piramids' that will outlive their builders, his speech expresses a desire that there will be 'lasting monumentes of [the Lord Mayors'] goodness and greatnes'; the City, he argues with an elegaic note, 'is still the same, and I hope the honor and dignity of the Citty shall still be the same' thereafter (BL Add. MS 18016, fol. 185r).

160 'Introduction to *The Monuments of Honour*', p. 235 (see also p. 246).

Appendix 1

The Lord Mayors' Shows, 1585–1639: summary

Year	Writer(s) / artificer	Title of printed work	Company / mayor	Printer / publisher	SR	Cost / print run
1585	George Peele	*The deuice of the pageant borne before Woolstone Dixi*	Skinners / Wolstan Dixie	Edward Allde		
1586	?Peele	?	Haberdashers / George Barne			
1587	?Peele	?	Haberdashers / George Bond			
1588	Peele	? 'The device of the Pageant borne before the Righte Honorable Martyn Calthrop'	Drapers / Martin Calthorp	?Richard Jones	Jones	

Year	Writer(s) / artificer	Title of printed work	Company / mayor	Printer / publisher	SR	Cost / print run
1589	?	?	Goldsmiths / Richard Martin			
1590	Thomas Nelson		Fishmongers / John Allot			
1591	Peele	*The deuice of the pageant*	Salters / William Webbe	'Printed for William Wright'		
		Descensus astraeae				
1592	?	?	Ironmongers / William Rowe			
1593	Plague year		Vintners / Cuthbert Buckle			
1594	?	?	Clothworkers / John Spencer			
1595	?Peele	?	Skinners / Stephen Slayne			
1596	?	?	Clothworkers / Thomas Skinner			
1597	?Munday	?	Skinners / Richard Saltonstall			
1598	?	?	Grocers / Stephen Soame			

Year	Writer / Artificer	Title	Company / Mayor	Printer	Place	Cost	Copies
1599	?		Clothworkers / Nicholas Mosley				
1600	?		Haberdashers / William Ryder				
1601	?		Haberdashers / John Garrard				
1602	?Munday / William Haynes / George Hearne		Merchant Taylors / Robert Lee			30s	
1603	Plague year		Mercers / Thomas Bennett				
1604	?Jonson (?and Munday) / John Grinkin		Haberdashers / Thomas Lowe	?Felix Kingston	Kingston	£1 10s	
1605	Munday / Grinkin	*The triumphes of re-united Britania*	Merchant Taylors / Leonard Holliday	William Jaggard			
1606	Plague year	?	Clothworkers / John Watts			£6	
1607	?		Mercers / Henry Rowe				
1608	?	?	Grocers / Humphrey Weld				
1609	Munday / Grinkin	*Camp-bell, or the ironmongers faire feild*	Ironmongers / Thomas Campbell	?			500 copies

Year	Writer(s) / artificer	Title of printed work	Company / mayor	Printer / publisher	SR	Cost / print run
1610	Munday / Grinkin	?	Merchant Taylors / William Craven			
1611	Munday / Grinkin	*Chruso-thriambos*	Goldsmiths / James Pemberton	William Jaggard		500 copies
1612	Dekker / John Heminger	*Troia-Nova triumphans*	Merchant Taylors / John Swinnerton	Nicholas Okes	Okes	
1613	Middleton / Munday / Grinkin	*The triumphs of truth*	Grocers / Thomas Middleton	Nicholas Okes	Okes	£4
1614	Munday / Grinkin	*Himatia-Poleos*	Drapers / Thomas Hayes	Edward Allde		
1615	Munday / Grinkin	*Metropolis coronata*	Drapers / John Jolles	George Purslowe		
1616	Munday / Grinkin	*Chrysanaleia*	Fishmongers / John Leman	George Purslowe	Purslowe	200 additional copies
1617	Middleton / Rowland Bucket	*The tryumphs of honor and industry*	Grocers / George Bolles	Nicholas Okes		500 / £4
1618	Munday / Grinkin	*Sidero-Thriambos*	Ironmongers / Sebastian Harvey	Nicholas Okes		
1619	Middleton / Garret Christmas / Robert Norman	*The triumphs of loue and antiquity*	Skinners / William Cockayne	Nicholas Okes		
1620	John Squire / Francis Tipsley	*Tes Irenes Trophaea*	Haberdashers / Francis Jones	Nicholas Okes		

Year	Author	Title	Company / Sponsor	Printer	
1621	Middleton / Christmas	*The sunne in Aries*	Drapers / Edward Barkham	Edward Allde	
1622	Middleton / Christmas	*The triumphs of honor and vertue*	Grocers / Peter Proby	Nicholas Okes	
1623	Middleton / Christmas Munday	*The triumphs of integrity*	Drapers / Martin Lumley	Nicholas Okes	
		The triumphs of the Golden Fleece		'T.[homas] S.[nodham]'	
1624	Webster / Terry / Patten /Lovett	*Monuments of Honor*	Merchant Taylors / John Gore	Nicholas Okes	
1625	Plague year		Drapers / Allan Cotton		
1626	Middleton / Christmas	*The triumphs of health and prosperity*	Drapers / Cuthbert Hacket	Nicholas Okes	
1627	Dekker / Christmas	*?*	Haberdashers / Hugh Hammersley	Nicholas Okes	
1628	Dekker / Christmas	*Brittannia's honor*	Skinners / Richard Deane	Nicholas Okes	
1629	Dekker / Christmas	*Londons tempe*	Ironmongers / James Campbell	Nicholas Okes	500
1630	?No Show		Merchant Taylors / Robert Ducy		
1631	Heywood / Christmas	*Londons ius honorarium*	Haberdashers / George Whitmore	Nicholas Okes	300 / £2

Year	Writer(s) / artificer	Title of printed work	Company / mayor	Printer / publisher	SR	Cost / print run
1632	Heywood / Christmas	*Londini artium & scientiarum scaturigo*	Haberdashers / Nicholas Rainton	Nicholas Okes		300 / £2
1633	Heywood / Christmas	*Londini emporia, or Londons mercatura*	Clothworkers / Ralph Freeman	Nicholas Okes		
1634	John Taylor / Norman	*The triumphs of fame and honour*	Clothworkers / Robert Parkhurst	?	Henry Gosson	
1635	Heywood /John and Matthias Christmas	*Londini sinus salutis*	Ironmongers / Christopher Clitheroe	Robert Raworth		500
1636	No Show?		Fishmongers / Edward Bromfield			
1637	Heywood /John and Matthias Christmas	*Londini speculum*	Haberdashers / Richard Fenn	John Okes		500 plus unspecified additional number for 40s
1638	Heywood /John and Matthias Christmas	*Porta pietatis*	Drapers / Morris Abbot	John Okes		
1639	Heywood /John and Matthias Christmas	*Londini status pacatus*	Drapers / Henry Garway	John Okes		300 additional copies for 40s

Appendix 2

Governance of the City of London

The livery companies

The importance of the livery company system to the lives of the citizens of early modern London cannot be overstated. From the medieval period onwards there were several dozen livery companies in London, representing and regulating various trades and crafts in the city such as ironmongery, drapery, and shoemaking. The Companies had jurisdiction over much of the economic and social life of their members as both a regulatory body and welfare provider. Structurally divided into a larger body of freemen and a smaller privileged group of liverymen, the livery companies were governed by a senior elite of liverymen – the Court of Assistants – from whose ranks the important annual offices of Masters and Wardens (in some companies known as Renter Wardens, although in others Renter Wardens were separate officers) were drawn. Historically, only liverymen could take part in the election of the Lord Mayor, the sheriffs and the other officers of the City. Livery companies owned halls in London for their internal bureaucratic and social purposes; and they kept extensive records of their membership, their economic activities and their entertainments, such as the Lord Mayor's Show.

The 'Great Twelve'

The London livery companies were numerous, to reflect the numbers of active trades in the city, but within that diversity twelve of the Companies held priority. These were known as the 'Great Twelve', and their order of precedence (laid down in 1516) was taken very seriously and sometimes disputed. Custom dictated that Lord Mayors were members of the Great Twelve, and, in the mid-sixteenth century at least, the same was true for the aldermen.

Members of lesser Companies were obliged to 'translate' into one of the Great Twelve upon election to office. The Great Twelve, in their usual order of precedence, were: the Mercers, Grocers, Drapers, Fishmongers, Goldsmiths, Skinners, Merchant Taylors, Haberdashers, Salters, Ironmongers, Vintners, Clothworkers.

The Freedom of the City

From the early fourteenth century, to be a freeman of London – that is, an economically and politically active citizen – one needed to be a member of one of the livery companies. Entry to a Company came through four means: by the fulfilment of a fixed term of apprenticeship, by the inheritance of one's father's own company-specific status as a freeman (freedom by 'patrimony'), by a mixture of lobbying, patronage and purchase (freedom by 'redemption') or by the process called 'translation', where a man who was already a member of one livery company moved over into another.

The City Corporation

The City Corporation of London was the jurisdictional unit for city government over which successive charters operated. Although certain urban services (poor relief and the night-watch, among others) were administered at the very local level of parish and pre-cinct, the primary geographical units of government were the City's twenty-six wards. Each ward was represented by an alderman elected for life from the senior elite of the citizenry; the aldermen sat together in a twice-weekly Court in Guildhall, presided over by an annually elected Lord Mayor. Their executive rule was prima-rily supplemented by two annually elected Sheriffs, the Common Council (a large legislative body of regularly elected freemen that met perhaps half-a-dozen times a year) and the Common Hall (an electoral body of all the city's liverymen who met in June and September to elect the senior city officers). London also returned four MPs at every parliamentary election.

The jurisdiction of the City Corporation extended as far as the outer limit of the wards. The city walls do not necessarily reflect the boundary of the City, which in many parts of London went beyond the walls (thus some city wards are called 'Without', i.e. outside the walls).

Bibliography

Manuscripts

The 'Album Amicorum' of Michael van Meer. Edinburgh University Library MS La.III.283

Booth, Abraham, 'Englandts Descriptie'. University of Utrecht Library MS 1198

——, 'Journael van't gepasseerde op mijne reyse in Engelant'. University of Utrecht Library MS 1196

Clothworkers' Company Quarter and Renter Warden Accounts 1578–1598

Clothworkers' Company Quarter and Renter Warden Accounts 1598–1613

Clothworkers' Company Quarter and Renter Warden Accounts 1630–1639

Clothworkers' Company Orders of Courts 1581 to 1605

Clothworkers' Company Orders of Courts 1605 to 1623

Clothworkers' Company Orders of Courts 1623 to 1636

Court of Aldermen Repertories, vol. 23 (1592–96). London Metropolitan Archives MS COL/CA/01/01/025

Court of Aldermen Repertories, vol. 26 (1602–04). London Metropolitan Archives MS COL/CA/01/01/028

Court of Aldermen Repertories, vol. 27 (1605–07). London Metropolitan Archives MS COL/CA/01/01/030

Court of Aldermen Repertories, vol. 39 (1624–25). London Metropolitan Archives MS COL/CA/01/01/043

Court of Aldermen Repertories, vol. 44 (1629–30). London Metropolitan Archives MS COL/CA/01/01/048

Drapers' Company Court of Assistants Minutes. 1584 to 1594. MB 10

Drapers' Company Court of Assistants Minutes. 1594 to 1603. MB 11

Drapers' Company Court of Assistants Minutes. September 1603 to July 1640. MB 13

Drapers' Company Wardens Accounts 1621–1622. WA 7

Drapers' Company Wardens of Bachelors Accounts 1615–1691. YR 2

Drapers' Company Freedom List 1567–1656. FA 1

Drapers' Company Quarterage Book, 1617–1627. QB 2

Fishmongers' Company Court Ledger No. 1. 1592–1610. GH MS 5570/1

Fishmongers' Company Court Ledger No. 2. 1610–31. GH MS 5570/2

Fishmongers' Company Court Ledger No. 3. 1631–46. GH MS 5570/3

Goldsmiths' Company Wardens' Accounts and Court Minutes. O. Part 3, 1604–2. Jam. 1 to 1611–9. Jam. 1. Vol. 14

Goldsmiths' Company Wardens' Accounts and Court Minutes. P. Part 1, July 26 1611 – Jan. 22 1617. Vol. 14a

Grocers' Company: Orders of the Court of Assistants. 19th July 1591–14th July 1616. GH MS 11,588/2

Grocers' Company: Orders of the Court of Assistants. 26th July 1616–23rd March 1639. GH MS 11,588/3

Grocers' Company: Orders of the Court of Assistants. 22nd April 1640–15th June 1668. GH MS 11,588/4

Grocers' Company: Charges of Triumphs 1613–1614 [1640]. GH MS 11,590

Accounts of the Wardens of the Haberdashers' Company, 1633–1653. GH MS 15,866/1

Haberdashers' Company, Triumphs' Accounts, 1604–1699. GH MS 15,869

Haberdashers' Court of Assistants Minutes, 1582–1652. GH MS 15,842/1

Haberdashers' Company Register of Freedom Admissions 1526–1642. GH MS 15,857/1

Haberdashers' Yeomanry Accounts, 1601–1661. GH MS 15,868

Ironmongers' Company Court Minute Books, 1555–1602. GH MS 16,967/1

Ironmongers' Company Court Minute Books, 1602–11. GH MS 16,967/2

Ironmongers' Company Court Minute Books, 1612/13–1629. GH MS 16,967/3

Ironmongers' Company Court Minute Books, 1629–46. GH MS 16,967/4

Ironmongers' Company Rough Court Minutes, 1593–1612/13. GH MS 16,969/2

Ironmongers' Company Rough Court Minutes, 1613–1674. GH MS 16,969/3

Merchant Taylors' Accounts, 1601–1604. GH MS 34,048/8

Merchant Taylors' Accounts, 1604–1609. GH MS 34,048/9

Merchant Taylors' Accounts, 1609–1615. GH MS 34,048/10

Merchant Taylors' Accounts, 1623–1625. GH MS 34,048/13

Merchant Taylors' Accounts, 1629–1633. GH MS 34,048/15

Merchant Taylors' Memorandum Book concerning processions and pageants, 1556–68. GH MS 34,105

Index to the Court Book of the Skinners' Company 1551–1617 [1697]. GH MS 30,710/1

Skinners' Company Court Book, 1551–1617. GH MS 30,708/1

Skinners' Company Court Book, 1577–1617. GH MS 30,708/2

Skinners' Company Court Book, 1617–51. GH MS 30,708/3

Skinners' Company: Receipts and Payments, 1564–1596 (Wardens' Account Books). GH MS 30,727/4

Skinners' Company: Receipts and Payments, 1596 [1597]-1617 (Wardens' Account Books). GH MS 30,727/5

Skinners' Company: Receipts and Payments, 1617–1646 (Wardens' Account Books). GH MS 30,727/6

Smith, William, 'A Breeff Description of THE FAMOVS CITTIE OF LONDON Capitall Cittie of this Realme of England. &c. Ann°. 1588'. BL Harley MS 6363 [transcribed by Andrew Gordon]

'Speeches on several occasions of Sir Heneage Finch, Recorder of London, 1620–1627'. British Library Add. MS 18016

Vintners' Register of Accountes from the Year 1582 to 1617. GH MS 15,333/2

Primary works

Lord Mayors' Shows

Bulteel, John (ascr.), *Londons triumph* (London: printed for N. Brook 1656; Wing B5455)

Dekker, Thomas, *Troia-Noua triumphans* (London: Nicholas Okes 1612; STC 6530)

——, *Brittannia's honor* (London: Nicholas Okes and John Norton 1628; STC 6493)

——, *Londons tempe, or, The feild of happines* (London: Nicholas Okes 1629; STC 6509)

Heywood, Thomas, *Londons ius honorarium* (London: Nicholas Okes 1631; STC 13351)

——, *Londini artium & scientiarum scaturigo. Or, Londons fountaine of arts and sciences* (London: Nicholas Okes 1632; STC 13347)

——, *Londini emporia, or Londons mercatura* (London: Nicholas Okes 1633; STC 13348)

——, *Londini sinus salutis; or, Londons harbour of health and happinesse* (London: Robert Raworth 1635; STC 13348a)

——, *Londini speculum: or, Londons mirror* (London: I. Okes 1637; STC 13349)

——, *Porta pietatis, or, The port or harbour of piety* (London: J. Okes 1638; STC 13359)

——, *Londini status pacatus; or, Londons peaceable estate* (London: J. Okes 1639; STC 13350)

Jordan, Thomas, *London's Resurrection* (London: printed for Henry Brome 1671; Wing J1040)

——, *London triumphant* (London: printed by W. G. for Nath. Brook and John Playford 1672; Wing J1036)

——, *The Goldsmiths Jubile [sic]: Or, Londons Triumphs* (London: printed by W. Godbid for John Playford 1674; Wing J1033)

——, *The Triumphs of London* (London: printed by J. Macock for John Playford 1675; Wing J1068)

——, *London's Triumphs* (London: printed for John Playford 1676; Wing J1042)

——, *Londons Triumphs* (London: printed for John Playford 1677: Wing J1043)

——, *London's Joy* (London: printed for John and Henry Playford 1681; Wing J1038)

Middleton, Thomas, *The triumphs of truth* (London: Nicholas Okes 1613; STC 17903)

——, *The triumphs of truth . . . Shewing also his Lordships Entertainement vpon Michaelmas day last* (London: Nicholas Okes 1613; STC 17904)

——, *The tryumphs of honor and industry* (London: Nicholas Okes 1617; STC 17899)

——, *The triumphs of loue and antiquity* (London: Nicholas Okes 1619; STC 17902)

——, *The sunne in Aries* (London: Edward Allde 1621; STC 17895)

——, *The triumphs of honor and vertue* (London: Nicholas Okes 1622; STC 17900)

——, *The triumphs of integrity* (London: Nicholas Okes 1623; STC 17901)

——, *The triumphs of health and prosperity* (London: Nicholas Okes 1626; STC 17898)

Munday, Anthony, *The triumphes of re-united Britania* (London: W. Jaggard 1605; STC 18279)

——, *Camp-bell, or the ironmongers faire feild* (London: William Jaggard 1609; STC 18265)

——, *Chruso-thriambos. The triumphes of golde* (London: William Jaggard 1611; STC 18267)

——, *Chruso-thriambos. The triumphes of golde* (London: William Jaggard 1611; STC 18267.5)

——, *Himatia-Poleos. The triumphs of olde draperie, or the rich Cloathing of England* (London: Edward Allde 1614; STC 18274)

——, *Metropolis coronata, the triumphes of ancient drapery: or, Rich cloathing of England, in a second yeeres performance* (London: George Purslowe 1615; STC 18275)

——, *Chrysanaleia: the golden fishing: or, Honour of fishmongers* (London: George Purslowe 1616; STC 18266)

——, *Sidero-Thriambos. Or Steele and iron triumphing* (London: Nicholas Okes 1618; STC 18278)

——, *The triumphs of the Golden Fleece* (London: T. Snodham 1623; STC 18280)

Nelson, Thomas, *The deuice of the pageant: set forth by the worshipfull companie of the fishmongers, for the right honorable Iohn Allot* (London 1590; STC 18423)

Peele, George, *The deuice of the pageant borne before Woolstone Dixi Lord Maior of the citie of London* (London: Edward Allde 1585; STC 19533)

——, *Descensus astraeae the device of a l'ageant* [*sic*] *borne before M. William Web* (London: printed for William Wright 1591; STC 19532)

Settle, Elkanah, *The Triumphs of London* (London: printed by J. Orme 1693; Wing S2723)

——, *The Triumphs of London* (London: printed by Richard Baldwin 1694; Wing 2727)

——, *The Triumphs of London* (London: printed by Jer. Wilkins 1695; Wing S2726)

——, *Glory's Resurrection* (London: printed for R. Barnham 1698; Wing S2688)

Squire, John, *Tes Irenes Trophaea. Or, the Tryumphes of Peace* (London: Nicholas Okes 1620; STC 23120.5)

Tatham, John, *Londons Tryumph* (London: printed by Thomas Mabb 1658; Wing T225)

——, *London's Tryumph* (London: printed by Thomas Mabb 1659; Wing T223)

——, *The royal oake with other various and delightfull scenes presented on the water and the land* (London: printed by S. G. for R. B. 1660; Wing T232)

——, *London's Tryumphs* (London: printed by Thomas Mabb 1661; Wing T228)

——, *Londons Triumph* (London: printed for H. Brome 1662; Wing T224)

——, *Londinum Triumphans* (London: printed by W. G. for Henry Brome 1663; Wing T221)

——, *Londons Triumphs* (London: printed by W. G. for H. Brome 1664; Wing T227)

Taubman, Matthew, *London's Triumph, or the Goldsmiths Jubilee* (London: printed by J. Leake 1687; Wing T243)

Taylor, John, *The triumphs of fame and honour* (London: [s.n.] 1634; STC 23808)

Webster, John, *Monuments of Honor* (London: Nicholas Okes 1624; STC 25175)

Other primary works

Anon., *The king of Denmarkes welcome Containing his ariuall, abode, and entertainement, both in the citie and other places* (London: printed by Edward Allde 1606; STC 5194)

——, *The Magnificent, Princely, and most Royall Entertainments giuen to the High and Mightie Prince, and Princesse, Frederick, Count Palatine* (London: printed [by Thomas Snodham] for Nathaniel Butter 1613; STC 11357)

——, *Hic mulier: or, The man-woman* (London: printed for I. T. 1620; STC 13375.5)

——, *The Several speeches made to the Honorable Sir Richard Brown lord mayor of the city of London* (London: printed by R. Wood 1660; Wing S2812A)

——, *The excellent and renowned history of the famous Sir Richard Whittington* (London: printed by J. Conyers 1690; Wing E3780A)

Babington, John, *Pyrotechnia or, A discourse of artificiall fire-works* (London: printed by Thomas Harper for Ralph Mab 1635; STC 1099)

Barriffe, William, *Mars, his triumph* (London: printed by I. L. for Ralph Mab 1639; STC 1505)

Bate, John, *The mysteryes of nature, and art* (London: printed by Thomas Harper for Ralph Mab 1634; STC 1577.7)

Calver, Edward (ascr.), *The foure ages of man* (London: to be sold by P. Stent [i.e. J. Hind] 1635; STC 197.7)

Chapman, George, *Homer's Odysses* (London: printed by Richard Field for Nathaniel Butter 1614; STC 13636)

——, Ben Jonson and John Marston, *Eastward hoe* (London: printed for William Apsley 1605; STC 4970)

Cooke, John, *Greenes Tu quoque, or, The cittie gallant* (London: printed by Nicholas Okes for John Trundle 1614; STC 5673)

Davies, Richard (ascr.), *Chesters triumph in honor of her prince* (London: printed [by William Stansby] for I. B[rowne] 1610; STC 5118)

Dekker, Thomas, *The magnificent entertainment giuen to King Iames, Queene Anne his wife, and Henry Frederick the Prince, vpon the day of his Maiesties tryumphant passage (from the Tower) through his honourable citie (and chamber) of London* (London: printed by Thomas Creede, Humphrey Lownes, Edward Allde and others for Tho. Man the yonger 1604; STC 6510)

——, *The magnificent entertainment giuen to King Iames, Queene Anne his vvife, and Henry Frederick the Prince, vppon the day of his Maiesties tryumphant passage (from the Tower) through his honourable cittie (and chamber) of London* (Edinburgh: Thomas Finlason 1604; STC 6512)

——, *The whole magnificent entertainment giuen to King Iames, Queene Anne his wife, and Henry Frederick the Prince; vpon the day of his Maiesties tryumphant passage (from the Tower) through his honorable citie (and chamber) of London* (London: printed by E. Allde, Humphrey Lownes, and others for Tho. Man the yonger 1604; STC 6513)

——, *The seuen deadly sinnes of London* (London: printed by E[dward] A[llde and S. Stafford] for Nathaniel Butter 1606; STC 6522)

——, *Iests to make you merie* (London: printed by Nicholas Okes for Nathaniel Butter 1607; STC 6541)

——, *West-ward hoe* (London: printed by William Jaggard 1607; STC 6540)

——, *The guls horne-booke* (London: printed for R. S. 1609; STC 6500)

——, *Warres, Warre[s], Warres* (London: [By Nicholas Okes] for I. G[rismand?] 1628; STC 6531)

——, *The second part of The honest whore* (London: printed by Elizabeth Allde for Nathaniel Butter 1630; STC 6506)

——, *A tragi-comedy: called, Match mee in London* (London: printed by B. Alsop and T. Fawcet, for H. Seile 1631; STC 6529)

Dugdale, Gilbert, *The time triumphant declaring in briefe, the ariual of our soueraigne liedge Lord, King Iames into England* (London: R. Blower 1604; STC 7292)

Fennor, William, *Cornu-copiae, Pasquils night-cap* (London: printed for Thomas Thorp 1612; STC 10782.5)

Fitzgeffrey, Henry, *Satyres: and satyricall epigrams with certaine obseruations at Black-Fryers* (London: printed by Edward Allde 1617; STC 10945)

G., B., *The Ioyfull receyuing of the Queenes most excellent Maiestie into hir Highnesse Citie of Norwich* (London: printed by Henry Bynneman 1578; STC 11627)

'G. M.', *Certaine characters and essayes of prison and prisoners* (London: printed by William Jones 1618; STC 18318)

Harrison, Stephen, *The arch's [sic] of triumph erected in honor of the high and mighty prince. Iames. the first of that name* (London: John Windet 1604; STC 12863)

Heywood, Thomas, *Troia Britanica: or, Great Britaines Troy* (London: William Jaggard 1609; STC 13366)

——, *An apology for actors* (London: Nicholas Okes 1612; STC 13309)

——, *A marriage triumphe Solemnized in an epithalalium* (London: printed [by Nicholas Okes] for Edward Marchant 1613; STC 13355)

——, *The hierarchie of the blessed angells* (London: printed by Adam Islip 1635; STC 13327)

——, *A true description of His Majesties royall ship, built this yeare 1637* (London: printed by John Okes for John Aston 1637; STC 13367)

Jonson, Ben, *B. Ion: his part of King Iames his royall and magnificent entertainement through his honorable cittie of London* (London: printed by Valentine Simmes and George Eld for Edward Blount 1604; STC 14756)

——, *A pleasant comedy, called: The case is alterd* (London: printed by [Nicholas Okes] for Bartholomew Sutton, and William Barrenger 1609; STC 15748)

——, *Epicoene, or the silent woman* (London: printed by William Stansby 1620; STC 14763)

Jordon, Thomas, *London in Luster* (London: printed for John Playford 1679; Wing J1035)

Marston, John, *The Dutch Courtezan* (London: printed by T[homas] P[urfoot] for John Hodgets 1605; STC 17475)

Mayne, Jasper, *The citye match* (Oxford: printed by Leonard Lichfield 1639; STC 17750)

Middleton, Thomas, *Ciuitatis amor. The cities loue. An entertainment by water, at Chelsey, and White-hall* (London: printed by Nicholas Okes for Thomas Archer 1616; STC 17878)

——, *Honorable entertainments, compos'de for the seruice of this noble cittie* (London: printed by George Eld 1621; STC 17886)

—— and William Rowley, *The changeling* (London: printed for Humphrey Mosley 1653; Wing M1980)

Munday, Anthony, *Zelauto. The fountaine of fame* (London: printed by John Charlewood 1580; STC 18283)

——, *Londons loue, to the Royal Prince Henrie* (London: printed by Edward Allde for Nathaniel Fosbrooke 1610; STC 13159)

——, *The third booke of Amadis de Gaule* (London: printed by Nicholas Okes 1618; STC 543)

Ogilby, John, *The relation of his Majestie's Entertainment passing through the City of London* (London: printed by Thomas Roycroft for Richard Marriott 1661; Wing O181)

Prynne, William, *Histrio-mastix. The players scourge, or, actors tragaedie* (London: printed by Edward Allde, Augustine Mathewes, Thomas Cotes and William Jones for Michael Sparke 1633; STC 20464a)

Roberts, Henry, *Englands Farewell to Christian the fourth, famous King of Denmarke* (London: printed for William Welby 1606; STC 21079)

——, *The Most royall and Honorable entertainement, of the famous and remowmed* [sic] *King, Christiern* [sic] *the fourth* (London: printed for H. R. 1606; STC 21085)

Selden, John, *Table-talk, being discourses of John Seldon* [sic] (London: printed for E. Smith 1696; Wing S2438)

Sharpham, Edward, *The fleire* (London: printed by Edward Allde 1607; STC 22384)

Shirley, James, *A contention for honour and riches* (London: printed by Elizabeth Allde for William Cooke 1633; STC 22439)

——, *Honoria and Mammon* (London: printed by T. W. for John Crook 1659; Wing 3474)

Stow, John, *A suruay of London* (London: printed by John Windet for John Wolfe 1598; STC 23341)

——, *A suruay of London* (London: John Windet 1603; STC 23343)

—— (eds) Anthony Munday, Humphrey Dyson and others, *The survey of London* (London: printed for Nicholas Bourn 1633; STC 23345.5)

——, *A survey of the cities of London and Westminster: containing the original, antiquity, increase, modern estate and government of those cities. Written at first in the year MDXCVIII. By John Stow, citizen and native of London. . . . Now lastly, corrected, improved, and very much enlarged: . . . by John Strype* (London, 1720). 2 vols.

Tatham, John, *Londons Glory Represented by Time, Truth and Fame* (London: printed by William Godbid 1660; Wing T222)

Taylor, John, *Heauens blessing, and earths ioy* (London: printed for Joseph Hunt 1613; STC 23763)

——, *Prince Charles his welcome from Spaine* (London: printed by George Eld 1623; STC 23789.7)

——, *Taylors pastorall being both historicall and satyricall* (London: printed by George Purslowe 1624; STC 23801)

——, *Taylors feast* (London: J. Okes 1638; STC 23798)

——, *Englands comfort, and Londons ioy* (London: printed for Francis Coules 1641; Wing T456)

Webster, John, *The tragedy of the Dutchesse of Malfy* (London: printed by Nicholas Okes 1623; STC 25176)

Whetstone, George, *The right excellent and famous historye, of Promos and Cassandra* (London: printed by John Charlewood for Richard Jones 1578; STC 25347)

Whitney, Geffrey, *A choice of emblemes, and other deuises* (Leyden: Francis Raphelengius 1586; STC 25438)

Wither, George, *Britain's remembrancer* (London: to be sold by John Grismond 1628; STC 25899)

Secondary works

Adams, Elizabeth D., 'A fragment of a Lord Mayor's pageant', *Modern Language Notes*, 32:5 (1917), 285–9

Aldous, Vivienne, 'Cockayne, Sir William'. *Oxford DNB*. www.oxforddnb.com/view/articleHL/5824. Accessed 23.7.07

Andersen, Jennifer and Elizabeth Sauer (eds), *Books and Readers in Early Modern England* (Philadelphia: University of Pennsylvania Press 2002)

Anderson, Susan, ' "A true Copie": Gascoigne's princely pleasures and the textual representation of courtly performance', *Early Modern Literary Studies* 14:1 (2008) 6.1–43. http://purl.oclc.org/emls/14-1/article5.htm. Accessed 23.6.09

Anglo, Sydney, 'William Cornish in a play, pageants, prison, and politics', *The Review of English Studies*, 10:40 (1959), 347–60

——, *Spectacle, Pageantry, and Early Tudor Policy* (Oxford: The Clarendon Press 1969)

Anon., *Civic honours; or, a succinct historical display of the . . . election of the chief magistrate of the city of London: together with some particulars of his inauguration . . . show . . . and . . . banquet . . . on Lord Mayor's Day* (London: Sherwood 1816)

——, *Handbook of Ceremonials, &c.: A Revised Edition of the Book of Ceremonials of the City of London* (London: Whitehead Morris 1933)

Arber, Edward (ed.), *A Transcript of the Registers of the Company of Stationers of London* vols 2–4 (London: privately printed 1875–77)

Archer, Ian W., 'The London lobbies in the later sixteenth century', *The Historical Journal*, 31:1 (1988), 17–44

——, *A History of the Haberdashers' Company* (London: Phillimore and Co. 1991)

——, *The Pursuit of Stability: Social Relations in Elizabethan London* (Cambridge: Cambridge University Press 1991)

——, 'The nostalgia of John Stow', in David Smith, Richard Strier *et al.* (eds), *The Theatrical City* (Cambridge: Cambridge University Press 1995), 17–34

——, 'The arts and acts of memoralization in early modern London', in J. F. Merritt (ed.), *Imagining Early Modern London* (Cambridge: Cambridge University Press 2001), 89–113

——, 'The livery companies and charity in the sixteenth and seventeenth centuries', in Ian Gadd and Patrick Wallis (eds), *Guilds, Society and Economy in London 1450–1800* (London: CMH/IHR/Guildhall Library 2002), 15–28

——, 'Discourses of history in Elizabethan and early Stuart London', *Huntington Library Quarterly*, 68:1–2 (2005), 205–26

Archer, Jayne Elisabeth and Sarah Knight, 'Elizabetha Triumphans', in Jayne Elisabeth Archer, Elizabeth Goldring and Sarah Knight (eds), *The Progresses, Pageants, and Entertainments of Queen Elizabeth I* (Oxford: Oxford University Press 2007), 1–23

Ashton, Robert, *The City and the Court* (Cambridge: Cambridge University Press 1979)

——, 'Popular entertainment and social control in later Elizabethan and early Stuart London', *The London Journal*, 9:1 (1983), 3–19

Astington, John H., 'The ages of man and the Lord Mayor's Show', in Helen Ostovich, Mary V. Silcox and Graham Roebuck (eds), *Other Voices, Other Views: Expanding the Canon in English Renaissance Studies* (Newark: University of Delaware Press 1999), 74–90

——, 'The succession of sots, or fools and their fathers', *Medieval and Renaissance Drama in England*, 20 (2007), 225–35

Bach, Rebecca Ann, *Colonial Transformations* (New York and Basingstoke: Palgrave 2000)

Bald, R. C., 'Middleton's civic employments', *Modern Philology*, 31 (1933), 65–78

Barbour, Reid, 'Peele, George'. *Oxford DNB*. www.oxforddnb.com/view/article/21768. Accessed 23.7.07

Barker, William, 'Mulcaster, Richard'. *Oxford DNB*. www.oxforddnb.com/view/articleHL/19509. Accessed 23.7.07

Baron, Xavier, 'Medieval traditions in the English Renaissance: John Stow's portrayal of London in 1603', in Rhoda Schnur and Ann Moss (eds), *Acta Conventus Neo-Latini Hafniensis* (Binghamton, NY: Medieval & Renaissance Texts & Studies 1994), 133–41

Barrett, Robert W., 'Royal freight: City-Crown negotiations in Anthony Munday's 1610 *London's Love to the Royal Prince Henry*', *Research Opportunities in Medieval and Renaissance Drama*, 47 (2008), 1–24

Barron, Caroline, 'Chivalry, pageantry and merchant culture in medieval London', in Peter Coss and Maurice Keen (eds), *Heraldry, Pageantry and Social Display in Medieval England* (Woodbridge: Boydell 2002), 219–41

——, 'Pageantry on London Bridge in the early fifteenth century', in David N. Klausner and Karen Sawyer Marsalek (eds), *'Bring furth the pagants'*: *Essays in Early English Drama Presented to Alexandra F. Johnston* (Toronto: University of Toronto Press 2007), 91–104

Barton, Anne, 'The London scene: city and court', in Margreta de Grazia and Stanley Wells (eds), *Shakespeare* (Cambridge: Cambridge University Press 2001), 115–28

Barty-King, Hugh, *The Salters' Company 1394–1994* (London: The Salters' Company 1994)

Bath, Michael, *Speaking Pictures: English Emblem Books and Renaissance Culture* (London: Longman 1994)

Bawcutt, N. W., 'A crisis of Laudian censorship: Nicholas and John Okes and the publication of Sales's *An Introduction to a Devout Life* in 1637', *The Library*, 1 (2000), 403–38

Beasley, Gerald, 'Shute, John'. *Oxford DNB*. www.oxforddnb.com/view/article/25483. Accessed 23.6.09

Benbow, R. Mark, 'Sixteenth-century dramatic performances for the London livery companies', *Notes and Queries*, 29:227 (1992), 129–31

Bentley, Gerald Eades, *The Profession of Player in Shakespeare's Time, 1590–1642* (Princeton: Princeton University Press 1984)

Berek, Peter, 'Genres, early modern theatrical title pages, and the authority of print', in Marta Straznicky (ed.), *The Book of the Play: Playwrights, Stationers and Readers in Early Modern England* (Amherst: University of Massachusetts Press 2006), 159–75

Bergeron, David M., 'Harrison, Jonson and Dekker: The Magnificent Entertainment for King James (1604)', *Journal of the Warburg and Courtauld Institutes*, 31 (1968), 445–8

——, 'The Christmas family: artificers in English civic pageantry', *English Literary History*, 35:3 (1968), 354–64

——, 'The emblematic nature of English civic pageantry', *Renaissance Drama*, 1 (1968), 167–98

——, 'Heywood's "Londons Ius Honorarium"', *Studies in Bibliography*, 22 (1969), 223–6

——, 'Symbolic landscape in English civic pageantry', *Renaissance Quarterly*, 22:1 (1969), 32–7

——, 'Charles I's Royal Entries into London', *Guildhall Miscellany*, 3:2 (1970), 91–7

——, 'The Elizabethan Lord Mayor's Show', *Studies in English Literature*, 10:2 (1970), 269–85

——, 'Thomas Dekker's Lord Mayor's Shows', *English Studies*, 51:1 (1970), 2–15

——, 'Venetian state papers and English civic pageantry, 1558–1642', *Renaissance Quarterly*, 23:1 (1970), 37–47

——, 'The wax figures in *The Duchess of Malfi*', *Studies in English Literature*, 18:2 (1978), 331–9

——, 'Gilbert Dugdale and the royal entry of James I (1604)', *Journal of Medieval and Renaissance Studies*, 13 (1983), 111–25

——, 'Middleton's moral landscape: *A Chaste Maid in Cheapside* and *The Triumphs of Truth*', in Kenneth Friedenreich (ed.), *'Accompaninge the players': Essays Celebrating Thomas Middleton, 1580–1980* (New York: AMS 1983), 133–46

——, 'Urban pastoralism in English civic pageants', *Elizabethan Theatre*, 14 (1983), 129–43

——, 'Middleton's *No Wit, No Help* and civic pageantry', in David Bergeron (ed.), *Pageantry in the Shakespearean Theatre* (Athens: University of Georgia Press 1985), 65–80

—— (ed.) *Pageants and Entertainments of Anthony Munday: A Critical Edition* (New York and London: Garland 1985)

——, 'Representation in Renaissance English civic pageants', *Theatre Journal*, 40:3 (1988), 319–31

——, 'Pageants, politics, and patrons', *Medieval and Renaissance Drama in England*, 6 (1993), 139–52

——, 'Thomas Middleton and Anthony Munday: artistic rivalry?', *Studies in English Literature*, 36 (1996), 461–79

——, 'Stuart civic pageants and textual performance', *Renaissance Quarterly*, 51:1 (1998), 163–83

——, *Practicing Renaissance Scholarship* (Pittsburgh: Duquesne University Press 2000)

——, 'King James's civic pageant and parliamentary speech in March 1604', *Albion*, 34:2 (2002), 213–31

——, *English Civic Pageantry 1558–1642* Revised edition (Medieval and Renaissance Texts and Studies vol. 267. University of Arizona 2003)

——, *Textual Patronage in English Drama, 1570–1640* (Aldershot: Ashgate 2006)

——, 'The "I" of the beholder: Thomas Churchyard and the 1578 Norwich pageant', in Jayne Elisabeth Archer, Elizabeth Goldring and Sarah Knight (eds), *The Progresses, Pageants, and Entertainments of Queen Elizabeth I* (Oxford: Oxford University Press 2007), 142–59

Berlin, Michael, 'Civic ceremony in early modern London', *Urban History Yearbook*, 19 (1986), 15–27

Billington, Sandra, 'Butchers and Fishmongers: their historical contribution to London's festivity', *Folklore*, 101:1 (1990), 97–103

Blanchard, Ian, 'Gresham, Sir Richard'. *Oxford DNB*. www.oxforddnb. com/view/article/11504. Accessed 23.7.07

Blanchard, Joël, 'Le spectacle du rite: les entrées royales', *Revue Historique*, 627 (2003), 475–519

Blayney, Peter, *The Texts of* King Lear *and Their Origins*, vol. I (Cambridge: Cambridge University Press 1982)

——, 'The publication of playbooks', in John D. Cox and David Scott

Kastan (eds), *A New History of Early English Drama* (New York: Columbia University Press 1997), 383–422

Boffey, Julia and Pamela King (eds), *London and Europe in the Later Middle Ages* (London: Centre for Mediaeval and Renaissance Studies 1995)

Bonahue, Edward, 'Citizen History: Stow's *Survey of London*', *Studies in English Literature*, 38:1 (1998), 61–85

Borg, Alan, *The History of the Worshipful Company of Painter-Stainers* (London: Jeremy Mills Publishing Co. / The Painter-Stainers 2005)

Bowers, Rick, 'Dick Whittington, Stow's *Survey*, and "Catte Streete"', *English Language Notes*, 43:1 (2005), 33–9

Bowles, Edmund A., 'Musical instruments in civic processions during the Middle Ages', *Acta Musicologica*, 33 (1961), 147–61

Bradbrook, M. C., *John Webster, Citizen and Dramatist* (London: Weidenfeld and Nicolson 1980)

——, 'The politics of pageantry: social implications in Jacobean London', in Antony Coleman *et al.* (eds), *Poetry and Drama, 1570–1700: Essays in Honour of Harold F. Brooks* (London: Methuen 1981), 60–75

——, 'London pageantry and lawyers' theater in the early seventeenth century', in Peter Erickson and Coppélia Kahn (eds), *Shakespeare's 'Rough Magic': Renaissance Essays in Honor of C. L. Barber* (Newark and London: University of Delaware Press 1985), 256–68

Breight, Curtis, 'Realpolitik and Elizabethan ceremony: the Earl of Hertford's entertainment of Elizabeth at Elvetham, 1591', *Renaissance Quarterly*, 45:1 (1992), 20–48

Brenner, Robert, 'The civil war politics of London's merchant community', *Past and Present*, 58 (1973), 53–107

——, *Merchants and Revolution* (Cambridge: Cambridge University Press 1993)

Brigden, Susan, 'Religion and social obligation in early sixteenth-century London', *Past and Present*, 103 (1984), 67–112

——, *London and the Reformation* (Oxford: Clarendon 1989)

Bromham, A. A., 'Thomas Middleton's *The Triumphs of Truth*: City politics in 1613', *The Seventeenth Century*, 10 (1995), 1–25

Bryant, Lawrence M., 'Configurations of the community in late medieval spectacles: Paris and London during the dual monarchy', in Barbara A. Hanawalt and Kathryn L. Reyerson (eds), *City and Spectacle in Medieval Europe* (Minneapolis: University of Minnesota Press 1994), 3–33

Burden, Michael, '"For the lustre of the subject": music for the Lord Mayor's Day in the Restoration', *Early Music*, 23:4 (1995), 585–602

Burrage, Michael C. and David Corry, 'At sixes and sevens: occupational status in the City of London from the fourteenth to the seventeenth century', *American Sociological Review*, 46:4 (1981), 375–93

Butler, Martin, 'Jonson's London and its theatres', in Richard Harp and

Stanley Stewart (eds), *Ben Jonson* (Cambridge: Cambridge University Press 2000), 15–29

—— and David Lindley, 'Restoring Astraea: Jonson's *Masque for the Fall of Somerset*', *English Literary History*, 61:4 (1994), 807–27

Butterworth, Philip, *Theatre of Fire: Special Effects in Early English and Scottish Theatre* (London: The Society for Theatre Research 1998)

Byrne, Maurice, 'Instruments for the Goldsmiths Company', *The Galpin Society Journal*, 24 (1971), 63–8

Calendar of State Papers Domestic 1591–1603, vol. V (London 1872)

Calendar of State Papers Venetian 1558–1580, vol. VII (London 1890)

Calendar of State Papers Venetian 1603–1607, vol. X (London 1900)

Calendar of State Papers Venetian 1607–1610, vol. XI (London 1904)

Calendar of State Papers Venetian 1616–1617, vol. XIV (London 1908)

Calendar of State Papers Venetian 1617–1619, vol. XV (London 1909)

Callaghan, Dympna, *Shakespeare Without Women: Representing Gender and Race on the Renaissance Stage* (London: Routledge 2000)

Cannadine, David, 'Introduction', in David Cannadine and Simon Price (eds), *Rituals of Royalty: Power and Ceremonial in Traditional Societies* (Cambridge: Cambridge University Press 1987), 1–19

Cannon, Debbie, 'London pride: citizenship and the fourteenth-century custumals of the City of London', in Sarah Rees Jones (ed.), *Learning and Literacy in Medieval England and Abroad* (Turnhout: Brepols 2003), 179–98

Capp, Bernard, *The World of John Taylor the Water Poet 1578–1653* (Oxford: The Clarendon Press 1994)

——, 'Taylor, John'. *Oxford DNB*. www.oxforddnb.com/view/article/27044. Accessed 7.8.08

Carlyle, Ursula, *The Mercers' Company* (London: The Mercers' Company 1994)

Carnegie, David, 'Galley foists, the Lord Mayor's show, and the early modern English drama', *Early Theatre*, 7:2 (2004), 49–74

——, 'Introduction to *Monuments of Honour*', in David Gunby, David Carnegie and MacDonald P. Jackson (eds), *The Works of John Webster: An Old-spelling Critical Edition*, vol. 3 (Cambridge: Cambridge University Press 2007), 223–50

Carr, H. G., 'Barge flags of the City livery companies of London', *Mariner's Mirror*, 28 (1942), 222–30

Cartwright, John, 'The Antwerp *Landjuweel* of 1561: a survey of the texts', in Robert A. Taylor *et al.* (eds), *The Centre and Its Compass: Studies in Medieval Literature in Honor of Professor John Leyerle* (Kalamazoo: Western Michigan University 1993), 71–86

Chambers, E. K., *The Elizabethan Stage*, vol. I (Oxford: The Clarendon Press 1923)

City of London (England), Public Relations Office, *The Lord Mayor of London's Jacobean Thames Pageant* (London: The Corporation 1988)

Clark, A. M. (ed.), *Two Pageants by Thomas Heywood, 1632, 1633* (Oxford: Theatre Miscellany, Luttrell Society Publications no. 14, 1953)

Clark, Peter, 'The ownership of books in England, 1560–1640: the example of some Kentish townsfolk', in Lawrence Stone (ed.), *Schooling and Society* (Baltimore and London: Johns Hopkins University Press 1976), 95–111

Clark, Sandra, *The Elizabethan Pamphleteers* (New Brunswick: Associated University Presses 1985)

Claus, Peter, 'Recalling the City: the Lord Mayor's Show and pageants of memory', *Ranam: Recherches Anglaises et Nord-Américaines*, 36:3 (2003), 139–44

Clegg, Cyndia Susan, 'Renaissance play-readers, ordinary and extraordinary', in Marta Straznicky (ed.), *The Book of the Play: Playwrights, Stationers and Readers in Early Modern England* (Amherst: University of Massachusetts Press 2006), 23–38

Clode, Charles, *The Early History of the Guild of Merchant Taylors* (London: privately printed, 1888)

Cockagne, G. E., *The Lord Mayors and Sheriffs of London* (London: Phillimore and Co. 1857)

Collections Volume V (Oxford: The Malone Society 1960)

Collections Volume XIII: Jacobean and Caroline Revels Accounts, 1603–1642 (Oxford: The Malone Society 1986)

Collington, Philip, ' "A puppet-play in pictures": Thomas Middleton's emblematic drama', in Helen Ostovich, Mary V. Silcox and Graham Roebuck (eds), *Other Voices, Other Views: Expanding the Canon in English Renaissance Studies* (Newark: University of Delaware Press 1999), 91–131

Corns, Thomas N., 'Literature and London', in David Loewenstein and Janel Mueller (eds), *The Cambridge History of Early Modern English Literature* (Cambridge: Cambridge University Press 2002), 544–64

Cowan, Alexander and Jill Steward (eds), *The City and the Senses: Urban Culture since 1500* (Aldershot: Ashgate 2007)

Crawford, Anne, *A History of the Vintners' Company* (London: Constable 1977)

Cressy, David, *Bonfires and Bells: National Memory and the Protestant Calendar in Elizabethan and Stuart England* (London: Weidenfeld and Nicolson 1990)

Cuthbertson, David, 'The Stam Boeck von den Michiel [sic] van Mer. Being a brief narrative regarding the water colour illustrations, and an account of the noblemen and others whose contributions are contained in the volume' (unpublished: Edinburgh University Library 1919)

Dart, Thurston, 'The Triumphs of Oriana', *The Musical Times*, 103 (1962), 406

Davidson, Clifford, *Technology, Guilds and Early English Drama* (Kalamazoo: Medieval Institute Publications, 1997)

——, *Festivals and Plays in Late Medieval Britain* (Aldershot: Ashgate 2007)

Davies, Matthew (ed.), *The Merchant Taylors' Company of London: Court Minutes 1486–1493* (Stamford: Richard III and Yorkist History Trust / Paul Watkins 2000)

—— and Ann Saunders, *History of the Merchant Taylors' Company* (London: The Merchant Taylors' Company 2004)

Dekker, Thomas, ed. Fredson Bowers, *The Dramatic Works of Thomas Dekker: Volume IV* (Cambridge: Cambridge University Press 1961)

DeMolen, Richard L., 'Richard Mulcaster and Elizabethan pageantry', *Studies in English Literature*, 14:2 (1974), 209–21

Doolittle, Ian, *The Mercers' Company, 1579–1959* (London: The Mercers' Company 1994)

Dutton, Richard, '*King Lear, The Triumphs of Reunited Britannia* and the "matter of Britain"', *Literature and History*, 12:2 (1986), 139–51

—— (ed.), *Jacobean Civic Pageants* (Keele University: Ryburn Publishing 1995)

Easterling, Heather C., *Parsing the City: Jonson, Middleton, Dekker, and City Comedy's London as Language* (London: Routledge 2007)

Englefield, W. A. D., *The History of the Painter-Stainers Company of London* (London: Hazell, Watson and Viney Ltd. 1950)

Enterline, Lynn, 'Rhetoric, discipline and the theatricality of everyday life in Elizabethan grammar schools', in Peter Holland and Stephen Orgel (eds), *From Performance to Print in Shakespeare's England* (Basingstoke: Palgrave 2006), 173–90

Ewbank, Inga-Stina, 'Masques and pageants', in Boris Ford (ed), *The Cambridge Guide to the Arts in Britain. Volume 4: The Seventeenth Century* (Cambridge: Cambridge University Press 1990), 110–17

Fairholt, F. W., *Lord Mayors' Pageants*, vols. I and II (London: The Percy Society 1843–4)

——, *The Civic Garland* (London: The Percy Society 1845)

Farmer, Alan B. and Zachary Lesser, 'Vile arts: the marketing of English printed drama, 1512–1660', *Research Opportunities in Renaissance Drama*, 39 (2000), 77–165

——, 'The popularity of playbooks revisited', *Shakespeare Quarterly*, 56:1 (2005), 1–32

Fisher, Margery, 'Notes on the sources of some incidents in Middleton's London plays', *The Review of English Studies*, 15:59 (1939), 283–93

Fletcher, Alan J., 'Playing and staying together: sixteenth-century Dublin', in Alexandra F. Johnston and Wim Hüsken (eds), *Civic Ritual and Drama* (Amsterdam: Rodopi 1997), 15–37

Ford, L. L. 'Wedel, Lupold von'. *Oxford DNB*. www.oxforddnb.com/view/articleHL/92463. Accessed 23.6.09

Forker, Charles R., 'Two notes on John Webster and Anthony Munday:

unpublished entries in the records of the Merchant Taylors', *English Language Notes*, 6 (1968), 26–34

——, *Skull Beneath the Skin: The Achievement of John Webster* (Carbondale and Edwardsville: Southern Illinois University Press 1986)

Foster, Frank Freeman, 'Merchants and bureaucrats in Elizabethan London', *The Guildhall Miscellany*, 4 (1971–3), 149–60

——, *The Politics of Stability: A Portrait of the Rulers in Elizabethan London* (London: Royal Historical Society 1977)

Fryer, Peter, *Staying Power: The History of Black People in Britain* (London: Pluto 1984)

Fumerton, Patricia, 'Introduction: a new new historicism', in Patricia Fumerton and Simon Hunt (eds), *Renaissance Culture and the Everyday* (Philadelphia: University of Pennsylvania Press 1999), 1–17

Gadd, Ian, 'Early modern printed histories of the London livery companies', in Ian Gadd and Patrick Wallis (eds), *Guilds, Society and Economy in London 1450–1800* (London: CMH/IHR/Guildhall Library 2002), 29–50

——, 'Allde, Edward'. *Oxford DNB.* www.oxforddnb.com/view/article/363. Accessed 29.10.07

Gasper, Julia, *The Dragon and the Dove: The Plays of Thomas Dekker* (Oxford: The Clarendon Press 1990)

Geertz, Clifford, 'Centers, kings and charisma: reflections on the symbolics of power', in Joseph Ben-David and Terry Nichols Clark (eds), *Culture and Its Creators* (Chicago and London: Chicago University Press 1977), 150–71

Gentles, Ian, 'Political funerals during the English Revolution', in Stephen Porter (ed.), *London and the Civil War* (London: Macmillan 1996), 205–24

Gibson, Strickland, 'Brian Twyne', *Oxoniensia*, 5 (1940), 94–114

Girtin, Thomas, *The Golden Ram: A Narrative History of the Clothworkers' Company, 1528–1958* (London: The Clothworkers' Company 1958)

Glover, Elizabeth, *A History of the Ironmongers' Company* (London: The Ironmongers' Company 1991)

Goldring, Elizabeth, 'The funeral of Sir Philip Sidney and the politics of Elizabethan festival', in J. R. Mulryne and Elizabeth Goldring (eds), *Court Festivals of the European Renaissance* (Aldershot: Ashgate 2002), 199–224

Gordon, Andrew, 'Performing London: the map and the city in ceremony', in Andrew Gordon and Bernhard Klein (eds), *Literature, Mapping, and the Politics of Space in Early Modern Britain* (Cambridge: Cambridge University Press 2001), 69–88

Gordon, D. J., 'Poet and architect: the intellectual setting of the quarrel between Ben Jonson and Inigo Jones', *Journal of the Warburg and Courtauld Institutes*, 12 (1949), 152–78

Grady, Hugh, 'Shakespeare studies, 2005: a situated overview', *Shakespeare*, 1 (2005), 102–20

Grantley, Darryll, *London in Early Modern English Drama* (Basingstoke: Palgrave 2008)

Greg, W. W., *A Bibliography of the English Printed Drama to the Restoration*, vol. I (London: Bibliographical Society 1939)

——, *A Bibliography of the English Printed Drama to the Restoration*, vol. II (London: Bibliographical Society 1951)

——, *A Bibliography of the English Printed Drama to the Restoration*, vol. III (London: Bibliographical Society 1957)

——, *A Bibliography of the English Printed Drama to the Restoration*, vol. IV (London: Bibliographical Society 1959)

Griffiths, Paul, 'Secrecy and authority in late sixteenth- and seventeenth-century London', *The Historical Journal*, 40:4 (1997), 925–51

——, 'Building Bridewell: London's self-images, 1550–1640', in Norman L. Jones and Daniel Woolf (eds), *Local Identities in Late Medieval and Early Modern England* (Basingstoke: Palgrave 2007), 228–48

——, *Lost Londons: Change, Crime, and Control in the Capital City, 1550–1660* (Cambridge: Cambridge University Press 2008)

Grupenhoff, Richard, 'The Lord Mayors' Shows: from their origins to 1640', *Theatre Studies*, 18 (1971–2), 13–21

Guillory, John, 'A new subject for criticism', in Henry S. Turner (ed.), *The Culture of Capital* (New York and London: Routledge 2002), 223–30

Gunby, David, 'A sonnet by John Webster?', *The Review of English Studies*, 43:170 (1992), 243–5

Guppy, Henry, *The John Rylands Library Manchester: 1899–1935* (Manchester: Manchester University Press 1935)

Gurr, Andrew, *The Shakespeare Company, 1594–1642* (Cambridge: Cambridge University Press 2004)

Hackel, Heidi Brayman, *Reading Material in Early Modern England: Print, Gender, and Literacy* (Cambridge: Cambridge University Press 2005)

Halpern, Richard, *The Poetics of Primitive Accumulation* (Ithaca and London: Cornell University Press 1991)

Hamilton, Donna, *Anthony Munday and the Catholics* (Aldershot: Ashgate 2005)

Hardin, William, '"Pipe-pilgrimages" and "fruitful rivers": Thomas Middleton's civic entertainments and the water supply of early Stuart London', *Renaissance Papers* (1993), 63–73

——, 'Spectacular Constructions: ceremonial representations of city and society in early Stuart London' (PhD dissertation, University of North Carolina 1996)

——, 'Conceiving cities: Thomas Heywood's *Londini Speculum* (1637) and the making of civic identity', *Comitatus*, 28 (1997), 17–35

Harding, Vanessa, 'Citizen and mercer: Sir Thomas Gresham and the social and political world of the city of London', in Francis Ames-Lewis (ed.),

Sir Thomas Gresham and Gresham College (Aldershot: Ashgate 1999), 24–37

——, 'City, capital, and metropolis: the changing shape of seventeenth-century London', in J. F. Merritt (ed.), *Imagining Early Modern London* (Cambridge: Cambridge University Press 2001), 117–43

——, 'Pageantry on London Bridge', in Bruce Watson, Trevor Bingham and Tony Dyson, *London Bridge: 2000 Years of a River Crossing* (London: Museum of London Archaeological Service 2001), 114–15

——, *The Dead and the Living in Paris and London, 1500–1670* (Cambridge: Cambridge University Press 2002)

Harrison, Jennifer, 'Lord Mayor's Day in the 1590s', *History Today*, 42:1 (1992), 37–43

Heal, Felicity, *Hospitality in Early Modern England* (Oxford: Clarendon Press 1990)

Heath, Baron, *Some Account of the Worshipful Company of Grocers of the City of London* (London: privately printed 1869)

Hegarty, A. J., 'Twyne, Brian'. *Oxford DNB.* www.oxforddnb.com/view/article/27924. Accessed 26.10.07

Heinemann, Margot, *Puritanism and Theatre* (Oxford: Oxford University Press 1980)

Henderson, Frances, 'Clarke, Sir William'. *Oxford DNB.* www.oxforddnb.com/view/article/5536. Accessed 7.12.07

Hentschell, Roze, *The Culture of Cloth in Early Modern England* (Aldershot: Ashgate 2008)

Heywood, Thomas, *Edward IV*, ed. Richard Rowland (Manchester: Manchester University Press 2006)

Hickman, David, 'Religious belief and pious practice among London's Elizabethan elite', *The Historical Journal*, 42:4 (1999), 941–60

Higgins, Anne, 'Street and markets', in John D. Cox and David Scott Kastan (eds), *A New History of Early English Drama* (New York: Columbia University Press 1997), 77–92

Hill, Janet, *Stages and Playgoers* (Montreal and London: McGill-Queen's Press 2002)

Hill, Tracey, *Anthony Munday and Civic Culture* (Manchester: Manchester University Press 2004)

——, '"Representing the awefull authoritie of soueraigne Maiestie": monarchs and mayors in Anthony Munday's *The triumphes of re-united Britania*', in Glenn Burgess, James Lawrence and Rowland Wymer (eds), *1603: The Historical and Cultural Implications of the Accession of James I* (Basingstoke: Palgrave 2006), 15–33

Hillebrand, Harold Newcomb, *The Child Actors* (New York: Russell & Russell 1964)

Hirschfeld, Heather Anne, *Joint Enterprises: Colllaborative Drama and the Institutionalization of the English Renaissance Theater* (Amherst and Boston: University of Massachusetts Press 2004)

Holland, Peter, 'Introduction: printing performance', in Peter Holland and Stephen Orgel (eds), *From Performance to Print in Shakespeare's England* (Basingstoke: Palgrave 2006), 1–10

Homer, Ronald F., 'The Pewterers' Company country searches and the Company's regulation of prices', in Ian Gadd and Patrick Wallis (eds), *Guilds, Society and Economy in London 1450–1800* (London: CMH/IHR/Guildhall Library 2002), 101–14

Hone, William, *Ancient Mysteries Described . . . Including Notices of Ecclesiastical Shows &c* (London: printed for William Hone 1823)

Horne, David H., *The Life and Minor Works of George Peele* (New Haven: Yale University Press 1952)

Howard, Jean E., 'Competing ideologies of commerce in Thomas Heywood's *If You Know Not Me You Know Nobody, Part II*', in Henry S. Turner (ed.), *The Culture of Capital* (New York and London: Routledge 2002), 163–82

——, *Theater of a City* (Philadelphia: University of Pennsylvania Press 2007)

Howe, Nicholas (ed.), *Ceremonial Culture in Pre-Modern Europe* (Notre Dame: University of Notre Dame Press 2007)

Hulse, Lynn, '"Musick & poetry, mixed": Thomas Jordan's manuscript collection', *Early Music*, 24:1 (1996), 7–24

Hunt, Alice, *The Drama of Coronation* (Cambridge: Cambridge University Press 2008)

Hunting, Penelope, *A History of the Worshipful Company of Drapers of the City of London* (London: The Drapers' Company 1989)

Hutchings, Mark and A. A. Bromham, *Middleton and His Collaborators* (Tavistock: Northcote House 2008)

Hutton, Ronald, *The Rise and Fall of Merry England: The Ritual Year, 1400–1700* (Oxford: Oxford University Press 1994)

Ingram, William, 'Minstrels in Elizabethan London: who were they, what did they do?', *English Literary Renaissance*, 14 (1984), 29–54

Ioppolo, Grace, *Dramatists and Their Manuscripts in the Age of Shakespeare, Jonson, Middleton and Heywood* (Abingdon: Routledge 2006)

Jackson, MacDonald P., '*Titus Andronicus* Q: Shakespeare or Peele?', *Studies in Bibliography*, 49 (1996), 134–48

——, 'Textual introduction [to *Monuments of Honour*]', in David Gunby, David Carnegie and MacDonald P. Jackson (eds), *The Works of John Webster: An Old-spelling Critical Edition*, vol. 3 (Cambridge: Cambridge University Press 2007), 251–2

Jackson, Michael, (ed.), *Records of the Court of the Stationers' Company 1602 to 1640* (London: the Bibliographical Society 1957)

Jackson, William A., 'Humphrey Dyson's library, or, some observations on the survival of books', *Papers of the Bibliographical Society of America*, 43 (1949), 279–87

James, Mervyn, 'Ritual, drama and social body in the late medieval English town', *Past and Present*, 98 (1983), 3–29

Jansson, Maija and Nikolai Rogozhin (eds), *England and the North: The Russian Embassy of 1613–1614* (Philadelphia: The American Philosophical Society 1994)

Jenstad, Janelle Day, 'Institutional uses of pageantry: the case of the Goldsmiths' (unpublished conference paper, March 2002)

——, '"The City cannot hold you": social conversion in the Goldsmith's shop', *Early Modern Literary Studies*, 8:2 (2002) www.shu.ac.uk/emls/08-2/jensgold.html. Accessed 17.05.09

Johnson, A. H., *The History of the Worshipful Company of the Drapers of London*, vol. II (Oxford: Oxford University Press 1915)

Johnson, Gerald D., 'The Stationers versus the Drapers: control of the press in the late sixteenth century', *The Library*, 10:1 (1988), 1–17

Johnson, Paula, 'Jacobean ephemera and the immortal word', *Renaissance Drama*, 8 (1977), 151–72

Johnston, Alexandra F., 'Introduction', in Alexandra F. Johnston and Wim Hüsken (eds), *Civic Ritual and Drama* (Amsterdam: Rodopi 1997), 7–14

Jones, Ann Rosalind and Peter Stallybrass, *Renaissance Clothing and the Materials of Memory* (Cambridge: Cambridge University Press 2000)

Jones, Eldred, *Othello's Countrymen* (London: Oxford University Press 1965)

Kastan, David Scott, '"Shewes of honour and gladnes": dissonance and display in Mary and Philip's entry into London', *Research Opportunities in Renaissance Drama*, 33:1-2 (1994), 1–14

Kathman, David, 'Grocers, Goldsmiths and Drapers: freemen and apprentices in the Elizabethan theatre', *Shakespeare Quarterly*, 55:1 (2004), 1–49

——, *Biographical Index of English Drama Before 1660*. www.shakespeareauthorship.com/bd/. Accessed 14.10.08

——, 'Heywood, Thomas'. *Oxford DNB*. www.oxforddnb.com/view/article/13190. Accessed 23.8.07

——, 'Smith, William'. *Oxford DNB*. www.oxforddnb.com/view/articleHL/25922. Accessed 13.3.09

Kellett, J. R., 'The breakdown of gild and corporation control over the handicraft and retail trade in London', *Economic History Review*, 10:3 (1958), 381–94

Kiefer, Frederick, *Shakespeare's Visual Theatre* (Cambridge: Cambridge University Press 2003)

Kiessling, Nicolas K., *The Library of Robert Burton* (Oxford: Oxford Bibliographical Society 1988)

——, *The Library of Anthony Wood* (Oxford: Oxford Bibliographical Society 2002)

King, John N., 'Queen Elizabeth I: representations of the Virgin Queen', *Renaissance Quarterly*, 43:1 (1990), 30–74

Kinney, Arthur F., (ed.), *Renaissance Drama: An Anthology of Plays and Entertainments* (Oxford: Blackwell 2002)

Kipling, Gordon, 'Triumphal drama: form in English civic pageantry', *Renaissance Drama*, 7 (1977), 37–56

——, '"A horse designed by committee": the bureaucratics of the London civic triumph in the 1520s', *Research Opportunities in Renaissance Drama*, 31 (1992), 79–89

——, ' "He that saw it would not believe it": Anne Boleyn's royal entry into London', in Alexandra F. Johnston and Wim Hüsken (eds), *Civic Ritual and Drama* (Amsterdam: Rodopi 1997), 39–79

——, 'Wonderfull spectacles: theater and civic culture', in John D. Cox and David Scott Kastan (eds), *A New History of Early English Drama* (New York: Columbia University Press 1997), 153–71

——, *Enter the King: Theatre, Liturgy, and Ritual in the Medieval Civic Triumph* (Oxford: Clarendon 1998)

——, 'The deconstruction of the Virgin in the sixteenth-century royal entry in Scotland', *European Medieval Drama* (2005), 127–52

——, 'The King's advent transformed: the consecration of the city in the sixteenth-century civic triumph', in Nicholas Howe (ed.), *Ceremonial Culture in Pre-modern Europe* (Notre Dame: University of Notre Dame Press 2007), 89–127

Klein, Benjamin, 'Between the bums and bellies of the multitude: civic pageantry and the problem of audience in late Stuart London', *London Journal*, 17 (1992), 18–26

Lake, Peter, 'From Troynovant to Heliogabulus's Rome and back: "order" and its others in the London of John Stow', in J. F. Merritt (ed.), *Imagining Early Modern London* (Cambridge: Cambridge University Press 2001), 217–49

Lancashire, Anne, 'Plays for the London Blacksmith's Company', *Records of Early English Drama Newsletter*, 1 (1981), 12–14

——, 'Medieval to Renaissance: plays and the London Drapers' Company to 1558', in Robert A. Taylor *et al.* (eds), *The Centre and Its Compass: Studies in Medieval Literature in Honor of Professor John Leyerle* (Kalamazoo: Western Michigan University Press 1993), 297–313

——, 'Continuing civic ceremonies of 1530s London', in Alexandra F. Johnston and Wim Hüsken (eds), *Civic Ritual and Drama* (Amsterdam: Rodopi 1997), 81–105

——, *London Civic Theatre* (Cambridge: Cambridge University Press 2002)

Lang, R. G., 'Social origins and social aspirations of Jacobean London merchants', *The Economic History Review*, 27:1 (1974), 28–47

Larsen, T., 'The father of George Peele', *Modern Philology*, 26:1 (1928), 69–71

Leahy, William, 'Propaganda or a record of events? Richard Mulcaster's

The Passage Of Our Most Drad Soveraigne Lady Quene Elyzabeth Through The Citie Of London Westminster The Daye Before Her Coronacion', *Early Modern Literary Studies*, 9:1 (2003) http://purl.oclc.org/emls/09-1/leahmulc.html. Accessed 23.6.09

——, *Elizabethan Triumphal Processions* (Aldershot: Ashgate 2005)

Leech, Roger H., 'The symbolic hall: historical context and merchant culture in the early modern city', *Vernacular Architecture*, 31 (2000), 1–10

Lefkowitz, Murray, 'The Longleat papers of Bulstrode Whitelocke: new light on Shirley's "Triumph of Peace"', *Journal of the American Musicological Society*, 18:1 (1965), 42–60

Leinwand, Theodore B., 'London triumphing: the Jacobean Lord Mayor's Show', *Clio*, 11:2 (1982), 137–53

Lesser, Zachary, *Renaissance Drama and the Politics of Publication* (Cambridge: Cambridge University Press 2004)

——, 'Topographic nostalgia: play-reading, popularity, and black letter', in Marta Straznicky (ed.), *The Book of the Play: Playwrights, Stationers and Readers in Early Modern England* (Amherst: University of Massachusetts Press 2006), 99–126

Letts, Malcolm, 'Three foreigners in London, 1584–1619', *Cornhill Magazine* (1922), 316–28

Lindenbaum, Sheila, 'Ceremony and oligarchy: the London Midsummer Watch', in Barbara A. Hanawalt and Kathryn L. Reyerson (eds), *City and Spectacle in Medieval Europe* (Minneapolis: University of Minnesota Press 1994), 171–88

Lindsay, Jean S., 'So slendre effect', *Renaissance News*, 8:3 (1955), 131–6

Loach, Jennifer, 'The function of ceremonial in the reign of Henry VIII', *Past and Present*, 142 (1994), 43–68

Lobanov-Rostovsky, Sergei, 'The Triumphes of Golde: economic authority in the Jacobean Lord Mayor's Show', *English Literary History*, 60:4 (1993), 879–98

Lublin, Robert I., 'Costuming the Shakespearean Stage: visual codes of representation in early modern theatre and culture' (PhD dissertation, Ohio State University 2003)

Lusardi, James P. and Henk Gras, 'Abram Booth's eyewitness account of the 1629 Lord Mayor's Show', *Shakespeare Bulletin*, 11 (1993), 19–23

Lyell, Laetitia (ed.), *Acts of Court of the Mercers' Company, 1453–1527* (Cambridge: Cambridge University Press 1936)

MacAloon, John J. (ed.), *Rite, Drama, Festival, Spectacle* (Philadelphia: Institute for the Study of Human Issues 1984)

McGee, C. E., 'Mysteries, musters and masque: the import(s) of Elizabethan civic entertainments', in Jayne Elisabeth Archer, Elizabeth Goldring and Sarah Knight (eds), *The Progresses, Pageants, and Entertainments of Queen Elizabeth I* (Oxford: Oxford University Press 2007), 104–21

—— and John C. Meagher, 'Preliminary checklist of Tudor and Stuart entertainments: 1588–1603', *Research Opportunities in Renaissance Drama*, 24 (1981), 51–155

McGowan, Margaret M., 'The Renaissance triumph and its classical heritage', in J. R. Mulryne and Elizabeth Goldring (eds), *Court Festivals of the European Renaissance* (Aldershot: Ashgate 2002), 26–47

McGrath, Elizabeth, 'Rubens's Arch of the Mint', *Journal of the Warburg and Courtauld Institutes*, 37 (1974), 191–217

MacIntyre, Jean and Garrett P. J. Epp, ' "Cloathes worth all the rest": costumes and properties', in John D. Cox and David Scott Kastan (eds), *A New History of Early English Drama* (New York: Columbia University Press 1997), 269–85

McKenzie, D. F., *Stationers' Company Apprentices 1605–1640* (Charlottesville: Bibliographical Society of the University of Virginia 1961)

McKerrow, Ronald B., *Printers' and Publishers' Devices in England and Scotland 1485–1640* (London: the Bibliographical Society 1913)

McKitterick, David (ed.), *The Making of the Wren Library* (Cambridge: Cambridge University Press 1995)

McRae, Andrew, 'The peripatetic muse: internal travel and the cultural production of space', in Gerald MacLean, Donna Landry and Joseph P. Ward (eds), *The Country and the City Revisited* (Cambridge: Cambridge University Press 1999), 41–57

Manley, Lawrence (ed.), *London in the Age of Shakespeare: An Anthology* (London: Croom Helm 1986)

——, 'From matron to monster: Tudor-Stuart London and the languages of urban description', in Heather Dubrow and Richard Strier (eds), *The Historical Renaissance: New Essays on Tudor and Stuart Literature and Culture* (Chicago: University of Chicago Press 1988), 347–74

——, *Literature and Culture in Early Modern London* (Cambridge: Cambridge University Press 1995)

——, 'Of sites and rites', in David Smith, Richard Strier and David Bevington (eds), *The Theatrical City* (Cambridge: Cambridge University Press 1995), 35–54

——, 'Criticism and the metropolis: Tudor-Stuart London', in Glyn P. Norton (ed.), *The Cambridge History of Literary Criticism*, vol. III: The Renaissance (Cambridge: Cambridge University Press 1999), 339–47

——, 'Civic drama', in Arthur Kinney (ed.), *A Companion to Renaissance Drama* (Oxford: Blackwell 2002), 294–313

Manley, Lawrence E., Jennifer Ashworth and David Rosend, 'London 1590: a conference', *Studies in Philology*, 88: 2 (1991), 201–24

Manningham, John, (ed.) John Bruce, *Diary of John Manningham, of the Middle Temple, 1602–1603* (London: J. B. Nichols 1868)

Marcus, Leah Sinanoglou, '"Present occasions" and the shaping of Ben Jonson's masques', *English Literary History*, 45:2 (1978), 201–25

———, 'The occasion of Ben Jonson's *Pleasure Reconciled to Virtue*', *Studies in English Literature*, 19:2 (1979), 271–93

———, 'City metal and country mettle: the occasion of Ben Jonson's *Golden Age Restored*', in David Bergeron (ed.), *Pageantry in the Shakespearean Theatre* (Athens: University of Georgia Press 1985), 26–47

Mardock, James D., *Our Scene is London: Ben Jonson's City and the Space of the Author* (London: Routledge 2008)

Marotti, Arthur and Michael Bristol (eds), *Print, Manuscript and Performance* (Columbus: Ohio State University Press, 2000)

Masten, Jeffrey, 'Playwrighting: authorship and collaboration', in John D. Cox and David Scott Kastan (eds), *A New History of Early English Drama* (New York: Columbia University Press 1997), 357–82

Meagher, John C., 'The London Lord Mayor's Show of 1590', *English Literary Renaissance*, 3 (1973), 94–104

Meredith, Peter, 'Fun, disorder, and good government in York, 1555; some thoughts on House Book 21', in David N. Klausner and Karen Sawyer Marsalek (eds), *'Bring furth the pagants': Essays in Early English Drama Presented to Alexandra F. Johnston* (Toronto: University of Toronto Press 2007), 41–57

Merritt, J. F., 'Puritans, Laudians, and the phenomenon of church-building in Jacobean London', *The Historical Journal*, 41:4 (1998), 935–60

——— (ed.), *Imagining Early Modern London* (Cambridge: Cambridge University Press 2001)

———, *The Social World of Early Modern Westminster* (Manchester: Manchester University Press 2005)

Middleton, David and Derek Edwards (eds), *Collective Remembering* (London: Sage Publications 1990)

Middleton, Thomas, ed. R. C. Bald, *Honourable Entertainments* (Oxford: the Malone Society 1953)

Milford, Anna, *Lord Mayors of London* (West Wickham: Comerford and Miller 1989)

Miller, John, *Cities Divided: Politics and Religion in English Provincial Towns 1660–1722* (Oxford: Oxford University Press 2007)

Morrissey, L. J., 'English pageant-wagons', *Eighteenth-Century Studies*, 9:3 (1976), 353–74

Mortimer, Ian, 'Tudor chronicler or sixteenth-century diarist? Henry Machyn and the nature of his manuscript', *Sixteenth Century Journal*, 33:4 (2002), 981–98

———, 'Machyn, Henry'. *Oxford DNB*. www.oxforddnb.com/view/articleHL/17531. Accessed 23.7.07

Muir, Edward, 'The eye of the procession: ritual ways of seeing in the Renaissance', in Nicholas Howe (ed.), *Ceremonial Culture in Premodern Europe* (Notre Dame: University of Notre Dame Press 2007), 129–53

Mulryne, J. R., 'Introduction', in J. R. Mulryne and Elizabeth Goldring (eds), *Court Festivals of the European Renaissance* (Aldershot: Ashgate 2002), 1–14

Munday, Anthony, *Chrysanaleia, the Golden Fishing*, ed. J. G. Nichols (London: printed for the Worshipful Company of Fishmongers 1844)

——, (ed.) J. H. P. Pafford, *Chruso-thriambos. The Triumphs of Gold* (London: privately printed 1962)

Munro, Ian, *The Figure of the Crowd in Early Modern London: The City and Its Double* (Basingstoke: Palgrave 2005)

Munro, Lucy, *Children of the Queen's Revels* (Cambridge: Cambridge University Press 2005)

Murdoch, Tessa, 'The Lord Mayor's procession of 1686: the chariot of the virgin queen', *Transactions of the London and Middlesex Archaeological Society*, 4 (1983), 207–12

Musvik, Victoria, '"And the King of Barbary's envoy had to stand in the yard": the perception of Elizabethan court festivals in Russia at the beginning of the seventeenth century', in J. R. Mulryne and Elizabeth Goldring (eds), *Court Festivals of the European Renaissance* (Aldershot: Ashgate 2002), 225–40

Myhill, Nova, '"Judging Spectators": dramatic representations of spectatorship in early modern London, 1580–1642' (PhD dissertation, University of California, Los Angeles, 1997)

Neill, Michael, ' "Exeunt with a dead march": funeral pageantry on the Shakespearean stage', in David Bergeron (ed.), *Pageantry in the Shakespearean Theatre* (Athens: University of Georgia Press 1985), 153–93

Newman, Karen, *Cultural Capitals: Early Modern London and Paris* (Princeton: Princeton University Press 2007)

Nichols, John Gough, *The Progresses and Public Processions of Queen Elizabeth*, vol. III (London: John Nichols and Son 1823)

——, *The Progresses, Processions and Magnificent Festivities of King James the First*, 4 vols (London: J. B. Nichols 1828)

——, *London Pageants* (London: J. B. Nichols 1837)

—— (ed.), *The Fishmongers' Pageant on Lord Mayor's Day, 1616: Chrysanaleia, the Golden Fishing* (London: The Worshipful Company of Fishmongers 1844)

—— (ed.), *The Diary of Henry Machyn, Citizen and Merchant Taylor of London, from AD 1550 to AD 1563* (London: J. B. Nichols and Son 1848) www.british-history.ac.uk/source.asp?pubid=324. Accessed 4.10.07

——, 'Preface' to *The Diary of Henry Machyn: Citizen and Merchant-Taylor of London (1550–1563)* (1848), pp. V–XIII. www.british-history.ac.uk/report.aspx?compid=45504. Accessed 14.11.08

Norbrook, David, '"The masque of truth": court entertainments and international Protestant politics in the early Stuart period', *The Seventeenth Century*, 1 (1986), 81–110

Northway, Kara, '"I desyre to be paid": interpreting the language of remuneration in early modern dramatic archives', *Comparative Drama*, 41:4 (2007), 405–22

——, '"To kindle an industrious desire": the poetry of work in Lord Mayors' Shows', *Comparative Drama*, 41:2 (2007), 167–92

Novarr, David, 'Dekker's gentle craft and the Lord Mayor of London', *Modern Philology*, 57:4 (1960), 233–9

O'Callaghan, Michelle, *Thomas Middleton, Renaissance Dramatist* (Edinburgh: Edinburgh University Press 2009)

O'Connell, Laura Stevenson, 'Anti-entrepreneurial attitudes in Elizabethan sermons and popular literature', *The Journal of British Studies*, 15:2 (1976), 1–20

Orgel, Stephen, 'The book of the play', in Peter Holland and Stephen Orgel (eds), *From Performance to Print in Shakespeare's England* (Basingstoke: Palgrave 2006), 13–54

Orlin, Lena Cowen (ed.), *Material London, ca. 1600* (Philadelphia: University of Pennsylvania Press 2000)

Osberg, Richard H., 'Humanist allusions and medieval themes: the "Receyving" of Queen Anne, London 1533', in Ricard Utz and Tom Shippey (eds), *Medievalism in the Modern World: Essays in Honour of Leslie J. Workman* (Turnhout: Brepols 1998), 27–41

Osteen, Mark and Martha Woodmansee, 'Taking account of the New Economic Criticism', in Martha Woodmansee and Mark Osteen (eds), *The New Economic Criticism* (London and New York: Routledge 1999), 3–50

Ovenall, R. F., 'Brian Twyne's library', *Oxford Bibliographical Society Publications*, 4, 1950, 1–42

Overall, W. H. and H. C. Overall (eds), *Analytical Index to the Series of Records Known as the Remembrancia* (London: E. J. Francis and Co. 1878)

Palmer, Daryl W., *Hospitable Performances: Dramatic Genre and Cultural Practices in Early Modern England* (West Lafayette, Indiana: Purdue University Press 1992)

——, 'Metropolitan resurrection in Anthony Munday's Lord Mayor's Shows', *Studies in English Literature*, 46:2 (2006), 371–87

Palmer, Kenneth Nicholls, *Ceremonial Barges on the River Thames* (London: Unicorn Press 1997)

Palmer, Jane, 'Music in the barges at the Lord Mayor's triumphs in the seventeenth century', in Kenneth Nicholls Palmer, *Ceremonial Barges on the River Thames* (London: Unicorn Press 1997), 171–4

Parry, Graham, *The Golden Age Restor'd: The Culture of the Stuart Court, 1603–42* (Manchester: Manchester University Press 1981)

——, 'Wood, Anthony'. *Oxford DNB*. www.oxforddnb.com/view/article/29864. Accessed 7.12.07

Paster, Gail Kern, *The Idea of the City in the Age of Shakespeare* (Athens: University of Georgia Press 1985)

——, 'The idea of London in masque and pageant', in David Bergeron (ed.), *Pageantry in the Shakespearean Theatre* (Athens: University of Georgia Press 1985), 48–64

Patterson, Catherine F., 'Married to the town: Francis Parlett's rhetoric of urban magistracy in early modern England', in Norman L. Jones and Daniel Woolf (eds), *Local Identities in Late Medieval and Early Modern England* (Basingstoke: Palgrave 2007), 156–77

Perry, Curtis, *The Making of Jacobean Culture: James I and the Renegotiation of Elizabethan Literary Practice* (Cambridge: Cambridge University Press 1997)

Pettitt, Thomas, '"Here comes I, Jack Straw": English folk drama and social revolt', *Folklore*, 95:1 (1984), 3–20

Phythian-Adams, Charles, 'Ceremony and the citizen', in Peter Clark and Paul Slack (eds), *Crisis and Order in English Towns* (London: Routledge and Kegan Paul 1972), 57–85

Plomer, H. R., *Dictionaries of the Printers and Booksellers who Were at Work in England, Scotland and Ireland 1557–1775* (Ilkley: the Bibliographical Society 1977)

Postlewait, Thomas, 'Theatricality and antitheatricality in Renaissance London', in Tracy C. Davis and Thomas Postlewait (eds), *Theatricality* (Cambridge: Cambridge University Press 2003), 90–126

Prideaux, Walter, *Memorials of the Goldsmiths' Company, vol. I* (London: Eyre and Spottiswoode 1896)

Quilligan, Maureen, 'Renaissance materialities: introduction', *Medieval and Early Modern Studies*, 32:3 (2002), 427–31

Ramsay, G. D., 'The recruitment and fortunes of some London freemen in the mid-sixteenth century', *The Economic History Review*, 31:4 (1978), 526–40

Randall, Dale B. J., *Winter Fruit: English Drama 1642–1660* (Lexington: University Press of Kentucky 1995)

Rappaport, Steven, *Worlds Within Worlds: Structures of Life in Sixteenth-century London* (Cambridge: Cambridge University Press 1989)

Ravelhofer, Barbara, *The Early Stuart Masque* (Oxford: Oxford University Press 2006)

Reddaway, T. F., *The Early History of the Goldsmiths' Company, 1327–1509* (London: Edward Arnold 1975)

Rees, J. Aubrey, *The Worshipful Company of Grocers: An Historical Retrospect, 1345–1923* (London: Chapman and Dodd 1923)

Richardson, Catherine, 'Introduction', in Catherine Richardson (ed.), *Clothing Culture, 1350–1650* (Aldershot: Ashgate 2004), 1–25

Robertson, James, 'Stuart London and the idea of a royal capital city', *Renaissance Studies*, 15:1 (2001), 37–58

——, 'The adventures of Dick Whittington and the social construction of Elizabethan London', in Ian Gadd and Patrick Wallis (eds), *Guilds,*

Society and Economy in London 1450–1800 (London: CMH/IHR/ Guildhall Library 2002), 51–66

——, 'Persuading the citizens? Charles I and London Bridge', *Historical Research*, 79:206 (2006), 512–33

Robertson, Jean and D. J. Gordon (eds), *Collections Volume III. A Calendar of Dramatic Records in the Books of the Livery Companies of London, 1485–1640* (Oxford: The Malone Society 1954)

Rowland, Richard, *Thomas Heywood's Theatre, 1599–1639: Locations, Translations and Conflict* (Aldershot: Ashgate 2010)

Sanford, Rhonda Lemke, 'Playing in the street: civic pageantry in early modern England', *Shakespeare and Renaissance Association of West Virginia: Selected Papers*, 25 (2002), 35–50

Saunders, Ann, 'A cloke not made so orderly: the sixteenth-century minutes of the Merchant Taylors' Company', *The Ricardian*, 13 (2003), 415–19

Sayle, R. T. D., *Lord Mayors' Pageants of the Merchant Taylors' Company in the 15th, 16th and 17th Centuries* (London: privately printed 1931)

Scherb, Victor, 'Assimilating giants: the appropriation of Gog and Magog in medieval and early modern culture', *Journal of Medieval and Early Modern Studies*, 32:1 (2002), 59–84

Schlueter, June, 'Michael van Meer's Album Amicorum, with illustrations of London, 1614–15', *Huntington Library Quarterly*, 69:2 (2006), 301–13

Schofield, John and Ann Saunders (eds), *Tudor London: A Map and a View* (London: London Topographical Society 2001)

Seaver, Paul, *Wallington's World* (London: Methuen 1985)

Sharpe, Kevin, 'Representations and negotiations: texts, images, and authority in early modern England', *The Historical Journal*, 42:3 (1999), 853–81

Shaw, Phillip, 'The position of Thomas Dekker in Jacobean prison literature', *PMLA*, 62:2 (1947), 366–91

Shohet, Lauren, 'The masque in/as print', in Marta Straznicky (ed.), *The Book of the Play: Playwrights, Stationers and Readers in Early Modern England* (Amherst: University of Massachusetts Press 2006), 176–202

Smuts, R. Malcolm, 'Public ceremony and royal charisma: the English royal entry in London, 1485–1642', in A. L. Beier, David Cannadine and James M. Rosenheim (eds), *The First Modern Society* (Cambridge: Cambridge University Press 1989), 65–93

——, 'Occasional events, literary texts and historical interpretations', in Robin Headlam Wells, Glenn Burgess and Rowland Wymer (eds), *Neo-Historicism* (Woodbridge: D. S. Brewer 2000), 179–98

Society of Antiquaries, *A Catalogue of a Collection of Works on Pageantry Bequeathed to the Society of Antiquaries of London by the late Frederick William Fairholt, Esq., FSA* (London: Society of Antiquaries 1869)

Somerset, J. A., 'New facts concerning Samuel Rowley', *The Review of English Studies*, 17:67 (1966), 293–7

Sponsler, Clare, 'Alien nation: London's aliens and Lydgate's mummings for the Mercers and Goldsmiths', in Jeffrey Jerome Cohen (ed.), *The Postcolonial Middle Ages* (New York: St Martin's 2000), 229–42

——, 'The culture of the spectator: conformity and resistance to medieval performances', *Theatre Journal*, 44:1 (2002), 15–29

Steedman, Carolyn, *Dust: The Archive and Cultural History* (New Brunswick: Rutgers University Press 2002)

Steen, Sara Jayne, *Ambrosia in an Earthern Vessel: Three Centuries of Audience and Reader Response to the Works of Thomas Middleton* (New York: AMS Press 1993)

Stevenson, Christine, 'Occasional architecture in seventeenth-century London', *Architectural History*, 49 (2006), 35–74

Stevenson, Laura, *Praise and Paradox: Merchants and Craftsmen in Elizabethan Popular Literature* (Cambridge: Cambridge University Press 1984)

Stock, Angela, '"Something done in honour of the city": ritual, theatre and satire in Jacobean civic pageantry', in Dieter Mehl, Angela Stock and Anne-Julia Zwierlein (eds), *Plotting Early Modern London* (Aldershot: Ashgate 2004), 125–44

Streitberger, W. R., *Court Revels, 1485–1559* (Toronto: University of Toronto Press 1994)

Strickland, Ronald, 'Pageantry and poetry as discourse: the production of subjectivity in Sir Philip Sidney's funeral', *English Literary History*, 57:1 (1990), 19–36

Strong, Roy C., 'The popular celebration of the Accession Day of Queen Elizabeth I', *Journal of the Warburg and Courtauld Institutes*, 21:1/2 (1958), 86–103

Stubblefield, Jay, '"Very worthily sett in printe": writing the Virginia Company of London', in Christopher Cobb and M. Thomas Hester (eds), *Renaissance Papers 2003* (Columbia, SC: Camden House 2003), 167–87

Sullivan, Ceri, *The Rhetoric of Credit: Merchants in Early Modern Writing* (London: Associated University Presses 2002)

——, 'London's early modern creative industrialists', *Studies in Philology*, 103:3 (2006), 313–28

——, 'Summer 1613: Middleton's fluid credit', *Review of English Studies*, 233 (2007), 1–13

——, 'Thomas Middleton's view of public utility', *Review of English Studies*, 234 (2007), 162–74

——, 'Thomas Middleton', in Andrew Hiscock and Lisa Hopkins (eds), *Teaching Shakespeare and Early Modern Dramatists* (Basingstoke: Palgrave 2007), 146–57

Sullivan, Garrett A., *The Drama of Landscape* (Stanford: Stanford University Press 1998)

Supple, B. E., *Commercial Crisis and Change in England 1600–1642* (Cambridge: Cambridge University Press 1970)

Sutton, Anne, 'Civic livery in medieval London', *Costume*, 29 (1995), 12–24

Sweetinburgh, Sheila, 'Clothing the naked in late medieval East Kent', in Catherine Richardson (ed.), *Clothing Culture, 1350–1650* (Aldershot: Ashgate 2004), 109–21

——, 'Mayor-making and other ceremonies: shared uses of sacred space among the Kentish cinque ports', in Paul Trio and Marjan de Smet (eds), *The Use and Abuse of Sacred Places in Late Medieval Towns* (Leuven: Leuven University Press 2006), 165–87

Sykes, Winifred, 'Lord Mayor's Day', *Notes and Queries*, 191 (1946), 80–1

Symonds, E. M., 'The Diary of John Greene (1635–57)', *The English Historical Review*, 43:171 (1928), 385–94

Taylor, Gary, *Buying Whiteness: Race, Culture, and Identity from Columbus to Hip Hop* (Palgrave, New York 2005)

——, 'Making meaning marketing Shakespeare 1623', in Peter Holland and Stephen Orgel (eds), *From Performance to Print in Shakespeare's England* (Basingstoke: Palgrave 2006), 55–72

—— and John Lavagnino (eds), *Thomas Middleton: The Collected Works* (Oxford: Clarendon Press 2007)

—— and John Lavagnino (eds), *Thomas Middleton and Early Modern Textual Culture: A Companion to the Collected Works* (Oxford: Clarendon Press 2007)

Thomas, Max W., 'Urban semiosis in early modern London', *Genre: Forms of Discourse and Culture*, 30:1 (1997), 11–28

Thomson, Peter, 'Kemble, John Philip', *Oxford DNB*. www.oxforddnb. com/view/article/15322. Accessed 1.2.08

Thrush, Andrew, 'Clitherow, Sir Christopher'. *Oxford DNB*. www. oxforddnb.com/view/articleHL/5691. Accessed 23.6.09

——, 'Finch, Sir Heneage'. *Oxford DNB*. http://www.oxforddnb.com/ view/article/9432. Accessed 23.11.09

Tittler, Robert, *Architecture and Power: The Town Hall and the English Urban Community c.1500–1640* (Oxford: Clarendon Press 1991)

——, *The Reformation and the Towns in England: politics and political culture, c. 1540–1640* (Oxford: Clarendon Press 1998)

——, 'The Cookes and the Brookes: uses of portraiture in town and country before the Civil War', in Gerald MacLean, Donna Landry and Joseph P. Ward (eds), *The Country and the City Revisited* (Cambridge: Cambridge University Press 1999), 58–73

——, *The Face of the City: Civic Portraiture and Civic Identity in Early Modern England* (Manchester: Manchester University Press 2007)

Tumbleson, Raymond D., 'The triumph of London: Lord Mayor's Day pageants and the rise of the City', in Katherine Z. Keller and Gerald J. Schiffhorst (eds), *The Witness of Times: Manifestations of Ideology in*

Seventeenth Century England (Pittsburgh: Duquesne University Press, 1993), 53–67

Turner, Henry S., 'Plotting early modernity', in Henry S. Turner (ed.), *The Culture of Capital* (New York and London: Routledge 2002), 85–127

Twyning, John, *London Dispossessed: Literature and Social Space in the Early Modern City* (Basingstoke: Macmillan 1998)

Unwin, George, *The Gilds and Companies of London* (London: Methuen 1908)

Wall, Cynthia, 'Grammars of space: the language of London from Stow's *Survey* to Defoe's *Tour*', *Philological Quarterly*, 76:4 (1997), 387–411

Wall, Wendy, *The Imprint of Gender: Authorship and Publication in the English Renaissance* (Ithaca and New York: Cornell University Press 1993)

Walsh, Brian, 'Performing historicity in Dekker's *The Shoemaker's Holiday*', *Studies in English Literature*, 46:2 (2006), 323–48

Walsh, Martin W., 'St Martin in the City: the Lord Mayor's Show of 1702', *Studies in Medievalism*, 4 (1992), 70–8

Ward, Joseph P., *Metropolitan Communities* (Stanford: Stanford University Press 1997)

——, 'Imagining the metropolis in Elizabethan and Stuart London', in Gerald MacLean, Donna Landry and Joseph P. Ward (eds), *The Country and the City Revisited* (Cambridge: Cambridge University Press 1999), 24–40

Watanabe-O'Kelly, Helen, 'Early modern European festivals: politics and performance, event and record', in J. R. Mulryne and Elizabeth Goldring (eds), *Court Festivals of the European Renaissance* (Aldershot: Ashgate 2002), 15–25

—— and Anne Simon, *Festivals and Ceremonies: A Bibliography of Works Relating to Court, Civic and Religious Festivals in Europe 1500–1800* (London and New York: Mansell 2000)

Watt, Tessa, *Cheap Print and Popular Piety, 1550–1640* (Cambridge: Cambridge University Press 1991)

Wayne, Don E., '"Pox on your distinction!": humanist reformation and deformations of the everyday in *The Staple of News*', in Patricia Fumerton and Simon Hunt (eds), *Renaissance Culture and the Everyday* (Philadelphia: University of Pennsylvania Press 1999), 67–91

Wedel, Lupold von, 'Journey through England and Scotland made by Lupold von Wedel in the years 1584 and 1585', trans. Gottfried von Bulow, *Transactions of the Royal Historical Society*, 9 (1895), 223–70

Weinstein, Rosemary, 'The making of a Lord Mayor, Sir John Leman (1544–1632): the integration of a stranger family', *Proceedings of the Huguenot Society*, 24 (1986), 316–24

Welch, Charles (rev. Trevor Dickie), 'Myddleton, Sir Thomas'. *Oxford DNB*. www.oxforddnb.com/view/article/19685. Accessed 14.7.08

Werner, Hans, 'A German eye-witness to *Troia-Nova Triumphans*: is

Dekker's text a reliable description of the event?', *Notes and Queries*, 46 (1999), 251–4

Westhauser, Karl E., 'Revisiting the Jordan thesis: "white over black" in seventeenth-century England and America', *The Journal of Negro History*, 85:3 (2000), 112–22

Wheatley, Chloe, 'The pocket books of early modern history', in Henry S. Turner (ed.), *The Culture of Capital* (New York and London: Routledge 2002), 183–202

White, Adam, 'Christmas family'. *Oxford DNB*. www.oxforddnb.com/view/article/73261. Accessed 23.7.07

White, Martin, 'London professional playhouses and performances', in Jane Milling and Peter Thomson (eds), *The Cambridge History of British Theater, Volume 1* (Cambridge: Cambridge University Press 2004), 298–338

White, Micheline, 'A biographical sketch of Dorcas Martin: Elizabethan translator, stationer, and godly matron', *Sixteenth Century Journal*, 30:3 (1999), 775–92

Whitney, Charles, '"Usually in the werking daies": playgoing journeymen, apprentices, and servants in guild records, 1582–92', *Shakespeare Quarterly*, 50:4 (1999), 433–58

——, 'The devil his due: Mayor John Spencer, Elizabethan civic antitheatricalism, and *The Shoemaker's Holiday*', *Medieval and Renaissance Drama in England*, 14 (2001), 168–85

Wickham, Glynne, *Early English Stages 1300–1660, vol. I 1300–1576*, 2nd edition (London: Routledge & Kegan Paul 1980)

——, *Early English Stages 1300–1660, vol. II 1576–1660* (London: Routledge & Kegan Paul 1972)

Williams, Sheila, 'The Pope-burning processions of 1679, 1680 and 1681', *Journal of the Warburg and Courtauld Institutes*, 21 (1958), 104–18

——, 'A Lord Mayor's show by John Taylor, the water poet', *Bulletin of the John Rylands Library*, 41:2 (1959), 501–31

——, 'The Lord Mayor's Show in Tudor and Stuart times', *Guildhall Miscellany*, 1:10 (1959), 3–18

——, 'Two seventeenth century semi-dramatic allegories of truth the daughter of time: Middleton's *The triumphs of truth* (1613) and Heywood's *Londons ius honorarium* (1631): both Lord Mayor's shows', *The Guildhall Miscellany*, 2:5 (1963), 207–20

Wilentz, Sean (ed.), *Rites of Power: Symbolism, Ritual, and Politics since the Middle Ages* (Philadelphia: University of Pennysylvania Press 1999)

Withington, Philip, 'Two renaissances: urban political culture in post-Reformation England reconsidered', *The Historical Journal*, 44:1 (2001), 239–67

Withington, Robert, 'The early "Royal-Entry"', *PMLA*, 32:4 (1917), 616–23

——, 'The Lord Mayor's Show for 1590', *Modern Language Notes*, 33:1 (1918), 8–13

——, 'A note on "A fragment of a Lord Mayor's pageant"', *Modern Language Notes*, 34:8 (1919), 501–3

——, 'Additional notes on modern folk pageantry', *PMLA*, 37:2 (1922), 347–59

——, 'A Note on *Eastward Ho*, I, ii, 178', *Modern Language Notes*, 43:1 (1928), 28–9

——, *English Pageantry: An Historical Outline* (2 vols, New York: Arno Press 1980)

Wood, Julia K., '"A flowing harmony": music on the Thames in Restoration London', *Early Music*, 23:4 (1995), 553–81

Woodbridge, Linda (ed.), *Money and the Age of Shakespeare: Essays in New Economic Criticism* (New York: Palgrave 2003)

Woolf, Daniel, 'Of Danes and giants: popular beliefs about the past in early modern England', *Dalhousie Review*, 71:1 (1991), 166–209

——, *The Social Circulation of the Past* (Oxford: Oxford University Press 2003)

Wortham, Simon, 'Sovereign counterfeits: the trial of the pyx', *Renaissance Quarterly*, 49 (1996), 334–59

Wren, Melvin C., 'The disputed elections in London in 1641', *The English Historical Review*, 64:250 (1949), 34–52

Wright, Nancy E., '"Rival traditions": civic and courtly ceremonies in Jacobean London', in David Bevington and Peter Holbrook (eds), *The Politics of the Stuart Court Masque* (Cambridge: Cambridge University Press 1998), 197–217

Wunderli, Richard M., 'Evasion of the office of Alderman in London, 1523–1672', *London Journal*, 15:1 (1990), 3–18

Yamey, Basil S., 'Peele, James'. *Oxford DNB*. www.oxforddnb.com/view/article/56446. Accessed, 23.7.07

Yates, Julian, *Error Misuse Failure: Object Lessons from the English Renaissance* (Minneapolis and London: University of Minnesota Press 2003)

Index